Abbey Boys

FORT AUGUSTUS ABBEY SCHOOLS

MICHAEL T R B TURNBULL

corbie.com

PERTH 2000

First published by
corbie.com
Mountview, Kinnoull Hill Place, Perth PH2 7DD

ISBN 0-9539002-0-7

British Library Cataloguing in Publication Data
A catalogue record of this book
is available from the British Library.

ISBN 0953900207

Photographic sources in the art section and throughout the text have been acknowledged where known. If any source has been omitted, please inform the Publisher for future acknowledgement.

Typeset in Bembo and Charlemagne.
Cover design by Mark Blackadder.
Cover photograph courtesy of Lovat Estates.
Printed and bound in the United Kingdom by Bell & Bain Ltd., Glasgow

Contents

SAINT ANDREW'S PRIORY, CARLEKEMP PRIORY
AND SUMMER SCHOOLS

Foreword

EARLY last century an Apostolic Visitor proposed that Blairs should become the senior seminary for Scotland, and the junior seminary be transferred to the Abbey School, Fort Augustus. It is sad to see both Blairs and Fort Augustus now abandoned, and it is interesting to speculate on what might have been had that advice been taken.

Former boys of both institutions are now collecting their memories, and we can begin to appreciate how profoundly both institutions have influenced the Catholic Church in Scotland. Michael Turnbull has done this with great regard to Fort Augustus Abbey School and in so doing has rendered not just former pupils but the whole community a signal service.

The vision shared by Dom Jerome Vaughan, the Marquess of Bute and Lord Lovat to convert a military fort into a Benedictine Abbey was a magnificent one. In the heart of the Highlands, on one of the most beautiful sites in Scotland, a place radiating the Gospel, would, like so many of the Hydro Electric schemes which now dot the area, turn to energy the waters of life.

Given this vision the Abbey School was a natural progression from the establishment of the Abbey itself. It is easy to identify the influence of the Abbey through some of its more distinguished Old Boys such as Lord Lovat, Sir James Calder, Lord Carmont and the two Archbishops, Archbishop Andrew Joseph McDonald of St Andrews & Edinburgh, himself sometime Abbot of Fort Augustus, and Archbishop Maurus Caruana of Malta. Bishop George Bennett of Aberdeen was a former pupil, as was Bishop Ansgar Nelson of Sweden. Many others, lay-men as well as priests, though less well known perhaps, are remembered by those still living, as making their own valuable contribution to life in Scotland and beyond.

The School was of course also the recruiting ground for the monastic community whose surviving members continue to serve the Church, two of them in the Aberdeen Diocese, and one as parish priest at Fort Augustus.

I recall with pleasure my visits to the Abbey and the Abbey School over the years, whether for the consecration of the great Church, or for a Prize-giving within the School. I recall especially my confirmation visits when the red-coated boys made a splendid sight!

Sport was an important part of the School curriculum, and it is good that the book includes the names of those awarded Colours for Rugby, Hockey and Cricket.

Record is made of the two Priories – Saint Andrew's Priory, Edinburgh and Carlekemp Priory, North Berwick, the closure of which preceded that of Fort Augustus and perhaps made way for the latter's eventual ending.

At the closure of the Abbey some of the heritage items, coming originally from the Abbey of St James at Ratisbon, were given to the Blairs Museum thereby ensuring that the name of Fort Augustus will not be forgotten as long as the Catholic Church in Scotland values its heritage.

Right Rev. Mario Joseph Conti KCHS PhL STL DD FRSE
Bishop of Aberdeen
SEPTEMBER 2000

Acknowledgements

THIS book could not have been written without the encouragement and support of the Fort Augustus Old Boys' Association and, in particular, Ralph Giulianotti KSG, Mike Drummond, Chris Stephenson and Andrew Dempster. I am especially indebted to the Very Rev. Francis Davidson OSB, Giles Foster of Lovat Estates, and to the monks, Old Boys and Old Girls who responded with patience to my many requests for information. I am also very grateful for the unfailing assistance given me by Dr Christine Johnson, Keeper of the Scottish Catholic Archives and by the Graphics and Multimedia Section of the University of Edinburgh.

Michael T R B Turnbull
SEPTEMBER 2000

To all
who lived, prayed or played
at the
Fort Augustus Abbey Schools.

*St Benedict's College
and the
Abbey School*

'THE MONASTERY GARDEN' BY PETER ANSON (1934).

CHAPTER 1

St Benedict's College
1876-78

IN June 1993 the Abbey School, Fort Augustus, closed – the first and last post-Reformation monastic boys' school in Scotland. So was brought to an end an association with the Highlands which began in 1876 when Simon, 15th Lord Lovat, gave the former Hanoverian fort to the Order of St Benedict for an annual 'peppercorn' rent.

Little has been written about the history of the School, or rather, Schools, for the Benedictine community at Fort Augustus also staffed and administered three other educational establishments: Saint Andrew's Priory, Edinburgh (1930-45), Carlekemp Priory School, North Berwick (1945-77), and the Summer Schools (1975-93).

★   ★   ★

St Benedict of Nursia (c. 480-547) is generally credited as being the founder of Western monasticism. He wrote his pioneering *Rule for Monks* (*Regula monachorum*) in Monte Cassino around the year AD 515, directing his monks in the *Rule's* 73 chapters to engage in working with their hands, in teaching the young and, in an era before printing was invented, in transcribing books. In 1964 St Benedict was declared Patron Saint of Europe by Pope Paul VI.

The Rule of St Benedict is aimed at maintaining the physical, mental and spiritual health of a monastic community. Characteristically, the Prologue to the *Rule* is positive in its encouragement, while very down to earth in its understanding of the weaknesses of human nature. Benedict urged his monks: 'Let us open our eyes to the light that comes from God', but the motto of the Benedictine Order is 'Peace among thorns'.

The Site

The premises chosen for the new Scottish monastic community was the barracks at Kilcumein, strategically placed at the southern end of Loch Ness, Inverness-shire.[1] Kilcumein ('church of Cumein') was named after a successor of St Columba, so testifying to the long pedigree of Christian devotion where the River Tarff flows into Loch Ness. According to Adamnan (*c.* 625-704) in his *Life of St Columba*, the saintly Bishop of Iona had succeeded in preventing the death of one his followers at the hands of a water monster (*aquatilis bestia*) in the River Ness.

Built in 1716, the original barracks to the west were replaced in 1729 at General George Wade's (1673-1748) suggestion, with a military fortification designed by Captain John Romer. The new building was completed in 1742 and named after George II's third son, Prince William Augustus, Duke of Cumberland. Fort Augustus, as it was now called, was captured in 1746 by the Jacobite forces who then proceeded to destroy significant parts of the fortification.[2]

GROUNDPLAN OF THE FORT

After the Battle of Culloden (1746) – where Prince Charles Edward's chaplain had been the Benedictine monk, Dom Gall Leith – and the defeat of the Jacobite forces, the victorious Duke of Cumberland spent some time at Fort Augustus, laying waste the whole of Lochaber and much of Badenoch, breaking the back of the clan system. Cumberland referred to Fort Augustus as 'this diamond in the midst of hell'.[3]

In the subsequent reconstruction of 1747-48, a dry moat and *glacis* (sloping bank) were added. Joseph Mitchell, in his *Reminiscences of my life in the Highlands,* describes the garrison at Fort Augustus:

ELEVATION OF THE FORT

At that time [1805-6] *the fortress was in military occupation. There was a governor, with from eighty to a hundred old soldiers* [invalids *as they were called*], *who kept regular military guard. The governor, in full uniform, with cocked hat and epaulettes, inspired great awe amongst the simple inhabitants of the village.*[4]

By 1818 the outer defences had been dismantled and the ordnance and most of the garrison transferred further north to Fort George.

In 1867 the Fort was bought by Thomas, 14th Lord Lovat. He used the building partly as a shooting lodge, partly to house tenants. In 1876 Simon Lovat, his son and the 15th Lord, presented the Fort to the English Congregation of Benedictines. As the final headmaster of the School, Fr Aelred Grugan OSB has observed, 'two quite starkly contrasting communities of men have occupied these premises in succession, with only a short break between their tenancies'.[5]

A Vision

Abbot Alban Boultwood OSB (himself a former pupil of the Abbey School), points out that the proposal for restoring monasticism to Scotland came from that visionary patron, intellectual and connoisseur, the 3rd Marquess of Bute, the driving force and investor behind so many initiatives aimed at restoring the Roman Catholic tradition in Scotland.[6]

The Marquess presented his idea to the General Chapter of the English Benedictine Congregation in 1874. It was felt that this would be a good opportunity to revive the English abbey of Saints Adrian and Denis, formerly at Lamspring near Hildesheim in Hanover, Germany (founded by the English Benedictines in 1644), a community that had been suppressed in 1803. This was also an opportunity to revive the Scoto-Irish abbey of St James, Ratisbon at Regensburg in Bavaria, dissolved in 1862 (but which still retained compensation money given by the Bavarian government).

Following dissolution, a few survivors of Lamspring (including Dom Augustine Birdsall), had set up a small community at Broadway in Worcestershire, supported by the Lamspring funds.

On the 11 May 1875 at St Osburg's, Coventry, the Chapter General of the English Benedictine Congregation agreed to a foundation at Fort Augustus (significantly on land that, in pre-Reformation times, belonged to the monks of Beauly). The new foundation would incorporate Lamspring Abbey and the ancient Scots Abbey (*Schottenkloster*) at Ratisbon.[7]

The Marquess of Bute offered financial support for a new monastery, provided it was established north of the Border. Lord Bute's chief objective was to restore the Benedictine Order in Scotland, and the General Chapter of the English Benedictine Congregation agreed that if three separate monasteries could be founded in Scotland they might be formed into a distinct Scottish Congregation.[8]

When, in September 1876, the time came for the first novice (Br Andrew Delaney) to be clothed at Belmont for what was to become the new St Benedict's Abbey, Fr Anselm Robertson, the last surviving monk of St James of Ratisbon, also took part in the rite so that he might provide a living connection between the old and the new congregations.

The newly-appointed Prior, Fr Jerome Vaughan, a relative of Bishop (afterwards Cardinal) Vaughan of Salford (and of Lord Lovat by marriage), was joined in the new Community by other monks who were members of the extended Lovat family (such as Frs Benedict and Adrian Weld-Blundell). The new Community would be almost exclusively English and largely aristocratic by birth.

On the morning of 9 February 1876, Fr Jerome Vaughan was travelling from Invermoriston, along the shore of Loch Ness, in Lord Lovat's carriage, accompanied by Abbot Burchall, when he reached the summit of the road. In front of them lay Fort Augustus, an oasis of green below the snow-covered hills. In later years Fr Vaughan used to recount his conversion-experience as if he had been Paul on the road to Damascus:

> … *coming out from Invermoriston and seeing the old Fort against the sun, saying,* Hic habitabo, quoniam elegi eam ['In this place will I dwell, for I have chosen it'].[9] *In any case it was his energy and his begging that founded Fort Augustus after the late Lord Lovat had given the site to the Benedictines.*

Lord Lovat handed over the buildings of the Fort and promised the equivalent of the rent of the neighbouring farm of Borlum for a term of 19 years. The entire gift by Lord Lovat amounted to more than £8000.[10]

The foundation stone of the Monastery was laid by Lord Lovat on 15 September 1876; the foundation stone of the School was laid by the Marquis of Ripon, while the foundation stone of the Guest House was jointly laid by Mr Maxwell-Scott of Abbotsford and Mr Monteith of Carstairs. A letter from Pope Pius IX was read in which he expressed his joy at learning of a military establishment being converted to a House of Prayer, whereas in Italy so many religious houses had been confiscated for secular purposes.[11]

Opening

On 16 October 1878, enough of the Monastery and St Benedict's College had been completed to justify a solemn opening ceremony. Pontifical High Mass was celebrated in one of the rooms which had been fitted out as a chapel. Chief celebrant was Bishop MacDonald of Aberdeen (a former student of St James, Ratisbon), assisted by Dr Burchall (Abbot President of the English Benedictine Congregation), Abbot Smith, and the resident Community at St Benedict's. The sermon was preached by the Rev. Dr Sweeney OSB of Bath.[12]

Also present at the opening ceremonies was the architect, Peter Paul Pugin. The assembled guests had an opportunity to marvel at the many different types of stones which had been used in the Abbey building. The original local whinstone of the old Fort was too porous to be watertight and had to be protected by a thick covering of harling. Pugin also designed the renovation of the southern parts of the fort into what became the Guest House. Later, however, Joseph Hansom, the English

THE ABBEY AS SEEN FROM THE LOCH.

15

architect who designed the rest of the Monastery, removed the harling and so let in the rain.

The College

The new St Benedict's College catered for an exclusive educational market. It was 'more particularly intended for the education of boys of the upper classes' and was 'designed to provide for the sons of gentlemen a liberal education, and to combine the refining influences of home life with the manly and invigorating spirit of a public school'.[13] The cubicles of the student dormitories were furnished with carpet, wardrobe, chair, lavatory, bath and heated with hot water pipes; students were required to take a sponge bath every morning.[14]

Five days later, monastic observance and the recitation of office began. The Community itself was twelve-strong, consisting of five priests, four juniors and three lay-brothers.

In those early days the accommodation was still relatively primitive. Masons and other tradesmen were hard at work on the new structure. The monks had to make do with a temporary wooden church.

Three Ampleforth monks and one from Ramsgate were in charge of teaching and discipline in the College, which at that time only contained 15 boys – English, Scottish and Irish (some of whom had arrived as much as two months earlier). The College masters were known as 'professors'. The Headmaster was styled 'prefect of studies'. Two of the teachers were Cambridge graduates – Mr Wall (later Fr Martin) and Mr Poynter. They taught a curriculum which, according to the somewhat ambitious prospectus, was of intimidating intellectual breadth: 'all the dead languages and most of the living – astronomy, geology, natural and mental philosophy, agricultural chemistry, domestic architecture, political economy, general law of contracts and property.'

Weather

Abbot Hunter Blair recalled that the first three Winters of life at Fort Augustus were exceptionally severe. Furious gales alternated with unusually prolonged frosts. The heating apparatus was not yet in working order; the cloisters were still entirely open to the weather, and there were, for some months after the opening, no front doors to Monastery or College.

But there were compensations. The boys and younger members of the Community enjoyed wonderful skating during those biting Winter days, but incurred the wrath of some of the locals for venturing on the ice on Sundays. Both the ministers of the Village called officially on the Prior to protest against 'Sabbath-breaking'.

Hostility

Relations with the world outside the Monastery became rather strained. One correspondent in a local paper protested:

> *This Summer they are at it again, boating, &., on the Sabbath. Now, sir, if this be not attempting to bring French Sundays, French sins, and I may add French judgements, into British territory, I know not what it is!*

On balance, nevertheless, noted Abbot Hunter Blair, the immediate neighbours, Protestant as well as Catholic, were all as a rule pleased with the new life brought into their quiet Village by the opening of the monastic School.

Nationwide there were, however, still areas of deep distrust. In June 1888 the Monastery and School were officially denounced by the General Assembly of the Free Kirk, one of whose speakers declared that 'if they allowed the Popish system to operate with its monks and nuns, its bribes and appliances, a great change would speedily come over the Highlands'.

CHAPTER 2

St Benedict's College
1879-1919

A Solemn Celebration

BY August 1879 the monastic and collegiate buildings were finally completed. The fledgling Community consisted of Frs Jerome Vaughan (Prior), James Bernard Murphy (Sub-prior); Anselm Robertson, Nicholas Frie, George Elphege Cody, John Sigebert Cody and William Alexius Eager.

Three days of solemn celebration on 24, 25 and 26 August, marked the 14th centenary of the birth of St Benedict. Rome granted a plenary indulgence to all who visited the monastic chapel and received holy communion or went to confession on the last of the three days.

There were two special functions – the procession of the Relics and the blessing of statues. In the former, relics of St Andrew, St Benedict and St Marcellus were carried round the cloisters with lights and banners, accompanied by 100 clergy and 300 lay-people.

The end of the year, however, was marked by disaster. The weather took a turn for the worse on 28 December 1879 when a terrific gale destroyed the Tay Bridge. Abbot Hunter Blair recalled:

Fort Augustus was the very centre of this appalling storm as it swept across Scotland and suffered great damage. I was in the Prefect's room in the tower, listening in dismay to the howling of the elements, when a boy rushed in, and with unholy joy in his countenance which always accompanies the telling of bad news, shouted 'Please, Father, the monastery's blown down!' What had happened was the demolition of one

THE MARY BELL

of the two great stone gables for the new calefactory wing which was just waiting to be roofed. The gable crashed down through three floors, smashing through ponderous joists and beams as if they had been matchwood.

Schoolboy memories

The Census in 1881 reveals that there were now six monks, six Divinity students and one lay-brother, 27 year old Englishman Peter McKenna. There were 38 scholars in the new College, eight of them from Ireland, three from France, one from Uruguay and one from Brazil.

In September 1881 a new boy, John Calder, arrived at Inverness Station:

I was met by Mr McDonald, formerly Lord Lovat's factor, but then a wine merchant, a fine looking, benevolent old Highlander, very popular in Inverness and known, I believe, as 'Sample Sandie', for reasons not difficult to guess. He took me to the horse brake which Macrae and Dick then ran to the steamer at Muirtown. I think it was the Glengarry, then a very old boat, as were also the Gondolier and the Loch Ness with their red and black funnels .... Presently the Glengarry started, after I had said goodbye to Mr McDonald who had so kindly piloted me, and I sailed down the Canal and Loch, the steamer being at that time the only method of getting to St Benedict's, not yet an abbey.

Tensions, however, had begun to build up in the monastic Community. Some of the monks felt that the daily life of the monks was too secular and lax. In 1880 they had demanded, for example, that no novices should be employed in the College; that there should be no eating or drinking in the Calefactory (warm monastic common room). They wanted the serving of claret wine at dinner to be discontinued.

Two years later other demands were made for stricter observance: the exclusion of the schoolboys from the Cloister; greater use of silence during the monastic day; fixed times for the recitation of the Office; more frequent periods of abstinence and fasts. Some of these demands were eventually met, but still there was a feeling that a new style of monasticism, recapturing the original Benedictine spirit, was needed and that only separation from the English Benedictine Congregation could bring this about.

Lord Lovat did not spare himself in pressing for Fort Augustus to

19

distance itself from its parent body. On 30 September 1882 he wrote to Archbishop Strain of St Andrews and Edinburgh:

> *It has always been my wish in giving land … for the establishment of the Monastery that it should be, if possible, an entirely Scotch foundation, my object being to benefit Religion in our own Country. At present the Monastery belongs to the English Benedictine Congregation and at any time, any one or all the best men might be called off to England.*[1]

In December 1882 Pope Leo XIII ordered the separation of Fort Augustus from the English Benedictine Congregation. St Benedict's Priory was constituted into an independent Abbey, immediately subject to the Holy See. It was the first post-Reformation Abbey of the English Benedictine Congregation in mainland Britain.

The Community broke away from the English Congregation on 7 January 1883, becoming directly subject to Rome:

> *On the Feast of the Epiphany, 1883, Archbishop Strain of St Andrews and Edinburgh came to Fort Augustus for the purpose of singing Pontifical High Mass there. In due course the Mass began, and after the Gospel had been sung, the Archbishop, standing at his Throne, suddenly* [and, apparently to the astonishment of almost all present], *drew out a document which he proceeded to read aloud. This was the Papal Brief* Summa cum animi *which declared Fort Augustus an independent monastery, cut off from the English Benedictine Congregation and placed directly under the Holy See.*[2]

After the service ended it was reported that the first manifestation of triumph took the form of the English Benedictine habit being rolled up into footballs and kicked round the Calefactory and the Cloisters![3]

The Prior, Fr Vaughan, who was strongly opposed to the break with the English Benedictine Congregation (EBC), had been experiencing considerable difficulty in his relations with other members of the community at Fort Augustus. 'The monks do not want Fr Jerome for Abbot and have been petitioning against him,' Fr James Campbell wrote to Archbishop Strain from Rome.[4] Paradoxically, within a few hours of the reading of the Brief, a letter arrived from the EBC declaring Prior Vaughan to be deposed from office (presumably for allowing the separation to take place). Fr Vaughan left soon after and was succeeded as Prior by Fr Kentigern Milne.

One of the first results of the new emphasis on a purer form of monasticism was adoption of the Italian pronunciation of Latin. The Fort Augustus monks' habit was changed to one with a longer hood and a leather belt round the waist instead of a cloth one. The monks' hairstyle was also changed from a simple tonsure to a *corona* (double cut round the head). Later that Spring a wall and a bank planted with trees was constructed between the Monastery and the College to emphasise the finality of separation and the inviolability of the *enclosure* (to no part of which women were henceforth permitted to enter).

Prior Milne in turn was replaced in 1887 by the dynamic German Benedictine, Fr Leo Linse, who brought with him the fervour of his former community at Beuron in Germany. Beuron, founded in 1863 by the brothers Maurus and Placidus Wolter through the generosity of Princess Catherine of Hohenzollern, was (with Solesmes) one of the leaders of the revival in monastic life, liturgy, and music.

Under the influence of Prior Linse the community at Fort Augustus strove to remodel itself more closely on what it saw as the authentic medieval tradition and rather less on establishing an ongoing relationship with the world around it – such as the contemporary English Benedictine foundations did through the running of schools or parish work.

On 15 July 1888, with suitable ceremony, Prior Linse, after due process of consultation and election, was consecrated the first Abbot of Fort Augustus, an office he was to hold until 1909, when he would be obliged through increasing ill health to retire. Among the many dignitaries attending the ceremony was the founder of Fr Linse's old monastery, Arch-Abbot Maurus Wolter of Beuron. In his consecration address the new Abbot assured the congregation that 'the sons of St Benedict would always be ready to do all in their power, and as far as lay within their monastic vocation, for the good of religion in Scotland'.

On 24 September 1890 the foundation stone of an Abbey church, designed by Peter Paul Pugin in the Gothic style, was laid by the Archbishop of St Andrew's and Edinburgh. Other portions of the church were later changed to the Norman style, designed by Reginald Fairlie.

Transport

Having surveyed the Highlands in 1724, General George Wade had begun the construction of a network of roads in 1726 designed to facilitate the transport of military wheel-carriages and artillery trains. The

roads were completed by 1737. Fort Augustus was a pivotal part of this system.

In spite of Wade's roads access by land to Fort Augustus was still difficult, but this made the journey all the more picturesque.

Financial arrangements for the monastic community were equally adventurous. As there was no bank in Fort Augustus at that time, the Prior used to ride out on his grey horse every Friday to the even smaller village of Invergarry seven miles away, where there was a branch of the Caledonian Bank. He would return, it was rumoured, with his saddlebags full of silver for the payment of the masons and other workmen.

Recreation

Students at St Benedict's College were not always able to return home during their holidays. Christmas 1888, for example, was celebrated at Fort Augustus by most of the pupils.

In September 1887 the monastic Community and the School were saddened to learn of the death of 58 year old Lord Lovat, the 14th Baron and 23rd chief of the Frasers. He had died on the Mackintosh grouse moors at Moy one afternoon when preparing to join a shooting party.

The new head of the Lovats was still only a schoolboy at Fort Augustus. The young Lord Lovat became Captain of the School in January 1888.

In a number of ways the College was well ahead of its time. When, in April 1889, electric light was installed throughout the whole building, Abbot Hunter Blair asserted: 'I believe our monastery and school were the first institution in Scotland by many years … to introduce the new illuminant.'[5]

By the time of the 1891 Census, the Community at Fort Augustus consisted of 16 priests, twelve English-born and only two Scottish (Fr David Hunter Blair and Fr Alexander Milne, both from Wigtownshire). There were 14 students of Theology or the Humanities and one Clerk in Orders. The Community also included 16 tradesmen – four shoemakers, two tailors, a miller, a carpenter, a printer-compositor and a wheelwright. The School itself had 36 pupils – 13 from England, eight from Scotland, five from Ireland, four from Argentina, two from Tasmania and one each from Australia, France and Italy.

In the Summer, boating was the most popular sport. The greatest day was the annual boat race from the first lock at Fort Augustus, two miles up the Canal to Kyltra. The College was given a half-holiday and accompanied the boats as they were taken to the start in farm carts on the morning of the race. The race itself started at one o' clock in the afternoon, with the College, the monastic Community and most of the Village crowding the banks of the Canal.

Cricket and Football were the only organised games, but the boys also enjoyed a wall game (squash rackets) and a special wall was built for that purpose. Mr Shaw, groundsman and cricket professional, had joined the staff in April 1888, often turning out for St Benedict's against other schools. Games were compulsory twice a week and a fine of sixpence was imposed on boys who did not appear or who were late.

That year the *School Chronicle* began. In its pages are detailed the Athletic Sports held on 2-3 April. Over 300 people took dinner in the Cricket Pavilion at the Abbot's expense. Records set that day were:

100 Yards	10.5 seconds
Hop, Step and Jump	32 feet
Throwing the Cricket Ball	76 yards 2 feet
Throwing the Hammer	75 feet 10 inches
Pole Jump	6 feet 10 inches
Putting the 16lb Weight	36 feet 1 inch

The first Cricket match recorded in the *School Chronicle* was against the Village. The College made 58 runs in the first innings and 146 in the second; the Village made 22. Perhaps this was due to the fact that the School's professional, Mr E. Shaw, also turned out for the boys.

The first Football match recorded in the *Chronicle* was against Fort William. The College lost 8-0!

One sport which the boys loved was fishing. One February night in 1885 a boy laid a night-line out from the end of the pier right into the Loch. Just to make sure, he attached a medal of the Holy Father to the line. When he went to inspect his catch the next morning he found he had caught the biggest fish of the season.

The Organ

In 1894 Fort Augustus was agog at the arrival of the great Abbey organ. Originally built in 1875 by Bryceson for a Mr Holmes for his house in Regent's Park, London, it was taken out in 1884 and placed in the Albert Palace, Battersea Park. Ten years later, when the Palace was demolished, the organ was bought by the monks of Fort Augustus:

> *A special train, a procession of lorries through Inverness and finally a special steamer down Loch Ness, brought this gigantic 'Kist of whistles' from Battersea to our monastery; and there it lay for a score of years, thousands of pipes, with the action bellows, keyboards filling the largest room in the Abbey, the calefactory or recreation-room, from floor to ceiling.*

Closure

At Christmas 1894 St Benedict's College closed, partly because numbers were falling due to competition from other Catholic boarding schools, and because the monks at Fort Augustus were inspired by Prior Linse and the Beuronese tradition to turn away from the world and devote their energies to prayer, painting and sacred music. The College changed in function and was very much reduced in size, now operating as a junior seminary for boys intending to be monks – holding, for example, 16 students in 1900 and only seven in 1903.

One of the last batch of the 230 pupils at the original College was John Carmont, later a King's Council and a Senator of the College of Justice.

The College was replaced by a class (with less than 20 pupils) which studied Latin, Greek, English, French, German, Science and Maths in a curriculum designed mainly to prepare boys for the priesthood.

Abbot Linse, who was discovered to be suffering from diabetes, was finding it increasingly difficult to fulfil his duties. Eventually, in 1906, a Visitation was made by the Abbot Primate. Abbot Linse's health steadily deteriorated. He had to return to Germany to be treated for his condition. In his absence the everyday administration of the monastery was in the hands of his Prior, Fr Kentigern Milne.

Abbot Linse stayed on the Continent for almost a whole year. He returned in the Autumn of 1909, ill and very weak. Finally he resigned and retired to St James', Letterfourie, near Buckie, where the monks of

Fort Augustus had a retreat house. He continued in office until his death at St James' in March 1910.

That year St Benedict's Abbey ceased to be an independent monastery under Rome and rejoined the English Congregation. For two years St Benedict's Abbey was under the jurisdiction of a claustral prior, Prior Hilary Willson from Ampleforth. In 1912 Sir David Oswald Hunter Blair, a flamboyant Oxford-educated Scottish aristocrat and man of letters, succeeded as the second Abbot of Fort Augustus.

On 15 March 1911, Abbot Hunter Blair's diary recorded the arrival at Fort Augustus of two British submarines. He described them as weird, wicked-looking brown things, whose officers dined in the monastic refectory.

During the First World War the Abbey and the day-school at the Convent nearby continued to function. The premises of the former St Benedict's College, however, were used as a military hospital, primarily to care for wounded Belgian soldiers.

A number of the monks went to France and Italy as military chaplains.[6] One of them, Fr John Lane Fox, was in the Irish Guards. In the Spring of 1916 he was involved in a horrific accident:

Father Lane Fox, the late chaplain to the Irish Guards, lost his right eye and hand in a bombing accident. He was standing by the Colonel, Lord Desmond Fitzgerald, watching a bombing practice. The Colonel said 'Now, Padre, you have a try'. Lane Fox took a bomb, pulled out the pin, and then, before the proper time, the bomb exploded in his hand, destroying his right eye and hand, killing Lord Desmond Fitzgerald and wounding or killing two officers and several men.[7]

Subsequently Fr Lane Fox was awarded the Military Cross for valour:

He is absolutely the idol of the regiment .... This is Father Lane Fox, the chaplain of the London Irish, who joined in the famous charge of the battalion at Loos, absolving those who were shot as they fell and arriving in the German trenches with the foremost.[8]

Odo Blundell

Prior to the First World War, Fort Augustus played an important part in Scottish archaeology. Fr Odo Blundell, who had investigated Cherry

Island in August 1908, was behind an initiative for the systematic investigation of Scottish pile-dwellings (crannogs) which was first proposed to the Society of Antiquaries of Scotland and subsequently funded by them. It was later also taken up by the British Association.

In his investigations he used a water-telescope (a zinc box with a glass bottom which was lowered one foot into the water).

Fr Odo sent out a preliminary circular to local antiquarians as a result of which about 50 new crannogs were added to the 100 known to exist. In 1914 he was asked to start a detailed investigation of a crannog in Loch Kinellan near Strathpeffer.[9] From 1912-14, as RC Chaplain, he said Mass on Sundays for the Fleet then based at Lamlash in the Firth of Clyde. By the outbreak of the War, he had established a tradition which was accepted by each Commanding Officer, without question. The need for RC chaplains was pressing.

Doggedly Fr Odo won the support of the Commander in Chief, Admiral Jellicoe, and resisted attempts by Prince Louis of Battenberg to prevent public celebration of Mass.

Throughout the War, Fr Odo served as a Naval chaplain, seeing much action, including the Battle of Jutland, where he served on the HMS 'Collingwood' alongside the future King George VI.

Meanwhile, in Fort Augustus considerable progress had been made in the building of the Abbey. The completed portion of the new Church, the Choir and Blessed Sacrament Chapel (which had been started in June 1914) was solemnly blessed on 13 November 1917 by Bishop Aeneas Chisholm.

Abbot Oswald Hunter Blair resigned that month. After a brief inter-regnum when Fr Hilary Willson of Ampleforth again acted as claustral prior, he was succeeded by Fr Andrew Joseph McDonald, who was elected Abbot on 27 August 1919.

CHERRY ISLAND CRANNOG

CHAPTER 3

The Abbey School
1920-29

THE revived Abbey School, Fort Augustus, unlike its nineteenth century predecessor, was not designed for the education of boys of the upper classes, nor was its curriculum as erudite.

The new School, with only 18 boys, was kick-started into life on 10 September 1920 by the dynamic new Abbot, Andrew Joseph McDonald.

The new Abbot was the first Gaelic-speaking abbot since the Reformation. He had the reputation of being a sound manager who had also had wide pastoral experience as a missionary priest in the city of Liverpool. He took over at a time when change was badly needed:

The Abbey itself was much depleted owing to the war and the earlier closing of the School; very few novices had been received during almost twenty years, so that there were scarcely any young men to carry on the work of the house, added to which difficulty, funds were at a low ebb.

The first headmaster of the new School was Oxford graduate, Fr Anselm Parker. At Ampleforth for five years, he had spent twelve years as Master of St Benet's Hall, Oxford. His prefect was Fr John Lane Fox.

The new School administration set out to educate their charges in the broadest sense: they were loth to impose a strict regime for the boys, preferring instead to persuade them that good behaviour would be in their own interest. They decided not to have 'rigid laws ... and discipline at every turn', preferring to persuade the boys (who were, after all, 'Catholic and gentlemen') to chose to behave themselves of their own accord and through their innate goodwill. 'This,' added Fr Parker in his first end of year speech, 'marked off our own school from the ordinary kind of school'; there were 'almost no penances' and 'the ferrula [strap] was getting more and more dusty in his room'.[1]

One of the changes instituted by Abbot McDonald was to the School colours:

> *The old School colours for … games, chocolate and white, had to be changed owing to the difficulty of obtaining a good chocolate, as good dyes after the war were unprocurable. The Abbot, therefore, gave up the chocolate colour and, being told that the colours of Corpus Christi College, Cambridge were scarlet and white (to represent the Body and Blood of Christ), he decided upon these colours in honour of the Holy Eucharist. In this way the well-known scarlet and white blazers of the School representing the colours of the Blessed Sacrament, were chosen specially by Abbot McDonald.*

Under the provisions of the 1918 Education (Scotland) Act the new institution at the Abbey was intended as 'a boarding School at a moderate pension (35 guineas a term as opposed to the 90 guineas charged by St Benedict's College), catering for the professional and commercial classes'.

In November 1923 Fr Anselm Parker's health broke down irretrievably. He was forced to retire and was succeeded immediately by Fr Ninian Macdonald.

The first fledgling School magazine, *Jottings from the School Chronicle* (which replaced *The Raven* of the pre–1894 College) did not appear until 1924. The Editor wrote:

> *We hope that the day is not far distant when the School will publish its Magazine … at present the circulation would be too limited to justify such a financial outlay … and we trust that in the meantime these 'Jottings' will be welcomed as stepping-stones to future higher things.*

THE RAVEN (ABOVE)
AND THE EDITOR OF JOTTINGS
AT HIS DESK.

When the School reopened in January 1924 there were 59 names on the roll.

The School staff consisted of Fr Ninian Macdonald (Headmaster), assisted by Frs Ambrose Geoghegan, Cyril Dieckhoff, Luke Cary-Elwes, John Lane Fox (Prefect of Studies), Victor Le Jeune, Francis Blackwell, Basil Wedge, Aelred White and Romuald Alexander.

Commander G. F. Farie was Prefect of Discipline, assisted by T. Byrne Esq, J. McNally Esq and Miss Ellis.

J. J. Robertson Esq was the Medical Officer and the Matron was Miss Tyler.

Physical Training was conducted by courtesy of the Cameron Depot, Inverness, who provided the services of Staff-Sergeant Hoban (Featherweight Boxing Champion of the Army for the previous four years). Dancing classes were held by a Miss Williamson.

For academic purposes the School was divided into three Sets. Already three boys had gained certificates in the Scottish Intermediate Examinations. Prizes were distributed for Maths, Latin, English Literature, Science, Band and Orchestra, Sports, Public Service and Industry.

There was a Dramatic Society (which presented William Shakespeare's 'The Merchant of Venice' on 8 December 1924 and 'Macbeth' on 8 December 1925 in the Abbey School theatre), an Orchestra (under Fr Luke Cary-Elwes), a Brass Band and a Choir (trained by Fr Ambrose Geoghegan). Other societies included the Debating, Photographic, Philatelic, Music, Natural History and Natural Science, as well as the Association for the Propagation of the Faith (APF) which met monthly and raised money for the Foreign Missions.

Relations with the local community outside the School were strengthened when the Abbot and the Headmaster were elected parish councillors in December 1925 and the Headmaster re-elected Hon. President of the Mactavish Shinty Association.

It was Fr Ninian who created the School magazine *The Corbie* from the earlier *Jottings* and laid the foundations of the policy which guided the publication:

To chronicle events of special interest to those who claim the Abbey School as theirs and to publish articles with a wider appeal.

Abbot McDonald left Fort Augustus for Liverpool in September

1924 and then set sail for America with a band of monks who had completed their year's Novitiate at Fort Augustus, in order to establish the new St Anselm's Priory at the Catholic University of Washington DC.

During the year 1923-24 the School games were still Shinty (the School team winning the Schools' Championship and the Mactavish Trophy for 1924-25), Football and Cricket, the latter played in front of the wooden Pavilion. Boating was also popular, especially the Masters versus School race and the Glasgow District versus The Rest:

> *The oft-mooted question, as to which games should be officially adopted during the Winter months, seems to be settling itself by the old rule of 'demand and supply'. The possible number of out-matches must necessarily be the determining factor. The present turn of the wheel indicates that Association football is on the decline. The Schools in our neighbourhood devote themselves in increasing numbers to Shinty and Rugby Football. The ideal solution, doubtless, would be to play one game in the Third Term, and the other in the First. Unfortunately, weather prophets cannot assure us with any degree of certainty in which term King Frost is more likely to reign. For the present, therefore, we shall continue to play both games before and after Xmas.*

On Sunday afternoons the boys played Abbey Ball, a game 'with nothing barred but kicking'.

In June 1926 Francis Corballis, an Old Boy and then Chief Scout's Commissioner, spent some days at the School, explaining the history of the Scout movement to the boys. The first official parade of the Scout Corps in uniform and carrying the Troop Colours was to come on Armistice Day, 11 November 1926, at the Village War Memorial.

The School Orchestra gave two concerts in aid of local charities. The first, at Roy Bridge to raise funds for a new church, included three arias sung by Abbot McDonald's niece, Miss Ryan. The instrumentalists returned through the Great Glen, arriving at 1.30 am. The second was held in the Drill Hall in aid of the Nursing Association. There was also a very successful choir picnic to Torgoyle in the middle of July.

The new Organ

Abbot Hunter Blair recalled that the presence of the mighty organ created its own hazards even before the instrument was finally assembled in all its glory:

One pipe alone, the mighty 32 foot cylinder, had to be left in all its length in the cloister, close to where we assembled for the daily offices; and there, one Summer evening, as we stood in silent lines at the vesper hour, waiting to enter the choir, was heard an indescribably confused sound of scratching and squeaking. Had the monastery cat got into the great pipe and lost her way out? Could it be a dog? A gigantic rat? A family of whimpering mice? Could it be – surely not, yet it was, a small boy (I think the smallest in our school), who had crawled head first into the mighty open tube, with the firm purpose of emerging at the other end. Alas! He found himself in a cul-de-sac, and nearly smothered; and only with incredible struggling, scrabbling, panting and groaning was he extricated backwards, but alive, from his perilous position.

From St Anselm's Priory, USA, came the gift of a Balopticon. This was an instrument which not only was capable of showing lantern slides, but was also able to project on a screen illustrations derived from prints, books and postcards, reproducing the colours exactly.

It was at this time that the notion of starting an Old Boys' Association was first mooted. However, as the Editor of *The Corbie* pointed out:

We feel that the opportune moment for this has not yet arrived; nevertheless our readers may rest assured that the project is being steadily borne in mind.

Midsummer 1926 saw the arrival of two lay-masters, Mr Scholes and Mr Hickey. By now, boys of Scottish descent were coming from far-flung parts of the globe – Australia, India and even Japan. Relations with the wider community outside the School were helped by the diplomacy of Sport: the Headmaster, Fr Ninian Macdonald, had the satisfaction of being promoted to vice-president of the Mactavish Camanachd Association and made a member of Council.

January 1927 brought a great gale of wind which did considerable damage to trees in the neighbourhood. Nevertheless, Spring fishing on Loch Ness that year was very successful. Abstinence days were eagerly looked forward to as a plentiful supply of clean-run salmon was added to the School rations.

Later that year Abbot McDonald was re-elected. It was a glorious Summer which affected the boys in particular:

It happens that in the month of June we have practically twenty-four hours of continuous daylight. The only disadvantage of this is the difficulty of getting to sleep at the hours of nine or ten o'clock. An interesting experiment has been made this year: all the large dormitory windows have been thoroughly 'smoked' and a twilight effect has been obtained, which encourages drowsiness.

On 29 September there was additional cause for rejoicing when four Old Boys entered the Novitiate – George (Edmund) Carruth, Joseph (Clement) King, John (Ethelbert) McCombes, and John (Oswald Eaves). The Autumn term also saw the arrival of the new Classical Master, Mr Pimley, who would in due course achieve the status of legend.

After 45 years of exposure to wind and weather, the dials of the Tower Clock needed protection and were encased in glass. The clock, in spite of having lost its dial glasses in transit before installation, was only losing one second per week (less than a minute per year).

Abbot Hunter Blair left Fort Augustus that Winter to spend some time in Brazil, where in 1895 the Abbey of Beuron had restored the Benedictines at the request of the Holy See. One of the fruits of this expedition was the rosewood screen in the Blessed Sacrament Chapel, made by the São Paulo School of Arts and Crafts.

At the end of January 1928 consecutive days of heavy rain and a rapid thaw of snow on the hills brought the rivers down in roaring spate. The surface of Loch Ness rose several inches above the boathouse pier. The Editor of *The Corbie* complained:

Much damage was done to the Tarff bridge by uprooted trees which were swept down and became wedged between the concrete pillars. The water eddying around the bases quickly ate into the bed of the river and caused such a displacement of the pillars that traffic had to be suspended for several days. Our football pitch was turned into a miniature lake.

However, the Spring fishing in the Tarff was very successful, both the large-scale operations carried out by the lay-brothers with the salmon net and the efforts of small anglers, netting a considerable quantity of well-fed trout.

BBC radio broadcasts by prominent members of the Community took place during 1927: one on 'Scottish Monasticism' delivered by Abbot Hunter Blair and two given by Dom Gregory Ould ('Christmas Carols' and 'Plainsong').

Around this time, Fr Ninian made arrangements to present candidates for the Oxford and Cambridge Schools Examination Board in addition to taking the customary Scottish Leaving Certificate. In July 1928 eight boys sat the Oxford and Cambridge School Certificate. When the results were known one boy had achieved seven credits, one six, and two had five credits. Prizes for academic and sporting activities were awarded annually from contributions given by Old Boys Sir James Calder CBE, Bishop Bennet and Lord Lovat.

On 20 July Abbot McDonald returned from his visit to the American priories:

> *The School turned out* en masse *to meet him at the main entrance to the grounds and accompanied him (with music from the Scout Corps Band) to the door of the Guest-house, where he was met by the assembled Community. Meanwhile, the flag was hoisted on the College Tower and the big bell was swung.*

October saw an arrival of a different kind – a covey of sea-planes, which created much excitement:

> *Two came down close by the boat-house pier; and the officers very kindly allowed the School to see over the strange 'birds'. The gracefulness with which the planes alighted upon and rose from the surface of the water was very much admired.*

On 7 December Fr Basil's production of Shakespeare's 'Hamlet' (slimmed down by judicious cuts) was given in the School theatre. H. Boultwood played the Prince and P. Conacher successfully interpreted the role of the bumbling official Polonius.

For the Rugby season a new field was rented on Borlum Farm. It was so perfectly drained that even the heaviest fall of rain left no water lying on its surface. There was only one fall of snow that Winter, so the fixture list was not disrupted.

The frost at the beginning of 1929 allowed several of the boys to acquire basic skating skills:

> *Loch Uanagan provided an excellent sheet of ice, and the Shinty on its surface attracted a large number of players. Many individuals, however, seemed to find boot leather a better balancing medium in a scrimmage than the blade of a skate!*

On 21 March 1929 an Old Boy, Edward A. Douglas, was nominated a Judge of the Supreme Court in Brisbane, Australia; but the year was most notable for the nomination of the Abbot of Fort Augustus to the Archbishopric of St Andrews and Edinburgh, news of which reached the Abbey on the day the School was breaking up for the Summer holidays.

What made Archbishop McDonald's consecration ceremony in St Mary's Cathedral, Edinburgh so memorable was that the new Archbishop was supported during the long and trying function by two Old Boys, themselves bishops – Louis Caruana, Archbishop of Malta (1915) and George Bennett, Bishop of Aberdeen (1918).

THE CORBIE (BY FR PHILIP HYNES)

CHAPTER 4

The Abbey School
1929-35

THE election of an Abbot to succeed Archbishop McDonald took place on 11 November 1929. The Community chose Fr Wulstan Knowles who had been Superior of a Priory in America for a number of years. Formerly he had been on the teaching staff of the Abbey School at Fort Augustus. On the same day Br Anthony Mattes, shoemaker to the Community, had a stroke. He died a few days afterwards.

Abbot Knowles returned to Fort Augustus on 12 December and was welcomed by the Community and the School. A holiday was declared to celebrate his solemn Blessing five days later. The Headmaster, Fr Ninian Macdonald, left to work in America. His place was taken by Abbot Knowles.

During the few holidays that term the boys enjoyed a taste of mountaineering. Meallfuarmhonaidh was tackled on 8 October, offering a fine view of the surrounding countryside. On 28 November the School mountaineers set out for Sròn a' Choire Ghairbh (3066 feet). Unfortunately a thick mist on the top obscured the view.

The School Rugby team performed well that season, largely due to the coaching of two of the masters, Mr Hughes and Mr Hamilton. The team was also putting in more practice and the powers-that-be had allowed some of the Junior clerics to play in the practice games, so providing sterner practice opposition.

For the first time ever, four Fort Augustus boys worked as *brancardiers* (stretcher-bearers) on the September Pilgrimage to Lourdes led by the Bishop of Northampton. The Comte de Beauchamp, head of the *brancardiers*, was greatly impressed by the boys' cheeriness, piety and their readiness to obey orders.

On 14 July 1930 a meeting was held in the Headmaster's room to discuss the revival of the now moribund Old Boys' Association. Representatives of both the 'old' School and the existing one expressed

OLD BOYS' GOSSIP

the hope that the meeting would give an impetus to the movement to create a really active Association.

On the following day the Golden Jubilee of the Abbey was marked with a Pontifical High Mass of Thanksgiving, celebrated by Archbishop McDonald. Photographs were taken in the quadrangle afterwards, and then the whole Community – monks and visitors – assembled for luncheon in the long northern cloister. In the absence of Lord and Lady Lovat, the young Master of Lovat acknowledged the toast. After supper the festivities were closed by a concert in the School theatre.

Some weeks later Fr Alphonsus O'Connell, an enthusiastic proponent of 'muscular Christianity', returned from the United States and took up his joint (and perhaps conflicting) posts as spiritual adviser and boxing instructor!

Perhaps the most dramatic event that Winter was the change in the games from Shinty to Hockey. The Prefect of Discipline, Commander Farie, explained the reasons: first, it was becoming increasingly difficult (in fact almost impossible) to arrange away matches; second, it was felt that it was much better to learn a game which could very likely be a source of much enjoyment in later years, whereas a knowledge of Shinty would be of very little use outside the North of Scotland.

Meanwhile, news came that Fr Ninian Macdonald, former head-master of the Abbey School, had received an invitation to attend the celebrations to held in October in Carinthia, a province of Austria.

Immediately after the First World War the disposal of Carinthia was one of the problems faced by the Peace Conference. In 1920 an inter-allied Commission was nominated to conduct a plebiscite of the inhabitants over their future government.

Fr Ninian, having worked as a British diplomat after the War, was asked to join the Commission. He received a letter of appointment from the Secretary for Foreign Affairs, Lord Curzon, because of his unique knowledge of local Carinthian affairs. In addition to other posts, he was Secretary to the British Section of the Commission.

Unhappily, since Fr Ninian was working in USA and not in Europe, he was debarred from accepting the invitation to be present at the annual celebrations in Carinthia.

Fr Aloysius Carruth, meanwhile, was studying in Germany and Fr Alban Boultwood was in Rome. Both wrote to the Editor of *The Corbie* to say they were delighted to receive their copies. Fr Aloysius' brother, D. Carruth, a monitor, Vice-Captain of Rugby and a Cricket 'cap', had at this time just entered the Novitiate.

In sport J. McLaughlin (later Fr Thomas) excelled. He was not only a speedy rugby player, but also managed to win the 100, 220 yards, and the Long Jump. He came second in the Half Mile and in the 440 yards.

The first annual dinner of the Catholic Public Schools Scottish Association was held in Glasgow on 5 February 1931, presided over by the Archbishop of St Andrews and Edinburgh. The object of the Association was 'to provide and promote fellowship among old boys of Catholic public schools; its ultimate and main aim was to enable old boys of Catholic public schools to participate, with the strength that only organisation can give, in all spheres of Catholic life'.

Fr Anselm Parker, the first headmaster of the new School, paid a brief visit to Fort Augustus. During one of the holidays the annual ascent of Ben Nevis took place and on another occasion, Glengarry was explored as far as Tomdoun.

When the School returned after the Summer holidays they found that a new lighting system had been installed throughout the building, including the stage lights in the School theatre.

A ripple of expectation ran through the School because the Latin and French Master and Prefect of Studies, Mr Pimley, had just got married. Another cause for celebration came on 29 September 1931 at the Solemn Profession of Fr Oswald Eaves, the first boy from the new School to be professed.

At the Spring retreat held at Fort Augustus, a number of Old Boys played Rugby against the School. During an informal meeting it was decided to form branches of the Fort Augustus Old Boys' Association in Glasgow, Liverpool and Inverness.

In the Summer term one of the most interesting events was a visit from Squadron-Leader F. Noakes, who demonstrated the reliability and safety of modern aircraft by his daring and skilful handling of his Gypsy Moth. Three boys were given flights, the aircraft taking off from the field south of the Tarff in front of the eyes of the whole School, the Community and members of the public.

The warm weather encouraged many to bathe in the Canal and Loch Uanagan (with its higher temperature). Inside the School a craze for yo-yos swept through the student body.

In the Autumn, after ten years at the School, Commander Gilbert Farie RN (Retired) was not in good health and it seemed uncertain whether he would be able to take up his work again.

He had come from a teaching post at Rugby to be master of Mathematics at Fort Augustus. Soon after, he had succeeded Fr Ninian Macdonald as Prefect of Discipline, in which capacity he tried to further the interests of the boys in every direction, particularly in the improvement of the standard of Athletics, Rugby and Cricket. He had a dry sense of humour – 'If you want to make a good school, burn all the books and get on with it,' was one of his favourite remarks.

There was a note of sadness too for the death of a very distinguished Old Boy, Colonel Sir James Reynolds, Bart, MP. He had come to St Benedict's College in 1879. *The Corbie* observed:

> *Frank, straight-forward and high principled with an abhorrence of anything which savoured of meanness or injustice, vigorous, rollicking, happy-go-lucky is but a partial description of Jimmy. His outstanding qualities both in his school days and in after life were however his charitableness, thoroughness, determination and energy.*

The Winter of 1932 was notable for the appearance of two books written by members of the Community – Fr Cyril Dieckhoff's *Gaelic Dictionary* and Fr Ninian Macdonald's *History of Shinty*.[1]

In the school theatre, meanwhile, Fr Alphonsus worked hard to make the scenery as efficient as possible. He introduced methods of rapid scene-shifting which were in use in the best theatres of the time. The stage was now completely equipped with lights and scenery. A door had also been placed at the side of the stage to prevent noisy scene-changing.

The new arrangements were shown off to the full in 'Bluebeard', produced by the Junior Dramatic Society. The actors were well 'made up' by Fr Luke (who also painted the scenery). Fr Alphonsus was an indefatigable stage manager and the very realistic killing of Bluebeard was due to the fencing instruction given by Fr Victor.

On 18 February 1933 Lord Lovat died suddenly. Mass was sung at Beauly by Archbishop McDonald. Fr Abbot was present in the sanctuary and a choir of monks under Fr Prior was responsible for the music.

★   ★   ★

Transport was always a problem. The Fiat which had given years of yeoman service was replaced by an Albion which now would have to face bouncing along paths at the foot of Ben Nevis with a load of 35, or negotiating precarious wooden bridges and tortuous bends.

There was excitement in the Senior Literary and Debating Society during a Mock Trial. Mr Hughes had been accused of the murder of his aunt and was proving to be a very amusing prisoner, when the lights suddenly went out. During the darkness the air was thick with missiles of all kinds, and when the lights went up the court presented an extraordinary appearance (alarming various members of the Community who were present!).

Summer 1933 was notable for Commander Farie's return to full vigour, and for heightened public interest in the Loch Ness Monster. Two students of the Abbey School were reported to have had an excellent view of the creature.

During the Winter term of 1933 the weather was remarkably good. Excavations for the swimming pool continued steadily. Many Old Boys responded to Fr Bernard's appeal for funds. Later in the year snow never descended from the hill-tops, but in December there were several days of hard frost which made skating possible. 'Monster fever' continued and one correspondent in *The Corbie* was convinced it was nothing more than a big water-lizard.

One of the entertainments in the School theatre during the term was 'The Monster', which had the beast invading the mansion of the Laird of Bunoich. It was eventually disposed of, disgorging in its death-throes a baby, a live chicken, and a clergyman!

The death of a distinguished Old Boy, F. F. Corballis, robbed the School of a good friend. Fred Corballis was a Chief Scout's Commissioner, President of the Catholic Scout Advisory Council, a Member of the Catholic Educational Council, and a Member of the Council of St Vincent de Paul. In 1927 the Pope created him a Privy Chamberlain, and in 1929 he received the medal *Bene merenti* for his work as organiser of the British Section of the International Scout Pilgrimage to Rome.

On 18 March, Passion Sunday, Fr Oswald Eaves and Fr Aidan O'Flynn were ordained priests. Fr Celestine Haworth was ordained a sub-deacon.

First seen in September 1934 was the new laboratory which replaced the old Science room. Designed by Reid & Forbes, Edinburgh, and built by the lay-brothers, the laboratory was fitted into the gap between the Study Hall and the Gymnasium where, in former times, a wooden ramp joined the two. A cellar was demolished and its stones used to construct the front of the laboratory so as to disguise the addition. The laboratory was nearly three times the size of the old Science room. It was now possible to offer a practical Science course up to the standard of pre-University examinations.

On the cricket pitch, meanwhile, another innovation appeared, aimed at honing the skills of the Cricket teams. Colonel Gordon had designed and built a catapult, constructed out of a wooden stand, two rake handles, a few feet of rubber and a piece of carpet. The result was a very efficient instrument for producing any length and any pace of bowling. A skilled operator could pitch on a handkerchief nine times out of ten. This came in useful at the time of the first ever properly organised Old Boys' game with the School XI on 18 and 19 July (which the School won by 20 runs).

On Monday 7 January 1935, preceding dinner at the Caledonian Hotel in Edinburgh, the inaugural meeting of the reconstituted Fort Augustus Old Boys' Association was held.

In the chair was Abbot Wulstan Knowles, supported by the Bishop of Aberdeen and Abbot Hunter Blair. Abbot Knowles urged the Association to consider seriously the possibility that Old Boys might help those who had just left School to find employment.

It was decided to change the name to 'The Fort Augustus Association'. Fr Luke, Chaplain to the Association, invariably included a Memento for living and dead Old Boys in his daily Mass. Life membership subscription was five guineas, annual subscription half a guinea.

Present at the dinner which followed were Charles George SSC (the Chairman of the steering committee), Fr Oswald Eaves, Mr W. D. Hamilton (Editor of *The Corbie*), Mr Reginald Fairlie RSA, and 30 Old Boys. The first toast was 'The Pope and the King'.

CHAPTER 5

The Abbey School

1935-38

DURING the early Spring of 1935 the new swimming pool was completed and equipped with a diving platform and a diving board. The whole School could now look forward to good bathing facilities in the Summer term.

Regrettably, due to increasing rheumatism and heart problems, Miss Tyler, the School Matron, was forced to resign. Her place was taken by Mrs Pimley. Commander Farie, who had been Prefect of Discipline for most of Miss Tyler's time at the School, commented:

For 15 years she has carried out the work of Matron. She never left off, her working week was seven full days, nothing was ever too much trouble; the Abbey School interests were her interests, and she has left a big gap, difficult to fill.

On 27 February the London Dinner of the Fort Augustus Association was held at the Rembrandt Hotel. Abbot Hunter Blair presided over 21 Old Boys and guests. Toasts were proposed by Fr Robert Steuart SJ and the Hon. Everard Fielding OBE. In his address Abbot Hunter Blair mentioned his coming visit to Rome and promised to ask a special blessing for the Association at his Audience with the Holy Father. He was given a tremendous ovation and the assembly, as one man, arose and sang 'For he's a jolly good fellow'.

One afternoon during the Summer term, when the School XI was playing on the Cricket pitch, fire broke out and destroyed the Gym and the Theatre. The fire had been caused by a boy smoking in the prop room of the Theatre. It was thanks to many of the villagers from Fort Augustus that the School itself was untouched. Plans were immediately made to build a modern complex comprising a theatre and gymnasium, form rooms, surgery and matron's quarters.

One consequence of this event was a plan for a new School building to be erected on the ground facing the School tower between the tennis court and the swimming pool. But the proposal was vetoed by the Monastery Chapter on the grounds that it would create a school that was too big for the Community.[1]

On 6 May the School Scout Troop set off to fire the Ben Nevis Beacon in honour of King George. They set off from Torlundy Farm at the foot about 4 pm, accompanied by Maclachlan the ghillie, leading a pony skilfully loaded with rockets, flares, flash powder, rope, electric torches, rations, wax tapers and matches. Another party began the ascent from Glen Nevis. After a gruelling climb, both parties met at the Half-Way House where they had a meal of sandwiches and cheese biscuits washed down with ginger wine.

The warm weather that Summer made the occasional School holidays very popular. This made possible full day tramps through the Highland landscape, two of the days being spent picnicking beside Loch Hourn. The Albion, now well broken in to the heavy West Highland roads, tackled them with the same doggedness as its predecessor, thanks to the attention of Br Joseph.

The new swimming pool proved to be an unqualified success. Most of the School were able to swim by the end of the term, thanks to the lessons given by Fr Bernard and Br Andrew. The Swimming Competition was enjoyed by competitors and spectators alike.

A well patronised Old Boys' Reunion was held at Fort Augustus on 21 and 22 September 1935 in the presence of Fr Abbot, Bishop Bennet and Abbot Hunter Blair. During the meeting on 21 September the rules of the Association were read and adopted.

The photograph of the Old Boys taken on the grass outside the cloisters shows that, out of 31 men present, 19 were now members of the Order of St Benedict.

Later that year a biography of Lord Lovat appeared, written by Sir Francis Lindley.[2] It was reviewed in *The Sunday Times,* with a contemptuous reference to Lord Lovat's 'obscure upbringing and meagre education' which he received at the Benedictine College of Fort Augustus, where he passed most of his school days.[3]

Abbot David Hunter Blair castigated the reviewer and the biography:

No such epithets as 'meagre' and 'obscure' are justified in reference to an educational centre which, in the course of a single generation, has turned out (to say nothing of so admirable a trio as Lovat and his two brothers) a remark-

able group of distinguished soldiers, merchant princes, eminent churchmen, three judges of the High Court in Scotland and Australia who achieved distinction in various walks of life .... The excellent Cricket played at the Abbey School, under first-rate professional training, may almost be said to have introduced the game into the Highlands .... Lovat himself thought very highly of his old school and loved his time there.

In the same issue of *The Corbie*, the School's academic record was defended. 'Attacks subtle and open have been made on the School,' wrote the Editor. 'Fair criticism is feared by none, but unjustifiable and ungrounded misrepresentation is not to be tolerated.'

The Corbie went on to point out that the School was visited annually by His Majesty's Inspectors from the Scottish Education Department and 'a series of very good reports has been received on the various activities of the School, inside and outside the class room'. During the period 1928-35 only one boy had failed the Scottish Group Certificate (Higher Leaving Certificate). In the Oxford and Cambridge Examinations a very high average of 70 per cent of possible successes was maintained, with an average of nearly five credits per candidate.

In the Winter term of 1935 a new Matron, Miss Macdonald, arrived. A Boxing instructor, Mr Morrison, was another newcomer to the staff.

During School picnics to Invergarry and Torgoyle, Dr Flood acted as chef, with the help of a hay-box and a new oven.

When the School returned after Christmas, it found the Fort under snow in Arctic conditions which lasted for about three weeks. Rugby and Hockey were out of the question, so Winter sports were the order of the day – sledging and skating on Loch Tarff.

On 3 March Fr Martin Wall died. Born in 1843, he always claimed to have introduced the word 'bicycle' into the English language in 1868, while an undergraduate at Emmanuel College, Cambridge.

Among the lectures delivered to the School was 'Germany under Hitler' by Frau Müller and 'Distilling' by Captain Smith Grant MC.

The Old Boys' Dinner took place that Spring in the Caledonian Hotel, Edinburgh, with Abbot Hunter Blair presiding over a company of 27 members. The guest of the evening was Lord Moncrieff who, in his address, paid tribute to the contribution made to Scottish education by the Benedictine Order.

The Summer term was given over to the construction of the new tennis court. This was done by bringing stones from the bed of the

River Tarff just above the bridge and filling the bowling green with them.

The School staff gave the lead. Mr Pimley was site manager, Mr Hughes, with strings round his trousers, was a first-class navvy. Mr Hamilton knocked down trees, while Mr Morrison dug drains with great efficiency. Mr Scholes carted stones about, while Br Maurus used a barrow! In four days the court was half done. In seven days it was completed. In ten it was ready for use. Commander Farie, who had umpired on the Centre Court at Wimbledon, gave the School some hints on how to play.

The usual School one-day holidays were as popular as ever, but it was now remarked on that the seniors preferred to go off in small groups rather than as a large body.

There were 46 at the Old Boys' weekend on 11 July, including those who were members of the Community. There was first a general business meeting in the Calefactory on the Saturday night. 'Old Boys sprouted from everywhere,' commented *The Corbie*. 'I doubt if you could have thrown a stone from the top of the tower without hitting one.'

For the next edition of *The Corbie*, the outside cover was re-designed. *The Corbie* had been on display at the Catholic Press Exhibition in Rome, but there had been no way of telling from the cover where the magazine was printed. Hence the change.

On 14 October, while Mr Dames and Mr Maclennan were working to remove a sandbank in the Abbey vegetable garden, they found what they thought to be a stone drain.

However it turned out to be three ancient graves (cists) built of stone slabs. In one cist was found parts of a human skull, in another larger parts of a human skeleton.

That term the third volume of Abbot Hunter Blair's autobiography was published. *A Last Medley of Memories*, illustrated by Peter F. Anson, brought his reminiscences into the contemporary era.[4]

There were technological changes at Fort Augustus. Great excitement surrounded the assembly of the gigantic church organ. Another innovation was the good ship 'Mañana' which was due to arrive at the School to be used by Staff and School for cruising during the holidays.

On 2 August, Frs Denys Rutledge and Celestine Haworth were ordained to the priesthood. Frs Edmund Carruth and Anselm Richardson were ordained to the diaconate on the same day.

The Fort Augustus Association met on 28 November 1936 at the

Grand Hotel, Charing Cross, Glasgow. Abbot Wulstan Knowles presided over the meeting.

After toasts to 'The Pope' and 'The King', Archbishop McDonald of St Andrews and Edinburgh told the meeting that a great deal was expected of them and tradition would be shaped largely by their hands. He hoped it would be a tradition of social service, in an age which seemed to have forgotten the fundamental principles of justice, principles laid down by Pope Leo XIII in his encyclical *Rerum Novarum*, when the tide of Communism threatened society with class warfare. It was only by working for the welfare of the less fortunate that Catholics could show to the world the value of their principles.

Early in the following year came the sad news of the death of Miss Winifred Tyler on 25 February 1937. Miss Tyler, who had been Matron at the School for 14 years, had died as bravely as she had lived. The Requiem Mass at St Peter's, Edinburgh, and the funeral at Mount Vernon, Edinburgh, were carried out by Archbishop McDonald for whom she had worked for so long at Fort Augustus.

The good ship 'Mañana' proved to be the 'Ann Cook', a *Fifie*, 69 feet overall, 21 feet beam, her shallow draft essential for the East of Scotland's tidal harbours. The rig was originally a large dipping lug and standing mizen with no head sail, the foremast an enormous spar, nearly

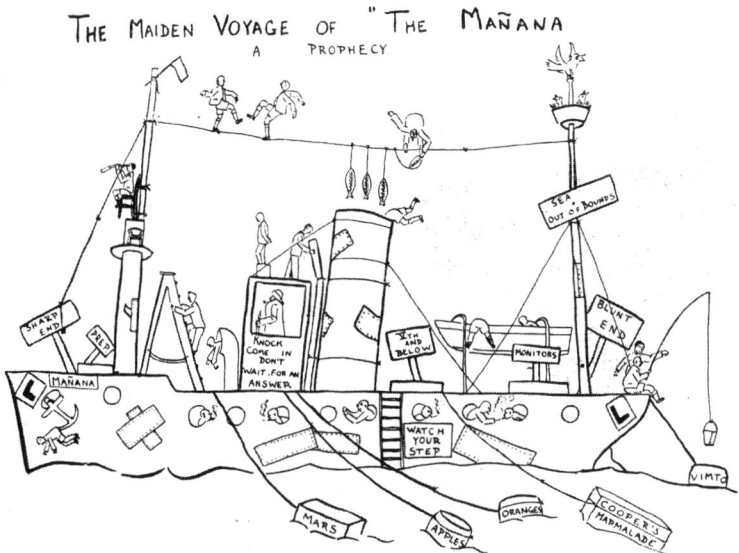

THE MAIDEN VOYAGE OF "THE MAÑANA"
A PROPHECY

two feet in diameter, stayed only by the halliards. The 'Ann Cook' was now powered by a Gardener semi-Diesel engine which replaced the spars and sails, with only small masts now carrying a trysail and mizen. However, the hull was as sound as the day she left Millar's yard at St Monance.

There were two memorable holidays that Easter term. The first, on Monday 8 February, was to Invergarry via Loch Lundy, a long and pleasant walk. The day was frosty with a good deal of snow lying about. The whole party was entertained by Miss Grant at Invergarry.

On Thursday 4 March a School party set off for Stratherrick, but, because the road was blocked by snow-drifts, they only reached Glencoe. In spite of these difficulties they had an excellent meal in Mr Macdonald's barn, the food being prepared by Dr Flood.

On Coronation Day, after High Mass, the School sang 'God save the King' with great enthusiasm. Cricket in the afternoon was interrupted to receive Coronation Medals. A bonfire was lit at night and the School Tower was floodlit.

On St Benedict's Day a large contingent of Old Boys arrived. One of them, Colonel A. W. McDonald, presented the prizes in the Study Hall. Commander Farie read an account of the School's educational and sporting achievements during the year. At the end of his remarks he called for three cheers. The roof nearly came off!

That Summer the 'Prep' class moved to the new Saint Andrew's School in Edinburgh. This meant, pointed out Commander Farie, that the Matron, Miss Ellis, would regrettably have to leave the Abbey staff.

In July a number of Old Boys visited the School for their Annual Reunion. It was decided that, in future, the Headmaster should always be, *ex officio*, a member of the Committee.

Old Boys abroad included L. Connolly who had joined the Palestine Police and was due to sail for Haifa in September, and J. E. McFall who would shortly begin his career in the RAF at Hatfield Aerodrome, Hertfordshire, before being drafted to Egypt.

On 1 August 1937, Frs Edmund Carruth and Anselm Richardson were raised to the priesthood by Bishop Bennet; Brs Ethelbert McCombes, Andrew McKillop and Maurus Whitehead received the diaconate; and Brs Alban Boultwood and Aloysius Carruth received the sub-diaconate.

Intriguingly, seven officers from the German Navy visited the Abbey on 20 August, accompanied by the Provost and Chief Constable of Inverness and several other dignitaries.

On 4 November 1937 Abbot Wulstan Knowles was re-elected. The School was delighted, particularly when he granted them a holiday the day after his election. Perhaps to mark the re-election, T. C. Barry, the previous year's School Captain, produced a series of sports statistics for 1926-37. During that period 34 School Cricket matches were played, of which 23 were won. Since the inauguration of Hockey as a school game, 16 matches were played, of which 13 were won. In Rugby the School had played 47 matches and won 21. However, the 1936-37 Rugby season was the only one in which the School XV was undefeated. Perhaps that was because American football seemed to have arrived at Fort Augustus. Coach W. Kelly had often been seen in a huddle with members of the XV. The 'flying wedge' and 'blocking' had been practised.

Archaeological excavations had again been taking place in Fort Augustus, but were now nearing completion. During the previous four months Stone Age artefacts had been discovered and the site of the first occupation tumulus and burial definitely established.

The Organ had now been electrified and re-erected. More speaking stops had been added, the pedal work had been increased and the tonal resources improved to make it one of the best instruments in Europe.

On 30 May 1938, Br Meinrad Grimm died. He was born in a village near Baden in 1884 and served as a baker/confectioner and then as a soldier in the German Army before joining the Abbey of Beuron.

Abbot Linse persuaded him to join him at Fort Augustus and he was professed in 1893. He then worked as a baker at the Abbey. However, during the First World War the British Government asked for him to be transferred to the Abbey of Belmont. When the War ended, he returned to Fort Augustus and continued to work as a baker and confectioner in the foul air of the old dungeons.

Towards the end of his life he suffered from insomnia, cataract and diabetes. He died in his sleep.

Around the same time Br Francis Kennedy also died. He had been responsible for the Abbey electrical plant, the upkeep of the auxiliary engine, the supervision of batteries and water power, the refrigeration plant and for the various motors supplying power for the organ, bells and workshops, all functions expertly performed by Br Francis.

The value of a School magazine was increasingly appreciated. *The Corbie* mixed domestic and global material, School tittle-tattle, and hard international news gathered by monks and boys from all parts of the world acting as 'special correspondents'.

During the Summer of 1938 an Old Boy, Fr Adrian Weld-Blundell, returned as Novice Master, and Fr Luke Cary-Elwes came back from Malta looking tanned and fit and was soon to be found on his beloved square – the Cricket pitch. The School Cricket team benefited from the arrival of a professional coach, J. W. Day, late of Notts. Meanwhile Dr John McQuillan, teacher of Religious Knowledge over the previous two years, left to take the post of Professor at St Peter's College.

The Fort Augustus Association's annual general meeting took place at Fort Augustus on 10 July, presided over by Abbot Wulstan Knowles. The new Constitution was proposed for acceptance by Commander Farie and accepted unanimously by the 37 Old Boys present. The Association was now divided into four areas: North of Scotland, South of Scotland, North of England, South of England.

Old Boys were making their mark in academic and literary life. John C. Barry had recently gained a Double First in French and German at Cambridge University and was proceeding to Fribourg in September. Fr Gregory Brusey had been awarded the degree of Bachelor of Music at Edinburgh University. Fr Aloysius Carruth had just written a pamphlet on the Loch Ness Monster, published and printed by the Abbey Press.

There was, however, more tangible marine disturbance when, on 31 July 1938, at Strangford Lough on the east coast of Ireland, the School boat, the 'Ann Cook', ran aground. Commander Farie, who had been at the helm, was distraught.

There were now 56 boys in the School, led by Commander Farie, a Headmaster with outstanding leadership qualities. However, the Commander now decided it was time to retire. The School Inspector described him as 'a headmaster who for 17 years directed its [the School's] activities with outstanding ability, impressing upon it his own vigorous personality and turning out manly and independent boys, well prepared physically and intellectually to take their place in the world'.[5]

CHAPTER 6

The Abbey School
1938-40

The imminence of War was brought home to Fort Augustus when the monastic Community began training as air wardens and carried out gas drill. The boys of the School were measured for gas masks and given two lectures on how to use them.

Lord Lovat, who was married on 10 October, visited the School later in the term. The School Captain, W. MacDonald, had sent him a telegram conveying the boys' good wishes. 'The School owes much to Lord Lovat's family,' commented *The Corbie*, 'and it is fitting that Fort Augustus maintain a close contact with him.'

There were several changes in the teaching staff: Fr Ethelbert McCombes was appointed Assistant Headmaster and Fr Maurus White-head made Prefect of Discipline.

In spite of these changes the boys continued to show the personal qualities which Commander Farie tried so hard to instil. The School Inspector noted that ' … the spirit and discipline of the School are admirable, while the bearing of the boys, a blend of frankness, independence and deference, was very attractive'.[1]

An entertainment was presented by the School under the direction of Br Alban. A particular feature of the evening's entertainment was the Jazz Choir which sang 'Highland Swing' and 'Lambeth Walk', and there were excerpts from Gilbert and Sullivan's favourite light operas.

The inaugural dinner of the North of Scotland branch of the Fort Augustus Association was held in the refectory of the Abbey School that term. The Abbot, Fr Wulstan Knowles, presided over 26 Old Boys, including Commander Farie, Headmaster of the School, and ten members of the monastic Community. The company was interested to hear that Acting Pilot Officer J. McFall, serving with the RAF in Palestine, had already been mentioned in dispatches.

An Old Boy and a solicitor from Beauly, Mr J. Paterson, gave the main address, urging the Old Boys to advise young students still at school on how to choose a career and suggested they should also find employment for boys about to enter business or industry. The Old Boys had entered, he continued, upon one of the greatest struggles the Catholic Church had ever known – a battle of mind and personality, the vanguard fight against Communism and militant Atheism.

On 10 February 1939 Pope Pius XI died. His successor, Pius XII, was elected on 2 March. Fr Ethelbert succeeded Commander Farie as Headmaster and Fr Maurus was replaced as Prefect by Fr Laurence Kelly.

Commander Farie, who had come to Fort Augustus in 1922 after several years on the staff of the RN College, Keyham, and at Rugby School, had for many years taught Geography and Mathematics at the Abbey. He had served as Prefect of Disciple under Fr David Parker and Fr Ninian Macdonald and had himself been Headmaster for the past eight years.

Abbot Wulstan Knowles had wanted to gather some of the 200 young men who had passed through the Abbey School during the previous 17 years and celebrate Commander Farie's retirement at Easter. The Commander, however, did not want any special demonstration in his honour.

At the annual Prize-giving, Lord and Lady Lovat distributed the prizes. Abbot Wulstan emphasised that his aim was to make the School 'a vital force in the religious, social and academic life of the country'. Lord Lovat added that Fort Augustus more than held its own among the public schools of Britain, and he exhorted the boys to uphold the great tradition of this Highland School.

The Abbot of Dunfermline, Sir David Oswald Hunter Blair, retired Abbot of Fort Augustus, died on 12 September 1939 and was buried in the Abbey cemetery.[2] Writing in *The Corbie*, one admirer recalled his diplomatic skill:

> *The purpose his charm achieved was the deft concealment of the intensity of his devotion to duty. Men yielded without feeling the fact of surrender. His early life provided him with an invaluable gift for patiently understanding prejudice, wherever it might arise.*

After ten years on the teaching staff, Mr Hamilton, Editor of *The Corbie*, Rugby coach and Scout Master, left Fort Augustus. Meanwhile, Mr Murphy arrived to teach Maths and Science.

On Sunday 30 July, Bishop Bennett of Aberdeen (himself an Old Boy) ordained Frs Aloysius Carruth, Alban Boultwood, Cyprian Gibson and Thomas McLaughlin. The diaconate was conferred on Frs Jerome Ireland, Laurence Kelly and John-Baptist McBride.

The array of cups in the Boys' Refectory was added to that year by the Scholes Batting Cup, presented by Mr Scholes and first awarded to V. Birch.

On 4 August Fr Abbot sailed for the United States where he was due to visit the Abbey's two priories at Washington and Portsmouth, Rhode Island.

In spite of a heatwave in the earlier part of the term, it was a good Summer for fishing. The biggest fish was a 50 lb trout caught by Fr Bernard. It was also an enjoyable end of year for the Choir. For their annual Picnic, Fr Prior took the singers round the time-honoured route of a bathe at Torgoyle, lunch, 'big-game hunting', another bathe, tea and the return trip by Cluanie, Tomdoun, Loch Garry and home.

Things were looking promising for the coming Rugby season. Mr Mackenzie, who had been capped for Scotland the previous year, promised to come down for a game, as did Lord Lovat and the Irish international, Aidan Bailey.

The First Cricket XI won five games and lost five. It was judged a poor season, the main fault being the lack of good bowlers. Home matches, nevertheless, were specially enjoyable owing to the high standard of catering supervised by the Matron.

For the under-14s the 'three-weekly' holidays were unfailingly popular. The first was over the water by the whaler to Glen Doe boat-house with Matron, Fr Andrew and Br Laurence. It was a very hot day and the boys enjoyed themselves swimming, taking photographs and fishing. The second holiday (also to Glen Doe) was enlivened by Br Aloysius frying bananas and making scrambled eggs.

At the annual General Meeting of the Old Boys 28 members were present. The treasurer's report showed a deficit, but not a serious one. Collecting subscriptions by letter from one centre was found to be a waste of time. It was agreed in future that the real collectors would be the local secretaries. At the close of the meeting a presentation was made to Fr Luke from the Old Boy members of the Orchestra. It consisted of a conductor's baton in ebony, with an ivory rose at its base. It bore an inscription on a silver plate in memory of Fr Luke's creation of and work in the Orchestra.

That August Fr Gregory Brusey set off from Fort Augustus to Hungary to spend a whole year studying theology and the organ. From Munich he took a train. His (third class) carriage was very crowded. He dozed off but was rudely awakened at the first stop by German soldiers crowding onto the train. The loading up of troops continued throughout the night.

His journey continued through Vienna to Budapest and then to the Abbey of Pannonhalma, a stronghold of Benedictine life – 'a magnificent building of radiant white stone on a hilltop.'

On 17 October Fr Abbot returned from his visit to the American priories. With him he brought Fr John Lane Fox, formerly a teacher of Geography and Prefect of Discipline at Fort Augustus. By now three of the Community had left the Abbey to serve as chaplains to the Forces – Fr Peter Walter, Fr Cuthbert Wilson and Fr Denys Rutledge.[3]

Within the School several changes took place. Fr Celestine took over the teaching of Maths. Fr Thomas McLaughlin and Fr John-Baptist McBride came to help with the languages.

The School now had to cope with the black-out. Returning from a match with Gordonstoun, the last two hours' travel that evening took place in total darkness. The School had now become accustomed to moving around the building in a ghostly blue light. The trunk room (one of the old dungeons of the '45), had also been converted into an ARP bomb-proof shelter.

Among the Old Boys there was great sadness in hearing of the death of Colonel A. W. MacDonald of Blarour, a very popular member of the Association. During the South African War, as adjutant to the Lovat Scouts, he was mentioned in dispatches and awarded the Queen's Medal and the DSO. In the Great War he saw service again with the Lovat Scouts in Egypt and Salonika and at the Dardanelles. After the War he was a member of Inverness County Council, Chairman of the Lochaber District Committee, and Deputy Lieutenant for the County. He was a strong supporter of the ancient game of Shinty, in which he had excelled in his youth.

The first Old Boy known to be in France was D. R. B. Duffy (RASC), followed shortly by J. Chapman and N. Connolly. Commander Farie, meanwhile, was in charge of the 'Impregnable', a training ship, where he was producing young naval officers by the hundred.

Among those following a career in religion, John Fair was preparing to be ordained at Downside, Laurence Davison was in a seminary in

Bordeaux, John Barry was at Oscott, and H. Curran at St Peter's College, Wexford.

The new year (1940) brought another departure. Miss Cusack, after four years as Matron, left for a post elsewhere. *The Corbie* made the comment:

> *In her four years with us Miss Cusack has not only set a new level in the many departments in which the Matron plays so important a part in a school, but she has won the respect and real affection of the boys and their parents, the school staff and the community.*

On 1 February 1940 Fr Abbot and a choir of monks went to Inverness for the funeral of Captain John Macdonald, skipper of the Loch Ness steamers for 50 years and father of Fr Ninian.

News now came of a number of Old Boys serving in the Forces. J. Clark was with the BEF in France, H. Doherty with The Greys; L. Young was in the RAF, while J. Singleton was with the Fleet Air Arm and W. D. Young was a second lieutenant in the Royal Artillery. Leonard Connolly was a police officer in Palestine.

On Low Sunday, Archbishop McDonald came to confer the Sacrament of Holy Orders. Frs Jerome Ireland and Laurence Kelly received the priesthood and Fr Gregory Brusey the diaconate.

By Mid-summer 1940, in view of his impending departure as chaplain to HM Forces, Fr Alban Boultwood retired from the post of Editor of *The Corbie*. 'During his period as Editor,' commented the editorial, 'Fr Alban brought about some improvements in *The Corbie* including a notable increase in its size.'

The Community and the School were saddened by the death of Fr Francis Blackwell on 1 July 1940. As a boy in London, his literary talents brought him into contact with the most prominent poets of the 1890s. He won scholarships to the City of London School and Dulwich College, showing a special aptitude for English.

After leaving school he became literary editor of *The Westminster Gazette*. After some months at the Redemptorist Novitiate in 1907, he joined the Benedictines and was ordained at Fort Augustus in 1916. He subsequently served as a military chaplain during the final year of the First World War where a gas attack left him with permanent heart trouble.

He worked for the community both at Fort Augustus and also in America, where he spent five years. At Fort Augustus he was parish priest, librarian and English master. Besides the play 'St Thomas More', he wrote many poems and contributed regularly to the American journal, *Homiletic Review.*

During the Headmaster's speech at Prize-giving, the year 1939-40 was declared to have been highly successful in both study and sport. Of the entrants for public examinations, all gained certificates and the majority won credits in many or all of their subjects. The new Matron, Miss Candon, received an ovation from the School, showing how popular she had already become.

The School Cricket XI lost only one of their matches, but a shadow was cast over this success by news of the death of Major T. M. Threlfall (Cameron Highlanders and presenter of the Threlfall Fielding Cup), who was killed while fighting with the BEF in France.

On 23 June news came of the death of a notable Old Boy, John MacDonald, elder brother of Archbishop McDonald (their names were spelt differently). He first came to St Benedict's College shortly after it opened in October 1878. He took up a business career, becoming a Justice of the Peace and a Major in the Lovat Scouts. He later emigrated to New Zealand where he died.

News also came of Old Boys serving in the Forces: J. Chapman was a commissioned officer in the Durham Light Infantry; P. Dunn was with the Highland Light Infantry; M. Loftus was an Acting Pilot with the RAF, while B. Parker was in the same unit; J. E. McFall DFC was adjutant of his squadron; M. Reilly was with the Cameron Highlanders; A. Stephen with the Mercantile Marine; J. Thompson was attached to GHQ at Dunkirk and acquitted himself with distinction; M. G. Walsh was a Second Lieutenant in the Royal Artillery. B. Brusey had been wounded in the thigh while with the Royal Artillery at Dunkirk. He was put into an ambulance which was later machine-gunned and he was captured by the enemy. He had been registered as missing.

Around 20 attended the Old Boys' May Reunion in Edinburgh. The meeting was chaired by Archbishop McDonald and the guest of honour was Fr Giles Black OP, Chaplain at Edinburgh University, who praised the Benedictine method of education which had the secret of so combining the education of the mind and the soul that the boys from Benedictine schools were not only fitted for their tasks in the world, but were also educated for their religion.

'Apart from the obnoxious black-out, life at Fort Augustus continues very much as in peace time,' wrote *The Corbie's* Editor. There had been a marked increase in numbers in the Schools and a flood of new boys added to the ranks of both Schools, mainly in the lower ranks. There were 20 new boys in the Abbey School, two, D. and J. Korczynski, from Poland.

Within the monastic Community there was a change of a different kind. Abbot Wulstan Knowles resigned his office in December. A constitutional election had been impossible under war conditions – many of the monks serving as chaplains with the Forces and the American priories being unable to send representatives. Fr Bede O'Donnell was on a hospital ship, Fr Bernard Sole was in Burma, Fr Denys Rutledge was to find himself eventually in Holland. Accordingly, Abbot President Trafford installed Fr Anselm Rutherford of Downside as Claustral Prior of Fort Augustus until such time as an election could take place.[5]

The retiring Abbot had a long career of achievement. In 1895 the young Wulstan Knowles had left his home in Worcestershire for Fort Augustus. He finished his school course in 1900, entered the Novitiate, and was professed two years later. He completed his studies at the College of Sant' Anselmo, Rome and was ordained in 1908.

On his return to Fort Augustus he was appointed assistant bursar and a few years later became parish priest of Glengarry and Abertarff. On the outbreak of war in 1914 he served as a naval chaplain at Invergordon.

After the war he became Sub-Prior, but in 1924 went to Washington as superior with a number of American priests who had spent a year training at Fort Augustus. Not long afterwards he was sent with Fr Hugh Diman to found the Priory and School at Portsmouth, Rhode Island. He stayed at Portsmouth as Prior until 1929, by which time the School was firmly established. Upon Abbot McDonald's consecration as Archbishop of St Andrews and Edinburgh, Fr Wulstan was elected Abbot of Fort Augustus.[6]

The four members of the Community who were chaplains in the Army were now joined by Frs Bede, Bernard and Anselm (who had volunteered some months before). On the lay-staff side, Mr Scholes and Mr Pimpley received invitations to act on the Panels of Teachers, while the Headmaster had been appointed to the Board of Assessors for the award of the Scottish Leaving Certificate.

Fort Augustus Abbey School was now fortunate to have the services of an outstanding musician, William Worden. On 2 November he gave a concert to the Community and the School. As well as playing pieces by Chopin, Schubert and Mendelssohn, Mr Worden played two of his own compositions – 'Miniature' and 'The Lost Cantref' – from his 'Welsh

Suite'. Mr Worden was also an expert in building model planes which he tested over the Rugby fields.

The War brought changes to the conditions under which Rugby was played by the School. Most of the fixtures had to be scratched, either because of transport difficulty or because many clubs and schools were unable to raise teams.

The Abbey School were beaten 18-3 at Invergordon and 12-3 at Inverness by RAF Coastal Command. They also lost 18-6 to Trinity College, Glenalmond's 2nd XV (the first time the School had been beaten at Glenalmond), but drew 6-6 with a Northern RAF Station.

Meanwhile encouraging news arrived about the fate of Bernard Brusey RA, who had been registered missing. According to the most recent report he was suffering from a wound in the thigh, sustained before his capture. D. A. P. Barry was now a Lance-Corporal in the East York Regiment; T. Fletcher was an Observer in the Fleet Air Arm; L. Laverty a wireless operator in the RAF; and W. MacDonald (Skye) was a driver in an Auxiliary Ambulance Corps in London.

Fr J. K. Birnie had left Dunfermline and was now parish priest at Kelso, while Fr Alban Boultwood was still a military chaplain. Fr Anselm Richardson was now chaplain to HM Forces in Iceland.

The death had occurred of Captain Herbert J. A. Throckmorton, aged 69, at his home in Beccles, Suffolk. Captain Throckmorton was an Old Boy of Fort Augustus and a member of the Old Boys' Association. He was a noted yachtsman. During the First World War he was the commander of HMS 'Havelock'. Captain Throckmorton had never really recovered from the death of his 20 year old son, Robert, during the Dunkirk evacuation.

THE ABBEY SCHOOL TOWER.

CHAPTER 7

The Abbey School
1940-44

As the War continued the Abbey Press ran up against a shortage of paper, in spite of the best efforts of the printers, Br Hugh and Br Patrick. However, 'we are determined to print as long as there is a sheet of paper in the office,' wrote the Editor of *The Corbie*.

In the School itself sweets were in very short supply at the shop, jam was rarely seen in the refectory and there had been one red air-raid warning during which the enemy planes were nowhere near. The boys, ever resourceful, were now 'digging for victory' in an allotment scheme.

Members of the Community did what they could to supplement food supplies. Br Joseph scrounged sugar to keep his hives of bees alive; Frs Gregory, Maurus and John with Brs Placid, Michael and Joseph, spent cold and weary hours out after salmon on Loch Ness from 15 January onwards in snow, sleet and rain. Fr Maurus even shot a hind which he then carried on his shoulders eleven miles back to the Abbey.

There was extraordinary news about the good ship 'Ann Cook' which had so ignominiously run aground in Ireland under Commander Farie some years before. It emerged the boat had been successfully raised, reconditioned and put into service. During the evacuation of the BEF from Dunkirk, the 'Ann Cook' carried over 300 men to safety in two days.

The Hockey season was affected by deep snow and a veneer of ice which put the fields out of action. When it became possible to play, Forms V and VI had to spend a couple of hours brushing and scraping the frozen snow off the field.

The first game was against the Camerons, who played in gym shoes and found it difficult to retain their balance. Need-

less to say, the School won 4-2. In the return match at Inverness, the Camerons were much stronger and fitter and won 5-1. During a day of foul weather the School played an Invermoriston XI, their team reinforced by Fr Laurence and two of the School reserves. The School won 7-2, in a team that included Hamish MacDonald.

The Rugby season was a lean one with no hard individual effort to get down to practice. There was too much 'soft' tackling and not one goal kicked in matches, no practice ever having been put in!

Old Boys were saddened to learn of the death of Charles George SSC, KCSG of Edinburgh. He had started in the School in September 1879, went on to study Law at Edinburgh University and had been a solicitor of the Supreme Court for 50 years. In more recent times he had collaborated with Abbot Hunter Blair in launching the Old Boys' Association and giving it its first Constitution. In total some 59 Old Boys were listed as serving in HM Forces. Pilot Officer J. Kelly had been officially reported as 'missing'. His plane did not return from a night raid over Germany.

The outstanding event of the 1941 Summer term was the formation of the two Houses of Lovat and Vaughan. Fr Laurence Kelly was appointed housemaster of Lovat and Fr Celestine Haworth housemaster of Vaughan. The first new House prefects were A. McCawley and W. Hall (Lovat) and G. Dilworth and I. Lawson (Vaughan). 'Both Houses have settled down very well and a healthy rivalry is springing up between them,' noted the Editor of *The Corbie*. Both House Captains entered the Novitiate at the end of the year.

Among the Community members, Fr Cuthbert Wilson, who had been serving as a military chaplain, was now seriously ill in hospital. This resulted in many commendations from his fellow officers as to the effectiveness of his work with the Forces. Fr Aidan Trafford, after a brief stay at Fort Augustus, was recalled to Downside.

The death of Flt. Lt. John E. McFall DFC and Bar, was particularly poignant.[1] Captain of the Abbey School, an outstanding forward in the First XV, a boxer of note and a very successful Scout in the competitions of 1932, John McFall was also a fine Cricketer, winner of the aggregate prize at the School sports in his last year and of the Dunskey Cup for the Half-Mile championship.

He was also a good actor, leading many of the amateur dramatic shows at the Abbey, later joining the Marian Players and acting in many of their repertory shows in Glasgow.

He had an irrepressible sense of humour and developed a strength of character and personality which marked him out as a future leader of men. He was one of the boys whom Commander Farie regarded as his own product, a man with a natural sense of good conduct and fair play.

John McFall earned his first DFC for conspicuous gallantry in April 1939, unusually in peacetime. His second decoration, a Bar to the DFC, was announced only a few days before he died. His Commanding Officer gave the following account of his death:

> It was at 10.30 am on June 15th, 1941 that Mac took off on what proved to be his last flight. The Squadron was providing continuous air reconnaissance over a battle that was raging around Fort Capuzzo and Halfaya Pass. I had just landed and Mac was off next, so I passed on my information to him, wished him good luck and saw him off. That was the last time I saw Mac alive. At about 12.30, when Mac was just about to complete his reconnaissance and return home, he was attacked by three Messerschmitts. Mac was alone, but by skilful flying and clever manoeuvring he managed to reach our own lines. However, the enemy's advantage of number took effect and, with a riddled aircraft, useless engine and damaged controls, Mac was forced to land. Even that he managed successfully and was able, though wounded and hurt, to climb from his machine. The Germans, however, still continued to attack and a cannon shell hit Mac in the thigh as he got out. He was now mortally wounded and dying from shock and loss of blood. His sense of duty still urged him, in spite of the pain, to complete his mission. He had carried out the reconnaissance, but he had not passed on the information. This he now insisted on doing, giving valuable and important news of the enemy. Shortly after, he lost consciousness and died that afternoon.

★ ★ ★

The season's Cricket results made poor reading – played 7, won 3, lost 3, drawn 1, cancelled 7. In the first House match played on St Benedict's Day – 11 July –Vaughan were the winners by 54 runs.

On Saturday 17 May the annual Sports took place under grey skies and intermittent rain squalls. Timekeepers were Messrs Fraser, Michie and Lyons of the Scottish Amateur Athletic Association.

The following day the weather cleared and Roden was able to lower the 100 yards record by a tenth of a second to 10 seconds and four-fifths. In the inter-House relay, over a mile, the result was a dead heat in 3 minutes 54 seconds. In the Cricket Ball, Hamish MacDonald broke the School record with a throw of 90 yards, 2 feet, 7 inches.

For the Old Boys there was some good news in that Bernard Brusey, a prisoner in Germany, had recovered from his thigh wound. Sergeant J. D. Kelly RAF, however, who had been reported missing in January, was now officially presumed killed. In addition J. R. Stephen was not reported to be among the survivors of his ship torpedoed by enemy action in May.

John 'Archie' Stephen excelled in Rugby, Hockey and Cricket during his time at the Abbey School. He was only in the Third Form when chosen for the First XV. As a Monitor he was invariably cheerful, having a great fondness for practical jokes. When he left School he joined the Merchant Navy as an apprentice, rising to Third Mate and then gaining his Chief Officer's Ticket.

He was engaged to Miss Mary Scholfield at the time of his death. At what was to prove his final Old Boys' Gathering in Edinburgh two years before, Tom Barry recalled him passing the following comment:

The sea appears to me as the battleground between God and the Devil. Sometimes it is smooth and peaceful, at others it is a dark, raging demon. The calm is like God, the storm like Satan. If ever I go down in the sea in a storm, I will have the reassuring knowledge that although I am going into an angry, cold and devilish sea with death in every wave, I go with a better card in my hand than all those of Hell's put together.

News also reached the School of the death of Sgt. Pilot Felix Savvy RAF, killed in action in the Middle East the previous Autumn; and L-A/C Jerry Ryan, RAF, was killed on active service in Malta in January. The death was also announced of Alfred Gilbertson of Formby, Lancashire, who had died in Liverpool. He studied at St Benedict's College, Fort Augustus in the early 1880s and afterwards became an architect, designing several churches in the Cardiff Archdiocese, many commercial buildings in Liverpool, and the theatre and indoor swimming baths at Ampleforth.

In the Spring of 1942 there was a flurry of activity at the Abbey School:

Owing to the expansion of the School big changes have had to be made, the latest of which is that the Lodge is being turned into a sanatorium, the

Cottage taken over to relieve the congestion in the dormitories and most of the lay staff are now accommodated elsewhere.

There were also changes in the teaching staff. Mr Murphy, Science and Maths master since the Summer of 1939, left to join the RAF as a pilot officer. Mr Douglas, a Glasgow University man, joined the teaching staff, having previously worked in England.

Among the School societies came news of other changes. The Abbey School Boy Scout Troop was now defunct, replaced by the First Air Scout Troop. There were 20 members of the Air Training Corps Flight No. 1717. Before end of term the Cadets had a visit from a flying-boat.

Fr Oswald was asked to apply for a Commission in the Training Branch of the RAF Volunteer Reserve. Accordingly, he officially became the Officer of the Unit. The following instructors were appointed: Fr Cyprian (Signalling), Fr Andrew (Meteorology and PT), Wilfrid Worden (Aeronautics), J. Murphy (Mathematics), A. Scott (Anti-gas), Fr Oswald (Navigation, Aircraft Recognition, Law and Administration). Fr Oswald was also appointed Assistant County Commissioner for Air Scouts.

There was a marked increase in the supply of jam and golden syrup on the refectory tables. The School menu was enriched by several hours of the boys' free time spent the previous term lifting potatoes. The garden attached to the Abbey Cottage had been taken over by the boys who had worked on the School allotments the previous year. Vegetables and a few flowers were to be grown.

Among the Community there was sadness at the death of Fr Kentigern Milne on 7 March.[2] Fr Cuthbert Wilson had now received his discharge from the Army but was still seriously ill in hospital. Fr Luke was in a nursing home in Edinburgh. It was learned that Fr David was a parish priest in Lincolnshire and an auxiliary chaplain to the Army, being in charge of the spiritual welfare of a camp nearby.

Two Old Boys were now at sea. A. Jackson was in the Royal Navy, having gained further credits in the Oxford and Cambridge Certificate. R. Zukowski also gained the Certificate (in spite of his difficulty in understanding English). He was serving in the Polish Navy.

The School production of 'The Pirates of Penzance' (produced by Fr Thomas McLaughlin, with Wilfrid Worden and Fr Gregory at the piano, lighting by Fr John-Baptist, make-up by Fr Philip and costumes by Miss Doonan), was the first really ambitious musical play in the modern School, 21 years after it had opened.

Cyril Hall's well-trained treble in the part of Mabel was much admired, as was Hamish MacDonald's acting as the Pirate King. For the audience the enjoyment on stage was increased by the installation of a permanent heating system!

That term the Senior Debating Society had three meetings. Fr Ethelbert was replaced as chairman by Fr Celestine. Since September 1941 there had been four meetings of the Junior Debating Society.

In Rugby the season 1941-42 saw a drastic reduction in the number of fixtures played, principally because of transport difficulties. Only two School games were played but both were won: Inverness Academy were beaten 30-0; Trinity College, Glenalmond Second XV lost 20-9. Against RAF Lossiemouth the Abbey School lost 6-3 and were beaten 9-0 by RAF Invergordon.

A year passed before the next issue of *The Corbie* appeared in Spring 1942. The Editor explained it by a 'shortage of paper, the shortage of labour and similar hardships of war'. One effect of this cutting down of the number of issues was that more space had to be allocated to School activities at the expense of topics of more general interest. 'In short,' added the Editor, 'like most school magazines, we are becoming a mere chronicle.'

Over the previous twelve months the School had seen further staff changes. Fr Philip left for Liverpool to work in a parish. Mr Douglas and P/O Brack RN also left: the former for Glasgow University, the latter (an ex-medical student and ex-racing motorist) to gain his commission.

In their place came RSM Cassels, Mr Sobiecki (an MSc and Dip Ing of the University of Lwow, Poland), to teach Maths and Physics in place of Mr Murphy. A reserve officer in a Polish cavalry regiment, Mr Sobiecki had been in four wars since 1914. He was also at one time managing director of an armaments firm, in which capacity he supplied 200 AA guns to Britain.

The Operatic Society, with Fr Thomas McLaughlin as producer, gave several excellent performances of 'The Mikado' which raised £17 for the Prisoners of War Fund.

The ATC was thrilled to be visited by their president, Air Commodore R. Gordon. They all watched a film of Air Commodore Chamier's visit in March accompanied by Group Captain, The Duke of Hamilton and F/O J. Nairn who had filmed the proceedings. The 30 cadets enjoyed a number of short flights in various flying boats, both at Fort Augustus and at Camp. Their equipment officer was Fr Andrew, while Fr Benedict kept their accounts.

The 1942 School Sports included the House Relay, which Vaughan won in 4 minutes 4 seconds. The Sports were also won by Vaughan by 131 to 90 points. The Steeplechase was run across the River Tarff only once instead of twice (as the course had been the previous year). The runners also competed by Loch Uanagan and the Canal bank, the winner being Hamish MacDonald in 25 minutes 35 seconds.

At the height of the War the Abbey School had 102 Old Boys enlisted. In addition, three (Gunner Bernard Brusey RA, Private John S. Lewis RAOC and Major James F. Clark RAMC) were known to be prisoners of war; Second Lieutenant Maurice Walsh RA was missing. Five Old Boys had lost their lives: Sergeant John Kelly RAFVR, Chief Officer John Stephen MN, Flt. Lt. John McFall DFC and Bar RAF and Leading Aircraftsman Jeremiah Ryan RAFVR.

From the Spring of 1943 until the Winter of 1944, *The Corbie* remained firmly locked in its cage in the Print Room that lay at the end of an uneven cobbled floor in the Hanoverian 'dungeons' under the Abbey cloisters. *The Corbie* existed only in the imagination of its Editor, Fr Andrew McKillop, who apologised: 'One cannot argue with the Paper Control Board' and added: 'It is unavoidable that with the cutting down of issues and of size, the topics of general interest must give way to items of school activities, and so we apologise for any omissions.'

A special supplement issued with Volume 6, No 3 (Winter 1944) printed the Abbey School Roll of Honour: nine Old Boys killed, died of wounds or died on active service; six missing; three prisoners of war; five mentioned in dispatches; 92 serving in His Majesty's Forces. Captain Hamilton, formerly a teacher in the School, was recovering rapidly from wounds received on active service in Normandy.

The Community and School welcomed back Abbot Wulstan Knowles from his stay at Beccles. Another familiar face who had recently returned was Fr Ambrose Geoghegan, who had taken up post as a teacher of Latin. Fr Thomas McLaughlin, on the other hand, had relinquished his teaching duties, having been appointed Prior.

Physical training in the School was now under the eagle eye of Sergeant Bissel, an instructor in the Army Physical Training Corps, formerly self-defence instructor for the Metropolitan Police, Black Belt and undefeated National Champion of Catch-as-Catch-Can Wrestling (retired).

The Brass Band under Fr Gregory's leadership was frequently to be heard practising martial music in the Gym. The musicians had been enthused by a concert given in the School by the band of the Cameron Highlanders a few moths previously.

The Air Training Corps (ATC) was going from strength to strength, particularly in its work of pre-entry training. Fr Andrew received his Commission as Pilot Officer and had worked unsparingly as Adjutant, having attended the OTS at Cosford and returned full of 'gen'.

Among equipment received was the fuselage of a Westland Wallace and a Merlin engine. Br Joseph had agreed to explain the workings of the engine, while Br James did sterling work in training future electricians. A number of RAF volunteers from Fort Augustus and District had previously reported to the ATC for training. Now that they were in the Forces they contacted the Abbey from time to time with their news.

Visits had been paid to Alness and Dalcross aerodromes where the boys had been taken on flights. Fr Oswald could hardly contain his enthusiasm at being taken on an all-night Catalina trip and a 'Martinet' mock fighter-battle. Mr Scholes, instructor and expert in aircraft recognition, returned from a course in Southport with a Grade A.

On 24 July the ATC visited the Commando Training Base situated at Achnacarry. Lt.-Col. Vaughan OBE, his officers and men, presented the schoolboys with a breathtaking display of unarmed combat, machine carbine firing, wall-scaling, river-crossing (by Death Ride), and an incredibly realistic Opposed Landing. Later in the year, on 15 October, an inspection of the Flight was carried out by the Chief Commandant, Air-Marshall Sir L. Gossage, accompanied by Group Captain, the Duke of Hamilton. It was a red letter day in the history of the ATC.

As for the Air Scouts, Mr Scott, Scoutmaster since 1940, had to leave his post to take up new duties as an ARP Warden. The opportunity was taken to reconstruct the Scouts by only admitting those who were totally convinced and motivated.

On the artistic front the highlight of the year was the Operatic Society's performances of Gilbert and Sullivan's 'Pirates of Penzance' with J. D. I. Locke as the Major-General, C. J. Hall as Frederick and I. Atkinson as the Pirate King. The production was by the Headmaster, Fr Ethelbert, the orchestra being conducted by Fr Ambrose accompanied by Mr Worden and Fr Gregory. The costumes were the work of Mrs Matheson.

The Community and the School were saddened to learn of the death of the Archbishop-Bishop of Malta, Sir Maurus Caruana KBE, on 17 December 1943. Louis Caruana had come to Fort Augustus as a schoolboy in 1882. Two years later he became a novice and made his Vows in 1885. After preliminary studies in Philosophy he was sent to the Benedictine College of Sant'Anselmo in Rome to study Theology. He returned to Fort Augustus and was ordained a priest there in 1891.

From 1893-96 he was in charge of the *alumni* (junior seminarians) and was one of the chief singing Masters of the Abbey *Schola*.

In 1896 he was appointed Superior of the parish of Dornie on the West Coast of Scotland, which the Bishop of Aberdeen had asked the Abbey to take over for some years. Here he learnt Gaelic. Having a good ear and great linguistic talent, he became fluent in that language. After the Abbey gave back the parish to the Bishop in the first years of the twentieth century, Fr Maurus, along with the future Archbishop McDonald and other Fort Augustus monks, began the work of giving Missions and Retreats in the large parishes in and around Glasgow and Edinburgh with great success.

When the Maltese Benedictine, Archbishop Ambrose Agius, was appointed to the Philippines, Fr Maurus accompanied him as his secretary. Later he returned to Fort Augustus as parish priest.

In the Summer of 1914 he was sent by the then Abbot, Sir Oswald Hunter Blair, to the Benedictine Abbey at São Paulo, Brazil to teach in the College there. But he never reached South America. On the way he visited his family in Malta. While he was there he received word from Rome that he had been chosen to fill the vacant See of Malta.

Archbishop Caruana re-visited Fort Augustus in the Summer of 1921 and again in the Autumn of 1929. He lived through the aerial bombardment of Malta in 1943 and had the consolation of witnessing the end of the siege before he died.

Another Fort Augustus monk, Fr Swithun Bell, died on 4 December 1944. A convert at the age of 25, he became a Benedictine three years later, studying at Fort Augustus where he acted as assistant organist. From 1925-30 he was on the mission at Dowlais, South Wales. He then spent two years at Portsmouth Priory, Rhode Island, and a further two at Saint Andrew's Priory, Edinburgh. He returned to South Wales, where he was stationed in Cardiff, but ill-health forced him to return to the Abbey where he worked until 1941 as assistant organist, teacher in the Priory School, and instructor to the lay-brothers. He also acted as chaplain at Spean Bridge to the children evacuated from the South.

Another deceased Old Boy of the first School, George Charlton (born 1873), came to St Benedict's College in 1886, leaving in 1890. Although he spent most of his life in the Highlands, he made strenuous efforts to attend Old Boy functions. He died in 1943 in Inverness, while on holiday.

But it was the death in action of three younger Old Boys which touched all hearts most deeply.

James Chapman came to the School in 1933. He excelled in sport, especially in Swimming, winning the Levack Cup in 1937. He left school that July and entered the Army. By 1942 he was with the Durham Light Infantry in the Middle East. During the final push after El Alamein he was in command of a company and shortly after won the Military Cross at Mareth. Regardless of his own safety he brought back a wounded man who lay 20 yards in front of him. Later he led a bayonet charge which frustrated an enemy outflanking manoeuvre. On 11 July 1943, just after landing in Sicily, he was wounded. He died two days later in hospital at Syracuse, where he was buried.

The second Old Boy who fell was Angus MacKay, killed in action during heavy fighting in the Kohima sector of the Burma Front on 13 May 1944. He came to the School in 1928, becoming School Captain in his final year (1935-36). He represented the School in all games. At the outbreak of war he joined the forces. By 1942 he was commissioned with the Queen's Own Cameron Highlanders in India, moving up to the Burma Front in the early Summer of 1944. A week before he was killed he was recommended for immediate award of the MC and mentioned in dispatches.

The third Old Boy was Flt. Lt. Robert Levack who died in India on 14 May 1944. 'Podge' Levack went to Fort Augustus in April 1932 and distinguished himself both in games and studies. After leaving school he entered the firm of Cable & Wireless Ltd, where his father was highly placed in the administration. When war broke out he remained in this reserved occupation until France was over-run in 1940.

At the fall of Paris, his parents and sister were captured and interned. This made him determined to take a more active part in the fighting. He obtained his release in 1941 and joined the RAF. His pilot training was carried out in Rhodesia and he was commissioned early in 1943. He was then transferred to Ceylon, where he remained (except for a short break at Aden) until shortly before his death.

Finally, news had come of another intrepid airman who had contrived to cheat death yet again. Night-fighter Flt. Lt. J. Singleton DFC (Leyland), a Mosquito pilot, was reported to have shot down five Junkers 188 bombers, three of them in one night. For this he was awarded the Distinguished Service Order (DSO).

WAR MEMORIAL DESIGNED BY REGINALD FAIRLIE
(BUT NOT COMPLETED IN THAT FORM).

CHAPTER 8

The Abbey School
1944-52

BETWEEN Winter 1944 and Autumn 1946 *The Corbie* did not appear. The Editor (Mr Scholes) complained:

> *We don't know whether corbies come under the Protection of Wild Birds Act but we sometimes feel that some such favour should be granted to editors. We have become so used to the query, 'Wot, no Corbie?'*

The Editor went on to explain that during the war his team had continued to produce *The Corbie* under very difficult circumstances. Now conditions had slightly improved. The School was getting back to normal; Old Boys had returned or were returning. The paper shortage was less acute. He appealed for 'news, articles, anything'.

Fr Abbot, who had been suffering from eye trouble for three months, had also returned. Nearly all the chaplains were back in the Abbey after their war service. Fr Bede was now the Procurator; Fr Denys, for some time a most beneficent kitchen master, was now on mission. Frs Alban, Bernard and Anselm had also returned. Unhappily, Fr Luke Cary-Elwes and Fr Benedict had passed away since the last issue of *The Corbie*.

Commander Farie, looking fit after his strenuous war service, paid the School a visit, as did Mr Hamilton ('Hammy'), who had recovered from the amputation of his leg and was walking very well. He was due to resume his studies for the priesthood at the Beda College in Rome.

A new arrival to the teaching staff was Miss Jordan who replaced Mr Sobieski to teach Science.

Perhaps the most dramatic event of the year (apart from a short play entitled 'Money Makes a Difference' which was given by the boys on the last night of term), was the fire which broke out on the roof of the

ABBEY BOYS: FORT AUGUSTUS ABBEY SCHOOLS

Hospice and might well have been serious but for the gallant efforts of the Abbey Fire Brigade and the older boys.

A tremendous volume of water was poured onto the fire – this was before the Abbey took over the Fort Augustus and district Fire Service which (under the charge of the late Fr Bede), was very efficient (and also, from time to time, very entertaining).

During the season 1945-46 two Inter-House Athletic competitions were held. In both Lovat were the decisive victors! The outstanding feature was the running of Cyril Hall who set four School records in 1945 and then broke three of them again in 1946: 100 yards at 10.7 seconds; 440 yards at 54.1 seconds; 880 yards at 2 minutes 7 seconds; and Cross Country at 23 minutes 13.5 seconds. Hall had held the Dunskey Cup for four years in succession. Timekeepers at both meetings were representatives from the SAAA.

Because of the previous two lean seasons of infrequent practice, the Cricket team did not impress in 1945, nor was the House Match very exciting. By 1946, however, there had been an improvement. Batsmen, fielders and bowlers had been properly trained and the Cricket XI won all the matches played, most of them with wide margins. Captain Cyril Hall was outstanding as a fielder, winning the Fielding Cup.

In Rugby the School had a successful 1945-46 season. Of the nine matches played, seven were won and only two lost. 'Not for a long time,' commented *The Corbie*, 'has the School possessed a centre so capable and fast as C. Hall.'

On a sadder note, the School recalled with pride the sacrifice of Colin Hayens, who had been killed in action in North-Western Europe in December 1944.

Colin, from Newport, Fife, spent three years at Fort Augustus. He was a member of all three School first teams. After leaving in July 1942 he spent a short time at St Andrew's University where he obtained the A and B and STC certificates. He then volunteered for the Army and joined the Seaforth Highlanders in 1943. On D-Day he landed in Normandy and fought with his regiment through France, Belgium and Holland, where he was wounded but returned shortly to the fighting line. Details had come from one of his officers as to how he was killed:

The Brigade went into action on December 3rd. No. 16 Platoon was held up by small arms fire. Colin very gallantly led an assault against the enemy. Although he was killed before he reached them, he succeeded in distracting the enemy and removed the threat to 16 Platoon .... Colin held the respect and affection of all who knew him and to me he was one of the greatest friends I had in the battalion. His courage, cheerful spirit and sincerity influenced everyone. On December 5th he was buried in the presence of his friends with military honours.

News also reached Fort Augustus of the death of the Hon. Edmund Dwyer Gray. Born in Dublin in 1870, he was the son of Edmund Dwyer Gray, Member of Parliament for the Stephen's Green division of Dublin. He came to the Abbey School in 1881 and, on leaving, became a journalist on the staff of *Freeman's Journal*. In 1898 he went to Tasmania where he eventually became editor of the three Hobart papers, *The World, The Daily Post* and *The Voice*. Later he entered politics, becoming Treasurer and then Deputy-Premier of Tasmania in 1934, an office which he held to his death (apart from September 1939 to January 1940, when he was Premier).

Finally *The Corbie* carried the death notice of a long-time member of the Community with very close and productive links with the School: Fr Luke Cary-Elwes had died at St Joseph's Hospital, Manchester, where he was removed after becoming paralysed in 1940.[1]

Fr Luke, a man of multifarious talents and infectious humour, was the second son of Captain and Mrs Windsor Cary-Elwes. He came from an artistic family which produced the singer Gervase Elwes and Simon Elwes the portrait painter. Fr Luke (who had played the violin with Sir Edward Elgar in his village choir) was educated at Downside and the Abbey School. He studied art for 15 years in Paris and inspired the celebrated portraitist, John Singer Sargent, to portray him in a painting that later hung above the mantlepiece of the Chelsea Arts Club. In more belligerent times Fr Luke was also adjutant of the Artists' Rifles.

In 1899 he joined the monastery at Fort Augustus where he was responsible for the entire decoration of the walls of the Catacombs Chapel at the Abbey.

He singlehandedly formed and trained the School Orchestra at Fort Augustus which was eventually chosen to represent the Orchestras of the Public Schools of Britain at the World Scout Jamboree in 1929, playing in the presence of the Prince of Wales and the Chief Scout at the opening World broadcast of the proceedings from the BBC Station 2LO.

After a performance by the Abbey School Orchestra of Johann Strauss' 'Blue Danube' at The Arrowe Park, Birkenhead, in front of the Austrian and Hungarian contingents, Archduke Franz Josef of Austria, the leader of the contingents, came onto the platform. He kissed Fr Luke's hand and said: 'I have never heard "The Blue Danube" played like that, outside Vienna.'

Among the Old Boys there was as much activity as wartime would allow. Henry Curran was ordained in 1945 for the Archdiocese of St Andrews and Edinburgh. A dinner of the South Scotland Area was held at St Mary's Hotel, Edinburgh in January 1945 under the chairmanship of the Headmaster, Fr Ethelbert. Guests included Fr Francis Moncrieff OP, Chaplain to the University of Edinburgh, and Captain W. D. Hamilton, a former master at the Abbey School.

In 1946 the first post-war annual meeting of the South Scotland Area was held at Carlekemp Priory in North Berwick with Fr Oswald Eaves as Chairman. Paddy Connacher was elected Secretary-Treasurer, with his Committee made up of Fr Maurus and W. T. Doherty. The strong feeling of the meeting was that it was time a Reunion was held at Fort Augustus.

★   ★   ★

Once again *The Corbie* failed to appear. Having flown briefly into sight in the Autumn of 1946, it failed to materialise for two whole years. As the Editor commented in the Spring 1949 issue:

> *No!* The Corbie *has not fallen a victim to the direction of labour. After considerable difficulties it has at last emerged from the shades to begin a new and, we hope, an even more prosperous life.*

Several new members of staff had arrived. Fr Philip had returned from the mission to resume his Art classes. Fr Andrew was at his desk to

teach Geography, British and *Cricket* History. In Lower Maths, Fr Anselm had followed Fr Jerome who, regrettably, had just been 'stolen' by Carlekemp Priory School. Miss Candon had left to take a matron's post at Beaumont; the new matron, Miss Berridge, had left after all too short a stay. Mr Worden was back, but Miss Jordan was now teaching in the south of England. Another addition was Miss McCombes.

The old, rather dismal School Library with its musty tomes had now been replaced by an up-to-date and comfortable Library situated where the Billiard Room had been. Conversely, the former Library was now the new Billiard Room.

The School's production of Gilbert and Sullivan's 'The Gondoliers' was a great success. The teamwork was very impressive and *The Inverness Courier* singled out the principal 'ladies' – Angus Pirie Watson (later Fr Vincent) and T. McLaughlin – for 'their vivacity and true vocal rendering of the solos'. The gondolier-kings – Michael Crawford (brother of the film star, Ann Crawford) and Anthony Tobia – were well-matched by Michael Sloan as the Duke and Adrian Howarth as the Duchess. Mention was also made of the piano accompaniment by Mr Worden, the lighting (care of Br James) and the stage props (including a magnificent gondola) by Br Raphael.

The 1946-47 Rugby season was an outstandingly successful one, even though only three out of seven games were won. The Rugby XV exceeded all expectations. There was a tremendous enthusiasm and capacity for hard work.

The 1947-48 Rugby season was, in contrast, a mixed bag. There was great inconsistency of form. There seemed to be too much orthodoxy and not enough individualism.

The re-functioning of the Highland District Hockey Association in 1947 revived interest in the game and made possible outside fixtures after a lapse of four years. The game had continued at the School, but there were no outside fixtures. Then on the eve of the first match in the Spring term an epidemic broke out which forced the School to cancel all matches. So the game did not really start until the 1948 season.

Although ten fixtures had been arranged, only five of them were played. The other five were with Service teams who, at that time, were in a state of flux. Of the five games played, three were won and two lost.

In 1947 the School won all their Cricket matches, for the second year in succession. The strength of the team lay in the bowling, while the fielding was always good. In the House Match, A. Korcynski (Vice-Captain of the School team) took all ten Vaughan wickets for 8 runs (Vaughan 46, Lovat 48).

The first post-War AGM and Reunion of the Old Boys was held at Fort Augustus on the weekend of 12 to 13 July 1947. Thirty Old Boys were present and it was unanimously decided to continue the series as before. The Committee for 1947-48 was: Abbot Wulstan Knowles

(President); Fr Andrew (Hon. Secretary); Ian Kennedy (Hon. Treasurer); Fr Ethelbert (Headmaster). Three members were elected: Sir James Calder, Angus Macdonald and D. A. P. Barry. Fr James Birnie, Hawick, was elected Chaplain.

The great event of the 1947-48 season was the Shrovetide Buffet Dance at the Grand Hotel, Glasgow. This was organised in aid of the Abbey Church Building Fund. Over 400 tickets were sold and the proceeds of the dance, an auction of gifts and a supplementary Charity Matinee Film, realised £1250.

The 1948 Cricket season saw most of the previous year's XI still in the team. Despite some surprising uncertainty of form, the Cricket XI won five matches, lost two and drew one. Lovat again won the House Match (Lovat 152, Vaughan 70).

The Reunion and AGM of 1948 took place at Fort Augustus on 11-12 July. Thirty-six members were present. The question of a suitable memorial to Old Boys who fell in the War was raised. The matter was referred to a Committee who were to report the following year.

The Editor, writing in the next issue of The Corbie, recalled that it was 25 years since the School Chronicle had started under its then Editor, Fr Ninian Macdonald. Strictly speaking, he was not correct. There had been a real School Chronicle for the duration of St Benedict's College (1878-1894), a cheerful account of events in the College, with newspaper cuttings, handbills, some photographs, and a complete list of all the boys who had passed through the establishment. There had even been a College magazine called The Raven (copies of which do not appear to have survived). A second Chronicle had burst into life after the new School opened in the early 1920s. It had then ground to a halt – presumably the pen of the Chronicler had grown rusty?

The most notable event of 1950 was the death of Archbishop Andrew Joseph McDonald on 22 May. Born in Fort William on 12 February 1871 he was the youngest son of Donald Peter MacDonald [sic] and Jessie Margaret Carmichael. His family came originally from the MacDonalds of Cranachan in Glen Roy. Like his elder brothers he went to school at the Abbey. After the Summer of 1888 he entered the monastery as a postulant. He received the habit on 23 January 1889, taking the name of Joseph. On 3 February 1890 he made his profession as a Benedictine monk. After studying for the priesthood at Fort Augustus he was ordained priest by Bishop Hugh MacDonald of Aberdeen in 1896.

After the closure of the College in 1894, Fr Joseph was put in charge of the junior seminary which continued to prepare young boys who wished to become monks.

In 1898 he was made Sub-Prior, a post he held for 12 years. During these years he was looked upon by the rest of the monks as the man who would eventually re-open the School.

When in 1911 Abbot Smith of Ampleforth left Fr Hilary Willson to be Claustral Prior at Fort Augustus, he asked for the Sub-Prior to replace him on the mission. Accordingly Fr Joseph was appointed an assistant at St Anne's, Edge Hill, Liverpool. Shortly after the beginning of the First World War, Fr Joseph was made parish priest at St Anne's.

By August 1919 most of the monks had returned to Fort Augustus. Fr Joseph was elected Abbot. The new Abbot also took in around 20 late vocations from the Jesuit house at Osterley. Some of these eventually became novices – the first for many years.

Abbot McDonald immediately took steps to prepare the School for re-opening. It did so in September 1920. Three years later he accepted several American priests as novices in order to start a Benedictine monastery in Washington DC. In 1924 they returned to what was to become St Anselm's Priory, Washington with three monks from Fort Augustus, Abbot McDonald accompanying the party. Three years later he helped found St Gregory's Priory and School in Rhode Island with four monks from Fort Augustus.

In August 1929 Abbot McDonald was nominated to the See of St Andrews and Edinburgh. Fr John Lane Fox commented:

It is very difficult for a small community to find good leaders and this was the second Archbishop [the other was Maurus Caruana] *to be chosen from it within a dozen years.*

Writing 70 years later, Fr Julian Stead, a monk of Portsmouth, USA, who studied at Fort Augustus and was ordained there in 1948, explains:

The appointment of Abbot McDonald to be Archbishop of Edinburgh proved to be a mortal wound. I have seen other monasteries badly hurt by losing a key monk to a bishopric, it can be like the amputation of a leg or an arm. In Abbot McDonald's case, it was the amputation of the head.[2]

The deaths of a number of other Old Boys were also noted with sadness – Fr Placid Corballis OSB, the Hon. Alastair Fraser of Lovat and Lt.-Col. Charles Edmonstone-Cranstoun DSO.

By this time Commander Farie was back again at Fort Augustus, looking fit and well. One immediate consequence of his return was that boat crews started again and the boys' rowing improved enormously. 'The Man' was once again at the helm!

After much difficulty an adequate supply of blazers arrived in the School. At first the check border could not be procured, so the boys had to be content with a black border with a wavy white line. Membership of the Rugby, Hockey and Cricket teams was shown with the dates above the left pocket, colours being indicated by gold lettering. A slight modification had been made in the School tie; a thin black line above or below the white indicated the House – Lovat or Vaughan.

There were other signs of life in the School. The Art Society, first founded in September 1949 with ten members, held its first exhibition that Christmas in the Hospice parlour. The highlight of the year was the Competition for Schools organised by the Inverness Art Society where several of the boys exhibited and were commended.

After a lapse of some years, the School Orchestra had reformed and made its first appearance at a concert in the Abbey Theatre on Easter Sunday. After only a year of training under Mr Worden, the Orchestra (conducted by him and led by M. J. Foy), gave a very creditable performance of several works, including some of Mr Worden's own compositions, 'Boating Tune' (from 'The Dunvegan Suite') and 'Bourrée in C'. The Orchestra consisted of four violins, a viola, two cellos, two clarinets, a trumpet and a horn.

The Cricket season was a poor one, with only one game won out of eight. The great weakness lay in the batting where aggressiveness was lacking. Vaughan won the House Match by eight wickets. Swimming and Tennis offered an opportunity for the School to take on the Old Boys. The School won both.

Thirty-five Old Boys arrived for the 1949 Reunion in July. Suggestions were made and adopted for a memorial to Old Boys fallen in the War. At the 1950 Reunion there were 37 present. On this occasion the Old Boys won the Cricket match rather easily, although it seemed to rain almost all the time!

The Old Benedictines Hockey Club in the South Scotland Area (Edinburgh Branch) had a very successful season, playing 34 games, winning 17 and losing eight.

On 20 February 1950 the annual dance of the Glasgow section was held at the Beresford Hotel, Glasgow (managed by Angus Macdonald). Some 250 Old Boys, families and friends attended, along with Fr Abbot. At that time there were 152 Old Boys on the register, 20 of them priests (16 Benedictines and four Secular).

After the issue of Christmas 1950 *The Corbie* did not appear until Easter 1951. There had been a change of Editor.

When the School returned on 12 January, many of the boys did not appear. They were at home with flu! Even those who did appear had either already fallen ill, or were just about to. There were some compensations. The severe weather at the beginning of term gave many opportunities for sledging and skating. Much fun was had with the toboggan-run on Glen Doe Hill.

There were changes afoot all over Fort Augustus and district. After nearly sixty years of good service, the Abbey electricity plant was about to be switched off, so allowing Br James to look forward to years of rest after his self-sacrificing labours in the engine-house and the lade. Many houses in the Village already had the new power. Some of the shops had tubular lighting.

A branch of the Young Farmers' Club had started in the Village. Boys who were interested in agriculture began to attend the meetings, much to the satisfaction of the Club officials. On 6 March 23 boys attended meetings of a very different kind as they prepared to sit their Highers.

Rowing and sculling were very regular that term under the watchful eye of Commander Farie, but it was Br Placid whose skill on the water was most popular. On 7 February he caught a 20 lb fish; on 19 February an 18 lb salmon; on 1 March two lovely fish, one 19 1/2 pounds, the other 21 lb; on 16 March another fish at 18 lb. The fish received a royal welcome in the School Refectory.

Work on the Abbey Church had been interrupted in November. Sandstone for facing part of the wall near the Blessed Sacrament Chapel was needed but the quarry at Elgin did not have enough labour to meet the demand. The masons were recalled to Aberdeen until more stone could be quarried.

There were other changes in the Abbey. Br Adrian, who had so successfully conducted the poultry farm, had killed off his ducks, intending to start a fresh stock. Unfortunately, the outbreak of fowl pest in other parts of the country prevented him from getting the clutches of eggs he needed.

The School Orchestra was flourishing and attempting to enlarge its repertoire. The School Library, re-organised three years previously, continued to develop, while the Camera Club, although a recent institution, had already achieved considerable popularity. The School's darkroom was equipped with an enlarger and developing tanks (for which Mr Foy was largely responsible). Among the films shown to the School were 'A Song to Remember' (the story of Chopin) and 'Bulldog Drummond at Bay'.

The Abbey Press, meanwhile, issued a continuous stream of printed matter, such as the annual liturgical calendar (*Ordo Divini Officii*) of the English Benedictine Congregation. Another regular product was Abbot Hunter Blair's translation of the *Rule of St Benedict*.

On Tuesday 6 March, the same day that the Scottish Leaving Certificate Exam started, fire broke out in the back premises of Grant's Garage. At 5.30pm the fire alarm sounded. Fr Bede had his forces marshalled on the scene, complete with fire engine, in five minutes:

> However, quick as they were, some villagers were quicker. They were found running tyres and carrying spare parts out of the garage at high speed.

The Fire Brigade were fortunate to be on the scene so quickly. But for some members of the Kinloss Hockey XI who helped push the fire engine, the venerable machine would not have started!

Rugby in 1950 was blighted by snow. No games were played after the last weekend in November when the snow came and stayed till the end of term. Of the six games played, three were won and three lost.

On 5 February the Annual Ball of the South Scotland Area of the Old Boys' Association was held in the Beresford Hotel, Glasgow. Over 250 Old Boys and friends were present.

The third term that year was generally cold. Ascension Day was, by contrast, glorious:

FIRE!

> The School went out with the usual collections of frying pans, stoves, kettles and tin cans, and, garbed as only the Abbey School can garb itself on such occasions,

made for the hills, the streams and the lochs with the earnest determination to savour the pleasure ahead. In the evening, drifts of tinker-like humanity limped back to the fold. All were weary; all were cheery.

So dry was the Cricket field in early June that the Fire Brigade had to be enlisted to drench the ground. The Brigade also filled the swimming pool with 60,000 gallons of water.

While the School was on holiday at Easter, the stone masons returned. Soon the south wall of the Church was completed.

The 1951 Hockey season was well above average, with six wins and two defeats. P. Laing and F. Whitehurst represented the Highland District in the Easter Tour.

On 5 July an Inter-House Boat Race was held, which Lovat won by four lengths. Lovat also won the inter-house Sculling. Two days later came the Annual General Meeting of the Old Boys' Association. The latter managed to win the Cricket match but were beaten by the School in a boat race from the boathouse jetty to Freshwater Island and back.

THE "SCHOOL" PICNIC TO LOCH HOURN.

A GOOD TIME WAS HAD BY ALL IN SPITE OF THE RAIN.

BRO JOSEPH LOVED IT.

MR. SCHOLES LIKED IT

DR. FLOOD REVELLED IN IT

MR FARIE WALLOWED IN IT.

THE SEVENTY GUESTS (APPROX.) WERE POLITE & ENJOYED IT. THANK YOU

THE TWO (OR WERE THERE THREE?) BOYS WHO WENT, BECAUSE THEY COULDN'T THINK UP EXCUSES FOR DODGING IT, HAD A SWELL TIME.

At the Old Boys' Reunion the Committee was empowered to revise the Constitution and to advise the next meeting on any recommended alterations.

Changes were already afoot in the structure of the School year, largely instigated by the Minister of Education. The Summer Term was shortened and the Autumn Term lengthened to give candidates for the Senior Scottish Leaving Certificate more time to prepare. The old Oxford and Cambridge School and Higher Certificate examinations were dis-

continued and replaced by the General Certificate of Education (GCE).

One outcome of the change was an Old Boys v School Rugby match, played on 22 September before the former began their University term. The Old Boys narrowly won. A rematch the following day saw the School the victors – possibly because the Old Boys, flushed with success, may have spent too much of the night celebrating!

Throughout the Summer the stonemasons continued to build the Abbey Church. The west wall was well advanced and completed before November, when the masons returned to Aberdeen, with the aim of returning the following March.

On 20 October the first snows of Winter powdered the tops of the hills. It was only four days after the death of Mr J. Seed of Duns (father of a large family of Old Boys), as a result of a car accident, and of schoolboy John Burke who died at home after a short illness.

The Old Boys' generosity meant that the £500 mark was almost reached in the War Memorial fund.

A magnificent silver cup, the Macdonald Challenge Cup, recently donated by Angus Macdonald, was to be presented annually to the boy most proficient in Games and Athletics.

Twelve boys had left the School but there were 16 new boys, twelve of whom had come up from Carlekemp.

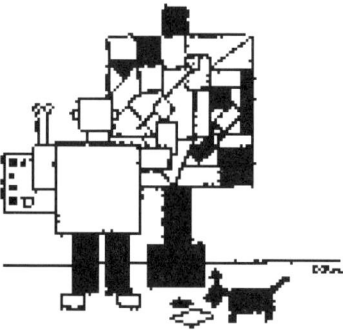

THE ABBEY THEATRE (NÉE GYM)

There had been some reconstruction in the School buildings as well as in the Church. The side and back walls of the theatre had been completely lined with celotex boards which improved the acoustics of the hall and acted as a heat insulator. An Aldis 300 film strip projector had been purchased and it was hoped to build up a film strip library to cover most subjects in the curriculum.

The Cricket season of 1951 was something of a non-event. Of the four matches against other schools, two were cancelled and the other two abandoned because of rain. The School lost against Mr H. B. MacDonald's XI, RAF Kinloss and the Old Boys' XI, but won against Col. F. Laughton's XI. The House Match was won by Lovat (135 runs to Vaughan's 81).

There was interesting news of a number of Old Boys. David Levie and

Angus Pirie Watson (who had left school the previous term), returned as novices in September. They were joined by Alasdair Rankin (who left in 1950). James W. Brown was now a Councillor of the City of Liverpool.

At the end of his third term of office, Abbot Wulstan Knowles retired from the post of Abbot of Fort Augustus to which he had been first elected in 1929. He was now living in retirement in his native Worcestershire.

Accordingly, on 9 January 1952 the Community took a momentous decision. On that day they elected Fr Oswald Eaves as the fifth Abbot of St Benedict's Abbey. He had long and strong links with Fort Augustus, having come to the School in 1924 and entered the Novitiate in 1927. He had taken a prominent part in all School activities, being a Monitor, Captain of Rugby and a member of the Cricket and Shinty teams.

Soon after his ordination in 1934 he went to the Priory, Canaan Lane as what *The Corbie* called 'an indefatigable second-in-command' to Fr Matthew Stedall; when the Priory transferred to Fort Augustus during the War, Fr Oswald was made a housemaster, a post 'in which his gifts of leadership and improvisation found more scope than ever'.

His outstanding achievement during the War was the raising and running of the Abbey School troop of Air Cadets with its junior bodies, the Air Scouts and Cubs. After the War Fr Oswald became the first Prior and Headmaster of Carlekemp. He was the first Old Boy of the new Abbey School to be ordained a priest and the first from it to be blessed as Abbot.

The Editor of *The Corbie* astutely assessed Abbot Oswald's charisms:

There is no need to relate how he fared in that capacity; his pupils, their parents and his staff are willing witnesses to his kindly but discriminating zeal.

CHAPTER 9

The Abbey School
1952-54

ON the 6 February 1952 King George VI died. At Fort Augustus there had not only been a change of Abbot – for Fr Anselm Richardson was the new Prior. He had just come back from parish work in Swansea (having previously taught Maths to the First and Second Forms). Fr Ambrose was Sub-Prior; Fr Jerome was Bursar; Fr Thomas was Novice Master, while Fr Cuthbert had succeeded the Headmaster as monastic Librarian.

After twelve years as Headmaster of the Abbey School, Fr Ethelbert was transferred to Carlekemp as Prior and Headmaster. He was succeeded at Fort Augustus by Fr Augustine Grene. A new Matron had also arrived – Mrs Mortimer. There was sadness at news of the death of Miss Mary Ellis, for many years in charge of the old preparatory department at Fort Augustus and, for a short period, a teacher at St Andrew's Priory School, Edinburgh.

The term opened with a howling gale that brought down a number of trees in the district, although its full force was not felt at Fort Augustus. After the great wind there came three or four weeks of snow and ice. No games were possible, but Winter sports became very popular. Some of the boys sledged on Glen Doe Hill, others skated on the big swamp, some were seen on skis, while the younger members of the School threw snowballs – everyone slid and slipped when they least expected it.

On St Gregory the Great's Day, 12 March 1952, Fr Oswald Eaves was formally blessed as the fifth Abbot of Fort Augustus by his friend of many years, Bishop Frank Walsh WF of Aberdeen.

The School also enjoyed a share in the material parts of the festivities. First came a solid breakfast of

bacon, eggs and sausage. Lunch was an elaborate affair of choice and varied meats. The boys were then free for the rest of the day and were urged to make for the hills. At the evening cinema show the boys found that Fr Abbot had provided ices.

That season's Rugby team was one of the very best ever. F. J. Whitehurst was Captain and T. E. McLaughlin Vice-Captain. The rest of the team included B. G. Paton, R. H. Duncan, V. Macari and A. Haworth. Of the twelve games played, nine were won and only three lost (against an Old Boys' XV, Aberdeen Grammar School and Gordonstoun).

The Hockey team, by contrast, was not quite so effective, losing three, drawing two and winning two.

There had recently been a change in the provenance of School sweaters and blazers. The new supplier was now R. W. Forsyth Ltd of Edinburgh.

An Old Boys' Dance at the Beresford Hotel, Glasgow was patronised by 250 guests and attended by Fr Abbot, Fr Ethelbert and Fr Augustine. The Edinburgh Dance in Easter Week at the Charlotte Rooms welcomed 166 guests, as well as Archbishop Gordon Gray of St Andrews and Edinburgh. A 15 lb Loch Ness salmon, brought to Edinburgh by Fr Abbot, was auctioned and the proceeds given to the Church Building Fund.

From Easter 1952 to the Summer of the following year *The Corbie* sat silent on its branch and failed to fly into print. Then it exploded into life. On 2 June 1953 the Coronation of Queen Elizabeth took place. With its new charismatic Abbot, Fort Augustus shared in the atmosphere of euphoria:

Like untold millions of Her Majesty's loyal subjects, we rejoice at this time in her happy and auspicious Coronation .... May God bless her. May she live long. May her reign be happy and glorious.

In the School, Fr Augustine had been replaced by Fr Thomas as Headmaster, the former taking up duties within the monastery. The presence of the new Abbot was immediately felt within the School. He took an active interest in the boys' daily life, studies and in their games.

News of the death of Fr Anselm Rutherford in June was received with deep regret. A monk of Downside Abbey and (at the time of his death) its Prior, he had been superior at Fort Augustus during the war, facing financial problems and the loss of priests serving as chaplains. He tackled all these difficulties with alacrity until his resignation in 1944 to make way for an abbatial election.

The death was also announced of Old Boy the Very Rev. Hugh Weld, for many years Prior of St Hugh's Charterhouse, Parkminster. Although not an Old Boy, the architect of the church, Reginald Fairlie (a generous benefactor), had also passed away.

Mr James Foy, an Old Boy and Science Master for five years, left at the end of the 1952 Summer term to take up a teaching post in Brighton. Then in January came news of his early death at the age of 37. The whole School assisted at a Solemn Requiem Mass in his memory.

Fr Basil, recently returned from Stanbrook Abbey, was now teaching English and History to the Juniors. Fr Anselm instructed the Middle school in Classics, Mr Pimley taught Classics to the Senior classes, while Commander Fogarty Fegen RN wrestled manfully with Junior Mathematics. The Science department had been taken over by Charles Palmer BSc.

Gymnastics and Boxing were revived that year under the eagle eye of Captain Flood. Br James rigged up a very efficient vaulting horse. A new Matron, Mrs Mortimer and a new Procurator (Fr John) ensured that the boys' health and their stomachs were in good order. Fr John was assisted by Br Adrian's 250 hens who now (coaxed by a cunning arrangement of alarm clocks and electric lights) were laying 130 eggs a day.

Sports for 1952 were dominated by F. J. Whitehurst who won the Dunskey Cup (half mile), the Captain Crawford (steeplechase), the Scholes (batting), the Threlfall (fielding) and shared the Macdonald (*Victor Ludorum*).

The Cricket season of 1952 was a disappointing one, with only one game won and seven lost! Rugby was a different matter – eight wins (including a 13-12 win over Aberdeen Grammar School) and one defeat.

Hockey in 1953 saw a better start to the season and a good ending, with the School Six reaching the final of the Highland District Tournament at Inverness.

The construction of the Abbey Church proceeded with the erection of six massive pillars of Burghead and Northumberland stone, crowned with 30 cwt granite capitals. Many of the construction workers had become old friends of the School – Mr Hendry, Ernie Skinner (a carpenter and trumpeter) and Edmund Ogg, the mason whose pipes could be heard night after night down by the river.

As part of a drive to raise money for the Abbey Church building, two celebrity concerts were given by the distinguished tenor Fr Sydney MacEwan, accompanied by Mr Wilfred Worden. The first, at the Empire Theatre, Inverness on 28 May, was followed by a second (equally successful) concert on 11 June at the Playhouse, Fort William.

In September a large party of Old Boys came up to Fort Augustus for the annual School versus Old Boys Rugby match. The first game was won 60-0 by the School, but the second went to the Old Boys (14-6).

During the same weekend Queen Elizabeth, the Queen Mother passed through Fort Augustus en route to unveiling the Commando War Memorial at Spean Bridge. On the Monday came tragedy, with the death on Loch Ness of John Cobb in his record-breaking speed-boat.

In April 1953 a large party of Old Boys gathered at Angus Macdonald's Bath Hotel. After dinner Abbot Oswald was presented with a magnificent set of breviaries as a mark of the Old Boys' gratification that a former pupil of the modern School had been elected Abbot.

In the field of sport, Hamish MacDonald was awarded an International Hockey Cap in 1953, playing for Scotland against Ireland, Wales, England and Holland. T. C. Barry was an international Hockey umpire and selector, while his brother Peter had captained Edinburgh Northern. Fr Laurence was President of the North of Scotland Hockey Association.

In Cricket, Hamish MacDonald captained the Northern Counties XI for the second year in succession. Under him they won both the League Championship and the knock-out Cup. In Racing, James McLean Jr had had a run of success with his horses, 'Royal Flush' winning the Caesarewitch.

The careers of some Old Boys had taken interesting turns. Lt.-Com. W. MacDonald (Fleet Air Arm), serving on HMS 'Eagle', was in command of the fly-past of aircraft at the Coronation Review on the Solent. Lord Carmont had gained widespread approval for his firm handling of gangs and razor-slashers in Glasgow and elsewhere. John MacGregor had won a further scholarship at the Royal Academy of Dramatic Art in London and been judged the best student of the year. Fr John Barry took part in the examination of the Cause for Beatification of Margaret Sinclair. He was a frequent contributor to periodicals and his article on the 'Medical Aspects of Miracles' attracted great interest.

In the monastic Community, the Autumn term of 1953 was notable for the solemn profession of Fr Robert McKenzie. Abbot Oswald had returned from three weeks at the Congress of Abbots in Rome and made his presence felt as a spectator at School games; while Frs Laurence and Celestine came back refreshed after a fishing holiday in Ireland.

One Old Boy, Lt.-Com. Willie MacDonald, made history at the beginning of term by landing his helicopter on the Abbey Rugby pitch!

Early in the term the Abbey was invaded by cameramen from the BBC who were filming the life of the School and of the Abbey for a forthcoming television feature. This followed the highly successful broadcast on 16 June of 'Vespers of the Feast of the Sacred Heart', with singing from monks and boys to the accompaniment of Fr Gregory on the organ. This was the first full-length service to be sent out on air from the Abbey. Already an earlier home-made film of life at Fort Augustus had proved to be very effective at Vocations exhibitions and lectures.

The power of prayer was not undervalued, although it could some-times be slightly misguided. According to the historian John Cornwell in his biography of Pope Pius XII, *Hitler's Pope* (1999), the chronic hiccup-ing which afflicted the Pope moved the Abbey School to pray en masse for his recovery:

> *An informant tells me that all the boys at the Benedictine monastic school of Fort Augustus in Scotland were instructed to write 'personal' letters of this kind to the Pontiff in 1953.*[1]

The distinguished Old Boy John Calder, managing director of Ind Coope and Allsop Ltd (who had come to the School over 70 years before), presented the prizes at the annual Prize-giving ceremony in the Summer term. Fr Thomas, Headmaster, reported that more boys than ever were going on to higher education. He went on to thank the School medical officer, Dr Kirkton, Mrs Mortimer the Matron, Captain Flood the physical training instructor, and Fr John-Baptist, Bursar.

On the last day of the Summer term a large and appreciative audi-ence enjoyed a performance of Gilbert and Sullivan's 'HMS Pinafore'. The show was produced by the headmaster, Fr Thomas, along with Mr Worden and Br Vincent (who was responsible for the scenery, the costumes *and* the make-up).

Sir Joseph Porter was played by Adrian Haworth, and Seumas Sweet-man made what *The Corbie* called 'a most ravishing Josephine'. Mr Palmer, the Science teacher, was a dastardly Dick Deadeye (able seaman), while, according to *The Corbie*, Iain McLaughlin made 'a very fetching bumboat woman'.

The performance of the School on the Cricket field was not, unhappily, quite as impressive. They lost seven, won two, drew one. Whitehurst, the Captain, gave a fine example in all departments and was an excellent all round player.

The Christmas term of 1953 was notable for its happy uneventfulness. Fr Thomas instituted a new system of alternating the usual films with lectures, to the approval of the boys. Patrick Maitland MP (Conservative, Lanark) spoke about his experiences as a *Times* correspondent; Mr Scholes entertained his audience with an account of his hobby – the discovery and exploration of caves and pot-holes; Mr J. Harvey Scott explained how Music was structured and the perils of being an orchestral conductor. Finally, BBC producer James Crampsey, then working on 'The Bride of the Lammermoor', explained the difference between a stage play and a radio play and the responsibilities of a radio executive.

Among the staff, however, there were some less welcome developments. Fr Celestine was having trouble with his hand and had to endure lengthy hospital treatment. Fr John's beloved boat, 'Grey Goose', buffeted by a sudden easterly gale and dogged by a faulty cable, was practically run aground in the Vegetable Garden.

A record number of Old Boys had come for the annual Rugby match against the School on 26 September. The Old Boys' dance held by the Edinburgh branch in October at the Charlotte Rooms attracted over 160 guests.

At a recent Old Boys' Hockey game against Edinburgh University, the Duke of Edinburgh, who was nearby, had sent over a note wishing the Old Boys good luck, and regretting he could not come over and see the game.

On the field of Rugby, the School XV had a torrid time. The team drew one match and lost eight! Some of the scores make depressing reading: 33-0 (Inverness Academy); 25-0 (Gordonstoun); 38-0 (Altyre); 44-0 (Aberdeen Grammar School).

In Boxing, Hyams, Boyd and O'Reilly were particularly promising, while Fencing and Small-bore Shooting attracted enthusiastic and hard-working aficionados. The Highland Dancing Society, founded at the beginning of the Christmas term, was an immediate success.

The Spring term of 1954 was one of the mildest on record. On Passion Sunday, after High Mass, all the members

of the Community, the School and many visitors attended the ceremony of the unveiling of the War Memorial in the south drive.

Fr Abbot made a brief but touching speech. He drew the analogy
between the Passion of Christ and the sacrifice made by the young men
whose memory was being honoured that day.

Commander Farie then came forward and lowered the Union Jack
which covered the Memorial. The Memorial was then solemnly blessed
by Abbot Oswald, assisted by Fr Prior. The ceremony closed with the
laying of a wreath of daffodils, tulips and other Spring flowers.

The War Memorial itself was seen to be a fine block of granite from
Royal Balmoral. On it was carved a simple Latin cross, with the words:

IN MEMORY OF OUR OLD BOYS OF THE ABBEY SCHOOL
KILLED IN THE WARS. RIP.
REMEMBER THEM AT THE ALTAR.

Older members of the School staff and the Community were saddened to learn of the death of Air Commodore Robert Gordon. A good
friend to the School and one of the pioneers of naval and military
aviation, he died at Newton Abbot, Devon at the age of 72.

Air Commodore Gordon was awarded the DSO for commanding
the operations which led to the destruction of the German cruiser
'Königsberg' in East Africa; he was four times mentioned in dispatches,
serving in Russia and Trans-Jordania.

On 30 May the Aberdeen Diocesan Rally was held at Fort Augustus.
Some 2500 pilgrims had gathered on the School Cricket pitch by 3.30
pm when the procession moved off from the Tower. The crossbearer
and his attendants were followed by the boys of the School, the Children
of Mary, Abbot Oswald, the monks of the Abbey, and a small group of
white-robed Benedictines from Pluscarden Priory. Then came the priests
of the diocese, led by Bishop Walsh, followed by the grey-clothed Sisters
of La Sagesse from Inverness and the Sisters of Mercy from Elgin and
Tomintoul. Behind the nuns came the pilgrims reciting the Glorious
Mysteries of the Rosary and singing hymns to Our Lady.

Assembled at an altar on the field in front of the School Tower, the
pilgrims were addressed by the Prior of Woodchester, Fr Anthony
Ross OP, who outlined in his sermon the work carried out by priests
during the Reformation to keep the faith alive in the Highlands. After
the sermon, Pontifical High Mass was sung by Bishop Walsh. At the

end he gave a Papal Blessing. So closed the largest rally held in the North of Scotland since the Reformation.

On 22 July 1954 nine members of the Abbey School accompanied the Headmaster, Fr Thomas, on a pilgrimage to Lourdes, led by Archbishop Gordon Gray of St Andrews and Edinburgh.

The year 1954 saw innovation in the Old Boys' affairs. The joint Kilgraston-Fort Augustus Ball held at the Central Hotel, Glasgow on 12 March was held in an atmosphere of good fellowship, sweet music and soft lights. The last was involuntary – the result of an electrical failure at Dalmarnock power station! Following this event the Old Boys held a very successful dinner in the Adam Rooms of the George Hotel, Edinburgh.

On the Old Boys' Committee, Commander Farie took over the post of Hon. Treasurer in succession to Mr Ian Kennedy. Among well-known Old Boys, Lord Carmont was conspicuous for his firm handling of those found guilty of razor or cosh attacks, handing out sentences of five to ten years. Further afield, Chicagoan Bill Kelly was now teaching in Evanston and also operating a Coca-Cola plant; Austin MacCaulay was in Hertford, Connecticut for a year of practical psychiatry, and David Levie (Royal Signals) was in Korea. Lt.-Com. Willie MacDonald was at Lossiemouth where he was in command of a squadron of the Fleet Air Arm.

The Hockey XI that year was 'by no standard a good team, and at no time did the eleven play well as a whole'. Of the eight games played, three were won and four lost. The Cricket XI won three of their eight matches. They were 'a curious mixture', as *The Corbie* put it; they 'played well against men, but allowed themselves to be completely dominated by any school team'.

After an initial wet start, the weather for the rest of that Summer was fine and balmy. This appeared to lull the School into a state of torpor: enthusiasm for Athletics was not as sharp as usual; little training was done. The result was that there were no outstanding achievements and the high standard of previous years was scarcely maintained. In the Junior Set, however, things were brighter, M. Cipolato only just managing to hold off D. Demarco and win the Championship.

Off the sports field the younger boys also did well. The Junior Debating Society enjoyed a particularly good year. Two new members (B. McCann and C. Dunn) were elected on the merits of their speaking.

Corbie readers were amazed to learn that Mr Pimley still held the record for throwing the Cricket ball at St Edmunds, Old Hall, established in 1912 (99 yards 6 inches). This distinguished senior linguist, however, had clearly not lost his projectile ability as the following anecdote revealed:

During a French period the aforesaid linguist produced his aged timepiece and chain and proceeded to swing it for the purpose of arousing one of his Lower Grade candidates from slumber. When an incredibly high velocity had been attained, the timepiece decided to part company with the chain. It flew with diminishing rapidity towards the ceiling whence it bounced and then made its return journey via a wainscoting, surmounting the windows, to the floor, narrowly missing one of the Higher Grade candidates. An expression of amazement mingled with ignorance of the chronometer's whereabouts, was depicted on the countenance of the celebrated poultry keeper. On being informed about what had happened he was enlightened as to why his examination class was exploding with bursts of ribald laughter. On being picked up and examined this both ancient and amazing piece of machinery was found to be in perfect chronological order!

CHAPTER 10

The Abbey School
1954-56

THERE was a significant change in the teaching staff at the end of the 1954 Summer term. Mr Wilfred Scholes, long time teacher of English and History, left to take up another post. He had first come to the School in September 1926. From the start he took an active interest in School activities. When a Scout Troop was formed, Mr Scholes became its Scout Master. During his time at Fort Augustus he produced many plays, acted as Chairman of the Senior Debating Society, and for a time edited *The Corbie*. A keen walker and climber, he would be remembered by those whom he took in conducted parties to the top of Corrieyarrick and Ben Nevis.

The outstanding event of the Summer term was the production of Gilbert and Sullivan's 'The Pirates of Penzance'. The part of Frederic was played with verve by J. McIntyre, H. Sweetman made a ravishing Mabel, while P. Mooney and R. Swift (sharing the role of the Pirate King) petrified the audience. The organiser-producer-singing teacher-director was Fr Thomas, while Mr Worden took care of the music, Br Vincent made the costumes, and Br Ignatius operated the stage lighting.

The Autumn term of 1954 saw the arrival of two new Masters, Mr P. Treadaway and Mr P. Daniel (who took over the Editor of *The Corbie*'s chair soon after his arrival), and, for the first time in its history, a Swedish boy joined the School, Nils Albrecht Ihre, who came to Fort Augustus through the good offices of Old Boy Bishop Ansgar Nelson of Stockholm.

Besides All Saints' Day and the Feast of the Immaculate Conception (when Pontifical High Mass was celebrated), there were holidays on 14 October and 17 November. Fine weather enabled Fr Aidan Duggan to take the First Form to Loch Buck, while the Second Form went with Fr Edmund, first to Loch Tarff and later up the River Tarff.

On 5 October at 8.05pm the eagerly-awaited film about Fort

Augustus Abbey and School was shown on television. As there was no television in the Abbey, the School and the Community had to be content with listening to enthusiastic accounts of the film or reading letters of appreciation, like the one that appeared in the *Radio Times* the following week.

On 27 October Mr Worden's Scottish Home Service concert was relayed to the School during lunch. He played Chopin's 'Fantaisie-Impromptu', his own Minuet from 'Salle des Glaces', and Schubert's 'Impromptu in A Flat' (Op. 90, no. 4).

A milestone in School leisure activities was the formation of the Apollo Society one October Friday in 1954. Fr Thomas outlined the scheme to the Third Form and above, saying that on Mr Treadaway's suggestion, a Society was to be established to promote artistic taste in the upper School. Within a few days a constitution had been drawn up and the Society held its first meeting in the Lodge Art Room, a great many boys being present.

A further innovation was the AAA (Abbey Automobile Association) which proposed to stage a number of events (Rallies, Speed Trials, Grands Prix) during the coming season under directors J. Pochon and J. Campbell.

The extreme youth (their average age was 15.7 years) and lack of experience of the 1954-55 Rugby team led to a poor season. Two of the games against other schools were won, but five were lost. Of the three club games played, one was drawn and two lost. G. Martin (Captain) was the best player in the team; at times he was a 'thrustful centre'; R. N. Swift, scrum-leader and Vice-Captain, was a very hard worker and by far the best forward.

Returning for the Spring term of 1955, the boys had to fight their way through the snow. The bus from Spean Bridge was held up for two hours at Laggan, arriving at midnight. The next night (15 January) the temperature was -1°(F) – another record for Fort Augustus. The new Editor of *The Corbie* (Mr Peter Daniel) wrote:

The snow and ice persisted, so that, in contrast to last year, Winter sports were well up to standard. There was skiing, tobogganing and skating on the Tarff every afternoon, while the weather lasted.

There were some staffing changes in the School. Fr Basil Wedge had returned to the School to take the First Form for History, while Mr

Pimley was now able to enhance his language instruction through the use of a new tape-recorder which slowly and solemnly repeated his voice announcing, '*Tous les matins à huit heures et demie, M. Desgranges quitte la maison*'.

There was sadness at the death at the age of 48 of Mr J. G. Hughes, former teacher of Maths and Science, who always took a keen interest in the School's activities outside the classroom. He had left Fort Augustus in 1939 to take up mushroom-growing at Ottery St Mary.

School holidays included expeditions conducted by Frs Edmund and John-Baptist, while on 23 January Fr Aidan took members of the First and Second Forms to see the vitrified fort at Tordoun. On 29 March the Fifth and Sixth Forms went with Fr Andrew by private bus to visit the Mullardoch and Benevean dams and the power station at Fasnakyle.

There was also some activity on the theatrical front. On 26 February 55 boys went with Fr Thomas to see the Inverness Amateur Opera Company perform 'The Mikado'; while a light-hearted performance of Sheridan's 'The Rivals', produced by Mr Treadaway on Easter Sunday, made a happy finish to a rather uneventful term.

The Junior Debating Society continued to flourish. During the debate on the motion 'That Classical Music is preferable to Modern Music', the speakers used gramophone records to illustrate their points. Brian McCann demonstrated his view that modern dancing was a disgusting affair by dancing the 'Be-Bop' (to the amusement of all) in the middle of the floor! In spite of his exertions, the motion was defeated by 8 votes to 5.

So severe was the weather after Christmas that it was only through good fortune that any Hockey games were played before March. A two-week break in the weather at the end of January was enough to get a team together and play three matches. Then the snow came again and no games were played until the first week in March. Of the twelve matches arranged, only four were played, two of which the School won.

J. K. Deady and A. Fava were the outstanding members of the team. Both played in the Final Schoolboy International Trial at Paisley and Deady achieved the honour of being selected to

play against the Irish Schoolboys in Dublin on 16 April. The School entered three teams in the District Six-a-Side Tournament at Lossie-mouth, the 'A' team coming within a point of winning their section.

At the end of the Spring term (1955) *The Corbie's* sub-editor R. S. Fothringham left and was succeeded in office by his brother.

On Sunday 22 May the Abbey and School broadcast a religious service in the BBC Scottish Home Service, led by Abbot Oswald. His talks were interspersed with hymns and plainchant, sung by the monks and by the boys. Fr Thomas was the choirmaster, Fr Basil the reader, and Fr Bernard the organist.

One new boy, P. Constable, joined the School; while another, G. Martin, went to Sandhurst in May to take his entry exam. A month later he heard that he had passed.

Athletics and Cricket were run concurrently that year and the Final Sports Day was held at mid-term at the beginning of June. Lovat were the winners for the fifth successive year; G. Martin won the Crawford Cup, the Dunskey Cup and the School Championship (for the second year running), while the outstanding achievement was J. K. Deady's equalling of A. Keegan's High Jump record of 5 feet 3 inches.

Mr Treadaway and Mr Daniel acted as supervisors for the Swim-ming. As the pool was empty for a while, some boys at first bathed in the Canal. The weather was so good that more and more people went in. Vaughan won the House Swimming competition at the annual Gala, while O'Reilly beat his last year's record by staying underwater for 56 seconds.

On Corpus Christi Sunday there was Vespers at 2.00 pm, followed by a procession round the Cricket field and cloisters. On 1 May (Whit-Monday) a large party of senior boys conquered Ben Nevis.

The author Sir Compton Mackenzie gave away the prizes in the Study Hall on Sunday 3 July. In his speech, Fr Thomas noted that three universities – Cambridge, Glasgow and Newcastle – had accepted candidates from the School, while J. Noblet had won a scholarship to the Royal Manchester College of Music and was studying singing with the tenor, Heddle Nash. Winner of the Sir James Calder Cup for the best all-round student of the year was R. S. Fothringham.

Sir Compton, in a witty speech, reminded the boys of their good fortune to be Catholics, free of the anxiety that affected so many in the world. He congratulated them on their good manners and hoped they would always hold fast to them. Politeness oiled the wheels of life.

Holidays that year were on Ascension Day, Whit-Monday, Corpus Christi, St Benedict's Day and St Peter and St Paul. On 4 July there was an extra holiday granted by Fr Abbot at the request of Sir Compton Mackenzie.

The 1955 production of 'The Mikado' was distinguished by the Japanese costumes sent from Osaka by Mr Forbes. Two debutants on the stage, John Airs (Katisha) and Brian McCann (Pooh-Bah), were outstanding. The latter's antics drew tears of laughter from all; the former was also favourably reviewed by Wilfred Taylor in his 'Scotsman's Log' (*The Scotsman*, 5 July 1955).

The 1955 Cricket XI was one of the best in the history of the School, winning eight matches, drawing one (Gordonstoun), and losing one (Nairn CCC). Much of the credit for the team went to G. Martin, the Captain, and to Vice-Captain G. Davidson who took 50 wickets and bowled consistently throughout the season. J. Deady was the best fielder and best all-rounder in the side.

Among Old Boys in religion Shaun Crowley was ordained at St Andrew's Cathedral, Dumfries on 17 July 1955. His brother, Diarmid, studying at the Scots College, Rome was now a deacon. Dom Robert McKenzie was ordained deacon at Monte Cassino; Dom Benedict Seed made his solemn profession on 15 August and was raised to the subdiaconate in Rome on 17 December.

During the Summer holidays the windows of the new church were glazed. Around 30,000 visitors inspected it.

Rugby in 1955 saw only moderate success. This was due to two weaknesses: failure, especially at forward, to rise above adversity led to two crushing defeats (23-6 against Aberdeen Grammar School and 31-0 against Glenalmond 2nd XV). A lack of scoring power behind the scrum deprived the team of two wins. But it was still a young side.

Since 12 October 1955 the Workshop above the Engine Room had been in use by the boys. Half was reserved to the crew of the 'Grey Goose' for storing their tackle, while in the other half canoes, sledges and suchlike were manufactured. O'Reilly, meanwhile, was to be found sitting in a tangle of wires making a short-wave radio set.

February 1956 will be long remembered for the tragic disappearance of Br Malachy Hanson who went for a walk on the afternoon of Monday 13 February and never came back. *The Corbie* reported:

He was last seen by Campbell and Airs near the Tarff Bridge, and the banks of the Tarff were the first place to be searched, notably on the following Wednesday, the 15th, by the whole School above the Second Form. We received every possible help from the police, who directed us on this and most other searches …. Volunteers from the Village helped in Sunday searches, and in the first few days we had the help of the Gordonstoun and Altyre mountain rescue squads, with their blood-hounds and walkie-talkies …. Amnesia being out of the question, it is feared that Br Malachy, who was very short-sighted, may have lost his spectacles and fallen, perhaps, into the river.

A Requiem Pontifical High Mass was held for Br Malachy on 22 February attended by the whole School and many local people. But still there was no news of him.

The Spring term of 1956 saw changes in the School staff. In Fr Andrew's temporary absence Commander Farie returned to the classroom to take over Senior Geography. Fr Aidan Duggan, who had only just come to Fort Augustus from Australia the previous year, had transferred to Carlekemp. In his place Fr Mark Dilworth came back to teach Languages. Mr Robertson, who had arrived as Physical Training Instructor from the Forces, had already enthused the School for Boxing, Fencing and Judo. Later in the term he arranged a number of public exhibitions.

On the Feast of St Michael the Archangel, the School attended High Mass in the choir as Brs Marian Lang and George Tolan were taking simple temporary vows. At Pontifical High Mass on All Saints' Day, the School again attended in choir and Br Vincent Pirie Watson made his solemn profession. Abbot Oswald presided over the annual Hallowe'en party given by the boys. This was followed by a display of fireworks on the lawn. At the Feast of the Immaculate Conception, Br Marian received the tonsure and Br Vincent the first two minor orders.

A dinner was held in the boys' refectory to celebrate the 356th meeting of the Senior Debating Society. Attending were Mr Pimley (President), Commander Fegen and Mr Treadaway (Vice-Presidents), Frs Anselm, Celestine and Thomas.

During the term over 70 books were added to the School Library, many the gift of boys or teachers, 30 of them from the County Library. Mrs Barry added a very popular present in the form of a subscription to *The Illustrated London News.* Examination of the School's borrowing habits revealed what *The Corbie* called a 'craze for espionage and escape books' which had continued unabated – one can only guess at the readers' motivation.

The School, however, also had other stimulants for their emotional development: Mr Treadaway's production of Shakespeare's 'Macbeth', for example, on 17 March for the Community and School and on 21 March for invited guests.

The most powerful acting in the play was by John Molleson as Macbeth and John Airs as Lady Macbeth. Molleson had had the advantage of sharing a railway sleeping compartment with an Old Boy, the actor John McGregor, who had gone through the whole play with him and later gave valuable help at a rehearsal in the Abbey theatre.

Other highlights of the production were the young Macduff's (John Kelly) 'splendidly harrowing and life-like screams as he was being murdered', the unnerving third witch of Jim Dollan, and Peter McCoy's ghost of Banquo, white of face and stained with blood.

The swordplay, under the direction of Mr Robertson, was carefully rehearsed and convincing; while the gory head of Macbeth, made out of newspapers, wax and red paint, sent a chill through the hearts of the audience.

Nearly all the costumes had been lent by Lewes Little Theatre Club, while the choice of Berlioz' 'Symphonie Fantastique' was due to Mr Worden's taste and perspicacity.

On the Hockey field, battles of a different kind were fought by the School XI. The team was 'fit and fast' wrote *The Corbie* of one game and they 'maintained a cracking pace from start to finish'. Only two out of nine matches were lost. The Captain and centre-half, J. K. Deady, was the pivot and mainstay of the XI. In defence G. Davidson was the other outstanding member of the team. In goal C. Dunn played effectively. Five of the School XI played in the Final Schoolboys Trial in Edinburgh, Deady and R. M. Beith being capped against Ireland. The School also fielded a Second XI and a Colts XI that year.

Returning after the Easter holidays the School found the partition between the old and the new Church had been removed, displaying the full grandeur of the nave. On 13 June the School attended Pontifical High Mass for Br George Tolan (who had died in Glasgow the previous Friday) and after Mass they were present at his funeral.

The swimming pool, newly painted maritime blue-green by Fr Bernard, Mr Robertson and many of the boys, was much in use. The tennis courts also proved popular, especially as they had been fenced in by Mr Robertson with netting.

On 16 May 'Macbeth' was given to a packed hall in Fort William. It

ABBEY BOYS: FORT AUGUSTUS ABBEY SCHOOLS

was a great success, 'one of its highlights being the occasion when Colin McAllister as Young Siward, carried away with martial ardour, laid about him with such lusty vigour in the battle scene that his sword broke in two, an unrehearsed touch of realism much appreciated by the audience'.

On 15 July, the Bishop of Aberdeen, the Rt Rev Francis Walsh WF, carried out the ordination of three Old Boys: Br Robert McKenzie was ordained a priest, Br Benedict Seed a deacon, and Br Vincent Pirie Watson a sub-deacon. Later in the term Abbot Wulstan Knowles visited and sang Pontifical High Mass on St Benedict's Day. On the same afternoon Prize-giving was held, followed by a performance of 'The Gondoliers'. The 1956 production of 'The Gondoliers' was the work of Fr Thomas and Mr Worden. It was notable for the gutsy lead given the male chorus by Mr Treadaway and for the acting of John Airs as the Duke of Plaza-Toro:

> John Airs, metamorphosed from shrewish harridan to foppish and frog-like aristocratic roué, caracoled about the stage in season and out of season with delightfully spontaneous abandon. His antics in the gavotte were a joy to watch .... We cannot conclude without mentioning J. Dollan's charmingly coy simper as a maiden approached by a gondolier ....

At the first night Michael Crawford (who had played the part of Marco in the 1948 production) presented a bouquet to the leading lady. This was followed by a speech from Fr John Barry.

In the Workshop, Fr John-Baptist presided over an impressive array of nautical gear; M. G. Smith sat quietly making model aeroplanes; while O'Reilly ran a hospital for senile or otherwise indisposed wireless sets. Much to everyone's astonishment (and not least their own), the canoes built there by J. Molleson and W. Dugmore proved perfectly water-worthy. On St Peter and St Paul's Day they proved this by paddling up the River Oich to Loch Oich, and back by the Canal, getting out and carrying their craft when they came to rapids or lochs. They had begun work on the canoes in the middle of the Christmas term, being certain that, without interruption, they would need no more than a month to complete the construction.

The record of the Cricket XI (played 13, won 10, lost 3) proved how strong it was in bowling and fielding. Only the batting, which depended too much on two or three players, let the side down on occasion.

G. Davidson (Captain) was the mainstay of the attack, capturing over 50 wickets for the second year running. B. Spary showed himself to be a fast and dangerous bowler. J. Deady was brilliant in the field, while P. Kelly and A. Duncan were equally fine batsmen.

In Athletics the outstanding achievements were J. K. Deady's new School Record of 5 feet 5 inches in the High Jump and M. Cipolato's three new records in the Intermediate Section (220 yards, 440 yards, and Long Jump).

The Old Boys' Annual General Meeting was held in the Calefactory with the President, Abbot Oswald, in the chair. It was unanimously agreed that a letter of thanks and appreciation should be sent to Fr Birnie on his retirement from the office of Chaplain. Fr John Barry was elected in his place.

A number of Old Boys had made their mark in public life: Michael Kerrigan was chosen to play Cricket for Scotland on several occasions; David B. Williamson was farming in Vancouver; Billy Mackenzie was serving in Cyprus; while Allardyce Smith (Seaforth Highlanders) was enjoying the sun in Gibraltar!

The ninth Annual Dance was held in the Central Hotel, Glasgow on 13 February. Some 360 guests attended – a large number of Old Boys, along with the Old Girls of Kilgraston, enjoyed a pleasant evening dancing to the music of Bill Lambert's Broadcasting Band. Two pipers of the City of Glasgow Police Pipe Band gave rendering of Scottish airs to which many of the company danced. Abbot Oswald and Fr Ethelbert moved among the guests meeting friends and benefactors.

The beginning of the new academic year (1956-57) saw the arrival of eight boys into Form I; seven (many of them from Carlekemp) into Form II; two to Form III; and one, John West, who had come from the Royal High School in Edinburgh.

Sadly, two outstanding masters left: Oxford graduates Mr Daniel and Mr Treadaway. In their place came the Rev. T. Johnstone (a former Church of England priest who replaced Mr Daniel as Editor of *The Corbie* and Chairman of the Senior Literary and Debating Society and Mr Treadaway as Chairman of the Apollo Society) and Mr D. Fowles (teacher of English and History who had taught for many years in Barbados).

Late in October Br Benedict Seed was ordained.

CHAPTER 11

The Abbey School
1956-58

THE School grew perceptibly in the year 1956-57. While 13 boys left in Summer 1956, 22 new boys arrived for the start of the Michaelmas term.

One of the highlights of the Autumn term was the visit of Lt.-Cdr. Willie MacDonald RN towards the end of October to speak about his career in the Fleet Air Arm. He had left Fort Augustus in 1939 and joined the Railways Catering Service. When war broke out he asked Commander Farie's advice and then obtained entry to the Royal Navy. After a brief training period in the United Kingdom, he went over to Florida, USA to continue his course. Returning to Scotland, he was sent to practise deck-landings in the Clyde and then served two years at sea with Captain Walker's Frigate Group. When the war was over, he continued to serve in the Fleet Air Arm.

On 1 December Brigadier G. L. Prendergast outlined his experiences in North Africa and in the Mediterranean theatre of war between 1939-45. The Brigadier had held high command in the Long Range Desert Group and had the celebrated 'Popski's Private Army' under his personal command.

An innovation that term was the introduction of Hospice study-bedrooms for selected boys, each study accommodating three or four students. In contrast to these new arrangements, there were other architectural landmarks at Fort Augustus which were to suffer severe damage:

The terrific gale of wind on the Twelfth of December transported trees bodily through the air, lifted the Abbot's garage from off its foundations (without, miraculously, damaging the car inside it), and deposited it upon one of the Abbey hen-houses. It also lifted the Rugger shed clean over a wall, placing it upside down on the other side. Fortunately, the gale brought no casualties, in spite of considerable damage to property; indeed, the only sufferers were a number of hens who were found in the morning wedged in the meshes of a wire fence in the hen enclosure.

The Camera Club continued to flourish under the guidance of Mr Worden and its darkroom now had a new roof. Since the old roof had been leaking prodigiously for three years, Fr John mended it during the Summer months. The members could now develop prints without being instantly and dramatically drenched by the Winter rains.

The 1956 Rugby season was disappointing. Seven School matches were played, of which the first was drawn and the other six lost.

The Matron, Mrs Mortimer, left at the end of December to take up a new job in the South, having been in post for five years. Mrs Fowles and Mrs Clark (Morrenish) stepped into the breach until the arrival of the new Matron, Mrs Bainbridge.

During the Christmas holidays the School Gym was used to stage a Nativity play in the form of tableaux by the Village schoolchildren, both Catholic and Protestant. Mr Worden had trained the choir and Fr Philip helped with the production. The result was highly successful.

During the Christmas gales, when wind speeds of 85 mph were recorded, Fr John's boat, the 'Grey Goose', dragged her ground tackle, weighing just over a ton, for about thirty yards.

It was in the early part of 1957 that Br Hugh, who had printed *The Corbie* for more than 25 years, gave up the unequal struggle with 'imperfect copy, editorial shortcomings and difficulties of understaffing and restrictions'. *The Corbie* was now no longer printed at the Abbey Press. *The Corbie* had been established originally to chronicle the life of the School from term to term, to print whatever Old Boys' news came to hand and to provide an outlet for the literary efforts of the boys. It also served a useful public relations function. Now that *The Corbie* was being printed outside the Abbey, the question of its finances became a priority. Costs would need to be balanced by sales and advertisements. Captain MacDermot-Roe had taken on the duties of Business Manager and had already done much to establish *The Corbie* on a sound financial basis.

The Apollo Society was still flourishing, even if only two meetings had been held during the term. Both were gramophone concerts which varied from Grieg to the Goon's 'Ying Tong Song'.

The Lent term began on Tuesday 15 January. Those who came by Spean Bridge did not arrive until 11 pm as the train was delayed.

Although the weather that term was exceptionally mild, strong winds caused damage for the third time that Winter. The weather vane from the School tower blew down and its point was driven into a window-pane on the front of the School, where it remained stuck. Because trees were uprooted, new ones were planted along the drive and lower road and in the swamp.

Br Raphael Auer died on 26 January. Born in Aberdeen in 1876, of Bavarian and Swiss parents, he attended Robert Gordon's College before entering the monastery in 1931. Previously he had worked in his parents' watchmaking and jewellery business (and had also been a representative of a firm of watch and clockmakers). At Fort Augustus he continued to use his expertise in a workshop full of bits of wood and the spare parts of watches. He was affectionately known as 'Gandhi' because of his resemblance to the great Indian politician and mystic.

On 20 February sung Votive Vespers of St Andrew were broadcast, prefaced by a short talk on Fort Augustus and the monastic life, given by Abbot Oswald. The boys' trebles alternated with the monks in the first and fourth psalms, and alternate verses of the Magnificat were harmonised. The programme was rounded off with a four-part 'Crux ave benedicta'.

The Loch Ness Monster reared its head again during the term. On 11 February, Fr Thomas, who had been attending a conference in Edinburgh, was persuaded, much against his will, to appear in a television programme about 'Nessie'. He firmly declared his disbelief. Exactly a month later, on 11 March, the creature appeared as Mr Fowles, with Mr Ian Grant from the Village, was driving along the Loch side near Drumnadrochit. Meanwhile, Fr Mark had also answered questions about the Monster in a BBC Overseas programme aimed at listeners in France.

Mr Fowles later told *The Corbie* what he had seen from the roadside:

About two miles this side of the AA box between Inverness and Drumnadrochit there is a lay-by on the Loch side of the road. It was when we were approaching this spot that I noticed what I first thought was surf breaking over the rocks two or three hundred yards off shore. The rocks were dark and there was a line of them, two rather larger than the third. They were perhaps sixteen to eighteen feet across. It was a few seconds before I realised there were no rocks at that distance from the shore anywhere along Loch Ness. I pointed out the disturbance to Mr Grant and he immediately looked and shouted, pulling the car into the lay-by. It was not until we were out of the car that I heard him say it was the Monster. While we were too far away to distinguish the finer details of the creature, it was clear enough to distinguish two lumps and a smaller one in the water. All three were moving in unison across a line of waves towards the other side of the Loch. The surf was much less now than when I first saw it. Gradually moving out all the time, it submerged, to leave an arrow-shaped trail as it moved just under the surface of the water. Soon it disappeared altogether, and though we looked for some time it did not appear again.

The Abbey Fire Brigade continued to operate successfully. Every Saturday at noon the siren was tested, but sometimes the emergency was real, as on the evening of 12 March when burning gorse bushes on the other side of the Village blazed out of control:

A team of Lay-brothers in blue battle-dress appeared from nowhere and disappeared at speed down the drive like a shot from 'Keep the Home Guard Turning'. Nor were the proceedings thereafter unlike one of Sir Compton's plots.

Since it was built in 1842 the Old Convent had seen more than a few changes. It had been in turn parish church, convent of two different orders of nuns, private house, Prep School, and again private house. It was now being turned into flats. When Mr Pimley retired from teaching at the end of the Summer, he continued to live in the Old Convent.

Although seven of the previous year's Hockey team were again playing in 1957, only two Colours were awarded (P. Gordon Smith and A. M. Duncan). The form of the 1957 team was erratic and the better players rarely did justice to their ability. Poor finishing and 'teeing-up' their shots cost countless goals. Three matches were won, three lost and two drawn. A. M. Duncan, right half, was the best man of the side, a neat player with good stick work and a very sound sense of position which made him a difficult man to get by. He went forward to the Schoolboys final Trial and was capped against Ireland.

The annual Fort Augustus-Kilgraston Ball was held on 5 March (Shrove Tuesday) in the Central Hotel, Glasgow, with over 400 guests and Old Boys present. Bill Lambert's Orchestra provided the music, while pipers from the Glasgow Police Pipe Band played for the reels.

According to the Mr Johnstone, Editor of *The Corbie,* 'The year 1957 will undoubtedly go down as a most important one in the history of the School'. He was referring to the decision to attach a new wing to the School in order to solve the accommodation problem. Through the generosity of Old Boy Sir James Calder, this became a reality. Plans were drawn up by Messrs McKillop and Lawrie of Inverness and approved by Chapter. The plan chosen would mean, unfortunately, the demolition of the bastion wall and part of the moat.

Another aspect of accommodation left a great deal to be desired. During the previous term the School Workshop had experienced considerable management difficulties. It was eventually closed down. Juniors did not appreciate how much trouble had been taken to provide the facility. Misuse of tools was commonplace. After a door had been left open, a burglary took place which resulted in the loss of tools and equipment to the value of £35.

Although Cricket began with the start of the Summer term on 26 April, the weather was unpleasant until the end of May when the sun finally broke through: 'The weather this term could be summed up as a month of fine weather sandwiched between two other months that were cold and wet.'

An attempt was made to smoke the rabbits from under the old tree opposite the corner of the Gym bastion. It succeeded too well, for the fire travelled to the centre of the roots and stayed there. Fire extinguishers proved to be useless. Finally a hole was made at the top of the trunk and water poured in, but it only acted as a chimney from which smoke continued to rise for the next seven days. Only a downpour of West Highland rain finished the job!

The steady drone heard in the monastic Choir on occasion was the doing neither of the monks nor of the organ, but of bees. Several colonies had made their home inside the corrugated iron of the temporary Choir, and on sunny days they made their way into the Choir itself.

A carved oak plaque with the Roll of Honour of the 14 Old Boys killed in the Second World War was fixed to the wall of St Andrew's Chapel at the end of June. A new granite altar was being erected and Br Cuthbert of Pluscarden was engaged on a wood-carving for the wall behind the Chapel which was to become an Old Boys' War Memorial. Around 40 Old Boys died during the South African War and the First World War. Three of them (Francis Wynter, William Macdonald and Simon Fraser) were awarded the Distinguished Service Order.

The most poignant event of 1957 was the finding of Br Malachy Hanson's body on 10 July, 17 months after his disappearance. The remains were in a ditch near the path, almost at the top of Corrieyarrack Pass, ten miles from Fort Augustus. His spectacles were found not very far away.

Evidently, Br Malachy was surprised by the sudden blizzard which followed that sunny afternoon, lost his glasses, wandered off the path, and so died of exposure.

On the day his body was found, his brother, Fr F. Hanson, by a happy coincidence, had arrived in Britain after seven years' missionary service in the Far East. He sang the Requiem Mass at his funeral three days later.

On 23 June, Br Anthony Freeman died of a heart attack at the Birmingham Oratory, with which he had been associated for most of his life. Percy Freeman was born in Birmingham in 1888 and orphaned at an early age. The family belonged to the Church of England and Percy was educated at the Royal Wolverhampton School. Afterwards he ran his own linen drapery business for a number of years. In 1912 he was received into the Catholic Church at the Birmingham Oratory where he served as sacristan and master of ceremonies for many years. In 1936 he received the monastic habit at Fort Augustus, being employed chiefly as sacristan and refectorian. In 1953 he was appointed to the lighter work of answering the door and telephone in the Hospice.

The BBC came on 17 May to make a film about the Abbey. This was later shown on television. Five days later they arrived again to film the two schools of thought about the Monster. This followed on from the four occasions the Abbey had featured in BBC programmes the previous term. The new station at Rosemarkie had brought TV to the Highlands and, in due course, an aerial appeared on the School tower.

Prizes were presented on Sunday 7 July by the Hon. Mrs Stirling of Keir, daughter of the founder (15th Lord Lovat), and a lifelong friend of the Abbey. She recalled coming to the Abbey to hear her brother singing in a Gilbert and Sullivan opera.

On the night of the Prize-giving, Fr Thomas' production of the Gilbert and Sullivan comic opera 'Patience' was performed to an audience of boys, friends and families:

It was a high-spirited gathering, ready to laugh at any hitches (it did laugh at one loud crash backstage), a trifle noisy and disinclined to break off conversation for the overture ....

As the dairy maid Patience, Mike Drummond acted successfully with a complete lack of sophistication; he forgot his lines occasionally and sometimes went off the note, but these were minor blemishes. J. Airs was the only one who was able to vary his voice for effect while singing, as when he put on a mincing tone.

The staging was by Mr Fowles (who had trained in stage managment at the Bristol Old Vic). Make-up was by Fr John-Baptist and Fr Vincent; Mrs Fowles made several of the costumes. Lighting was by Br Ignatius, general production by Fr Thomas, with accompanist Mr Worden in charge of the music. Five performances were given – four in Fort Augustus and one at Fort William.

Sport of a different kind was less successful. The 1957 Cricket team was of average ability. Ten games were played, of which five were lost. As there was no outstanding batsman or bowler in the side, the Bowling and Batting Cups were withheld. A. M. Duncan, the Captain, was very competent behind the stumps; B. C. Spary, Vice-Captain, did not have the success as a bowler which he had promised. However, with seven of the First XI in their team, Lovat had no difficulty in keeping up their winning sequence.

In Athletics the story was the same. There was no outstanding performance. Perhaps this was in part due to the weather which made it impossible to carry out a training schedule. In the Senior Section, M. Cipolato and B. C. Spary (both Lovat) carried all before them. In Swimming, Lovat won both the Relay and the Championship. The winner of the Cruickshank Golf Trophy for the second time was C. Dunn.

The Annual Old Boys' Reunion was held on Saturday 13 and Sunday 14 July. Many Old Boys had arrived by Saturday morning and, with the School, attended the burial of Br Malachy's remains. This was followed by the Cricket match (interrupted by heavy showers) which was won by the Old Boys, and the opera in the evening.

On the Sunday morning there was a boat race against the School from Battery Rock to the Canal. Fitness told – the School won. After High Mass the Old Boys sat down for lunch in the cloisters with the Community, during which a presentation of a wallet of notes was made to Mr Pimley.

The Annual General Meeting was the shortest for many years. All office-bearers were re-elected (Secretary, Fr Celestine; Treasurer, Commander Farie; the Committee was R. Phoenix, J. Marin, B. Murray; the Chaplain, Fr J. Barry).

On the last day of term the monitors went to the Old Convent to

present Mr Pimley with a silver cigarette case on behalf of the whole School. After 30 years teaching at Fort Augustus, he retired, having arrived at the School six years after it had been re-started. New teachers with degrees and experience had to be found outside the School. Mr Pimley possessed both. He came to the Abbey, married a Highland wife, and made Fort Augustus his home.

The Michaelmas Term was a time of confusion and bewilderment. On two occasions the Northern Lights gave colourful displays. With the Study Hall and nearby classrooms out of use, classes were being held in unlikely places. In the middle of this the Asian flu struck.

Rapidly classes ground to a halt as more and more boys succumbed. The first cases were taken to the Lodge. When full, the Hospice was used and then the Prep Dormitory. The Volkswagen plied briskly up and down the drive carrying boys and bedding. When Matron fell ill, Mrs Clark stepped into the breach. Strangely, hardly any of the staff or monks was affected.

Suddenly, the crisis was over. Classes began again on 2 October and things got back to normal (or as near normal as possible with building operations in full swing).

Meanwhile, a new boy Stefan (Istvan) Hegedus had arrived at Fort Augustus by a circuitous route. In 1956, fleeing from a Budapest in ruins, with the people on strike and Russian soldiers fighting in the streets, he and his family and a large group of friends had taken a train for the Austrian border. The train stopped and they had to escape across deep ploughed fields through the darkness.

The Hegedus family arrived in England in December 1956 at the military headquarters of the British Army in Aldershot. After a week or so there, they were taken to a former naval hospital at Wapping in the East End of London. By January 1957, through the Catholic Relief Agency, they were found a flat in Ealing, London and both he and his brother were accepted into St Benedict's School, Ealing, run by the English Benedictines. Subsequently he was brought to Fort Augustus by Abbot Oswald.

For the forseeable future the Fifth Form was in the monastic Calefactory, the Third Form in the Old Library, and the Second Form in the second floor of the Hospice (known to some Old Boys as 'The Itchery'). The Fourth Form were for a time transferred to the Art Room beside the Abbot's Chapel.

Some building alterations had already finished – the Study Hall had been robbed of two-fifths of its height, the centre dormitory had additional cubicles down the middle and the Old Convent was converted into flats. In the Hospice more rooms were allocated as studies. All these changes were the result of increased numbers in the School attracted by Abbot Oswald's networking skills and flair for publicity.

Ninety-eight boys (only two day pupils) assembled on 21 September for High Mass sung by the Headmaster. Twenty-eight were new boys. After a year's absence Mr P. Daniel came back to teach English. Old Boy Hamish MacDonald (a former Scottish Hockey international) was another new but well-remembered face on the staff. Fr Andrew had returned to teach Geography; Fr Edward had come from Carlekemp to take Middle School French; Fr Benedict, having satisfied the examiners in Rome, had come to pass on his knowledge to the Lower School.

On the following day, in the early evening, the Russian Sputnik satellite was reported to have been seen over Auchterawe in the early evening.

For the second time that year, a choir of monks and boys broadcast Vespers on the Home Service, this time at 7.45 pm on Sunday 8 December. Votive Vespers of the Immaculate Conception were sung. It was prefaced by a short talk on the feast and the antiphons and followed a short sermon, both given by Abbot Oswald. Boys and monks alternated in singing the verses of the psalm.

As the year drew to a close an assortment of unusual entertainments was provided. After the procession through the cloisters on Monday 9 December, a staff dinner was held in the Hospice where Commander Fegen astonished the guests with 'tricks from his repertoire'. The day before term ended, J. Molleson and his accordion accompanied the School in a very successful sing-song. The evening ended with an unaccompanied rendering of '*Adeste fideles*'.

The 1957-58 Rugby team had a good season. Out of eight matches, three were lost, but in two of these the margin of defeat was so narrow that the game could have gone either way.

The Corbie noted that the 1957 team was 'a strong combination and it was the combined effort, really good and intelligent team work, that brought the results; the pack was well led by C. R. Dunn and the scrum-half and Captain, A. M. Duncan, was an inspiration among the backs. E. R. Di Rollo at full-back was one of the finest in the history of the School. The game against Glenalmond College 2nd XV on 7 December ended with the following bizarre incident:

Five minutes from time it looked as if Demarco must score. Fielding the ball from a Glenalmond kick, he dodged his opponents; running strongly up the wing and with only the full-back to beat, he kicked over his head and must have scored, had the full-back not tackled him!

More strictly dramatic fare was given with two performances of Shakespeare's 'Julius Caesar' on 15 December (for the School and Community) and on 17 December (for the Village and other guests). There was a further performance on 1 April at the Empire Theatre, Inverness.

J. Molleson (Brutus) had the most difficult part and played it with a good measure of success; J. Airs, in spite of having a splint on his leg, gave a polished account of the role of Cassius. M. Turnbull as Mark Anthony showed ability in the delivery of his great speeches. K. Fryer, as Julius Caesar, gave an unusual interpretation of the part. Production was by Mr Fowles, make-up by Fr John, wiring and lighting by Fr Edward and Br Ignatius. Mr Worden was responsible for the sound-effects; costumes were by Mrs Fowles and M. Turnbull.

Mr Daniel's return had had an immediate effect in the founding of The Listeners (a record-playing group to replace the Apollo Society), The Library and the Senior Literary and Debating Society, where he resumed chairmanship.

Within the Community there were several interesting developments. Br Placid Grady was awarded the Diploma of Merit (First Class) in Tailoring and Cutting; Fr Edward had been appointed workmaster in charge of the routine and maintenance work done by Brothers and employees. One of the dungeon store-rooms under the School was converted into an Archive for valuable manuscripts and important documents. Fr Mark Dilworth was now the official Archivist.

Among the Old Boys the most significant event was the succession of former Coadjutor Fr Ansgar Nelson OSB to the See of Stockholm. I. R. Mackay became Convenor of the Mod Committee, while John McGregor accompanied Sir Laurence Olivier and his troupe on their Continental tour and also acted as understudy to Sir Laurence in a number of roles. V. P. Birch was now Chief Police Officer of the Northern Province Division of Sierra Leone.

At the beginning of the Spring term all electrical gear and wiring was removed from the Gym, making the showing of films impossible. Towards the end of term the Gym was speedily dismantled and then re-erected beside the old Engine-House.

For the first time in the history of the School there were over 100 boys, of whom four were day boys. There was a record of a different kind when Br Adrian's poultry produced 8000 eggs in February!

The term's weather could be characterised by a biting north-east wind, with snow every so often, never deep but lying for long spells. On one day Fort Augustus, with 26° of frost, was the coldest place in Scotland. Naturally the boys took advantage of the conditions for skating, sledging and even some skiing.

The Hockey XI enjoyed a very successful season. Six out of eight matches were won, the A team won the Kennedy Cup in the District six-a-side, and three boys (A. M. Duncan, I. F. Macdonald and I. M. Daly) were capped for the Scottish Schoolboys against Ireland.

The new Sailing Club, with Commander Farie as Commodore, was confined to the Third Form and above. The Headmaster arranged that adequate time would be made available throughout the year, not only for practical sailing but also for the maintenance and upkeep of the boats, and for the study of seamanship and navigation. The motto adopted by the club was 'Manus tua deducet me', the Vulgate rendering of the 138th Psalm: 'If I take my wings early in the morning and dwell in the uttermost parts of the sea, even there also shall Thy Hand lead me.' The monks of Iona always prayed this verse before putting out to sea.

Re-organisation of the Camera Club coincided with Mr Worden's return. With new subscriptions a 12 x 10 inch adjustable masking frame was purchased. This saved the time that used to be wasted fumbling in the dark with the old type of frame. The darkroom was besieged by members of the Fifth and Sixth Forms after the Scottish Leaving Certificate exams finished. Several experiments were carried out in connection with the use of different formulae, while the use of prismatic field-glasses as a telephoto lens was also investigated.

On Easter Sunday an Old Boys' team organised by Mr Beauchamp (then on holiday from Carlekemp) was beaten 7-3 by the School. In the evening the Fourth Form skiffle group played in the refectory. The following day (7 April) the School departed.

The Old Boys were saddened to learn of the death at the early age of 35 of Fr Edward Laverty, who was at the School from January 1935 to mid-Summer 1938. From Fort Augustus he went to Blairs and in 1948 was ordained priest in Motherwell, his native town. He served as a curate in various parishes of the diocese. He died after an illness which lasted almost two years.

CHAPTER 12

The Abbey School

1958-60

THE School returned on Friday 2 May. Classes began next day after High Mass. The weather all May was cold, with a biting East wind.

During the Easter holidays the Hockey Schoolboy International and the final of the Men's Inter-District Championship had been played. I. M. Daly, chosen as reserve, played at half-back in the Inter-District final at Arbroath, while M. J. Cipolato played at centre-forward. A. M. Duncan and I. F. Macdonald had already been picked. Duncan and Macdonald were also chosen to play for the Picts against a touring team of the Catalan Federation.

Mr H. MacDonald was now in charge of Cricket. Of the eleven matches played, six were won, three lost, one tied and one drawn. By far the weakest link in the chain was the batting which suffered from a lack of practice in the nets. Apart from A. M. Duncan and H. Sweetman, none of the batsmen did himself justice. By contrast the fielding was excellent, the Fielding Cup being awarded to the whole XI. I. M. Daly had the makings of a first class all-rounder, while L. F. Paterson had a good season of hostile fast bowling.

The Athletics final was held during the week ending Saturday 24 May. Conditions were horrendous. One photograph of the judges showed them huddled together, collars up and hands deep in pockets.

Vaughan won the championship by 121 points to 112. In the individual competition the three champions – M. J. Cipolato, I. F. Macdonald and M. E. Tate – faced little opposition and were clear winners in almost every event.

Fr Vincent had undertaken to help training the boat crews. Both Houses practised hard before the race. Lovat won for the first time in many years.

Soon it was time for the School's annual dramatic production. 'The critics [unofficial] were at their gloomiest as the first performance of "The Mikado" drew very near, with the opera in a dangerously un-finished state,' wrote *The Corbie*'s drama reviewer pessimistically. But through hard work the critics were proved wrong and the first perform-ance, on Prize Day, was a complete success:

The by-play and general funning of J. Airs as Ko-Ko riveted the attention of the audience to him whenever he was on stage .... M. Turnbull gave a most imperious and dominating performance as the Mikado himself, and was especially commendable in his singing role. I. Atkinson turned out to be a very able comedian; he rollicked through his part as a very entertaining Pooh-Bah. N. Gordon sang very well and played a convincing role as the young lover, Nanki-Poo, though he rather startled the first-night audience by appearing with a bald head! .... Of the three little maids, M. Wright as Yum-Yum showed most acting promise.

Five performances were given in the last fortnight of term under producer Fr Thomas, with Fr Edward as stage manager, and Mr Fowles responsible for the acting. Fr Andrew looked after costumes and Fr John created the effective make-up.

On 12 May a Glasgow steamer with a television crew arrived to look for the Monster. The following Thursday, Ascension Day, the School gathered to watch the TV programme. It was technically interesting but negative, the theme being the difficulty of obtaining evidence.

A choir of monks and boys broadcast Vespers of St Ephraem on 18 July on the Home Service. Fr Bernard had arranged a *faux-bourdon* for the *Magnificat*, to be sung by male voices.

Experts, making a survey of Hanoverian fortifications, visited the Abbey and spent four days photographing the remains of the old Fort. They scrutinised the north-west bastion in view of its approaching demolition.

At the height of the crisis in Lebanon, President Chamoun tele-phoned the School and gave a detailed description of events in his country. His purpose was to reassure his grandson, Munier, that he himself was safe and well.

That Summer 32 boys left the School. Prior to the McGowan twins leaving Britain to go to school at Portsmouth, Rhode Island, Mr McGowan made the generous gift of a Chevrolet car.

THE OLD FORT AND THE BASTION WALL.

Fr Ambrose Agius, after staying in the Abbey for over a year, also left in the summer.

On 21 July Mr Worden was given a great ovation when he played a farewell recital to the School and Community in the Gym on the last night of term. He was presented with a silver cigarette case from the School for his 18 years at the Fort. He would be sorely missed not only for his musical talents but for his expertise in photography and in wireless affairs.

On 2 September Br James Sherry died of cancer. Born in Govan in 1889, he was apprenticed early in life as a blacksmith in the Clydebank shipyards. He became a riveter on some of the famous battleships prior to the First World War.

He came to Fort Augustus at the age of 25 and turned his hand to a succession of trades. He was a tailor, then a mechanic and driver of the Abbey car. He acted as sacristan and was in charge of the beehives. He worked as a blacksmith, making gates, fire-escapes and candlesticks in wrought iron. He even became a steeple-jack on request. But he would be remembered chiefly for his work in plumbing and electricity. During these years he constructed the School washing basement containing 70 wash-bowls, nine baths and twelve showers. He set up an electric bell-ringing system connected to the tower clock, and until recently had been in charge of the electricity supply for the Abbey and the Village. He remained throughout his life a man of deep spirituality.

Among other members of the Community, Fr Cyprian Gibson had just undergone a serious operation in May but had made a good recovery. Fr Mark Dilworth had been in Germany to search for documents concerning Scottish Benedictines from the sixteenth to the nineteenth centuries; Br Leo Penman had gone to St Anselm's Priory in Washington; and Fr Edward had been appointed kitchen master.

The Annual Old Boys' Reunion was held on 11-13 July with 40 Old Boys present. On the Sunday the Community went in procession after High Mass to St Andrew's Chapel. There Abbot Oswald solemnly blessed the new memorial, with its polished granite altar, large wooden plaque of St Michael (the work of Br Cuthbert Swarbrick of Pluscarden Priory) and a carved oak board bearing the names of the Old Boys killed in the Second World War.

Abbot Oswald, along with Fr Ambrose Agius, led 36 Fort Augustus pilgrims for eight days in Lourdes. In front of the statue of St Margaret the Rosary was said for the conversion of Scotland. Nearly everyone had a bath in the Lourdes water and all attended a special Holy Hour given by Fr Ambrose and also Midnight Mass celebrated by Abbot Oswald in the upper basilica. Some kept an all-night vigil at the Grotto.

Michaelmas term 1958 saw 25 new boys, seven from Carlekemp. Fr Ambrose Geoghegan (Fr Gregory's uncle) returned to the staff to assist with Senior Latin. Mr Worden's place was taken by Mr Calvert who soon after his arrival formed a choral society.

One of the memorable events of the term was the work on the bastion wall. Demolition had begun early in October with little success and explosives were resorted to on 8 October.

After three days of blasting along the whole length of the bastion, about four feet from the ground, the wall had large breaches in it but refused to fall. As it was too dangerous to drill it for further charges, it was decided to pull it down.

On Thursday 9 October another bastion seemed in danger of crumbling. Pius XII (who had been Pope for almost 20 years), died in Rome. On 28 October Pope John XXIII was elected.

Mr Augustine Pimley died on 21 October. He was born in London in 1892, son of an Irish father and an English mother. While a schoolboy at St Edmund's, Ware he established a school record of 99 yards for throwing the Cricket Ball.

On leaving school in 1912 he settled in Paris. At the beginning of the First World War he returned to England and joined the Worcestershire Regiment, rising to the rank of Captain.

After the War he went to Canada and spent two years as a farmer, but eventually he returned to Britain to resume his French studies at London University. He came to Fort Augustus in 1927 at Abbot McDonald's invitation. There, as an increasingly valued member of staff, he taught French and Latin until his retirement in 1957. He was married twice, his first wife dying within a week of their return from honeymoon. In 1931 he married Miss Margaret Robertson, who survived him.

The record of the 1958 Rugby season was good. Only two matches out of eight were lost. Against Aberdeen Grammar School the team was weakened without the services of M. T. Turnbull (who had recently had a cartilage operation), not only a strong centre three-quarter but also an outstanding goal kicker. I. M. Daly (Vice-Captain) was the best and most convincing player. The most improved player behind the scrum was R. G. Sinclair at full-back. M. J. Cipolato (Captain) was the only forward from the previous year's team, a first-class leader and an outstanding performer.

Three-weekly holidays were one of the most enriching experiences available to boys at the Abbey School. On 27 November, five of the Third Form set out in blazing sunshine via Glen Buck to the Corrie-yarrack Pass. It was the best day of the month. One boy commented:

The tramp to the top nearly finished me. I was covered with sweat, and the uneven path, strewn with boulders, slid and slithered beneath my feet, tugging at muscles I wished I did not possess. As quickly as night falls in the tropics, the mist came down, shrouding us in a clammy, cold blanket. We did not think of turning back because of this, but decided to rely on our maps and compasses .... Suddenly the ground beneath us levelled out, and we knew that we had conquered the pass [2507 feet above sea level and ten miles from Fort Augustus].

Other outlets for creativity were the Workshop whose membership was large and keen. Model planes were made and work done for Fr Aloysius' shop; paper-knives were carved from soft wood and deer horn; Christmas cribs were also constructed. But the lathe could not be used because the current was not properly earthed. Owing to the demolition of the School laboratory, a large supply of plywood was available.

It was decided that membership of the Camera Club should be confined to the Fourth, Fifth and Sixth Forms. The departure of the Club's former president, Mr Worden, had also seen the loss of his enlarger lens, around which the Darkroom for so long revolved.

We are now reduced to what looks like the original meniscus lens. It has a widest aperture of f/11, and can only be described, in the words of one member, as 'a piece of bottle glass'! We are on the lookout for two second-hand lenses, one to cover 35 mm negatives and the other 3 1/2 inches by 2 1/2 inches.

There was one ordination in the Autumn of 1958. Fr Vincent Pirie Watson was ordained by Bishop Walsh of Aberdeen on 9 September. Mgr Valentine Mackenzie, Vicar-General of the diocese and a relative of Fr Vincent, was the assistant priest.

Fr Benedict Seed was studying for a degree in Science at Queen's College, Dundee, while Dom Francis Davidson had gone to Fribourg in Switzerland to study Philosophy.

An Old Boys' dinner was held in the Shap Wells Hotel, Shap, on 15 November. Abbot Oswald presided over a gathering of 34 members from the North of England, the Glasgow and Edinburgh areas.

M. Pirie Watson had recently been granted acting rank of Commander RNVR and appointed first Commanding Officer of the Headquarters Reserve Unit being raised at Rosyth. V. P. Birch was now Chief Police Officer of Freetown, Sierra Leone.

The Autumn term of 1958 saw the final removal of the bastion wall and the laying of the foundations of the new wing. During the Spring term of 1959 the frame for the entire building was erected. An enormous mobile crane put the pre-fabricated concrete beams into place. Then the shed and the garage were removed and the new stone shop began to rise rapidly.

The new term began with snow and ice. After a partial thaw it froze very hard, so that at the end of January and the beginning of February there was skating almost every afternoon. Loch Uanagan and Loch Tarff provided good skating.

On 28 February Br Paul Scott died at Fort Augustus. Born in Chatham in 1889, he first studied farming in Ireland. In 1912 he joined the Marines. He was shell-shocked at Gallipoli in 1918 and invalided out of the Services.

He came to the Abbey in 1919, but continued to suffer the after-effects of shell-shock. He became a lay-brother oblate. For almost 40 years Br Paul was a familiar sight as he chopped sticks or carried buckets or cleaned shoes. He was a deeply spiritual man who spent hours each day in prayer and in work.

Hockey started later that year. The weather and an epidemic of flu reduced the playing season to three weeks. Congratulations went to M. J. Cipolato, I. M. Daly and I. F. Macdonald who played for the Scottish Schoolboys XI against Ireland. Cipolato was centre-forward and Captain.

The Fort Augustus-Gordonstoun team was beaten 3-6 by the Picts, but five of the Picts' goals were scored by Mr Hamish MacDonald. Some consolation, at least. The score-sheet for the season was two games lost, two won and a draw.

At the request of the Bishop of Aberdeen, Pope John XXIII created Commander Farie a Knight of St Gregory, in recognition of his services to religion.

On 18 March Abbot Oswald celebrated the silver jubilee of his priesthood. This was combined with the laying of the foundation-stone of Kemnay granite in the new school wing. The Bishops of Aberdeen and Argyll and Abbot Wulstan were in choir, along with some monks of Pluscarden. During the Pontifical High Mass a choir of boys under the direction of Mr Calvert sang Mozart's '*Ave verum*' and '*Jubilate Deo*'.

With the return of the School on Friday 24 April, a new Preparatory timetable was put into force. In order to give the boys every opportunity of benefiting from the Highland Summer, the afternoon Prep periods on Mondays and Thursdays at 3.15 were transferred to Tuesday and Thursday evenings after supper. This gave more time for Crews, Sailing, Golf and other outdoor pursuits and hobbies.

The synthetic stone exterior walls of the new wing were now all but finished; the bitumen roof was laid and the glass was in the window frames. The new shop at the south end of the Hospice was completed. A cine camera was used to capture progress on the building during the term.

It was decided to continue Hockey into the first few weeks of the Summer term. To stimulate interest a Grand Hockey Tournament was arranged between three XIs drawn from the Senior School. The entry fee was a shilling a head and the prize a tea at the Golf-View Tearooms. The eventual winning team was The Loch Ness Monsters.

Henry Cotton, past holder of the Open Championship, paid a short visit to the Abbey on 24 May and gave a demonstration to the School on the Cricket field. His chip and mashie shots delighted all spectators.

During May the organ was given a complete overhaul and spring-clean. Many pipes were re-voiced and the large blower which had been in St Joseph's aisle was built into the walls of the Chapter House.

On Sunday 12 July, Group Captain Leonard Cheshire VC gave a short informal talk to the School on his work for the relief of those suffering from incurable disease and on his efforts to promote the veneration of the Holy Shroud. He visited the Holy Shroud exhibition outside the church before he left for Inverness, where he was to give a public lecture.

The Cricket team played eleven matches of which six were won, three drawn, one tied and one lost. In all, a successful season. The attack was led by L. F. Paterson, well supported by I. M. Daly and M. A. Coppin. Captain Ian Daly (winner of the Batting Cup) was one of the best all-rounders ever produced by the School. Vice-Captain Lewis Paterson (winner of the Bowling Cup) was a first-class cricketer who bowled with great fire and accuracy, taking 44 wickets in eleven matches. Iain Macdonald (winner of the Fielding Cup) was another all-round sportsman with a very quick eye.

The highlight of the Athletics competition was the House one-mile relay race. The excitement began in the second 440 when Moscardini so reduced Lovat's lead that he gave his colleague, L. F. Paterson, the chance in the final 220 to snatch a win for Vaughan at the tape. Both Houses recorded the same time, but Vaughan were justly given the verdict.

From the outset of the Summer term, many evenings were given over to rehearsals of the School's second production of Shakespeare's 'Hamlet', the first being in December 1928 with H. Boultwood (now Abbot Alban Boultwood) in the leading role. The first performance was given to the Community and the School on 15 June 1959. It was presented two nights later at the Empire Theatre, Inverness, and at the Town Hall, Fort William on 29 June.

It says much for the success of the production that serious thought was given to taking the play to the Edinburgh Festival Fringe.

As producer Mr Fowles preferred the naturalistic approach. He saw Hamlet as a tortured adolescent, maturing as the play goes on. M. Turnbull put this across with superbly intelligent sensitivity and vigour but, inevitably (in his adolescent near-hysteria), sacrificed some of the dignity one expects of a Shakespearean prince. The total effect was only rescued by the dignity J. J. Airs gave to the part of the King. J. M. Brown's impersonation of Polonius was far from negligible; I. R. Atkinson as Laertes improved as the play went on; M. C. Wright's Ophelia was almost beyond praise. J. A. B. Kelly and K. P. Fryer made a good thing of the negative parts of Rosencrantz and Guildenstern; while G. P. Mutrie's mirth-provoking gravedigger was outdone only by M. B. Conlin as Osric. The latter postured and pirouetted with no end of mincing absurdity. R. L. Giulianotti as Marcellus and D. A. Martin as Horatio gave life to their smaller but no less demanding roles.

Costume design of this landmark production was by Fr Vincent, with wardrobe management by Fr Andrew. Fr Vincent and Fr John-Baptist ably dealt with cast make-up; while Fr Edward, assisted by E. M. Marsh, made an efficient and effective job of the lighting and sound-effects. Old Boy and Shakespearean actor, John McGregor, loaned a number of beards, while the armour and most of the metallic props were created out of *papier-maché* by M. Turnbull and his minions.

Prize Day came on Sunday 5 July. Prizes were distributed by Brigadier G. L. Prendergast DSO of Inveroich House. Since Christmas, two new boys had arrived and 17 left the School. In his speech the Headmaster outlined what parents could reasonably expect from a fee-paying school. They were entitled to expect not only academic achievement, but the full preparation of a boy to enter society. But this could not be achieved unless parents and masters, home and school, worked together for a common purpose.

In December the Lord Lyon King of Arms granted new Heraldic Arms to the Abbey. These incorporated the double-headed eagle of the Abbey of St James at Ratisbon, the lamb of the Abbey of Saints Adrian and Denys at Lamspring and the triple-towered castle of Fort Augustus with the motto '*Pax in virtute*'.

Appropriately, Fr Mark Dilworth had recently published in *The Innes Review* a critical edition of the necrologies of the post-Reformation Scottish Benedictine Congregation, together with biographical notes on each monk.

On 22 June Fr Benedict Weld-Blundell, who had died in 1931 and was buried in Selby Park, was re-interred at Fort Augustus.

The Annual Old Boys' Reunion took place on 11-12 July. Mass was celebrated in St Andrew's Chapel on the Saturday morning for deceased

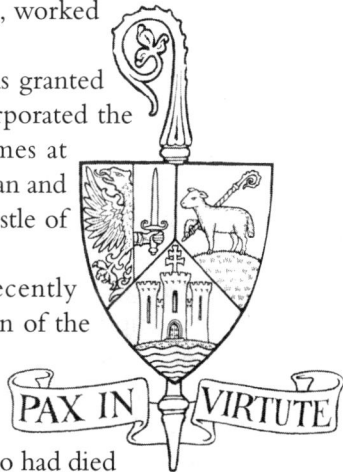

Old Boys. The Cricket match was played that afternoon in very bad weather and, when it had to be abandoned, a draw was declared. By supper-time the field was a quagmire!

On Sunday, after High Mass and lunch in the cloisters, Fr Celestine was elected Secretary and Commander Farie appointed as Treasurer.

Positive news continued about the careers of Old Boys. D. A. P. Barry was one of three Catholic representatives on a council set up by the Secretary of State for Scotland to advise on the treatment of criminal offenders. Lt.-Com. W. D. MacDonald had been flying jet planes in the Royal Navy until a year ago. Attached to RNAS Lossiemouth, he was the CO of Nos 736 and 806 Squadrons. Now, with his family of seven, he returned to Fort Augustus, where he had a successful first season in the Inchnacardoch Hotel. Meanwhile, actor John McGregor, who had worked with Scottish Television until June, had joined Granada where he made several appearances in the programme 'The Verdict is Yours'.

When the boys returned for the Autumn term of 1959 they found that the Headmaster, Old Boy Fr Thomas McLaughlin, had been replaced by another Old Boy, Fr Mark Dilworth. As Fr Ethelbert McCombes, Headmaster at Carlekemp, was still seriously ill, Fr Thomas was sent to replace him as Prior and Headmaster. Fr Philip joined the Abbey staff to teach Art in the Lower School and Fr Augustine to assist in Upper School French and Latin, taking a class of three for 'A' Levels.

In the new wing the plasterwork had already been started, much of the plumbing was well under way, and electrical conduit piping was being embedded in the walls and floors. Carpenters were busy fitting doors, cupboards and partitions. Towards the end of October, the exterior wall being finished, the scaffolding which had shrouded the building was removed.

The new 'dialogue' form was introduced into the School Mass from the beginning of term. Throughout October the School did not attend Sunday Vespers, being present only at Benediction. The tubular steel chairs and upright wooden chairs were all replaced with ones made of solid oak and leather. But there was one drawback, noted *The Corbie*, for 'the preacher can no longer judge the interest of his listeners by the rise and fall of that peculiar sound, canvas upholstery on tubular steel'.

The Corbie now had a new Editor – Fr Vincent – who, as usual, set about his new responsibilities with determination and vigour. He was to hold the post for seven years.

The 1959-60 Rugby season did not come up to expectations. They seemed to lack the determination to win. Of eight matches, four were won and four lost. There were some extenuating circumstances. During a home match against Gordonstoun on 17 October (which the School won 14-10), the Captain, R. G. I. Sinclair, playing at full-back, received a serious head injury while making a head-on tackle early in the second half. This resulted in his being kept out of the game for the rest of the season.

On 3 September, Br Dominic Fasseau died and was buried beside his father in the Monastery graveyard. He was born in London in 1887 but completed his schooling at St Cuthbert's, Slateford. At the age of 15 he came to Fort Augustus to be a lay-brother.

As his father was a chef at a hotel in Aberdeen, Br Dominic was put into the monastic kitchen. He was later joined by his father who worked in the Abbey kitchen until his death in 1917.

For many years Br Dominic was in charge of the kitchen and also spent considerable periods as sacristan. He was often *thurifer* at major choir functions. He kept a diary, noting the precise details of all the major functions at the Abbey since the turn of the century. Towards the end of his life he developed weakness of the heart and a form of dropsy.

For the Abbey and School, however, the most momentous event of the year took place three weeks after all the boys had gone home for the Christmas holidays.

On Wednesday 30 December 1959 (after many rounds of balloting in which a clear two-thirds majority did not emerge until the final simple majority vote), Fr Celestine Haworth was elected the sixth Abbot of Fort Augustus in place of Abbot Oswald Evans.

An Old Boy of the School, Abbot Celestine was professed in 1930. He made his theological studies at Fort Augustus and was ordained in 1936 by another Old Boy, Bishop George Bennett of Aberdeen.

In 1937, having already taught Mathematics at Fort Augustus, he was sent to the Priory School, Edinburgh where he taught and at the same time attended classes at the Heriot-Watt College. A year later he returned to Fort Augustus to take up work in the School.

When the House system was introduced in 1941, Fr Celestine became the first Housemaster of Vaughan. During the war years Fr Celestine taught Maths and also Science to Scottish Leaving Certificate level. He was a member of the monastic Council from 1951 onwards and a delegate to the General Chapter in 1953 and 1957.

The news that Abbot Oswald was no longer at the head of the Community at Fort Augustus surprised many in the English Benedictine

Congregation. In retrospect, the fact that Abbot Oswald Eaves was not given a second eight-year term seems to have been a turning-point in the history, not only of the School, but of the monastic Community which, by its decision not to elect him, opted for a more conservative style of management.

Abbot Oswald appreciated the influence of the aristocracy and others in positions of wealth or power. He persuaded them to help the Abbey and the Schools – much as Prior Jerome Vaughan had done eighty years before. He had also developed powers of leadership which were reminiscent of Abbot (later Archbishop) Andrew Joseph McDonald and would later find their full expression in his apostolate in Sweden.

His founding of the Air Scouts brought him into contact with members of the RAF such as the Duke of Hamilton, whose sons would later attend Carlekemp. While still Headmaster at Carlekemp, Fr Oswald had persuaded the golfer Henry Cotton to visit the School and demonstrate his skills to the astonished boys. Over subsequent years Henry Cotton presented a golf trophy and donated funds for the purchase of the wooden pews for the Chapel at Carlekemp.

Between 1953 and 1957 Abbot Oswald was instrumental in bringing to fruition at least seven radio or television broadcasts featuring Fort Augustus.[1] These and other initiatives led to the unprecedented rise in student numbers until the roll reached over 100 in 1958 for the first time in the history of the School.

CHAPTER 13

The Abbey School

1960-62

BY the time the School returned on 15 January 1960 the new Calder wing was in use, each study-bedroom being occupied by Seniors and one of the two dormitories by Vaughan Juniors.

Because of Abbot Celestine's election, changes in staffing became necessary. He himself combined his own duties with those of temporary Housemaster of Vaughan; Mr Palmer took over Fourth Form Maths; Abbot Celestine continued with his SLC candidates until the end of March. Mr MacDonald took over Third Form Maths and Second Form Science, while Fr Vincent relieved him of Lower School Geography. Replacing Fr John (who had moved to Carlekemp) as Latin teacher in the Middle and Lower School were Fr Anselm and Fr Aidan. In the absence of Mrs Bainbridge, Mrs Clark acted as Matron.

On 28 January Fr Cyprian Gibson died, after suffering from cancer for ten years. A man of enormous energy and a brilliant scholar, he had been born a member of the Church of Scotland in Glasgow. He had first worked as a clerk in the insurance and foreign exchange business. After serving three years in France as a signaller during the First World War, he joined the Anglican community at Nashdom but was eventually received into the Catholic faith by Abbot Wulstan Knowles at Fort Augustus in 1931.

Fr Cyprian studied Philosophy in Rome before being ordained at Fort Augustus in 1939, where he became Professor of Philosophy. He always had an abiding love of languages. During his service as a soldier in France, he used to tap the enemy telephones and listen to German conversations. In the trenches he taught himself Sanskrit!

THE DORMITORY

Over the years, his deep interest in liturgy and Scripture led him to learn Slavonic, Arabic and other Oriental languages.

Within the monastic Community, Fr Cuthbert Wilson was appointed Prior, Fr Maurus Whitehead became Bursar, and Fr Aidan Duggan was made Infirmarian. Fr Denys Rutledge, who had spent three years as a missionary in an Indian *ashram* ('spiritual centre'), a small community of Benedictines near Poona, was now back at Fort Augustus.[1]

From January the kitchen had been taken over by a firm of professional caterers who made a very good impression by providing cooked breakfasts on Sundays.

During February alterations were carried out to the Abbey Church. The High Altar was moved back to the east end, set half-way into the former sanctuary. The roof was barrelled over and the opening out into the Choir was arched. Both the choir-stalls and the throne were put back into their former positions. Fr Bernard designed and made the baldachino (canopy) and the throne.

The blessing of Abbot Celestine took place on Thursday 25 February. A southerly overnight gale caused a fast thaw of the snow which had fallen during the previous week and the morning dawned bright and dry. It was the commemoration of the Abbot, St Cumein, from whom the village of Kilcumein took its name centuries before the arrival of General Wade.

After Mass, Fr Abbot joined the guests at lunch in the monks' refectory. Afterwards, coffee and champagne were served in the Assembly Hall.

The Spring term of 1960 was also memorable for one especially tragic event – the accidental death of twelve year old Peter Tucker during the three-weekly holiday on Monday 29 February.

As part of the First Form outing to Glen Doe boathouse, led by Mr Calvert, Peter was following behind some companions up the path beside the burn. Evidently he slipped down the steep and rocky bank and was killed instantly, his body swept by the swollen torrent into the Loch where it was discovered almost immediately by a local fisherman who happened to be passing in his boat. Mr Calvert helped to bring the body ashore.

Peter's funeral took place on Thursday 3 March, after the Conventual Mass of Requiem, sung by the Headmaster and attended by the Community and School. The interment, accompanied by pall-bearers from the School, followed in the monastic cemetery where he was buried near the other young schoolboy Michael Caraher who had died on 15

February 1882. Some years later, Peter Tucker's father died and his ashes were scattered beside those of his son.

Peter Tucker had taken a lively interest in the activities of the Junior Debating Society, to which he contributed with wit and humour. Only a week before his tragic death, he had defended the motion 'That fried eggs contain more nutritional value than scrambled ones'.

That term there were changes in two of the most popular pastimes for the boys. Fr Edward took over showing of films as Fr Abbot's new duties took up an increasing proportion of his time. One of the cinematographs developed a fault in the sound and for the rest of the term all films were shown on one projector. The films ceased to be shown to the public when the new Assembly Hall began to be used for the weekly show.

Fr Vincent took over temporary supervision of the Workshop in place of Fr John-Baptist. Little work was undertaken in the first half of the term as the heavy snowfalls, though good for sledging, also meant that the workshop was freezing cold. Fr Vincent also took over the Sailing Club from Fr John and, in his characteristically energetic style, quickly enlisted the help of members to springclean the Club hut, build a small extension to the School pier, and fit out the boats.

The Hockey season was even worse than that of 1959. After a brief start at the beginning of term, the weather closed down on all games except Winter sports. At the very end of February, games resumed. Five matches were played (two won, two drawn and one lost). After playing with N. C. Taylor in the Schoolboys' Final Trial in Edinburgh, the Captain, I. F. Macdonald was again capped.

Old Boys' affairs revolved mainly around the very successful annual Fort Augustus-Kilgraston Shrovetide Ball held in the Central Hotel, Glasgow on Monday 29 February. In the Glasgow and South West Scotland Area Committee, a remarkable family double saw J. W. Dunn as President and C. R. Dunn as Secretary.

When the boys returned for the Spring term, they found that all the classrooms had been transferred to the new wing; the new Laboratory came into use and the space under the stage had been converted into a changing room, drying room and storage apartment.

The new Matron was Miss M. Burns, while Mr D. E. Roberts, who replaced Mr Calvert, took over piano tuition, Lower School music and the Polyphonic Choir. This was to be the last term at Fort Augustus for Commander R. Fegen, who had taught senior Mathematics for the past few years, and Miss Thomson, School Secretary for two years.

On 24 May, after a long illness spent in various hospitals in Glasgow, Fr Ethelbert McCombes died from a tumour on the brain. He was born in Glasgow in 1909 and came to the Abbey School aged 14. He entered the Novitiate four years later and on completion he was sent to Saint Andrew's Priory, Canaan Lane to study English at Edinburgh University where he graduated three years later.

In 1938 he was appointed Assistant Headmaster of the Abbey School under the Headmaster, Commander Farie. Fr Ethelbert took over as Headmaster in 1939, continuing in the post for 13 years. From 1941-45 he also took charge of the Preparatory School, which had been evacuated to Fort Augustus.

He succeeded Abbot Oswald Eaves as Prior and Headmaster of Carlekemp in January 1952. However, his health slowly deteriorated and finally broke down in 1959.

Fr Ethelbert's greatest innovation was the introduction of the House system (with monks as Housemasters), the administration of the School by members of the monastic Community, and the increasing importance given to Science.

While Fr Ethelbert had found a happy release from painful illness, a horizon of a different kind was opening up for the previous Abbot, Oswald Eaves, who sought new opportunities into which to channel his great enthusiasm and considerable gifts of communication and leadership.

In May 1960, Abbot Oswald set off for Stockholm in Sweden. He had been invited there at the urgent request of Ansgar Nelson OSB, Bishop of Stockholm and, thirty years before, a fellow-novice at Fort Augustus. The Bishop was in desperate need of priests. Within a week of his arrival in Stockholm he was sent to the city of Karlstad where the priest, Fr Söderberg, was ill, to supply for him until he recovered. Unhappily, Fr Söderberg died within four days. This was the beginning of Abbot Oswald's missionary activities in Sweden, which were to continue until 1974.

Among Old Boys who were members of diocesan clergy, a special opportunity came the way of Fr John Barry. Having worked as a Professor at St Andrew's Seminary, Drygrange from 1953-60, Fr Barry was appointed Rector of the Seminary by Archbishop Gordon Gray. As Rector, until his retirement from the post in 1977, he would exercise a positive influence on the formation of several generations of parish clergy.

When the boys returned on 21 September (including 24 new boys), they found a number of changes. During the Summer holidays, Fr Vincent Pirie Watson had been appointed to succeed Abbot Celestine as Housemaster of Vaughan. Fr Fabian Duggan had come to teach Latin to the Lower School, while Mr J. Duffy had taken over Middle School Science.

On St Michael's Day, Thursday 29 September, a holiday marked the formal opening of the Calder Wing in the presence of Sir James Calder, through whose generosity alone the construction had been possible.

At the beginning of September a nine foot bronze three-figure group of St Benedict and two Scottish boys (weighing almost half a ton) was put into place above the main entrance to the new Wing. The sculpture was the work of Mr Arthur J. Fleischmann, who also designed the Urquhart Memorial Altar in the Church, a Calvary group in bronze acting as a twelfth Station and as a shrine for the relic of the True Cross.

Abbot Oswald had first commissioned the sculptor Sir Jacob Epstein, but the latter's death ended the project. In 1958, however, Abbot Oswald had seen Mr Fleischmann's figure of the 'Risen Christ' on the front of the Vatican pavilion in the Brussels Exhibition and invited him to make the statue of St Benedict for the Calder Wing.

On 11 September, Br Stephen Cusick passed peacefully away. Born in Hamilton in 1887, he worked first as a clerk with various firms, including Singers in Clydebank and John Brown's shipyard. During the First World War he served in the Royal Scots and later in the Labour Corps. After the war he settled in Dalmuir, where he was organist at the parish church of St Stephen. In those days of silent films he used to play the piano during shows, improvising to suit the action.

He was attracted to Fort Augustus while attending men's retreats held during Glasgow Fair Week. He entered the monastery in 1931 and was clothed in 1933. He worked, first in the kitchen, then later as a sacristan and house Brother.

On 22 November 1960, Fr Andrew MacDonell died at the Bon Secours Hospital, Glasgow, at the age of 90. Born in Invermoriston, he spent his boyhood at Kintail, before being accepted as an *alumnus* by Prior Jerome Vaughan. He was sent to St Joseph's, Dumfries before entering the School at Fort Augustus in 1887. He was ordained in August 1896.

The first five years of his priesthood were spent in pastoral work in Fort Augustus parish. During this period he formed a pipe band, stimulated Shinty teams to compete for an annual cup, organised the Glen

Mor Gathering, and founded St Joseph's Hospital for orphans. His greatest achievement was to find and support a nursing post for the district. Two years later he set off to Vancouver Island, Canada with five girls from the Hospital and 18 others from England, hoping to find homes or positions for them.

In 1915 Fr Andrew enlisted as a chaplain and was sent to France, where he served with the Canadian Seaforths. During the battle of Vimy Ridge he worked with a field ambulance. While a chaplain he founded the Holy Name Society, to suppress the use of bad language by the troops and the taking of God's name in vain. Almost all the most senior Canadian officers of all denominations and thousands of the men signed the Society pledge. For his services as a chaplain he was awarded the Military Cross.

After the war he returned to Canada where, for almost 20 years, he helped to take settlers from Britain to various parts of Canada. He was managing director of the Scottish Immigrant Aid Society

His most lasting success was the Clandonald Settlement in Alberta. Perhaps the most publicised episode was the emigration of 300 Catholics from the Hebrides in 1924, over which there is still controversy. For his work in Canada he was awarded the MBE in 1937. He returned to Fort Augustus in 1956 before the decline in his health and memory made his transfer to St Raphael's, Edinburgh and the Bon Secours Hospital, Glasgow necessary.

During the term Fr Francis Davidson made his solemn profession, leaving shortly afterwards for the final year of his philosophical studies at Fribourg University. Australian Fr Chrysostom Alexander was ordained on 18 October by Archbishop Gordon Gray.

The 1961 Rugby team had a season of unfulfilled promise, winning three, losing three and drawing one game.

Both the Senior Literary and Debating Society (holding its 400th meeting) and the Junior Debating Society (holding its 376th meeting) continued to flourish: the first with five debates and a quiz that term, the second, with seven debates and a quiz. In the former, on 31 October, Mr Mike H. H. Drummond contested the motion that 'This House considers Rock 'n' Roll to be detrimental to the present teenage generation'. He claimed that the majority of Rock 'n' Roll singers sold their royalties and gave the proceeds to charitable concerns. He explained how Rock 'n' Roll had prompted the founding of many youth clubs, which kept teenagers off street-corners and out of trouble. He then played some

Rock 'n' Roll music from a tape-recorder. On being put to the vote, the motion was defeated by 15 votes to 10.

After the Christmas holidays, when the School returned on 16 January, they found a new Matron, Mrs D. Coppin. Later that term, an equivalent change took place in the monastery where Fr Fabian Duggan was appointed infirmarian.

On 7 March came the tragic news of the death of Old Boy Iain Macdonald in a road accident near Strathaven at the age of 18. He had left Fort Augustus only the previous Summer and was already one of Scottish Hockey's most promising youngsters:

> *He played a leading part in the match against Irish schoolboys in Glasgow last year, when the visitors were held to a draw, and early this season he received his first senior representative honour when he was selected to play left back for Home Scots against Ulster at Paisley. He has also played in preliminary trials for the full International side and last Saturday was in the Under-23 XI who did so well against the SHA XI in Edinburgh .... He had a likeable personality. His enthusiasm for the game, for his club, district and country, will be sadly missed.*[2]

For the School Hockey side it was a season much like 1959. The bad weather, sickness and cancellation meant that only half the fixture list was played. Two games were won, two lost and one drawn. However, individually the team members performed well with B. J. Mathieson, M. A. Coppin, A. J. Burns, R. N. Godfrey and J. G. van Bavel going forward to Edinburgh for the Final Scottish Schoolboys International Trials. Both Godfrey and van Bavel were selected, van Bavel also captaining the side.

When the School broke up on 3 April, Mr P. Daniel, who had been a member of staff for four years, also left to take up a new post. Head of the English Department, Chairman of the Senior Debating Society and founder of the Listeners and the Hill-Walking Club, Mr Daniel had made a memorable contribution to the cultural life of the School. His final expedition with the Hill-Walking Club was on 26 and 27 March, when a party of five boys walked along the north-west shore of Loch Lochy from Laggan to directly below Meall Dubh. The following day the party climbed Sròn a' Choire Ghairbh.

Among the Old Boys there was pride in learning that for the third year running, the Richard Smith Memorial Prize at St Andrews

University had been won by an Old Boy – Fr Benedict Seed. The two previous winners were D. W. G. Ardagh and D. Grisewood. Fr Benedict also captained the Queen's College Hockey XI, Dundee.

A presentation dinner to Abbot Celestine was held in the Eglinton Hotel, Eaglesham (Glasgow) on Tuesday 8 November and was attended by 30 Old Boys. A leather suitcase was presented to Abbot Celestine by the President of the Glasgow area, J. W. Dunn. The annual Shrovetide Ball, meanwhile, was held in the Central Hotel, Glasgow on Monday 13 February.

The Summer term of 1961 was largely uneventful. The Cricket season proved to 'one of bitter disappointment'. This was largely because the School XI contained so many experienced players and had the potential to win all its matches. The actual outcome of seven matches played, two won, one drawn and four lost was the sad reality which faced the Captain, John van Bavel and Vice-Captain, Neil Godfrey. In Athletics, Lovat took the House competition after a close-run fight with Vaughan, winning by 148 points to 142.

The highlight of the term was the Dramatic Society's 'The Pirates of Penzance', produced by Mr Fowles, with the music directed by Mr Roberts. Playing the Pirate King was H. S. Fothringham, who was 'clad in an imposing costume and produced an even more imposing voice from somewhere down in his boots'. As Major-General Stanley, R. N. Godfrey sang his lovely lyric to the rustling breeze in a nightshirt and still managed to put the song across. However, it was the singing of A. D. Wright as Mabel that lingered in the memory. Three performances in all were staged: one at Fort Augustus for parents and guests (Sunday 16 July); one to the public at Fort William; and a final one at Fort Augustus for the general public on Tuesday 18 July.

Following Mr Daniel's departure at Easter, Mr Fowles took over the management of the Library. As the number of books signed out exceeded all previous records, the Library was closed for two weeks for indexing, re-shelving and re-arranging the sections. One important acquisition was a new section on Highland History, including copies of books bequeathed to the Abbey by the late Mr Cameron-Head of Inverailort. These books, along with the School's 1896 edition of the *Encyclopaedia Britannica,* were housed in a large wooden bookcase with glass doors.

In the nautical sphere, the Sailing Club was prevented from leaving harbour by the strong winds which prevailed for much of the term. The former lifeboat was still being refitted by Fr Vincent who had burnt the paint off the bottom before beginning the arduous task (with the help of the sailors) of fitting on an extra eight inches of keel.

Since the lifeboat was not going to be ready in time for a week's outing on the Loch, it was decided that the Sailing Club's annual cruise should take place in one of the Graduate dinghies. Accordingly, over a period of five days in late July, 60 miles were logged, the dinghies and the crewboat sailing the length of the Loch and back in very varied weather conditions. Tents were carried and the crews, led by Fr Vincent, slept on shore at night.

Prize Day was on 16 July, the last Sunday of term (the final week for some 19 members of the School). The author Moray McLaren distributed the prizes, revealing that it was a pleasure to visit Fort Augustus under any pretext and at any time. Afternoon tea was served and all were invited to attend the evening performance of 'The Pirates of Penzance'.

During the Summer Fort Augustus became a place of pilgrimage to a number of religious groups. Early in July a Rally of the League of St Andrew was held for the first time, many parishes in Scotland being represented. In August the Aberdeen Diocesan Retreat was also held, the main preacher being Fr Anthony Ross OP.

Also in July, Old Boy Fr Alban Boultwood, Prior of St Anselm's, Washington DC, visited the Abbey, along with Fr Richard Flower of St Gregory's, Portsmouth, Rhode Island. There was news of the activities of Abbot Oswald Eaves, who was now acting as Vicar General of the diocese of Stockholm and administrator of the Cathedral.

A dramatic change in the design of *The Corbie's* cover took place in February 1962. The orange-pink and black quarters were done away with and the cover printed a darker red. The layout of the title was altered, the black corbie's head being reduced to a quarter of its original size.

Those with long memories might be forgiven for thinking that the changes in *The Corbie* reflected a change in direction within the School and the Monastery. It seemed to mirror Abbot McDonald's dropping of the old School colour of chocolate in favour of red, reflecting not only technological constraints but showing a new way of thinking within the monastic organisation, which saw decreasing value in public relations exercises represented by such vehicles as *The Corbie*.

There were changes too in the School building. The growth in the size of the School meant that it had become difficult to fit all the boys into the refectory at one sitting. Accordingly, the back wall had been removed during the holidays and the room lengthened. A swing door was now placed in the archway at the west end and the passage-way to the kitchen converted into a pantry.

Forty-four new boys assembled at Fort Augustus for the Michaelmas term. New to the staff were Frs Benedict Seed and Chrysostom Alexander. Fr Benedict, who had just returned from St Andrews University, had begun taking Middle school Maths and Science. Fr Chrysostom was helping out with History and RE. After 20 years teaching in the Latin department, Fr Aloysius Carruth had moved on to other duties. Mr A. K. Anderson had joined the senior Language departments and was shortly to take over senior English. Mr A. S. Fotheringham had arrived to teach in the Middle and Lower School and on the games field.

On 4 October, a fortnight after the School returned, a potentially major fire disaster in the early hours of the morning was providentially avoided. One of the new boys had deliberately started the fire. Had it spread, lives would almost certainly have been lost.

Within a short time of its discovery in the basements, the School buildings were evacuated and the fire brought quickly under control by the Abbey fire unit. When the Fort William and Inverness engines arrived, the fire was out, but they nevertheless carefully doused the embers to make sure it would not break out afresh. Meanwhile, the boys were in the Gym singing excerpts from 'The Pirates of Penzance' and listening to some strumming from the guitar group. Later on they had tea and biscuits before returning to bed for a few hours' extra sleep.

Damage was confined to the passage-way in which the boys' trunks were stored (most of them being either burnt or made unfit for further use by water damage) and to the floor between the Study Hall and Refectory. Had the fire progressed any further the Brothers' quarters would have been cut off and there would almost certainly have been considerable loss of life.

The Rugby season was marred by misfortune. There were many injuries: the XV were at full strength only once and in the final match five regular players were sent off! Out of six played, no matches were won and only one drawn.

Some new clubs and societies were formed. The Stamp Club met regularly under Fr Chrysostom's guidance. In the Senior School Fr Benedict and Mr Anderson organised and ran the Bridge Club which met on Wednesdays after supper.

The School and Community were saddened to hear of the sudden death of Captain Charles MacDermot-Roe on 12 December. Tall, courteous and distinguished, he had worked as advertising manager for *The Corbie* for a number of years and carried out various other administrative activities on behalf of the School.

A 'Festival of Music and Drama' was held on 17 December. During the evening four plays were presented, 'two of which were quite good, another seemingly interminable and the fourth consisting of the same word of affirmation (aye!) repeated at measured intervals'. There were also songs, recitations and musical items. The guitar group proved as popular as ever and the School was treated to the first-ever rendition of a new melody written for the guitar by G. I. McGlynn, the Captain of Rugby.

The Sailing Club found that their attempts to work on the 'Narwhal' (the lifeboat acquired the previous Winter) were constantly interrupted by the wet and cold weather. Fr Vincent, meanwhile, made several accessories for the boat in the carpentry shop: a new stem-head, shroud spreaders, dead-eyes and many other small items.

Owing to extra-curricular duties, Mr Fowles resigned as President of the Photographic Society. Mr Duffy succeeded him. The Dark Room continued to be in the West Wing. The Workshop moved from above the engine house and re-opened on the disused stage of the Gym where lighting had been fitted and heating was expected shortly.

A new Apollo Society was formed, presided over by Mr Anderson. Its aim was to develop an appreciation of the Arts. The first meeting was taken up by the first act of Gordon Daviot's 'Richard of Bordeaux', supervised by Mr Fowles in conjunction with Fr Vincent, Fr Chrysostom and Mr Anderson. The Society had applied for membership of the British Drama League.

Old Boys' activities centred round a very successful dinner at Shap Wells Hotel. Over 30 Old Boys from the North of England and Scotland were present and Abbot Celestine was guest of honour. The School and the Community were delighted to hear of the election of Old Boy Fr Alban Boultwood (1924-29) as the first Abbot of St Anselm's Priory, Washington.

Over the Christmas holidays the final repairs to the fire damage were completed. Work was also in progress preparing the sites for fire escapes.

Shortly after term began on 16 January there was a severe outbreak of flu. Boys and staff were struck down. At one time there were 52 patients. In some cases the epidemic was followed by mumps or chicken-pox.

The Corbie of May 1962 devoted the briefest-ever space to sport. The Hockey season, covered in half a page, was summed up in one sentence: 'It was a bad term and for all practical purposes the season was confined to ten days in the second half of March.' Nevertheless, three matches were won, only two lost and one drawn. The Captain, H. G. Young, and P. C. Bayliss were, in spite of all these difficulties, selected for the Scottish Schoolboys Hockey XI which played at Belfast on 14 April. Several Old Boys also gained Hockey honours, R. J. Chisholm (1948-53) playing for Scotland against Wales in the International Hockey match at Dalmuir, Glasgow (also on 14 April), and A. M. Duncan (1950-58) and I. M. Daly (1954-59) having taken part in the final Scottish Hockey Trial on 17 March.

A renewed interest in music came over the School. In the Lower School Mr Anderson had three recorder groups. Recorders were also popular among many in the Upper School and the revival of the School Orchestra now seemed less of a dream than it had once been. Chorally, the School was flourishing, with motets being sung by the Choral Society. In addition, the sonorous notes of the national instrument could often be heard reverberating around the buildings, since Fr Chrysostom started a group of fervent bagpipe and chanter blowers. This also raised the future possibility of a School pipe band.

The Summer term began with three weeks of dry, cold weather, so much so that there were few trees in bud before June. Then, beginning with a cloudburst, gale-force winds and heavy rain, a period of very wet weather followed.

The last Hockey matches of the year were played: Vaughan won the inter-House match 2-1 on 5 May, and the 1st XI beat Highland Hockey XI by the respectable score of 4-1 the following day.

The Cricket XI had a very successful season under Captain H. G. Young. All seven matches were won; none was lost and none drawn. The School also beat the Old Boys by 3 wickets. The bowling, spear-headed by M. C. Coppin, H. D. Shannon and R. C. Drummond, was never really mastered by any batsman. Although not always technically correct in every stroke, the School batsmen played with a determination and courage which had its effect.

In Athletics G. I. McGlynn was the outstanding performer, winning the 100 yards, 220 yards, 440 yards, and the Long Jump. He went forward to the Scottish Schools Championship in Glasgow to compete in the Long Jump. Although consistently hitting the 20 feet mark in the heats, his comparatively poor jump in the Finals was caused by the strong north-east wind which was blowing straight down the pit.

In mid-July the Dramatic Society's production of Shakespeare's 'Richard II' in the Assembly Hall and at Fort William was one of the highlights of the term. Produced by Mr Fowles, the play had excellent verse-speaking from N. A. R. Wright as King Richard and H. D. Shannon as a sturdy Bolingbroke. As Norfolk, V. Di Rollo gave an impassioned performance; while P. F. McFadyen, as a wizened, toothless old gardener, succeeded in establishing the mood of the play with his comic turn in the opening scene. M. C. Coppin, playing Gaunt, conveyed great pathos in his patriotic death-bed declamation.

The Golf Club and the Hill-Walking Clubs continued to flourish. In the former, H. G. Young, the holder of the Cruickshank Trophy, was beaten by his younger brother, R. A. Young. In the Hill-Walking Club, Mr Fotheringham led several trips, culminating in a two-day end of term expedition to climb Beinn a' Chaoruinn (3437 feet) and Creag Meaghaidh (3700 feet). In one term's climbing the Club had bagged two Munros and two tops over 3000 feet.

Prize Day was on Sunday 15 July. The prizes were presented by Bishop Stephen McGill of Argyll and the Isles. The winner of the Captain's Medal and the Macdonald Cup (*Victor Ludorum*) was G. I. McGlynn, one of the 16 boys whose final year at School it was.

A number of Old Boys were making a name for themselves in the Arts. J. I. Molleson (1954-58) was working with BBC Television in London; J. F. C. Noblet (1947-50) was now musical director at the Blessed Edmund Campion School in Preston; J. J. Airs (1954-59) had just given a noteworthy interpretation of the leading role of Berenger in Ionesco's 'The Killer' at an Edinburgh University Dramatic Society production on the Edinburgh Festival Fringe.

Old Boys were also to the fore in the Hotel and Catering industry. P. Moscardini (1955-59) was an assistant chef at Buckingham Palace, Balmoral and Holyrood; F. D. Cipolato (1949-53) was manager of the Governor's Harbour Hotel, 'Eleutheria', in the Bahamas; A. J. Macdonald (1922-25) had just opened the Macdonald Hotel at Eastwood Toll, Glasgow.

Sadly, news came of the death of two eminent Old Boys. John J. Calder JP, eldest son of James Calder of Ardagie, Perthshire died on 12 July in his ninetieth year. He was sent to the newly-opened College in 1881 and remained there for the next four years. On leaving school he entered his father's business and, on his death, succeeded to the estate. From managing his own business, he rose to be managing director of Ind Coope and Allsopps Ltd. He was a prominent member of Alloa Burgh Council for 14 years and held the office of Provost for three years. He was a Justice of the Peace for both Clackmannan and Perthshire and a member of the Catholic Education Council for nearly a quarter of a century.

His brother, Sir James Calder, died on 23 August. Born in 1869, he attended the College with his older brother until they both left in the Summer of 1885.

James also entered his father's business and was successful in everything he undertook. He founded the firm of Calders Ltd, one of the major timber importing firms in Britain; he was director of The Distillers Company and chairman of Macdonald Greenlees and Williams Ltd, the whisky distillers and wine merchants. His knowledge of timber led to his being appointed an adviser on Scottish Home Timber Production to the Raw Materials branch of the Ministry of Supply in the early years of the First World War, for, along with the late Lord Lovat, he had been one of the pioneers in the experimental growing of timber in the Highlands. It is therefore greatly owing to his efforts at that time that the afforestation of the Highlands became fundamental to the Scottish economy. In 1917 he was appointed Deputy Controller of the Timber Supply Department of the Board of Trade, until taking over as Controller in 1919. His services to the nation were rewarded by a CBE in 1920 and a knighthood the following year.

When Sir James came to Fort Augustus in 1954 to distribute the prizes, he learnt that an extension to the School was being contemplated. He readily offered financial help. Accordingly, through his generosity the work was completed and he was present on 29 September 1960 when the new Calder Wing was officially blessed and opened.

CHAPTER 14

The Abbey School
1962-65

WHEN the School returned on 20 September they found a number of minor structural changes had taken place in the building. The passageways on either side of the Assembly Hall had been partitioned to make a room large enough for the Upper School to study in. The former Second Form classroom had been fitted out as a Physics laboratory. The stage had been cleared to provide an Art Room, and Lovat House Assembly Room had been converted into a lower School classroom. The Masters' Common Room had moved to the Hospice, Fr Laurence's study was also enlarged, the wall dividing it from the Prefects' Room being knocked down and one of the doorways closed up.

Replacing Fr Philip Hynes in the Art Department was Mr W. Owen. Mr R. W. MacEachen took over as Head of the French Department from the Headmaster. Fr Edmund Carruth had left the staff to take up new duties as Superior at Carlekemp. At the end of term Mr A. S. Fotheringham would leave for another teaching post.

Coverage of Rugby in *The Corbie* of February 1963 was unusually brief – a mere two pages. The XV had a disappointing season, losing six matches, winning only one and drawing one. The biggest defeat was against Glenalmond 2nd XV (away), when the School lost 32-0.

School societies were, however, flourishing. The Senior Literary and Debating Society had its 414th meeting, while the Junior held its 399th. The new Choral Society, practising on Monday and Thursday afternoons, grew in vocal strength and confidence. The first work of the new year, Pitoni's '*Cantate Domino*', was sung during High Mass on All Saints. Palestrina's '*Alma Redemptoris Mater*' was performed on the Feast of the Immaculate Conception. As Christmas approached, the Choir learnt a selection of traditional and modern carols which they sang at Benediction on 16 December and repeated at the Catholic church in Fort William at the invitation of the parish priest, Fr Morrison.

At half term Mr Fotheringham led the Hill-Walking Club in an attack on Càrn a' Chuilinn ('Little Siberia') from Loch Tarff. There was heavy rain and snow on top, and a raging blizzard drove them back. The following Thursday another party tackled the same hill the easy way up. Although there was a great deal of snow, the day was clear and cold and the summit was reached in two and a half hours. The last walk of term was up Ben Tee where a complete white-out forced the walkers back 200 feet from the top.

The XXI Club, guided successfully by Mr Fotheringham, also had a number of successful meetings. These included one debate on the Common Market, one evening of ghost stories, and then a balloon debate. Since Mr Fotheringham was leaving, Mr Fowles stepped into the breach. The latter also entertained the Upper School as a lugubrious undertaker in a performance of 'Wanted – One Body', given by the Fort Augustus Players at the Drill Hall on 22 November.

Many members of the School enjoyed pony riding at Inchnacardoch organised by Mr Anderson. Old Boy Mr MacDonald of Inchnacardoch Hotel supplied the facilities and Mr Cameron lent the ponies.

The School watched the opening of the Second Vatican Council on television on 11 October, mindful of the fact that Old Boy Fr J. C. M. Barry (1926-35) was in Rome acting as adviser in Canon Law to the Archbishop of St Andrews and Edinburgh.

Many were saddened by the death of Mrs Pimley who passed away on 10 October. She was especially remembered for the unselfish way she offered her house during the Second World War for the use of the Preparatory School.

On 20 December Dom Anselm Parker, Titular Abbot of Westminster, died. He was the first Headmaster of the new School which opened in September 1920, but was forced to retire in December 1923 because of strain and overwork.

Succeeding Fr Oswald Hunter Blair as Master of St Benet's Hall, Oxford in 1908, Fr Anselm held that post until 1920 when he came to Fort Augustus. There he founded many of the societies in the School: Debating and Literary, Natural History, Philatelic, Dramatic, Photographic and Musical. In all these he took a personal interest. Compulsory games occupied a part of the curriculum. He took part in these as well, even though he was in his forties and irrespective of weather conditions. He also passed on his love of the countryside to the boys with day-long expeditions over moor and mountain.

From 15 January, when the School returned, the weather curtailed most outside activities and made games quite impossible. Black frost gripped the earth and there was snow till nearly the beginning of March. On most afternoons there was Skating or Ice-Hockey, at first on the old Mill pond and then on Loch Uanagan.

In the Abbey Church the School Mass was now celebrated at the High Altar with the two Houses seated on opposite sides of the nave. During Lent, the Stations of the Cross on Fridays replaced the usual Tuesday Benediction.

This was the third consecutive year when the weather seriously affected School games. However, now that the all-weather pitch presented by Mr Angus Macdonald was complete, it was hoped that this would no longer be a problem.

Although the Hockey season was short, the results were good. Three of the four matches were won. All were played away because of the bad condition of the School grounds. During the holidays H. D. Shannon, P. R. Perrin, W. C. Chisholm and R. C. Drummond played in the Scottish Schoolboys Trial held in Edinburgh. Drummond and Perrin were subsequently capped and played in the International Hockey Festival held at Port Talbot, South Wales on 19 and 20 April.

For over a year Piping classes had been held each week in the School. It all started when J. H. T. Slight arrived from Rhodesia with a set of bagpipes and instructions from his father that he should learn how to play them. The first instructor was Major Haig who travelled down from Drumnadrochit each week. Encouraging the boys was Fr Chrysostom, who also helped in the instruction.

The sudden death of Old Boy Dr Wilfred K. Christopher, at his home in Dunbar on 17 January, came as a shock to those who knew him. He had been forced to give up his practice because of ill health, but then went to Edinburgh University to train as a clinical pathologist. He worked as a Registrar up to his death. Dr Christopher was survived by his wife and six children, the eldest of whom was 13.

Fr Victor Lejeune, for many years Novice Master at Fort Augustus, died on 10 March. Fr Basil Wedge, due to his increasing infirmity, was under constant care at Twyford Abbey in London.

With the Summer term new staff member Mr M. Bolton arrived. Although he was to leave at the end of the term, he made his mark supervising small study groups, coaching Junior Cricket, and running the Workshop.

In the School, the Locker Room in the new wing was cleared and the lockers moved to the passageway connecting the new wing with the old. During the holidays, ventilators had been installed in the dormitories. The heating had been turned off before the end of April, but the mountains seen in the distance through showers of sleet and hail were still snow-capped. Accordingly the heating had to be put back on again!

On Sunday 5 May the all-weather Iain Fraser Macdonald Memorial Hockey Pitch was opened by the Headmaster, the gift of Mr Angus Macdonald in memory of his son Iain. A great deal of preparation had gone on at the site, as it had to be raised three feet to bring it to road level, much of the material for the filling coming from the top garden.

The inaugural match was played against Glasgow's Western Hockey Club (with several Old Boys in the Western team). The visitors won 5-3.

The Cricket team won four matches, drew one and lost three. R. C. Drummond (Captain) and H. D. Shannon (Vice-Captain) bore the burden of the attack and bowled for long spells at a time. They were never really mastered by any batsman who was not thoroughly competent in defending his wicket. In 160 overs they took, between them, 59 out of the 70 wickets which fell.

Although Lovat won the Cricket, it was Vaughan who won the Athletics. J. P. Marshall, the outstanding Senior athlete, won both the Dunskey Cup (Half-Mile) and the Crawford Cup (Cross-Country). Marshall also won the 440 yards in a time of 56.2 seconds. H. D. Shannon received the Captain's Medal and was also *Victor Ludorum*.

On 1 June the new Denny Hovercraft passed through the Canal on its way to London from Dumbarton. Although exciting, its performance was not as impressive as expected due to a technical fault.

The term's theatrical highlight was Sheridan's 'School for Scandal', produced by Mr Fowles. Rehearsal time was very short, with the result that the production was reduced by an hour between the dress rehearsal and the final performance. Nevertheless, the actors did extremely well.

The 'ladies', in their splendidly contrived wigs and patches, acted most convincingly, with only an occasional gaucherie in movement or stance. P. A. Diviani played a blushing Maria, but was too tall by the side of her guardian's diminutive wife (a matter for the producer rather than the surgeon).

The Art Club was started at the beginning of the year by Mr Owen, running on Saturday evenings. In the Spring term many more materials were available – water colours, Indian ink, charcoal and lino-cutting tools. By the Summer there were 16 members. Most of them were heavily engaged in painting the scenery for 'The School for Scandal'.

During the Summer term the Piping class received instruction from the military pipers at Fort George, while a Drum-Major taught drumming. Major Haig continued to teach *Ceòl Mór* to four members of the Senior group, while Fr Aidan taught the recorder to the Lower School.

Other societies continued to grow in strength. There were now 40 members in the Riding Club, 30 in the Golf Club, 35 in the Sailing Club. Only the Photographic Society seemed in the doldrums due to a lack of enthusiasm, co-operation and ideas.

On 3 June, Pope John XXIII died. His successor, Cardinal Montini (Pope Paul VI), when still a Monsignor attached to the Secretariat of State, visited Scotland in 1933 and stayed for two nights at the Abbey.

On 5 June, Br Gerard O'Brien died and was buried in the monastic cemetery. Born in Lanarkshire in 1883, he left home at the age of 15 to enter the religious life with the Vincentians at Armagh. After a short time, he came to Fort Augustus in 1898.

There he was put under Br Henry to learn carpentry. He continued as a carpenter and joiner for the rest of his life. He was also a great hill-walker and a keen fisherman. In his old age he would spend his holidays at St James' in Buckie, setting off early in the morning with his rod and bicycle. In his later years he devoted much of his life to prayer. He died suddenly, having just finished saying the Rosary and having received the Sacrament of the Sick two days before.

The School Prize Day was on Sunday 14 July. At High Mass in the morning the Choral Society sang Byrd's 'Mass for Three Voices' and in the evening there was a performance of 'A School for Scandal'.

Dr J. A. MacLean, Director of Education for Inverness-shire, presented the prizes. The Headmaster, Fr Mark, pointing out that there were about 40 Old Boys studying for a first degree at that time, added that there was a need for parents to fund additional educational materials:

Anti-flu injections, pamphlets for television programmes, paperback authors to encourage wider reading, art materials, French magazines: the list is endless and all cost money. Things that are for the exclusive use of a boy are therefore charged. The various clubs need equipment, and this is expensive .... We therefore charge a subscription of varying amount for these voluntary activities .... The parent who said that my prize-day speech last year was like an annual report to shareholders was accurate in more ways than one.

141

From the beginning of term, Fridays were now set aside as Corps Day for the School Cadet Force. This had been established largely through the initiative of Fr Vincent who had succeeded Abbot Celestine as Housemaster of Vaughan. Increasingly Fr Vincent's dynamism, ceaseless energy and many gifts made him take on the role of the moral backbone of the School, a role originally developed by the first Prefect of Discipline, Commander Farie (at Abbot McDonald's invitation) and then by Fr Laurence Kelly.

Fr Augustine Grene succeeded Fr Mark Dilworth as Headmaster at the beginning of the Lent term. An Old Boy of the School and a First Class Honours graduate of the University of Edinburgh, Fr Augustine (a shy Anglo-Irishman with a sing-song voice and impeccable manners, known to all the boys as 'Gussie'), had previously held the post (1952-53). Subsequently, he taught Theology in the monastery for some years before returning to the School in 1959 to teach Advanced Level French and Latin.

Fr Mark, who now returned to continue his studies and research into Scottish Catholic history (particularly monastic history), had been Headmaster for four years during which great developments had occurred.

As Headmaster, Fr Mark had taken a close interest in the problems of staff, parents and boys. For the staff he had concluded the negotiations over the national superannuation scheme and to ease parents' burdens he had introduced various insurance schemes. For the boys he set an ambitious programme of studies and took personal charge of it. His goals he announced during a prize-day speech:

> We wish Fort Augustus to be not only a good Catholic school, but a good school by any standards. That means that our professional competence must be at least as good as in any other school.

It was also time, unhappily, to say goodbye to other members of staff – Mr D. E. Roberts ARCO (who had taught Music for four years) and Mr Dereck A. Fowles BA who, since 1957, had 'given unstintingly of his time and talents in a far wider field than merely the subject he taught'.

The success of 'Chick' Fowles as Senior History Master was outstanding. He would accept any willing candidate and achieved a long line of success where others would have held out little hope. He also assisted at various times in the English department. 'Many boys will be grateful,' wrote *The Corbie*, 'for the interest he aroused in them and the enthusiasm he generated for his subject.' He also presided over School debating societies, was a power in the Village Council, and produced plays for the Village Dramatic Society

It was the stage which gave him an ideal outlet for his enthusiasm. *The Corbie* judged that he was 'the most talented school producer that this writer has ever come across, and he has gained a reputation for his productions far beyond the confines of the School'. He introduced a three-year cycle of classical, modern and musical drama which ensured that each generation of boys would either take part in or witness a different facet of the theatre:

> *He was that rare and valuable man, a schoolmaster who would take endless time and trouble, and do it entirely for the sake of his pupils, not for himself.*

With 27 new boys there were other changes in the School staff. Joining on 19 September were Fr Aidan, Fr Robert, Mr M. Stone (Science) and Mr A. W. Hunkin (English and History). Fr Mark had resumed the position of Senior French Master after the departure of Mr R. W. MacEachan at the end of the previous term.

From the beginning of term the School Mass was celebrated at a moveable altar at the head of the nave, since the High Altar was considered too far away for convenience.

During the holidays repairs had been made to the plasterwork in the Calder Wing. An outbreak of dry rot in the School porch, however, was only corrected after the boys had returned, so leading to much inconvenience.

The weather in September and early October was dry and pleasant. The ground stood up well to the intensive games practice. However it turned cold at the start of the following month, the first snow falling on 8 November.

The Hallowe'en Party on Sunday 10 November saw fireworks let off from the School tower, although a rogue Roman candle fell among half the intended display and set them all off at once. The evening was rounded off with an informal concert of short plays, pop music and a lengthy and long-winded mock Bye-election.

The Rugby XV had a good season, winning five out of eight of their matches. One of the victories was a rare one – an away win against Aberdeen Grammar School (a penalty goal and a try to one try).

R. C. Drummond, the Captain, was the outstanding player. The pack was efficient, well-drilled and very good in the loose. Their loose play was the strongest part of their game. Behind the scrum, resources were so limited that a forward, A. B. F. Kasprowiak, had to be taken out of the pack and made into a full-back.

The School play was produced in the Christmas term, the last of Mr Fowles' productions – Gian-Carlo Menotti's 'Amahl and the Night Visitors', with C. J. Crouch as the crippled boy Amahl, A. D. MacLaren as his Mother, the Three Kings being played by A. D. Wright, H. C. P. Walker and R. C. Drummond.

The opera was given with an orchestra stiffened from outside – particularly the Training Depot of the Queen's Own Highlanders at Fort George. Mr Ian Bowman of Inverness Royal Academy conducted the Inverness performance and Mr Holloway of Gordonstoun played in the orchestra on the same occasion. Mr Alan Nichol, Drama Advisor to the Highland Division of the Scottish Community Drama Association, commented:

> *The whole production must stand or fall in the portrayal of the Mother. The technical assurance and polish of this performance belied the years and experience of the player. It was one of the most satisfying and exciting performances I have ever seen in Youth Drama.*

While Menotti's opera tells the touching story of a new-born child, the School that term also mourned the death of a much liked monk, Fr Basil Deller Wedge, a man of gentle charm and great culture.

Born a member of the Church of England in Southampton in 1889, he was educated at Taunton School in Hampshire before entering St Boniface College, Earminster with a view to taking Anglican orders.

In 1908, however, he became a Catholic and joined a new religious order, the Congregation of the Divine Pastor. Having taken simple vows, he taught in a secondary school but decided to become a Benedictine.

He came to Fort Augustus in 1913 and was ordained six years later. When the School reopened in 1920 he was on the teaching staff. Three years later he became Master of Ceremonies and Sacristan and was in charge of Fr Lester's students.

Fr Basil was in 1930 appointed the first Prior of Saint Andrew's Priory, Edinburgh, but was forced by ill-health to convalesce in Malta where he had been invited by Old Boy Archbishop Maurus Caruana.

During this period he flew from Malta personally to deliver an important dispatch to Cardinal Pacelli (later Pope Pius XII) at the Vatican.

Fr Basil returned to Fort Augustus, but the climate was not conducive to his health and, accordingly, he went in 1939 to reside at Ealing Priory. He remained in London throughout the War and experienced the bombing. He was present when the Priory church was destroyed in an air raid in October 1940. He then spent six years as chaplain to Standbrook Abbey, then to Douai School, returning to Fort Augustus in 1952 where he did some teaching. Towards the end of 1960 he was sent to hospital in Glasgow, and finally to Twyford Abbey nursing home where he died. He was subsequently buried in the Abbey cemetery.

For the Old Boys there was additionally the sad news of the death of L. J. McKenna (1885-89) at the age of 91.

Laurence McKenna, a native of Belfast, rode horses from his earliest years. Before entering his father's wine merchant and hatter's fur business he was a student at Oxford where he rowed for the University, was a star bicycle polo player, and excelled at Cricket. In later years he coached the Ulster Cricket team.

During the First World War he was active in Red Cross work in Ireland. At the end of the War he gently but firmly refused the knighthood offered him by George V. In 1924 he settled in the United States and was active in business in Brookfield, Connecticut up to ten years before his death.

The Editor of *The Corbie* (May 1965), after apologising for the non-appearance of the magazine since February 1964, signalled a subtle change in the ethos of the School, a new emphasis which had been evident for some time:

It will be noted that games' reports are given more briefly than in the past, and that more space is increasingly being taken up by Societies and Activities. That this is so, owes much to the unrivalled opportunities offered by the surrounding countryside and to the increased numbers which have allowed the School to be developed along broader lines.

There were other changes among the School staff, principally the departure of Mr A. Keith Anderson. He was not only in charge of the teaching of English, but also taught Latin and Spanish and encouraged the boys to take up horse-riding, dramatics and debating. His greatest success, however, was with Music. In less than three years, starting from scratch, he had formed an orchestra, persuading boys to play almost any instrument, giving instruction himself on several of them.

After reading Classics at Oxford he taught in Spain and then in Turkey. Not many years later he held a senior post at Ankara University. After he had come to Fort Augustus his knowledge of Turkish affairs led to his being asked to broadcast on the Overseas programme of the BBC. The basis of his success was his varied experience and wide range of talents.

Throughout the year a number of Scottish Arts Council productions were performed in the School theatre. These included Tennessee Williams' 'The Glass Menagerie'; Lennox Milne in 'The Heart is Highland'; and the Edinburgh Quartet playing Mozart and Brahms clarinet quartets with Derek Jones. There were also two visits from Intimate Opera.

The Holy Week retreat was given by the popular preacher, Fr Giarchi CSSR.

During the Summer term the option of playing Golf, Tennis or Cricket was offered to the Senior School. This was only possible since the opening of the Macdonald Memorial Pitch, converted into four tennis courts for the duration of the Summer.

The death of the School physician, Dr John Kirton, on 12 May 1964 was received with sorrow. A graduate of Aberdeen University, he had been awarded the Military Cross during the First World War. After practising in Orkney, he worked in Fort Augustus for 30 years, serving the whole district. His son Ronald now took his place as School Doctor.

Fr Gregory Brusey returned in September to take over musical activities in the School. Messrs F. H. Cochrane and M. Peart filled the vacancies caused by the departure of Messrs Anderson and Fowles. Mr J. P. Schweitzer came in May as Senior French Master, while Mr D. L. Cuming, who had arrived in the Summer term, coached the First XV. The Editor of *The Corbie* noted:

> *The School will ever be grateful for the 25 years' coaching by Fr Laurence Kelly, who has now retired from that post, though still remaining in charge of games.*

The 1964 Rugby XV had a disappointing season with seven matches played: two cancelled because of the weather, three won and four lost. In spite of the hard work put into coaching by Mr Cuming, the XV did not fulfil its potential.

The year 1965 was memorable for the wonderful weather and the use of the new Hockey pitch. The two previous bad winters had reduced the season to only a few weeks and this had had an effect on the Lower School where the basic skills had hardly been learned and some boys had not played Hockey at all.

Nine matches were played: four were won, three drawn and two lost. The XI had their moments, but form was inconsistent. R. C. Drummond (Captain) at centre-forward was in a class of his own. His stick-work, control of the ball, judgement and speed were of a very high standard.

Drummond and P. R. Perrin (Vice-Captain) were capped for Scotland a second time in the Schoolboys International Festival and E. F. Foley did well to win his first cap. W. C. Chisholm and D. I. Colquhoun played in the Final Trial.

After a depressing start, the Cricket XI improved greatly. In all School matches the XI scored faster, often *twice* as fast as their opponents. The School bowled 82 maiden overs to their opponents' 29. Of the eight matches played, four were won, two drawn and two lost.

R. C. Drummond (Captain) won the Bowling Cup; J. H. T. Slight (Vice-Captain) won the Batting and Fielding Cup.

In Athletics, Lovat won the House Championship (166 points to 135). R. C. Drummond won the Senior Competition (with wins in the 100 yards, 220 yards, 440 yards and the High Jump). The Dunskey Cup (Half-Mile) was won by D. M. Waters and the Crawford Cup (Cross-Country) by G. M. Devine.

The Army Cadet Corps held regular short exercises, each of the four platoons taking part alternately. A training weekend held at Fort George in November involved a night exercise. Sunday morning was spent on the range, and in the afternoon there was a platoon exercise against Cadets from 1st Ross-shire Battalion, the Seaforth Highlanders. A second weekend in February had the Cadets completing a 20 mile circuit in arctic conditions, bivouacking overnight at 1000 feet above sea level. On 20 March the Pipe Band played on parade for the first time.

Following the departure of Mr Fowles, Fr Vincent undertook the production of Shakespeare's 'Macbeth', as well as designing and making the costumes. The set (a druidical circle of stones) remained unchanged throughout the play, scene changes being indicated by lighting sequences and a few moveable props. There was one performance, on Sunday 13 December, for parents, guests and the School.

W. T. Hill as Macbeth looked every inch the part, but was only occasionally in command of the language and was unable to convey the profundity of the great soliloquies. Lady Macbeth was intelligently played by A. D. MacLaren, ice-cold in 'her' passions. A. F. Macdonald showed considerable comic talent as the Porter.

Other School activities continued to show healthy signs of growth. The School Orchestra met twice a week under the direction of Mr Anderson; the Choral Society now had additional help in the form of Fr Gregory; the seven-strong senior group of the Pipes and Drums were now taught by Corporal Moorcroft who had returned from a tour of the United States where he had been one of the pipers who played at the late President Kennedy's funeral. A week before the assasination he had played on the lawn in front of the White House for the benefit of Mr and Mrs Kennedy.

Outdoor activities generated great enthusiasm among the boys. The Hill-Walking Club, under Mr Stone's guidance, made good use of the three-weekly holidays, while the Sailing Club took good advantage of Old Boy J. R. Mackenzie-Reid's newly-launched ketch 'Tringa', Fr Vincent and two boys crewing in April from Wroxham via Great Yarmouth to Inverness.

Thirty-one boys left that Summer, to be replaced by a further 27. In his prize-day speech on Sunday 5 July, Fr Augustine explained that there were now 155 boarders: 'We cannot take any more, and the entry list for next year is already closed.' The number of candidates for the SCE exams was 59, with 58 entered for the GCE. The previous year's results included many passes at Credit and Very Good level. In the evening a substantial concert prepared by Mr Anderson and Fr Vincent was provided by the School Orchestra and the Choirs.

For the second year running the Old Benedictines' Hockey Club won the six-a-side tournament organised by the Scottish Schools and held at the Grange, Edinburgh.

Mgr John Barry (1926-35), Rector of St Andrew's College, Drygrange, had been appointed a Domestic Prelate. Hugh D. Shannon (1958-63) entered the College in September to study for the priesthood. The Annual Reunion, held in July, was one of the smallest gatherings for years, only 36 Old Boys being present.

On 20 March 1965, Fr Norman Baird (1936-43) died. In his last year at Fort Augustus he had been Captain of the three major sports, as well as Head Boy. After leaving school he spent a year teaching at the Preparatory School (then in Fort Augustus) before entering the RAF. When the War ended he went first to St Peter's College, Cardross, before going to Rome to complete his Theology. After his ordination in 1953 he was appointed to Holy Cross, Glasgow, where he stayed until his death.

On Tuesday in Holy Week 1965, Abbot Wulstan Knowles, who had been chaplain at Stanbrook Abbey, Worcestershire for 13 years, died and was buried in the Abbey cemetery. Born in Birmingham in 1881, he first came to Fort Augustus as a 13 year old *alumnus*. This was shortly after the first School closed. He completed his secondary education at the Abbey and entered the Novitiate in 1900, followed by two years of study in Rome. He was ordained in 1908.

Before his election as Abbot, he carried out the work of bursar, parish priest, naval chaplain and virtual founder of two priories in the United States (being Superior there variously in 1924 and 1926). He spent five years establishing the priories.

In 1929 he was elected Abbot (and re-elected in 1944). His great contribution was his policy of sending young monks to take university degrees, and his turning of Saint Andrew's Priory into a preparatory school for Fort Augustus.

Five Hockey matches were played, of which three were won and two drawn. The XI's defence was much better than its attack. During the Spring term of 1965, three boys – J. H. T. Slight, I. S. Brown and P. J. Diviani – were chosen to represent Scotland in the Schoolboys' International Hockey Tournament at Winnington Park, Norwich.

Five Cricket matches were played: four were won and one lost. Vaughan won the Athletics championship (138 points to 109); G. M. Devine was awarded both the Dunskey and the Crawford Cup.

The Army Cadet Corps continued to flourish, holding a Summer camp in late July at Fersit, Glen Spean, two days' march from Fort Augustus.

Among the many societies and groups, the Archery Club now had 36 members. Rock-climbing was introduced by Mr Cochrane, with expeditions to Buchaille Etive Mór in Glen Coe and to Ben Nevis. The Golf Club, with 40 members, and the Sailing Club with nearly 40, competed for the boys' attention, along with the Hill-Walking Club (under Mr Stone).

At Christmas 1964, 17 boys accompanied Fr Vincent on a Holy Land cruise, calling at Piraeus in Greece, Haifa and Naples. From Naples the party went to Cassino and then Rome.

For several terms the guitar group known as 'The Kraken Wakes' (previously 'The Christophers') had entertained the School. It consisted of the three Christopher Brothers – Brian, David, Michael – and Christopher Crouch.

Abbot Butler of Downside, who conducted the quadrennial visitation of the Monastery that year, spoke to the boys about the Vatican Council, in which he had notably participated.

The building of the baptistry and narthex of the Church began. By now the structural work had been finished and the workmen were engaged on the interior.

A large number of non-cricketers played Tennis on the Macdonald Memorial Hockey Pitch. Twenty-one pairs competed in a doubles competition held for the Fifth and Sixth forms. A prize of a dozen tennis balls was presented by Fr Laurence.

Fr Aidan and Fr Chrysostom left the staff – the former to be chaplain at Stanbrook Abbey, the latter to teach at Carlekemp. French teacher Mr J. P. Schweitzer also left.

With deep regret the School learnt that the Matron, Mrs D. Coppin, would be leaving at the end of the Summer term. Since her arrival in 1961, Mrs Coppin had her department systematically re-organised. No trouble or sacrifice was too great for her. In 1962 she introduced the Winter term anti-flu inoculations which had proved so successful. She also helped with the costumes for the Dramatic Society and acted as First Aid Instructor in the Corps.

The life of the Community saw two apparently minor but, in reality, truly significant changes. On 13 November 1965 (as a result of recommendations made by the general Chapter in August), the Lay-brothers adopted the same habit as the Choir Monks. This change was intended to show the internal unity of vocation and ideals in the monastic life. A few days later a number of priests in the Community offered a con-celebrated Mass. This too was an expression of unity.

The previous Headmaster, Fr Mark Dilworth, had spent three months in Rome and Germany on a travelling scholarship, gathering material for a PhD thesis on the Scottish abbeys in Germany in the seventeenth century.

On 15 October Fr Ambrose Geoghegan died, as a result of a serious operation, while being cared for at St Raphael's nursing home in Edinburgh. Born in London in 1882, he entered the Alumnate at Fort Augustus in 1895 when the College had just been closed down. He made his profession in 1903 and was ordained in December 1909.

In the Autumn of 1910 he went to Oxford to take a degree and entered Parker's Hall (previously known as Hunter Blair's Hall). The Master was now Fr Anselm Parker, later to be Headmaster at Fort Augustus. Some years later it became known as St Benet's Hall. Fr Ambrose, however, found life at Oxford uncongenial and felt his degree course was not relevant to his needs. He only remained at Oxford until the following Spring, when he returned to Fort Augustus. Already before his ordination Fr Ambrose had been assistant organist, now he became chief organist and cantor.

During the First World War he became an Army Chaplain. In 1918 he was severely wounded at the Western Front and it was not until 1921 that he finally left hospitals behind him and returned to the Abbey.

Fr Ambrose was gifted musically, playing the piano and the organ (skills which his nephew, Fr Gregory Brusey, also inherited). He had a very true tenor voice. With a deep and exact knowledge of the Classics, he showed professional expertise and incisiveness in everything he did. He had an infectious sense of humour.

In September 1923 he was appointed prior by Abbot McDonald, a post he was to hold for the next 17 years. He was also organist and choirmaster, taught Moral Theology to the student monks and took charge of the studies of the Lester students.

He went to Downside in 1940 (where he taught moral theology) and returned to Fort Augustus in 1944, resuming his duties as organist, cantor and professor of moral theology. He was appointed Sub-prior, a position he held until his death.

His two main recreations, according to season and weather, were bookbinding and scything. The monastic Library was full of his beautifully executed bindings. His visitors had to thread their way between large wooden contraptions to enter his room. When he travelled south he always wore an ancient Inverness cape in the manner of Sherlock Holmes. In Summer he scythed, dressed in a monastic habit and a white straw hat, a pipe clamped between his teeth to keep away the midges!

The death also occurred of Fr Laurence McGann. Born in Trenton, New Jersey in 1910, he was educated at Fordham University before becoming a postulant at the recently-founded Priory in Portsmouth, Rhode Island, at that time a dependency of Fort Augustus. He studied for the priesthood at Fort Augustus and at the Catholic University, Washington and was ordained at Fort Augustus on 8 August 1937. He then taught for a time at Portsmouth Priory School.

Six months before Pearl Harbour Fr Laurence had become a naval chaplain. He served at sea during the War, in the Pacific. Afterwards he was appointed District Chaplain of the First Naval District, Boston and was Executive Director of the Armed Forces Chaplains' Board of the Department of Defence. Having been diagnosed as suffering from cancer, Fr Laurence retired and died a month later. The funeral, with full military honours, was at Arlington National Cemetery.

The Annual Old Boys' Reunion was held in July. Among those present was Abbot Alban Boultwood, who was elected Chaplain for 1965-66. Thirty-six Old Boys attended.

On 7 August 1965 Lord Carmont, one of the most prominent of Old Boys, died. John Carmont (1880-1965), from Galloway, was at St Benedict's College, Fort Augustus under the headmastership of the late Abbot Oswald Hunter Blair. Two of his sisters were Benedictine nuns.

After studying Law at Edinburgh University he qualified as a solicitor and then trained for the Bar, being admitted to the Faculty of Advocates in 1906.

During the First World War he served with the Royal Scots and was later commissioned into the Black Watch. Afterwards he returned to his practice and took silk in 1924, specialising in commercial and shipping cases, and in reparation.

In 1929 he married. Among his several homes was the house at North Berwick which was now Carlekemp Priory School. During this period he stood as a Unionist candidate for East Edinburgh, but later stood down in favour of a Liberal.

In 1934 he was elevated to the Bench of the Court of Session and became the senior Lord Ordinary in the Outer House by 1937. He was then moved to the First Division where he sat until the end of his life. After the Pope had appointed him a Privy Chamberlain of the Cape and Sword, Lord Carmont spent a part of the long vacation each year carrying out his duties at the Vatican.

Lord Carmont, however, was best known as a criminal judge. This was because of the severe sentences he handed down in the Glasgow Circuit during the early 1950s. In criminal parlance, a severe sentence became known as a 'carmont'.

CHAPTER 15

The Abbey School

1965-69

W HEN the School returned in September 1965 there were 32 new boys, bringing the School roll to 145. The next issue of *The Corbie* saw a change of Editor. Fr Vincent, who had edited very successfully for the previous seven years, took the place of Fr Francis Davidson. Fr Francis also replaced Fr Chrysostom on the teaching staff.

Mr Quinn joined the staff to teach French. Miss A. Clarke was the new Matron.

Unusually early snow and frost upset the normal outdoor activities. For two weeks from 22 November organised games were impossible because of snow and ice. Sledging became the sport of the moment and produced two casualties – A. Drummond, trying to avoid some girls, ran his sledge into a fence and suffered a fractured arm; F. F. McGarity broke his arm too (but with less gallant intent).

One of the central heating boilers broke down, leaving the old School building with no heating. Towards the end of term a car crashed a few miles south of Fort Augustus and brought down an electricity power line. The School was without electricity from four o'clock in the morning till mid-day.

The Scottish Department of Education arranged a Consolidated Inspection which lasted from 8-17 November. There were visits that term from three touring theatrical companies, sponsored by the Arts Council of Great Britain. These presented Noel Coward's 'Hay Fever', the Harlequin Ballet and Miss Rosalinde Fuller with her own dramatisations of short stories by authors such as Chekhov and Dickens.

The Hallowe'en party given by the boys for the staff on 4 November was followed by a concert in the Assembly Hall in which 'The Kraken Wakes' featured prominently.

All seven First XV Rugby matches were lost. The School was beaten 25-0 by Rannoch and 32-0 by Aberdeen Grammar School. The main reason for the poor performances was that an unusually large number of senior players had left at the end of the Summer. The Colts XV lost four (notably a 62-3 defeat by Rannoch) and won one.

The Army Cadet Corps, however, went from strength to strength. The Instructors of the 30 Cadets entered for the Certificate 'A' Part I Exam, scored 1005 passes. A Fire Cadre was fully operational that term which received instruction from the Inverness Fire Brigade training officer. A short night exercise held in December at Kyltra had many exciting moments, including the capture of one of the umpires! From the noise of battle and illuminating ground flares, the locals must have thought the country had been invaded.

The School play, produced by Mr Cochrane, was Kenneth Woollard's 'Morning Departure'. It was given one performance only – on 18 December. Written during the War, the action took place in September 1941 inside H. M. Submarine S14 and at the Naval Staff Offices ashore.

Long hours were spent building a set which accurately recreated the mess deck of a submarine with the shore offices positioned above. T. J. Murphy competently portrayed the tired and cautious salvage officer, while D. E. Toms, as Commander Whately, very successfully played the conscientious officer tied by red tape. Perhaps the most genuine characterisation of all was given by J. M. H. Bailey as Higgins, the Steward. He was cocky, belligerent, subservient or casual in turn.

Building works of all kinds were brought to fruition in a flurry of activity. Just before Christmas the narthex and baptistry of the Church were completed; a new bicycle shed was built onto the bastion wall beyond the School tower and a road laid to the site of the new houses for the lay-staff in the upper garden. The Army Cadets' drill hall was also completed. Electricians had been working in the house for the previous few months. They planned to rewire the whole of the Monastery and School buildings in gradual stages.

The Cadets had an action-packed term, taking part in two training weekends. Two assault boats arrived during the Easter holidays and were put to good use in a water-borne assault on Battery Rock. After the exams were over, the Pipe Band was kitted out in green doublets used by the old School Pipe Band before the turn of the century. The drummers strutted around in scarlet ones.

A new interest in the School was the Forestry Group, under the supervision of Fr Andrew, as part of practical Geography studies. Mr Frater from the local branch of the Forestry Commission conducted the course, which involved activities such as planting trees and the study of their care and development.

Towards the end of March the School Choir joined forces with that of Inverness Academy to present two performances of Handel's 'Messiah': one in St Andrew's Cathedral in Inverness and the other in the School Assembly Hall at Fort Augustus.

The Hockey results for 1966 were poor, with five defeats and only three wins. On 13 March the first Schoolboys' Trial was held at Fort Augustus. C. T. Campbell and D. M. Shannon were chosen to play in the Final Trials, and Campbell was selected for the Scottish Schoolboys' International XI, playing in three games.

The Cricket season was dogged by rain. The season was fair, with two wins, one defeat and one draw. As no individual was outstanding, the Fielding Cup was not awarded.

Not much dedication was directed towards Athletics either. Only a few boys trained properly. Nevertheless Lovat shattered the Relay record in a time of 3 minutes 37.2 seconds but did not manage to defeat Vaughan overall.

During his Prize-day speech, Fr Augustine gave some examination statistics to boys (32 of whom were leaving) and to the parents. In 1964-65 some 35 boys passed Higher English; in the following year this number rose to 45, nearly a third of the School. More than 30 boys gained GCE passes and the same number achieved SCE passes. P. M. Shea, for example, gained seven GCE O Levels and eight SCE Highers.

The end of term concert featured not only choirs and instrumentalists, but 'The Kraken Wakes' playing a selection of classical, folk and popular music.

On 23 August 1966 came the sad news of the death of Commander Farie in hospital in Inverness. Born in London in 1882, Gilbert Harrison Farie was educated by the Jesuits at Wimbledon College. In 1895 he joined HMS 'Britannia' as a naval cadet and passed out as midshipman. In 1912 he left the Navy with the rank of Lieutenant and spent two years working in Canada. In 1914, at the outbreak of war, he rejoined the Navy as Lieutenant-Commander and served as an executive officer at Devonport in a training college for public school cadets. In 1917 he was promoted Commander and in 1919 joined the staff of Training Ship 'Mercury' at Hamble under C. B. Fry. Shortly afterwards he joined the staff of Rugby School where he spent two years.

From 1922-39 he was on the full-time staff at Fort Augustus, where he held the post of Master of Discipline and was, in effect, for most of this time acting Headmaster.

When war broke out he rejoined the Navy, this time as Captain of HMS 'Impregnable', Plymouth, engaged in training boys and signal ratings. In 1950 Commander Farie returned to Fort Augustus, taking a small supervisory role, but then retired completely. In 1959 he was made a Knight of St Gregory by Pope John XXIII as a mark of appreciation for his work in the education of youth.

Commander Farie was known as 'The Man'. He was a person of simple faith and manly piety; a man of few words, prompt action, spartan habits, simple tastes and extraordinarily good manners.

Forty-two new boys arrived at Fort Augustus in September 1966, twelve from Carlekemp. New to the School staff in September 1966 was History teacher Mr M. Haines, formerly at Rannoch School. From the beginning of term the distribution of exercise books and text books was centralised in a bookshop supervised by Fr Edward.

On 1 December Fr Andrew, Fr Francis and 40 boys visited the new paper and pulp mill at Anat Point near Fort William. The scale of the whole operation from trees to paper was very impressive.

Towards the end of the term the weather deteriorated and the barometer hit a record low of 28.2 inches. A gale soon followed after two days of heavy rain, and then severe flooding.

The snow on the hills melted, the river rose, the swamp and the vegetable garden by the River Tarff were completely flooded. Even the Loch rose five feet above normal, the water backing up the Tarff and flooding the playing fields. The old Hockey pitch was under five feet of water; the Macdonald pitch under 18 inches. When the water finally flowed off, it ate away at the edge of the laid surface and undercut it by six inches. The surface grit was swept into sand-like ridges. Another flood might have done more serious damage, but luckily none came and the surface was restored before the Hockey season started.

It was a poor year for Rugby. Much of the blame lay with the forwards who never used their weight to advantage in the pack. The result was that the backs never had enough of the ball. Seven matches were lost with only one victory. On the positive side, six of the team played in the Highland Schools' Trial in Inverness where D. L. Haworth was chosen for the Highland Schools' Select XV, captaining the team at inside centre.

At the beginning of the Spring 1967 term, Fr Laurence Kelly (Housemaster of Lovat since the House system was introduced in 1940) retired to take up the post of Community and School Bursar. Succeeding him was Fr Robert McKenzie, an Old Boy and formerly a member of Lovat who had been teaching Religious Knowledge, History and Latin since returning from Rome where he had taken the degree STL and another in Sacred Scripture. Shortly after, the Junior House was instituted. Fr Robert became its first Housemaster, while Fr Chrysostom succeeded him as Housemaster of Lovat.

With the resignation of Fr Laurence, one of the lynchpins of the Abbey School ethos was gone. At the end of the year, the headmaster, Fr Augustine, described Fr Laurence as 'an unchanging pillar of the School'. Few boys will ever forget him encouraging them on from the touchline with shouts of 'Hard! *Hard!*'

Fr Laurence continued, however, to be Vice-President of the Scottish Hockey Association.

During the first half of February and the whole of March the weather was so bad that games on grass were impossible. In March Fort Augustus had 11½ inches of rain (normally the average was 3¼).

The result was that the Hockey XI won only two of their ten matches, losing six and drawing two. Nevertheless, two boys were selected to play for the Scottish Schoolboys' XI. Under the eagle eye of Fr Laurence (Chairman of the Schoolboys' Sub-committee of the Scottish Hockey Association) D. L. Haworth and J. A. MacBride played in the International Quadrangular Tournament at Shotton, Flintshire in April. Haworth was chosen as Captain of the team. For many years the Abbey School had contributed one or more members of the Scottish Schoolboys' side.

The Army Cadet Corps continued to make progress, now emphasising advanced fieldcraft and battlecraft tactics. A Signals section was given the go-ahead and the Pipes and Drums both raised the standard of performance and widened its repertoire.

Nine cadets visited the 1st Battalion in Berlin, crossing the Iron Curtain in the process.

During the visit there were chances to fire grenades in the Grünewald, drive armoured vehicles and spy on the East Germans.

The Dramatic Society gave one performance in December of Molière's 'The Imaginary Invalid' (in English, adapted by Miles Malleson). Produced by Mr Quin, the old and gullible hypochondriac was played by D. E. Thoms. His hearty brother was portrayed by B. H. Johnston Stewart. C. F. Brown as Toinette, the resourceful maid, acted to perfection.

The Choral Society suffered early in the year when the tenor and bass sections dropped alarmingly in numbers and the confidence of the trebles and altos dwindled. Group carol singing at Christmas rescued the Society. In March the Society combined with Inverness Academy to give, among other pieces, Fauré's '*Requiem*' at St Andrew's Cathedral, Inverness and at Fort Augustus.

School debating societies also prospered: the Senior, Fourth Form, Junior and First and Second Form societies met several times during the Christmas term.

The Rowing Club, under the direction of Mr Stone, had six crews. Mr Stone, accompanying the Hill-Walking Club, spent a day at Morven where the climbers came across the wreck of a 'USAF Voodoo' that had crashed in the hills two years before.

A Clay Pigeon Club was started to keep its members in form during the close season. Fr Maurus was invited to be President. The first shoot took place on 19 January and was mainly devoted to showing how clays flew, for those members who had not previously shot.

The Photographic Society had now taken on a new lease of life. The attendance at the first meeting was relatively large. There was an influx of new members attracted by the prospect of mastering the enlarging process.

Many Old Boys attended a memorial service at St Anne's Oratory, Edinburgh for the late Commander Farie. The principal celebrant was Mgr John Barry, along with other Old Boys Frs Birnie, Curran and Rogerson. Fr W. D. Hamilton, formerly a colleague of the Commander's at Fort Augustus, was also present. After the service they all went to the Scotia Hotel for an informal reunion. It was perhaps the largest gathering of middle-aged Old Boys ever seen in Edinburgh.

In the Monastery, a change of horarium had been introduced in November on a trial basis. Conventual Mass was now celebrated at 7.55 am. Prime had been abolished and Sext and None were recited before lunch. Classes in the School started at 8.40 every morning. The Holy Week liturgy was celebrated for the first time in the *vernacular* (English). *The Corbie* commented: 'The undoubted gain in meaningfulness and intelligibility is offset by a loss in aesthetic quality.'

Fr Mark Dilworth was due to complete his doctoral thesis in the Summer. Over the past years he had written numerous articles on Scottish monasticism: three contributions to *The Innes Review*, three to *The Downside Review*, six articles in *The Clergy Review*, a short section in 'Essays on the Scottish Reformation', a paper in the *Transactions of the*

Gaelic Society of Inverness, and an edition in *The Bibliotheck* of five poems written by a Scottish monk.

Fr Denys Rutledge, now living the life of a virtual hermit in the southern part of Chile, had just had his third book published. *The Complete Monk* describes his search for the ideal monastery by way of travels in Chile, Bolivia and Peru, where Fr Denys had gone in answer to the Pope's appeal for help in that continent.

The SCE examination candidates' holiday was arranged in two groups of 15 each. Some of the first group went to Aviemore, lived in rented caravans and enjoyed the facilities of the new recreation centre; skiing, skating and dancing appeared to have been the principal amusements. Others went on a more energetic holiday: a cycling tour of the Moray Firth area, returning by way of Aviemore and Spean Bridge.

Another cycling event during the term was the mile race round the 440 yard running track. About 25 boys lined up for the start and, although several dropped out at various stages, some did finish. A. J. Reynolds was the first to cross the line. The organisers admitted later that in the excitement they counted five instead of four laps! The cycle trip to Inverness was made several times during the term. A non-stop attempt by M. Summerfield and I. C. Traquair came within three minutes of the previous year's time of 110 minutes.

Fishing was another popular spare-time activity. One notable catch, a pike of truly monstrous size, was taken from the Canal by G. F. Campbell. But the fishing event of the season (which also happened to be true), was J. A. D. Culshaw's dramatic rescue of a 20 month old baby in the River Avon during the holidays!

The usual practice of playing Hockey (rather than Cricket) in the early part of the Summer term continued. This was in the form of a league championship in which four teams – the Hairy Goats, Borlum Asses, Loch Ness Monsters and Ardachy Ghosts – paid an entry fee of a shilling a head and competed for the prize of a special meal. Two First XI matches were played, but both ended in defeat.

Cricket that season was a game of high scores and drawn matches. Eight games were played, two won, two lost and four drawn. The main reason for these results was the lack of real pace in the opening bowling and the inability of most batsmen to score quickly. The Bowling Cup was not awarded.

Because of the large number of boys in the School, a fourth Athletics section was introduced. The points system was also reviewed, with less points being awarded in the junior section. This made for a most exciting contest with the issue in doubt until the final event. The House Athletics competition was won by Vaughan by 146 to 134 points.

For a number of weeks that Summer, a helicopter was stationed at the Lovat Arms Hotel. It was often heard making noisy flights around the countryside, being used for re-surveying the Ordnance Survey.

For Prize Day on 18 July the novelist Eric Linklater came over from Easter Ross to present the prizes. In July 28 boys left the School. Fr Augustine pointed to several developments in the curriculum such as the Nuffield Course in Physics and Chemistry which had just been introduced. Examination passes were encouraging. Of the 27 candidates for the SCE exams, two boys were now leaving with six Highers, three with five, four with four passes. Twenty-six boys achieved passes at GCE 'O' Level.

Fr Augustine announced that, in accordance with the wishes of parents expressed some time ago to take a more active part in the development of the School, an organisation to be known as the 'Friends of Fort Augustus' had now been set up. Colonel Toms was Chairman and Mr Conacher agreed to be Treasurer.

The day after Prize Day eight boys, accompanied by Mr Stone, set off to cross the Grampian hills from east to west, from Drumochter Pass in Inverness-shire to Fettercairn in Kincardineshire. The route was covered in just over a week, with the party covering 130 miles of country and climbing the height of Mount Everest.

On 29 July 1967 Br Magnus O'Brien died, after suffering for many months from cancer. Born in Motherwell in 1899, he worked for some time on the old Caledonian Railway and visited the Abbey on numerous occasions with the Glasgow retreatants. In August 1919 he came as a postulant and was clothed the following year.

He lived the ordinary life of any Brother in any monastery, doing all the ordinary things – boilerman, cook, baker, groundsman – until the day came when he could no longer work.

A man with a big body, a big voice, a big laugh and a big heart, he went into every task given him with a large enthusiasm. He was, in the true sense of the word, a simple man.

In October, the recitation of the Office in English, with the Brothers participating in Choir, was introduced at the request of the Abbot President.

In November 1967, the Abbot President conducted a visitation of the

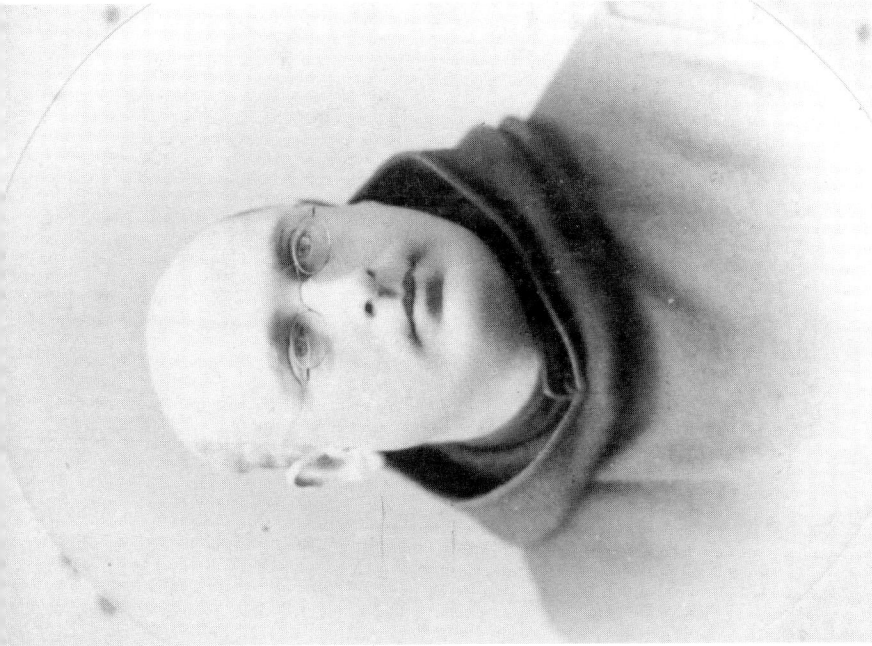

Dom Jerome Vaughan OSB

Old Boy Simon Joseph, 16th Lord Lovat

Cricketers at the Pavilion (*circa* 1880).

Old Boys' Reunion (in 1937) with Bishop Bennett, Abbots Knowles and Hunter Blair, and Commander Farie.

Fr Andrew McKillop MBE

Br Placid with 32lb salmon

Abbot Oswald Eaves and Pope Paul VI in Rome (1953).

Br Adrian and Br David.

The Abbey Church

Old Boys' Reunion (in the 1950s).

'Hamlet' (1959).

Brian McCann presenting a long-service quaich
to Hamish MacDonald (1988).

Three-Weekly Holiday (1960).

The 440 Yards (1960).

The CCF Platoon with Major Vincent Pirie Watson.

Ralph Giulianotti, Knight of St Gregory – with Frs Edward and Augustine,
Mark, Gay and Ralph Giulianotti jr, and Sir Robert Cowan (1991).

Summer School students on Loch Ness.

Miss K. O'Donnell at Saint Andrew's Priory.

Carlekemp Priory School

Open Golf Champion Henry Cotton with Fr Oswald Eaves

Monastery. This was in anticipation of the normal quadrennial visitation due shortly. Fr Laurence, who suffered a serious breakdown of health at the end of 1967, was now doing parochial work in Cumberland. Frs Maurus and Philip were also working in parishes in England.

At the end of December, Abbot Celestine Haworth's eight-year term of office ended. After a short holiday, he took up the position of chaplain to the Carmelite convent at Quidenham, Norfolk.

The Community welcomed the new Abbot, Fr Nicholas Holman, who was installed by the Abbot President on 9 January 1968.

Abbot Nicholas had entered Downside in 1928 and was ordained in 1935. Since that time he had been, variously, Bursar at Worth, Army Chaplain, Prior of Downside, Superior and Parish Priest at St Mary's, Liverpool, and also held administrative positions at Belmont and the Oratory School, Reading.

Abbot Nicholas paid a short visit to Abbot Oswald in Karlstad, Sweden. The Community had now formally adopted the mission of Abbot Oswald in Sweden and committed itself to providing assistance where it could.

There were further changes, this time in the School. Fr Augustine retired from the position of Headmaster and was replaced by Fr Mark Dilworth who had just been awarded a PhD by Edinburgh University for his thesis 'The Scottish Abbey in Wurzburg, 1595-1696'.

Thirty-four new boys arrived in September 1968, bringing the School roll to 147. Along with the rest of the School they were given the customary anti-flu injection and, as a consequence, there were no serious outbreaks of cold or flu.

During September a unit from Scottish Television was at Glen Buck filming outdoor scenes for a serialisation of D. K. Broster's 'The Flight of the Heron'.

The end of term was brightened by snow – rather unusual before Christmas.

The Rugby season resulted in eight defeats and only one victory. The Hockey team recorded five defeats and three victories with one match drawn. K. S. Janik, H. E. Murphy and J. A . MacBride were chosen to represent Scotland in the International Quadrangular Tournament at St Andrews in April. The Cricket team performed reasonably well, considering the youth of the squad, winning three, losing three and drawing one match.

Vaughan won the inter-House Athletics competition comfortably.

Abbot Nicholas presented a new cup for the boy who recorded the best time for the Mile. The Abbot Holman Cup was awarded to R. J. MacLaren, who also won the Dunskey and the Crawford Cups. In the Junior section, M. I. Bradley won the 100, 220, 440 and 880 yards in good times.

One of the highlights of the Combined Cadet Force's programme was a demonstration of riot control by the Advanced Infantry Section. A violent mob revolting against the rule of a certain President H–r–ld W–ls–n (the year being 1978 and Great Britain a republic) was dispersed, but only after the shooting of the leader, a wild Irishman with Chinese sympathies named D'Arcy. The missiles thrown by the crowd were mainly fruit and polythene bags filled with water, many of the latter scoring hits on the helmets of the Riot Control Party.

The timetable was modified in January. The 3.15 period was abolished, as well as the Prep from 9.00 to 9.30. Bedtime for the Seniors was brought forward by half an hour.

A cold, frosty spell occurred at the end of February. Snow lay on the ground, Hockey was impossible and skating on Loch Uanagan became a favourite occupation. Skiing was popular with one or two who went out with Fr Vincent on the hills above Loch Garry.

During the Summer term the School said goodbye to Miss Clarke, who had been Matron for three years. Her replacement was Mrs Blake-Mahon. Dr Kirton, who had looked after the boys' health for several years, took up a new position in Wales. The School presented him with a decanter and glasses. The new medical officer was Dr Buchanan.

Clubs and societies continued to flourish. A new Orienteering Club was started by Fr Andrew. The Car Club was another innovation. The Judo Club was re-started under Mr Cochrane, adding eight members. The Archery Club acquired one of the old hen-houses which they cleaned and painted.

In July 1968, along with Mr Cochrane (the Senior English Master for the previous four years), 29 boys left the School.

On 19 May, Bishop Foylan of Aberdeen ordained Fr Paul McCarron to the priesthood. Mass was concelebrated by the Community and by friends of Fr Paul.

The Autumn 1969 issue of *The Corbie* covered the School year from September 1968 to July 1969. The Editorial contained an apology from the Editor, Fr Francis, for the delay in its appearance. In fact, this was to be the last issue of *The Corbie* in its traditional format.

Twenty-five new boys arrived in September 1968. Mr Holland took over Mr Cochrane's position as senior English master. After many years of sterling service, Br Adrian retired from Refectory serving and maintenance. This was now all in the hands of an outside catering firm. Br Adrian now operated the School book and games equipment shops.

In December the Dramatic Society presented Robert Bolt's 'A Man for All Seasons'. The Common Man was played by N. J. Coppin and Sir Thomas More by V. R. Policella. Production was by Mr J. Holland.

The Rugby XV was mainly a young side, with only three of the previous year's team. Consequently five games were lost, two won and one drawn. The Hockey XI was one of the most successful for many years. Ten matches were won, five lost and one drawn. Four members of the team were selected for the International Trials – A. Cunningham, P. Greco and P. Doyle.

The Cricket XI won eight matches and only lost two. They were strong in all departments, most so in attack; Chlebowski bowled inswingers, J. Doyle moved the ball away, while F. Partridge mopped up the tails with his off-breaks. The real strength of the team was in their fielding.

In Athletics the Senior championship was again won by P. Doyle. In the Junior section High Jump there were two unorthodox techniques – the 'Bailey Bounce' and the 'Couttie Cartwheel'! C. T. Grieve won both the Mile and the Half-Mile.

The Combined Cadet Force had a year packed with purposeful activity. Section exercises were run on a Saturday night and Sunday morning. The inter-platoon competition included a race round Loch Tarff carrying two logs and a wooden crate. During the Christmas holidays six boys completed an Arduous Training expedition in western Inverness-shire. The 1969 Summer camp was held at Verden in Northern Germany. This included a 'flip' in a Scout Helicopter and an opportunity to drive Armoured Personnel Carriers.

Jimmy Savile, the disc jockey, while on a short trip to Fort Augustus on 26 February, spoke to the boys in the Library, signed autographs and talked to a senior Religious Knowledge class about his work for charities.

At the end of March Fr Augustine retired as Headmaster but continued to teach in the School.

Fr Mark took over from Fr Augustine as Headmaster at the end of April 1969. At the end of May, Mr Fifer joined the staff to assist in Music and Mathematics.

N. J. Coppin's play, 'After the Game', was taken to the Edinburgh Festival Fringe by his Kilcumein Players where it received encouraging reviews from *The Scotsman* and *The Daily Telegraph*. The playwright was also interviewed on Radio Four.

Forty-three Old Boys attended the annual lunch and about 60 went to the Weekend at the end of July.

Eighteen boys left at the end of July 1969, while in the Monastery there were equally dramatic changes. In the early part of the Summer, following the recommendations of the Second Vatican Council, the Brothers began to act as readers and antiphoners in Choir. Grace at meals was put into English. The Brothers moved into the main building of the Monastery, occupying vacant rooms and leaving their former accommodation for use as School studies.

Sanctus, * Sanctus, Sanctus Dómi-nus De- us Sá-ba-oth. Ple-ni sunt cae-li et ter-ra gló- ri- a tu- a. Ho- sánna in excél-sis. Be-ne-díctus qui ve- nit in nómi-ne Dó-mi-ni. Ho- sán-na in excél- sis.

CHAPTER 16

The Abbey School
1969-74

IN September 1969, just as *The Corbie* died, so the first edition of the *Fort Augustus News* appeared as an end-page of the monthly *Carlekemp Times* – perhaps a case of the tail wagging the dog?

In format it was a single sheet of yellow paper, hand-typed on both sides, sent out every month to regular readers of *The Carlekemp Times* and to all friends of Fort Augustus. The main purpose of the *Fort Augustus News* was to focus on former Carlekempians at the Abbey. Its tone was more informal than *The Corbie*'s had been and its articles much shorter. One other notable difference was that boys' first names were printed (unlike *The Corbie*, which always used initials only).

There were now 34 boys from Carlekemp in the senior houses at Fort Augustus. At Easter, Martin Chilver-Stainer was offered a place in the British 'B' Ski Team for the next Winter Olympics. Fr Robert McKenzie was the Abbey's delegate to the General Chapter of the English Benedictine Congregation and had also been elected secretary of the Commission for Monastic Renewal.

A new self-service cafeteria system in the School Refectory had solved the problem of keeping food hot in transit from the kitchen. Now the food was piping hot and almost unlimited in quantity. The men behind this scheme were Fr Edward and Fr Francis (who had been head boy both at Carlekemp and Fort Augustus).

There were now four Rugby teams at the Fort – the First XV, the Colts, the J-Colts and the Juniors. To date the First XV had played three and won two.

So far the weather had not been kind to outdoor activities.

In spite of near-arctic winds and fresh snow, the Hill-Walking Club had attempted two expeditions, one up Garbh Bheinn (2903 ft) in Ardgour, another to the hills around Glen Spean. The Orienteers held their first point-to-point against Lochaber High School. The course was run over two and a half miles of hilly, wooded country. The School won comfortably.

The Combined Cadet Force's work in fieldcraft and weapons instruction continued. The Motor Transport section had recently repaired the old 1-ton truck (which had blown a gasket), but spent most of their time on the Landrover, tuning, re-painting, washing and driving it.

The new boys' first 'three weekly' holiday was an expedition to Loch Buck with Br Adrian who had brought a load of half-cooked potatoes. The boys fully cooked them, finishing off their meal with milk and lemonade. A game of 'kick the can' kept most occupied during the afternoon. Before leaving the camp at 4.30 they ate rice crispies and had Jell-O for dessert.

The first touch of Winter arrived on 29 September when the School woke up to find the surrounding hills covered in snow. Sledges and skis were dragged out of the dungeons and the traditional battles between the Upper and Lower School were waged on the Cricket field.

A 'Riot' was staged on 4 December with the whole of the Senior School taking part. It was organised for the benefit of B Company, 1st Battalion, The Royal Highland Fusiliers who came down from Fort George to subdue the rioters. The idea was to give them some experience of dealing with student demonstrators, a situation they might have to face when they went to Northern Ireland in the New Year.

The area used for the exercise was the lower drive and engine house. All the roadways and buildings were given new names. The Church became 'Unity Flats' (from the roof of which some snipers opened fire on the advancing troops and temporarily halted them) and the Gym was made into a 'Gospel Mission'.

All sorts of missiles were used – flour bombs, water bombs, old and rotten fruit and vegetables. In a fierce battle many rioters were captured, put into 'cages', searched, interrogated and finally released. During the holidays the national press printed articles on the 'Riot'.

By December the fortunes of the Rugby XV had declined. There were defeats against Keil School, Aberdeen Grammar, Inverness Academy and Gordonstoun, relieved by a 17-0 victory against Glenalmond 2nds. Lochaber Rugby Club were also beaten 27-0.

George Bernard Shaw's three-act play 'Arms and the Man' was

performed at Christmas. The third act was later put on at the Youth Drama Festival in Inverness.

On 23 December Fr Benedict Seed sailed for New Zealand, where he was to take up a temporary teaching post in South Island. This experiment of monks diversifying their activities outwith the monastery had been given official recognition by the Second Vatican Council and the decisions of the General Chapter. He would be sadly missed as, apart from teaching Physics, Biology and Maths, he administered the Abbey *policies* (grounds) and tended the bees, as well as brewing a very acceptable beer. His place on the staff was taken by Dr Ian Campbell, a former lecturer in Biochemistry at Manchester University who had come up with his family from Hong Kong. Soon after his arrival, he formed a Science Club.

Since September, Peter Haworth and Selby Macduff-Duncan had been organising and running the Village Cub Scout pack. The School Matron, Mrs Blake-Mahon, had revived the local troop and helped them put on a Nativity play at Christmas. Jamie Edgar and Mike Christopher provided backing for the songs.

In spite of the School having been vaccinated against the flu during the first term, by January about 70 boys had suffered one type of infection or another. The Staff had not escaped either. When Matron succumbed, Fr Chrysostom stood in, but was soon himself confined to bed for nearly a week.

Five boys were present with Abbot Nicholas and Fr Mark at the inaugural meeting of the Friends of Fort Augustus held at Turnbull Hall, Glasgow on 23 January. About 180 were present, many Old Boys and parents. Fr Mark spoke of the gradual expansion at Fort Augustus over the previous two decades and of the desirability of boys from Catholic Clydeside increasing in number in the same proportion as boys from the rest of Scotland.

Arts Council tours continued to visit the School. Late in January the great-grandson of the poet William Wordsworth gave a solo performance drawn from the letters, diaries and poetry of the Wordsworth circle. In February the tiny Mull Theatre presented a triple-bill of one act plays. On another occasion the Figaro Ensemble played quartets and trios by Handel and Britten.

Old Boy Hugh Shannon was ordained priest by Cardinal Gray on 21 February. On leaving Fort Augustus, where he had distinguished himself on the sports field and in theatrical pursuits, Hugh decided to spend a year teaching in Africa. It was the time of the Congo crisis and he and his friends became involved in an incident on the border of Katanga which could have had nasty consequences. After being held in custody by the Congolese, they were all released and travelled home overland via the Sahara in a Landrover. Shortly after his return, Hugh decided to train for the priesthood at St Andrew's College, Drygrange, under Mgr John Barry.

The Hockey First XI had a very successful season, winning all their matches, with an aggregate of 41 goals for and only 7 against. Nevertheless, playing against the Picts (the Scottish International Touring XI), they were beaten 7-1.

Six boys played in the first Scottish Schoolboys Trial; three were chosen for the final Trial – Paul Greco, Graham Lumsden and William Chapman.

On 21 March the Choral Society joined with the Inverness Academy Choir to sing Vivaldi's '*Gloria*' and Mozart's '*Requiem*' in the Old High Church, Inverness. The following afternoon they gave a performance of the two works in the Abbey Church.

The School was buzzing with new activities. A Youth Club was formed, with Abbot Nicholas and Fr Vincent on the committee. Some of the senior boys were helping with the construction of a fireplace in their new quarters, and painting and decorating. At the first meeting of the Science Club, before more than 40 members, Frank Partridge gave a very interesting talk. A new ski slope was discovered within a mile of the School which gave excellent conditions for the shorter afternoons.

Unhappily, few Old Boys came to the Easter Retreat led by Fr Francis who took as his theme 'The basic Christian attitude of faith, hope and love in the modern world'. There was a similar lack of response to the Easter Sunday lunch.

At the end of April, members of the CCF took part in a night exercise aimed at testing their skills in concealment, patrolling and laying and breaking ambushes. The final phase involved crossing a minefield in the dark by following white tapes laid at 100 yard intervals, while the landscape was periodically lit up with parachute flares.

After a long illness, Br Hugh Shields died on 15 April. He had come to Fort Augustus in 1921 and was one of the founder members of St Anselm's Abbey in Washington DC. He would be remembered principally as a printer and photographer; and his wide knowledge and long experience of running the Abbey Press at Fort Augustus had brought him into contact with the printing trade throughout the UK. He was a friendly figure and a man of prayer.

On a happier note, Alan Grisewood (1948-54) was ordained a priest on 14 March.

For some years the boys had been able to take driving lessons locally. Now the number was snowballing and instructors were coming down regularly from Inverness on Wednesday afternoons.

In the last week of April the SCE exams began. There were 150 presentations at Higher Grade and 200 at Ordinary. Five senior boys enrolled with Wolsey Hall, Oxford to learn Italian by correspondence.

The School had again joined forces with Inverness Academy, this time to put on Mozart's opera, 'Così fan tutte'. The cast of 22 included Richard Lanni as Gulielmo and Mike Christopher understudying Ferrando. The production was a great success, the *Fort Augustus News* critic describing it as 'possibly the most successful ever seen in the School theatre, including those staged by visiting professional companies'.

After their exams were over, Steve Connolly and Johnnie Doyle filled in two days with some useful work around the grounds. The scorer's box in the Pavilion received a much-needed coat of paint and, when the weather was fine, they also painted the crosses in the monks' cemetery.

Four boys were entered for the Lochaber Junior piping competition. Patrick Grant won the Highland Homespun Challenge Cup for Strathspey and Reel.

Seven Cricket matches in all were played. In the first of the season the School beat Inverness Academy by 17 runs. Vaughan won the House Match by six wickets.

In Athletics it was a little difficult to adjust the records without a great deal of mental arithmetic. Frank Partridge swept the board in the Second Set (under $16\frac{1}{2}$), recording the best times in the 800 and 1500 metres and winning the Dunskey and Holman Cups for these open events.

Forty-three Old Boys attended the Annual Reunion on 27-28 June. Golf and Tennis were played on the Saturday afternoon but, in the Cricket match on Sunday, they were soundly beaten by the School.

The Annual CCF Inspection was conducted by Colonel P. G. Thompson from the Ministry of Defence. The Guard, drawn up on the front lawn, was commanded by Under Officer M. A. P. Grant who was later presented with the Sword of Honour as Senior Cadet. After the parade and march past, Colonel Thompson saw the training groups, including the Naval Section working in boats, the Fire Cadre putting out a burning 'house', and the Signals and Advanced Infantry setting up communications by radio and telephone and destroying a tank.

Around this time, nearly £1000 was raised for the homeless by the Shelter 'Round Britain' Walk. Over 100 boys walked some part of the 66 mile stretch between Inverness and Fort William. The total walked in the two days amounted to 2699 miles – the Headmaster and Fr Robert also being sponsored, and the whole event being organised by the Matron.

Cardinal Gordon Gray distributed the prizes on 8 July. In the morning he was received at the Church door by Under-Officer M. A. P. Grant. The procession into the Church for the sung Mass was headed by the Pipe Band. During Mass the choir led the singing at the Offertory, and rendered Britten's 'Hymn to St Peter'.

In the Assembly Hall Fr Mark spoke of the expansion of 'A' Level work in the Sixth Form over the previous year. Adam Dabrowski had gained a Grade A in French and 14 other 'A' Level passes were obtained. At the universities, Fort Augustus was well represented. Ninian Blackburn had gained First Class Honours in Chemistry at Dundee while, at St Andrews, John Robinson was taking a postgraduate course after obtaining a First in Medieval History.

The Prize Day concert consisted of musical items including Spirituals sung by the tenors and basses, and a performance of Benjamin Britten's 'The Golden Vanity'.

Four sporting trophies were won by Frank Partridge (including the Scholes Cup for Batting, Dunskey Cup for 1500 metres and a special award for the best time in the Cross Country).

Fourteen senior cadets from the Army Section spent a fortnight in Germany with the British Army on the Rhine. This included a three-day exercise at Minden and at a camp on the shores of the Edersee. The Naval Section spent some days at Loch Ewe.

Fr Andrew McKillop, after well over 30 years teaching in the School, went as chaplain to the nuns of Stanbrook Abbey. He replaced Fr Aidan Duggan, who returned to Fort Augustus as parish priest and to teach Spanish and Religious Knowledge (later, in December 1970, he would become Novice Master). In July Mr Hunkin and Dr Campbell left. Fr Francis replaced Mr Hunkin in the English Department, while Mr Gavine had taken over the Geography from Fr Andrew and would also take Biology for the lower Forms.

Over the last weekend of September the Monster Folk Festival was held at Fort Augustus. The Cricket pitch was used for the Sunday afternoon concert, but was anything but crowded, thus allaying the fears in some quarters that the Village and Abbey would be swamped by visitors.

Eight boys with First XV experience returned for the Rugby season. After a soft defeat 19-9 by Gordonstoun, the team had a decisive 33-0 victory against Inverness Academy. Against Keil they were beaten 16-3. Lovat won the House match 12-0.

In Hockey, five Old Boys and two present boys were selected for the district XIs. J. Doyle and G. Lumsden were chosen to play for Highland.

On 10 October Perth Repertory presented Tolstoy's 'War and Peace'. The setting was imaginatively designed with a sloping fore-stage jutting out into the auditorium, flanked by two towers. By all standards it was a memorable evening, with the battle scenes performed like armchair generals – with models.

A new once-a-term publication concocted by Francis Eves and Frank Partridge was in the process of preparation. Described as a 'compote', it was to contain articles on any subject. It would be targeted at the 'Establishment', with a certain amount of lively comment.

Mr Gavine launched a new Astronomical Society. The star-gazers were hoping for clear nights and used the tower for mounting their telescopes, hoping to see meteorites and even the *Aurora Borealis*. Mr Gavine had converted the IVB classroom into a Geography room, relieving the boredom of 'preps' by showing films and slides. Charts on the walls showed various rock formations and typical landscapes.

At the mid-term five-day break on 29 October, 16 boys remained in the School. Of these, eight went with Fr Vincent to the Kinlocharkaig bothy for three days.

Meanwhile, Fr Chrysostom had gathered a large piping class from the local population. Sergeant Mackillop of the Queen's Own Highlanders visited once a week and the battalion sent up a piper and drummer later in the month to stay for a week. The School was very grateful for this support from the Regiment now based in Edinburgh, the next commanding officer of which was to be Lieutenant Colonel J. C. R. Hopkinson, an Old Boy of the Priory while it was at Fort Augustus.

During October the rainfall was close on nine inches. In neighbouring Glen Shiel the monthly total was 23 inches. The pitches were hardly dry before the next great deluge. Even the Hydro Board complained.

A Guard of Honour paraded on Remembrance Sunday at the Village War Memorial. It was a very wet and windy morning, but it was the first time a joint service had been held, the prayers and readings being shared by the Revd Mr Hugh Gillies and Fr Aidan Duggan.

Oscar Wilde's 'The Importance of Being Earnest' was performed before a large and responsive audience on 14 December, the last night of term. Produced by Mr Quinn, with sets designed by Fr Vincent, painted by Mr Owen and stage-managed by Fr Edward, the play starred Fergus Brown and Bill Butchart as Algy and Jack, with Sjoerd Vogt as Gwendolen and David Lyon as Lady Bracknell. The costumes were made for less than £6! A fortnight earlier the international Scottish mime artist, Lindsay Kemp, visited with 'The Turquoise Pantomine'.

Despite the appalling weather only two fixtures had to be cancelled. The Rugby XV, having already defeated Inverness Academy in two games, won the Ness Trophy. Later, Lochaber defeated the School 26-9, avenging a thrashing they had received earlier in the season.

The *blaes* pitch was marked for Hockey, but the weather, turning frosty, prevented any games being played. Johnnie Doyle, Graham Lumsden, Willie Chapman and Johnnie Murray all represented Highland District at the Baxter Cup Tournament. Although Highland were knocked out early, this was an honour for the four boys.

The New Year brought in some of the mildest weather ever experienced in the Highlands. There had not been one sign of Winter in Fort Augustus since the early snows on Ben Tigh way back in October.

Early in January the 43 year old Abbot Primate of the Benedictine Federation, Abbot Rembert Weakland, came from Rome to visit Fort Augustus for the first time. Having celebrated an evening Mass for the School on 12 January, he talked to the boys who discovered that not only was he a gifted musician but had also been a star ice-hockey player.

New to the staff was Mr H. M. Bryce, Head of the Maths department. He replaced Mr Palmer who had been at the School for 18 years. His son was one of the five new boys who entered the School in January.

Two Hockey matches had been played. One, against Highland, was drawn; the other, against RAF Kinloss, was a win (3-2). Over mid-term the School goalkeeper, Willie Chapman, was invited to play for the

Home Scots against a combined Universities XI at Perth. Two further wins were registered against Dunrobin (11-0) and Gordonstoun (4-2). Willie Chapman and Graham Lumsden played in the Scottish School-boys' Hockey XI (of which Old Boy Paul Greco was the Captain).

Eighteen new Old Boys had joined the Association. A very distinguished Old Boy, 90 year old Fr John Lane Fox, had fully recovered from a broken hip and stubbornly refused to use his stick. The Old Boys' Committee had decided to add their own (second) page at the end of *The Carlekemp Times.*

In February the long-awaited Youth Club was finally opened. Performing the honours was Dr Ronnie Kirton, the former School doctor, who drove up from Wales. Already nearly two dozen from the Fourth Form and above had joined and the total membership of 12 to 20 year olds from Fort Augustus and district exceeded 80 in number.

Two CCF activity weekends had already taken place. In early March there was some excitement when the local police (whom the CO had forgotten to warn) began prowling around looking for deer poachers, as a report had gone out that six men with blackened faces and carrying rifles had been seen in the vicinity.

The Pipes and Drums featured in *The Press and Journal* with a front page photo of Fr Chrysostom and Sergeant MacKillop with the Band in the background. There was also a lengthy article about the 'Piping Monk'.

In March two boys brought the School into the public gaze. David Lyon, Head Boy and Senior Under-Officer in the CCF, was selected to represent UK Cadets in Canada, spending a month in the Rockies. David also had a scholarship to Sandhurst. Although still at School, Willie Chapman had been selected as reserve goalkeeper in the Scotland versus Ireland Men's Hockey International. With no more Hockey matches to be played, the School XI had once again completed an unbeaten season – the fourth in a row!

On 13 March the combined Academy and School Choirs performed Haydn's 'Nelson Mass' in the Ness Bank Church, Inverness and repeated the programme the next day at Fort Augustus.

Because of Fr Fabian Duggan's departure from Carlekemp to visit his ageing mother in Australia, Fr Robert had gone to North Berwick to replace him. Fr Chrysostom had relinquished charge of Lovat and been appointed to Junior House, while Fr Francis had now replaced him as Housemaster of Lovat.

The Hockey season came to an end with a superb display of open play by the School XI which won them the championship in the annual Quadrangular Tournament between Aberdeen Grammar School FPs, Western, Highland, and the School.

After a poor start the Cricket team's standard of play improved. Nevertheless they lost three, drew two and won only two.

On 27 June a televised Mass was broadcast with Fr Robert as narrator (operating with a monitor in the Chapter House). A 'Songs of Praise' programme was recorded the same day for nationwide viewing some weeks after. It featured Fr Mark linking the hymns. In both programmes Fr Gregory was the organist and Fr Vincent the choirmaster. A third programme recorded was a 'Meeting Point' between Abbot Nicholas and Fr William Anderson of the BBC. This was filmed in the entrance to the church and in front of St Andrew's Chapel.

About 50 Old Boys came for the annual Reunion. At the meeting Abbot Nicholas welcomed the opportunity to inform them that Fort Augustus was running smoothly on its course of service to God and Man through prayer and the two Schools.

Shortly before the new term began, acting parish priest Fr Bernard Sole was on his way to visit at Invermoriston when he was knocked off his scooter and suffered severe head injuries. He was quickly transferred to the intensive care unit at Raigmore. Fr Edmund Carruth was appointed to care for the parishes of Fort Augustus and Invermoriston.

Old Boys were saddened to hear of the sudden and tragic deaths in a car accident of Anthony Herraghty (1964-68) and Louis Caira (1964-70). It happened near Cullen, Banffshire on the evening of 22 September. The funeral took place at St Peter's, Buckie. Anthony was a gifted violinist studying music at the Royal College, while Louis was about to start a course in textile designing at Galashiels.

As the School matches were later in the term than usual, the Rugby XV played a number of friendly games. They were beaten 32-0 by Lochaber and 27-8 by Orkney RFC. A win by one point followed against Keil; then a 15-13 defeat by Inverness Academy.

Activities proliferated. New less formal discussion groups called 'Forum' met under the chairmanship of Fr Francis and Mr Haines. Mr Gavine and the Astronomy Club went star-gazing in a planetarium ingeniously constructed from old egg boxes with special torches to simulate the Northern Lights and meteorites. Their next project was a new four-foot telescope. Mr Gavine also ran the Archery Club; Mr Bryce attracted a good following to the Bridge Club, while Fr Chrysostom organised regular Band practices, and Mr Quinn was in process of directing a play.

The CCF managed to construct a ski slope beyond the junior Rugby field. Then a Territorial Army Unit from Stirling arrived to level an area behind the Village Hall for a car park and playing field.

The XV managed to beat Rannoch 13-12 thanks to a fine penalty goal by Butchart. They then lost to Gordonstoun 10-11; against Rubislaw (formerly Aberdeen Grammar) they lost 3-15 and then 4-33 against Gosforth Grammar School, Newcastle. Inverness Academy first came out on top 4-26, but in a second match were beaten 12-3.

The School Secretary, Miss Pam Turner, was seriously injured in an accident early in December. Tragically Mrs Hilda Johnson (mother of Chris in Form Two), who was also involved, later died.

Terence Rattigan's 'The Winslow Boy' was given one performance. Willie Beaton played Arthur Winslow convincingly; Bill Butchart's fine voice and ease of manner was especially effective in the cross-examination scene at the end of Act One. 'His words probed and pierced with rapier-like precision ....'

In January 1972 there were misgivings about some old habits in the School:

> *In the sewing room Cathie* [Sanach] *is forever lengthening and repairing, and one wonders if the time has not come to do away with trunks (which are the product of an earlier age when the railways collected and delivered very much faster than they do today) and substitute suitcases in their place?*

The First Hockey XI maintained their unbeaten record with a 4-2 win against Gordonstoun and a 1-0 against Highland.

Fr Chrysostom's classroom took on the appearance of a wartime plane-spotting lecture room. Aeroplanes of all types were suspended from the ceiling, the output of the Junior House.

Sadly, on 13 January Fr Bernard Sole died as a result of the road accident the previous September. Born in 1904 in Oxfordshire, he was educated at Douai and then came to Fort Augustus at the age of 18. As a student he went to the USA and was a founder member of St Anselm's Abbey in Washington DC and of Portsmouth Abbey, Rhode Island. He returned to Fort Augustus in 1929 and was ordained the following year. In the years leading up to the War he played an important part in the electrification of the organ.

During the War he served with the Army throughout the Burma Campaign. For years after his return his familiar figure topped by a wide 'burma' hat would be seen in his boat ('The Burma Star') as he waited patiently for the next trout to take the worm.

In these years he was organist and choirmaster and served locally on parish duties. He also composed a number of well-known hymns. In Stratherrick he was greatly loved, having worked there for nearly ten years.

In the middle of January, Br Patrick Cullen died suddenly and unexpectedly. He first came to Fort Augustus through Abbot McDonald's Glasgow Fair retreats – at that time he was working in the mines near Hamilton. Although he suffered from asthma for most of his life, he had once hoped to become a missionary priest like his brother. He was professed in 1928, working in the Hospice, the Printing Office, the Kitchen and, latterly, the Sacristy.

At the end of May 1972, Fr Mark Dilworth relinquished the post of Headmaster to take up a research fellowship at Edinburgh University. Fr Francis Davidson (who had studied at the University of Fribourg and had taught in the School for several years), succeeded him. Fr Francis had been head boy of both Carlekemp and Fort Augustus and was one of the first Scottish Schoolboy Hockey Internationalists produced by the School. On the Cricket field he had been a bowler of deadly accuracy.

Following the end of the SCE exams, the Geographers were busy surveying the School buildings and the raised beach around Fort Augustus with leveller and theodolite. The Biologists were studying the bug pond. Others were making a detailed study of mountain flora. In the afternoons, Orienteering proved a popular activity.

The wintry Summer did no justice either to Athletics or Cricket. There were no outstanding individual achievements, but a new record was set up by the Lovat Relay Team. Lovat also won the Athletics Championship.

Only two Cricket matches were won, with three defeats and three draws. After Vaughan had knocked up a modest 58, Lovat, who had the Inter-House Championship at stake, failed to close the gap by only 4 runs.

The Annual CCF Inspection was taken on 16 June by Colonel Stewart of HQ Scotland. The Beating of Retreat by the Pipes and Drums received great applause. David Lyon (1967-71), who was then an Officer Cadet at Sandhurst, came for the day and acted as ADC to the Inspecting Officer.

After a long illness bravely borne, Fr Ninian Macdonald died very peacefully on the morning of 18 May. A native of Fort Augustus, he was educated at the Abbey School and after the First World War (in which he served as a chaplain both in France and Italy) he was seconded to the Foreign Office Diplomatic Authority, whose particular mission at that time concerned the 'Fiume Problem' on the Italy-Yugoslavia border.

Fr Ninian served with great distinction and was sent on a further mission to Upper Silesia by the Plebiscite Commission.

On his return to Fort Augustus in 1923, he was appointed Headmaster of the newly re-opened School. Fr Ninian was a great Shinty fan, an authority who wrote a history of the game.

In the 1930s he went to the USA, returning after the War to become a chaplain at Kilgraston School. He retired from that post in 1967 and came back to Fort Augustus. Fr Ninian's charm would never be forgotten and his wit was there right to the end.

At the end of June, St Columba's, the tiny Catholic school which lay in the Abbey grounds close by the swing bridge across the Canal, closed down after nearly a century's use. The children were now catered for in the Primary Department of the Junior Secondary School. The Headmistress, Miss Brown, was transferred to Beauly. The buildings were offered to the School and were being altered to accommodate the Music and Art Departments.

Over 50 Old Boys came for the Annual Reunion on 1 July. Only 24, however, attended the AGM. In his welcoming address, Abbot Nicholas emphasised that only thoughtful and regular prayer would increase the size of the Community and suggested this was the best thing Old Boys could do for their *Alma Mater.*

On 17 August, after a short illness, Fr Philip Hynes died. Abbot Celestine was with him at the time. Fr Philip was Chaplain to the Benedictine Nuns at Talacre. Fr Maurus Whitehead (who had undergone a major operation on his hips in September but was already walking again) would succeed him as Chaplain when he was fully recovered.

Br Bill Bruening from California entered as a postulant in early September. He had been studying at Drygrange previously. Fr Aidan Duggan returned to Fort Augustus in early October after a year in Australia and had resumed his position as parish priest as well as teaching in the School.

In the Autumn Fr Benedict Seed returned after two years' teaching in New Zealand and was immediately appointed Housemaster of Lovat.

He took up teaching Maths and Chemistry and his interest in bee-keeping, wine-making and climatology was reawakened.

Mr Perry came to join him on the Science side (Chemistry and Biology) as Mr Duffy had left after twelve years at the School. In the French Department Mrs Pottage replaced Mr Quinn, who had also left in the Summer. Shortly after, Fr Chrysostom took three months' leave to visit his parents in Australia. Mr Gavine temporarily took over as Junior House Housemaster. On the Games side came Mr Trigg, who had lived in the Village in 1967 and was a former International Badminton coach.

In the first fixture of the Rugby season, the First XV beat Inverness Academy 56-18. Against Keil, the following weekend, they were thrashed 30-4.

The Rugby XV played five, won two and lost three. Points for were 108 and against 89. There were now seven teams – 1st XV, 2nd XV, Colts XV, Junior Colts A, Junior Colts B, Mini Colts, Puppy Colts. The most successful team of all was the Colts XV which played 4 and won 4, with 145 points for and only 38 against.

In spite of the appalling weather, the School's production of 'The Long and the Short and the Tall' attracted a large audience. Directed by Mr Holland and Miss Cameron, 'it was good drama competently performed'. Marco Coppola and Stephen McRory played their parts convincingly, while Hamish Johnston Stewart's patriotic Scotsman and Charles Greenwood's dumb Japanese prisoner were finely acted.

On 21 February Fr Peter Walter died. Born at Staines, Middlesex in 1891, he studied at an Anglican training college and then worked at giving missions for some time. In 1922 he left the Anglican ministry and was received into the Catholic Church. The following year he came to Fort Augustus as a student, being ordained in 1930. At the request of Archbishop McDonald, he was given charge of the parish of Haddington, remaining there until 1934. He was at Workington for two years and at St Anne's, Edghill from 1936 to the outbreak of War. He served as an Army Chaplain during the War and then spent the rest of his life on the English Benedictine Congregation mission. On demobilisation he was appointed to St Augustine's, Liverpool, where he remained for 16 years until moved to St Anne's, Ormskirk in 1961. Here he worked until ill-health made his return to the Abbey necessary. The Community would always remember his unfailing courage in the face of increasing paralysis. He was a zealous priest, greatly loved by his parishioners.

For the Old Boys, the death of Iain Sidgwick (1954–58) as a result of a car accident on 4 December was a tragic event, received with great sorrow.

For the previous two years the Sunday Mass had been enlivened by the singing of the Choral Society. Since the installation of amplifiers a greater unity of sound had been achieved.

On the Loch there was increased activity. The CCF had taken delivery of a 26 foot Motor Cutter, a gift from the Navy. It was beautifully fitted out with an illuminated nameplate atop the after cockpit which proudly read 'FORT AUGUSTUS'.

Archery went from strength to strength with the indoor range in frequent use. Mr Perry took Third Form small bore shooting on two afternoons. The Gun Club had acquired a second clay pigeon trap of some antiquity.

The School's first Old Girl had by now gone to university. Fiona MacDonald was now at Loughborough reading Sociology.

After seven years of faithful service to the School, Mrs Gloria Blake-Mahon retired at Christmas 1974. In her place came Miss M. Scanlin, whose nursing career had included periods of Voluntary Aid Nursing overseas.

In December Robert Bolt's 'The Thwarting of Baron Bolligrew' was presented by the Drama Society. Michael McCullough played the hero, Sir Oblong Fitz Oblong. Mr Holland produced and Fr Vincent provided the costumes. As usual Fr Edward was stage manager, with special effects by Mr Perry. Makeup was by Mr Gavine and Mr MacDonald.

The Hockey XI lost their first match against Highland Hockey Club 7-0 and the second 3-2. Against Inverleith Hockey Club (Edinburgh) they lost 4-1.

On 7 January Fr John Lane Fox died, just short of his 94th birthday. During the First World War he received the Military Cross after having been mentioned in dispatches by Winston Churchill. He also received a military decoration from the French Government.

In December 1973 David Grugan completed his postulancy and was clothed in the monastic habit. It was the first time in many years that a Scotsman had been clothed. Br Peter Bruening completed his Novitiate and made his religious profession in February 1974.

On 23 February the former Aberdeen Grammar School, now Rubislaw Academy, came to Fort Augustus with an unbeaten record. After an excellent game the Aberdonians were beaten 3-2. Next it was Gordonstoun's turn to be beaten (3-1) and then the Old Boys were defeated 2-1. Finally, Gordon's College were beaten 4-1. Michael Chapman and Paul Couttie took part in the Scottish Schoolboys Final Trial. Michael Chapman was selected. In May the School was host to Highland, Western and Aberdeen Grammar School FP Hockey Clubs for the third Annual Hockey Tournament.

During the first half of the Summer term, nine boys from Form Two organised themselves into a film production unit under the guidance of the Art Master, Mr William Owen. The film was to be a comedy which related the experiences of a new boy arriving at a school 'somewhere in the Scottish Highlands'. The boys hoped that the film, which was in colour, would have a synchronised sound track. David McSherry played the leading role.

Br Ignatius McNairn died on 15 May. Abbot Nicholas and members of the Community were called to his room and recited prayers for the dying. He had been an electrician before entering the monastery and continued to perform this duty for many years. He was buried in the Abbey cemetery, the School providing bearers, servers and pipers.

During the Summer term two classes, totalling more than 40 boys, took advantage of the tennis courts and enrolled for lessons. Enthusiasm was so high that two Tennis tournaments were held, with a cup and medallion trophy presented by the parents of a member of the monastic Community.

The Cricket XI beat Inverness Academy by four wickets after 21 overs. Against Gordonstoun they were 42 all out in reply to the former's 150 for 5 (declared). However, the School beat the Old Boys by 7 wickets! The House Match was won by Vaughan.

Lieutenant-General Sir Chandos Blair, General Officer Commanding the Army in Scotland, was the Inspecting Officer on 14 June. The exercise that year was 'Jack Tar', a demonstration of the withdrawal by sea of the beleaguered flank of an expeditionary force. The River Tarff was the base of operations for the naval rescue.

On 16 June the monastic Community and boys from the School made the Holy Year Pilgrimage to Pluscarden Abbey. About a mile before reaching Pluscarden, the Fort Augustus party disembarked from buses to walk the final distance along the Pilgrim's Way. They formed a procession with the thurifer, acolytes and crossbearer in front followed by pipers.

Sixty-eight year old Br Joseph McAuley, who had just celebrated his Golden Jubilee of monastic life, died suddenly on 28 May while on holiday in Bedford. Br Joseph was a 'jack of all trades' – carpenter, baker, mechanic, chauffeur, and he worked in the printing Press. He was a lynchpin among the Brothers and very important for their morale. His body was brought back to the Abbey for burial and the School provided readers and pall-bearers for the funeral.

A new literary publication, *FUG 320*, was compiled by the boys under the co-editorship of Michael Lombardi and Hubert Lorin.[1] The articles and cartoons were contributed during the course of the year and the financial backing came from paid advertisements supplied by local merchants. Three hundred copies were produced and the publication paid for itself. Some of the profits were kept for the next issue and the remainder used for buying new books for the Library.

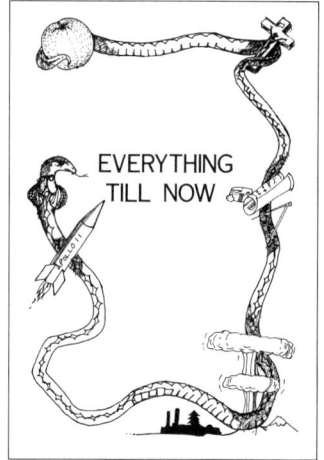

EVERYTHING TILL NOW

CHAPTER 17

The Abbey School
1974-78

WITH the beginning of the Autumn of 1974 many new faces were seen. The School had increased its numbers to 145 with boys and girls coming from every part of the world. Seventeen boys and three girls joined Junior House.

To cope with this influx, several innovations were made. The East Wing, for long the Sixth Form 'holy of holies', was now shared by Forms Five and Six, with every room in use. The dormitories had additional bunk beds and mattresses to help deal with the sleeping arrangements for the rest of the School.

There was also a new member of staff. Mr Charles Court was the new English Master and coached the Colts Rugby team. In addition, he held the rank of 2nd Lieutenant in the Army Section of the CCF.

As usual, School activities flourished, like the Pipe Band, Archery, Astronomy and the Film Club (8 mm movies). The Gun Club increased its membership; six members travelled to Comrie for a weekend shoot as guests of the Davenports. Although the grouse were fairly wild, $8\frac{1}{2}$ brace were taken as well as 21 hares. Mrs MacPherson, the School cook, made a superb game pie which the Club enjoyed for supper one night.

The CCF had its annual camp in Germany with the Queen's Own Highlanders. Six Senior Cadets also took part in a Royal Artillery Presentation in Edinburgh, staying the night at Redford Barracks. At the Junior Army Orienteering Championships in Peebleshire, Alexander Hay achieved the second best individual time.

The Rugby XV beat Inverness Academy 18-16 in a hard-fought game. The 2nd XV (the 'Tigers') beat Inverness 18-10, while the Junior Colts also won 20-8. They were beaten by Keil 18-10, but beat Gordonstoun 18-8 and lost 29-13 to Rubislaw Academy. In November the XV were beaten 30-17 by Rannoch and 18-14 by Inverness Academy. The Rugby House match was a 13-13 draw.

Old Boys learnt with regret of the death of Fr Hamilton ('Hammy'). Many attended his funeral Mass at St Mary's Cathedral, Edinburgh and heard Cardinal Gray describe him 'as man who wouldn't give up, who never gave in'.

Early in November, Fr Francis was elected to the Society of Head-masters of Independent Schools. This was a recognition of the development which had occurred over the past few years, both in numbers and in the academic and other facilities provided.

James Bridie's 'The Anatomist' was presented by the Drama Society on 11 December. It told the gory tale of body-snatchers Burke and Hare. Richard Bryce as Dr Robert Knox was superb. Sheena MacDonald as Mary Paterson added life to the play by her very good singing and acting. William Burke was played with sinister emphasis by Sjoerd Vogt. The play was presented to the public on 21 January. Mr William Owen and members of the Film Society made a series of film excerpts.

On 8 December Br Aelred Grugan made his religious profession in the Abbey Church. It was the first time in many years that a native Scotsman had joined the Community. Br Aelred had taken over the duties of Master of Ceremonies and was also in charge of training the boys for serving at the altar and reading.

On 8 January 1975, in Yorkshire, Abbot Oswald Eaves died of an aortic aneurysm after a happy Christmas visit to his relatives in Preston and to his old friend, Bishop Wheeler of Leeds. He took ill when with Bishop Wheeler, who immediately anointed him. Then Fr Michael Conlin (the Bishop's secretary and an Old Boy of Fort Augustus) rushed him to hospital. An Old Boy of Saint Andrew's Priory, Edinburgh, Br Casimir (Alistair Fegan, Prior at Scorton, Yorkshire and a Nursing Brother) was praying beside him when he died.

The Choir of the Church could scarcely contain the number of people who came to pay their last respects. Bishop Wheeler was present, along with the Abbots of Nunraw and Pluscarden and Abbot Celestine. The Bishop of Stockholm was represented by the Provincial of the Passionists in Sweden. Diocesan priests and monks from Ampleforth and Pluscarden filled the choir stalls. Among the mourners in the nave was Mother Agnes and friends from Karlstadt. One of them commented that Abbot Oswald 'had done more for the Church in Sweden than people in this country would ever realise'.[1]

The Requiem Mass was celebrated with the entire School attending, as well as many of Abbot Oswald's friends and relations. The homily was given by Fr Anselm Richardson, a life-long friend who had been Prior during his abbacy. Fr Anselm spoke very quietly and sincerely. A pin might have been heard to drop – so great and profound was the silence in the crowded Church.

Boys of the School served at the Mass. At the Offertory the School Choir sang a Russian Anthem in four parts. After Mass the monks sang the *'Libera me'* and absolution was given by Abbot Nicholas. Then six schoolboys carried the coffin on their shoulders as the Choir sang *'In paradisum'*.

The wind and rain died down to allow the congregation to move outside when he was buried in the monastic cemetery at the edge of the Loch. Sjoerd Vogt played a lament on the pipes and boys lowered the coffin into the ground. Bishop Wheeler sprinkled the grave and coffin with holy water.

In a long letter circulated to friends, Fr Thomas McLaughlin later pointed out that Abbot Oswald had had a distinguished career in the School, being a Prefect, Captain of Rugby, *Victor Ludorum,* Assistant Scout Master and a member of Fr Luke's Orchestra. *The Benedictine Yearbook* (1976) commented that 'Abbot Oswald's natural gifts were social – energy, enthusiasm and a sympathetic interest in his fellow men'.

In the School, Mountain Rescue activities continued under the guidance of Mr Haines. One group was making a classroom study of Mountain Rescue, learning skills such as map and compass work, snow climbing and acquiring a sound knowledge of the surrounding country-side. On 8 and 9 March the advanced group enjoyed two profitable days of rock climbing and stretcher-lowering with boys from Rannoch School.

The Hockey XI beat Highland HC 3-1, and RAF Lossiemouth 2-1, but were beaten 5-1 by Rubislaw Academy. In Athletics, under the careful eye of Mr Haines, improvements were made in the standards of performance. R. B. W. Milne won the trophy for the best individual performance at the North of Scotland Schoolboy Athletics Champion-ship in Inverness, winning the Senior Long Jump and then breaking the record for the 200 metres with a time of 22.9 seconds. He also broke records in almost every School event (except for the High Jump). T. A. S. Vogt won the 1500 metres in the record time of 4 minutes 34 seconds.

The Cricket XI lost to Inverness Academy after throwing the game away; they gained a time-draw against Gordonstoun and beat Highland CC with a score of 84 for six. The final tally was three victories, three defeats and three draws. Against the Old Boys the School were dismissed for less than 10 runs.

On 1 May, the Abbot President made a visitation of the Monastery. Since January, two monks from Pluscarden Abbey, Brothers Giles and Benedict, had been staying at Fort Augustus to take the Ecclesiastical Studies course. Br Gabriel, the senior member of the Community, celebrated the 52nd anniversary of his Profession on 18 May.

The Fort Augustus Fire Brigade was once again based at the Abbey. The volunteer firemen were Fr Vincent (in charge of the unit), Fr Benedict, and Brs John and Aelred. Br John had served in the Brigade for almost 30 years!

At the end of the Summer term Mr Young, Headmaster of George Watson's, Edinburgh, distributed the prizes. SCE results were excellent: P. J. R. Moore passed six Highers and C. P. Davenport five. Five Sixth Formers had 100% pass rates. K. S. Michelson passed five of his eight 'O' grades with over 90%, as did J. F. H. Greenwood and C. E. Grainger. No boys failed the GCE 'O' Levels.

The Old Boys' Pilgrimage took place at Ampleforth during the first week of September. The Grange Guest house was made available. Fr Vincent and Br Aelred joined the pilgrims and, as this coincided with the Ampleforth Old Boys Society Centenary, all benefited from the additional solemn liturgical celebrations. At Downside, meanwhile, Old Boy Fr Ninian Fair had been appointed Prior.

New members of staff in the School included Mr Angus who had come to teach Chemistry and Biology in place of Mr Perry. Mr Dowling, recently retired as a Headmaster, would also be joining the staff, having already given five boys the chance to go sailing on the Loch with him and Mrs Dowling.

In the School, meanwhile, the Astronomy Society polished its six inch telescope mirror, studied Jupiter's satellites, kept daily weather records and monitored the level of Loch Ness. The old seismograph was in operation again. It recorded the tremors of the Isle of Skye-Kyle of Lochalsh earthslip, the most powerful in the British Isles that year.

Members of the Camera Club pursued the bronze and silver levels of the Duke of Edinburgh awards. Mr Owen gave a preview of the slides which he would use in a new audio-visual programme in his local Highland Museum. An interesting question-and-answer session was held by the well known television documentary producers, Ray Gosling and Nicholas Broomfield.

The School play, Kesselring's 'Arsenic and Old Lace', produced by Mr Michael Liddell, was not the usual Christmas play. It was rehearsed in six weeks – snatched half-hours after games, with a final fortnight of nightly three-hour sessions until 10 pm on an unfinished set, pouring imaginary tea from imaginary teapots into imaginary cups. It was surprising that the end result was so good.

The 30 members of the Ski Club, with four new pairs of skis and sticks, and twice that number of boots, were able to enjoy good sport at Cairngorm and Glencoe.

In view of the new climate of sexual equality, the School authorities at last decided to pay attention to the clamours of the girls at the Abbey. There was now a Music and Movement class once a week (to encourage grace and poise), and a Sewing class. Three of the girls were in the Naval Section of the CCF. Sheena MacDonald ably acted in a very responsible post.

On 11 March the School welcomed Dundee Repertory Theatre to its stage, especially as this meant the return of Nicholas Coppin (1965-67) as Francis Flute in 'A Midsummer Night's Dream', and also the appearance of Maureen Beattie, sister of Paul Beattie (1970) as Hippolyeta and Titania. Special mention must be made of John Scrimger's music, given due prominence by Maureen Beattie's fine singing voice; of Bottom and Flute; and of Charles Nowosielski's Puck, whose acrobatics held the audience in awe.

Among the Old Boys there was news of W. G. Wilberforce (1961-64) who was to be ordained for the diocese of Plymouth on 21 April. Fr Alan Grisewood (1948-54), meanwhile, had written a letter to the School describing his work in Taiwan.

In competitive sport the School had a good year. The First Rugby XV beat a Rannoch Second XV 17-8. The First Hockey XI's school matches were even more successful. They beat Gordonstoun 5-2, Robert Gordon's College 7-0 and Rubislaw Academy 3-2. A. Sabin and S. C. Ross were selected for the final pool for the SSHA International XI. In the Abbey Tournament early in May, against Aberdeen Grammar School FPs, Highland HC and Western HC, the Abbey team won on goal average.

On 18 March, postulant Stuart Hain received the habit and became a novice, taking the name of Br Anthony. The Volunteer Fire Brigade, meanwhile, had already had eight minor outbreaks of fire in 1976. The Secretary of State subsequently awarded Br John Condon the Fire

Brigade Long Service and Good Conduct Medal in recognition of his 30 years' service with the Volunteer Fire Unit at Fort Augustus.

The 1976 Cricket XI drew with Inverness Academy in a game played on a time basis; they lost to Gordonstoun but, with the help of Dr Buchanan, Mr Sabin and Mr MacDonald, they beat Invergordon. In the final part of the term the XI lost to Gordonstoun, drew with the Old Boys, and lost to Northern Counties.

Prizes at the Prize-giving were presented by Sir Donald Cameron of Lochiel, Lord Lieutenant of the County of Inverness. At 11.00 am Mass the choir sang Schubert's 'Mass in G'. The solo parts were sung by Fiona MacDonald (1971-74) and P. J. Murray.

Among Old Boys came news of Jamie Edgar (1966-71) graduating with First Class Honours in Electrical Engineering at Edinburgh and C. G. Ferrard (1961-65), having taken his third degree – First Class Honours in Turkish – also at Edinburgh.

Over 85 Old Boys attended the meeting at Carlekemp in May. Thirty-seven were at the Reunion in July. Tennis, Golf, Cricket and reminiscing were the main activities, though some went water-skiing on Loch Lochy as Angus Macdonald (1950-53) brought up his speedboat and skis.

The standard of Tennis was the highest for many years. The Singles Champion was M. G. Cowling who beat R. de Kervenoael, the former's powerful serve and volley game contrasting with the delicate strokeplay and tactical game of de Kervenoael.

Bishop Michael Foylan of Aberdeen died suddenly on 28 May. Frs Andrew and Mark represented the Community at the funeral in Aberdeen. On 14 July, after an illness of some months, cheerful Cathie Sanach, maid and seamstress, died. She had given 40 years of unstinting service to the School and Community and was missed by all. She was buried in the monastic cemetery after a conventual Mass of Requiem.

The Centenary of the Abbey was celebrated on 14 September. In his commemorative address Abbot Nicholas drew attention to the achievements and aspirations of the Community and the School:

How blessed this Community has been in the quality of its membership .... Their educational work and apostolate has borne fruit the full extent of which is known to God alone .... Now we look forward to a new century .... We can be sure that we will be blessed with our cross and our crown of thorns ....

On 18 October, a half-holiday was enjoyed by the School in honour

---

of the new Scottish saint, John Ogilvie. D. Drummond, whose family had connections with the Ogilvies, was in Rome.

During the holidays the CCF's sailing and motor cutters were taken to Inverness for overhaul and repair. Fr Francis supplied some photographs of local scenes for use in the new air-rifle range in the Archery Hut. By using slides against a metal stop-plate, it was possible to simulate landscapes and targets for training purposes. It was hoped that battle noises could be added with the use of a tape-recorder.

The relatively small, young and injury-ridden First XV were heavily beaten by Rannoch, Inverness Academy and Keil School who fielded extremely strong and physical sides which dealt severe maulings.

On 21 December, at 10.30 pm, the film made the previous year by Ray Gosling and Nicholas Broomfield was screened on all the ITV networks. Not long before, a photographer from the *Radio Times* came to take publicity shots, armed with several Nikon bodies and lenses, which struck the School photographers with envy.

The old red Fire appliance JST 312, which had served the Abbey and district so faithfully since 1963, had now gone to be replaced by a spanking new Bedford with dual horns, revolving blue light and radio. It had already been called out – to a minor road accident three miles beyond Invermoriston.

The School play on 15 December was 'Dial M for Murder', produced by Fr Francis. A packed hall was held from first scene to last, totally involved in the lives of the characters. Mark Cowling as Tony Wendice had an enormous part to play and carried it off with relaxed, professional ease. Andrew Mitchelson and Colin Bryce as Sheila Wendice and Max Halliday were realistic foils. Gavin Johnston Stewart as the Inspector, and Raymond Atkinson as the killer, were very effective.

Within the Monastic Community, Fr Cuthbert Wilson was now resident at the Hospital of St John of God, Scorton in Yorkshire. Fr Edmund Carruth had taken up parish duties at Little Malvern near Worcester. Fr Thomas McLaughlin, who had been suffering from more cardiac trouble, was now resting with relatives in Dumbarton.

In the new year (1977) a group called the Muldoon Jazz Orchestra made the basements echo with music one afternoon in February. The leader was J. C. Steer, who had been composing blues on the piano for some time. Alongside him was A. J. Sabin on the trombone and synthesiser; M. Bell on the guitar; K. Vogt on the Frytol drums, the Pan flutes and the whistle; and K. Mitchelson on French horn and trumpet.[2]

Six boys attended the North of Scotland Schoolboys' Rugby Trial on 16 February. M. Sabin was chosen to captain the under-15 team (he was also a member of the International Hockey squad). The Senior selections would be made later.

The annual School Retreat was held in the third week of March. It was conducted by Fr Brian MacKean, Chaplain at St Andrews University. The personal reconsiderations and taking of stock that a retreat provides were not wholly unsuited to that time in the School calendar: the end of the term which immediately precedes examinations.

The Junior House operated on an independent timetable during the Retreat. Fr Chrysostom organised a pilgrimage to Invergarry Chapel, with everyone contributing something, either in sandwich-making, preparing Mass equipment, or selecting and composing intercessions. Some walked barefoot part of the way (P. Marko and T. Welsh did the whole eight miles). Everyone, however, made the return journey by car.

The two Fifth and Sixth Form syndicates in the Capitaliser Game sponsored by the Bank of Scotland and the Junior Chamber of Commerce suffered mixed fortunes. Syndicate 'A' showed a small profit of £603 from their investment of £20,000; Syndicate 'B' had a much healthier figure of £3,085. The students were also taking part in the Business Decision Game, an exercise which was a computer simulation of a business economy.

The fortunes of the Chess Club continued to fluctuate. Serious thought was given to the purchase of a kettle in order to recover some strays from the coffee-drinking Astronomers.

The Ski Club enjoyed its best year with over 800 man-hours spent on the slopes. M. Mackay and G. Hay were both selected for the team which entered the Army Ski Championships at Aviemore.

In the groups taking the Duke of Edinburgh awards, J. Cottriall and M. Tabona produced a simulated Napoleonic battlefield in their playroom. During the term they had made scenery and painted miniature period soldiers, including cavalry, cannons, French and British infantry and Highlanders.

The Hockey XI scored 22 goals in four matches, beating Robert Gordon's College 5-1, the Old Boys 7-1, Grammarians 3-1 and Rubislaw Academy 9-1. Lovat won the House Match 4-1. Due to a breakdown in communication between the School and the Secretary of the SSHA, A. J. Sabin and J. MacDonald (who had been in it earlier) were not in the final International Pool.

In Rugby, L. Vallot had been selected to play hooker for the senior North of Scotland Schoolboy team. A. J. Sabin (stand-off) was also chosen as Captain of the Under-15 North of Scotland team.

Old Boys were saddened to learn of the death of Francis Cipolato (1949-53) in the USA after a long illness. In the Community, Br David had been seriously ill after complications following an operation. He was now out of danger and making good progress.

Mr Court had founded a Fishing Club. With 15 members, its emphasis was on fly-fishing, although it did not close its doors to the worm and line angler. Casting lessons took place on Tuesdays evenings, and during the Winter there would be fly-tying instruction. Prizes were offered for the best fish. Colin Boyle was in the lead with a 1lb 2oz brown trout, taken in Boathouse Bay on a blue black.

In March the School Hockey XI won the mini-tournament at the Heriot-Watt playing fields with ease. In other matches, however, the School lost 2-3 against Ruthrieston and 0-4 against Gordonians in the Kennedy Cup six-a-side in Inverness.

Old Boy Dr S. Barrett (1937-39) died at the end of March. He had interrupted his medical career at Edinburgh to serve in the War where he was awarded the Military Cross in 1943 and a Bar the following year.

In May 1977 it was announced that in September the Prep School at Carlekemp would transfer to Fort Augustus.[3] The enlarged Junior House was renamed Calder House. In preparation, Fr Vincent had designed a Calder House tie which incorporated the blue and green colours of Carlekemp against the red Fort Augustus base.

The Lodge was to be transformed on the ground floor to accommodate the youngest two Years, with a dormitory, changing and washing rooms, playroom and reception room. On the first floor the Matron and Junior Form Mistress would have independent flats. The Hospice would be altered and decorated to provide two classrooms, a French room, small library and workroom for Staff. In the main School building there would be one new classroom, a new Junior Science room and two new playrooms. The disused bakehouse was converted into a laundry, while the kitchens were re-equipped with two large gas-fired ranges, replacing the oil-fired ones which were less flexible to use and more expensive to run.

Also in May a large number of Old Boys, their wives and families attended a sunny gathering in Carlekemp. In future the Old Boys' venue would be Paddy Crossan's Edinburgh pub, 'The Tilted Wig', on the first Tuesday of the month at 7.00 pm.

Bishop Mario Conti presented the prizes at the annual Prize-giving. This was also the occasion of the School and the Community's formal reception of the new Bishop. He was welcomed by the Community at the Church door, after processing *in cappa magna* from the Hospice with two Army and Navy Cadet orderlies, with Archie Lightfoot as personal piper.

The Headmaster, Fr Francis, commented on how successful the amalgamation of Carlekemp and the Abbey School had been, as over 80% of the Carlekemp pupils were to come up to Fort Augustus in September.

On 18 June the Fort Augustus Jubilee Celebrations were held in glorious sunshine. With the support of the Village Council and voluntary bodies, the CCF undertook the organisation of the event, tying it up with the Annual Inspection on 16 June.

Tentage and a public address system were supplied by the Army; the Royal Marines contributed an Unarmed Combat Display Team; the Royal Navy staged a diving display in the swimming pool and in the Canal; the Cadets put on a Drill Squad and an Inter-Service Gun Obstacle Race, while the younger Cadets created a medieval jousting tournament.

There was Highland Dancing by local children, a mini-Shinty match, the Girl Guides Dance team, archery, bottle-stall shies and shooting. The Abbey grounds were packed, the stalls sold out, the personnel exhausted but exhilarated.

The Cricket XI lost five matches and won two. The batting was generally unreliable, bowling erred in line and length, the fielding was adequate but never brilliant. Vaughan won the Athletics House Match by 14 points, but Lovat won the Badminton by 2 matches to 1, and also the Tennis.

Some 40 Old Boys attended the weekend in early July. The Mass for deceased Old Boys was celebrated by Fr Vincent in the Memorial Chapel before a large congregation. After supper there was a Beer Social in the Hospice Gallery. During the Association meeting the next day, Tom Kelly appealed to all Old Boys to act and not just speak in support of their old School. Old Boys should be active public relations men for Fort Augustus, fully committed Catholics working for each other and for the benefit of the School.

Among Old Boys graduating that Summer was Duncan Wilson who gained First Class Honours in Electrical Engineering at Edinburgh University.

The extended School opened its doors on 15 September to welcome

65 new boys. There were now 146 pupils in the School. The new Matron was Mrs O' Riordan; the Junior Form Mistress was Miss Ogni. Another newcomer was Mr Keith, also from Carlekemp.

The beginning of term was saddened for all by the death of the School Doctor, Dr Buchanan, in a car accident on 2 October. He had been hurrying to a road accident on a Sunday evening when his Range Rover crashed. He died early the next morning in Raigmore Hospital.

Dr Buchanan was so much more than a colleague to the Staff and a doctor to the School; his death was a personal loss to everyone. He was a friend and fellow sportsman, who gave of his time, energies and enthusiasm in so many ways to so many of the boys. He would be missed for his care and concern for the sick, as an unfailing supporter at School matches, on the Cricket field as a coach, umpire and player, on the Loch as a sailor, in the School as an instructor in First Aid, and as a kindly and gentle counsellor in so many ways.

Seven Sixth Formers acted as pall-bearers at the funeral and each Form chose a representative to attend. Everyone also attended one of the several Masses said for the repose of his soul.

In the School Library the arrival of several hundred books from Carlekemp gave the 20 library workers plenty to register, catalogue and shelve. Cataloguing would take over a year to complete. The new books did not, on the whole, duplicate existing titles.

The first Rugby match was against Inverness Academy. There had been very little time to prepare the squad. The XV lost 17-3. Two weeks later came a 30-16 victory against Keil School. Then followed defeats against Gordonstoun (15-6) and Aberdeen Grammar School (48-8).

Numbers in the Community increased with the arrival of Fr Andrew (now parish priest of Stratherrick), Fr John-Baptist (teaching in the School) and Fr Thomas (who taught theology to the Junior monks and helped in the School). A party of 14 boys was expected at mid-term to live with the Community and gain practical experience of monastic life.

The Standard 1 and Standard 2 classes were now ensconced in the rooms directly above the Bursar and Headmaster. Early in November, Mr H. Walker, a regional HM Inspector, visited the School on two occasions to look at the Primary department in Calder House. He seemed to be satisfied and pleased, commenting favourably on the Classical and French studies in Standard 3.

The two youngest Years, who lived in the Lodge (known as 'Lodgers'), were now developing their own brand of social life. Members' birthdays were celebrated with a party; Miss Ogni took them for walks and rambles. Young monks or senior boys played 'tag' and 'hide and seek' with them. On Thursday evenings the 'Lodgers' had their own Eucharist in the Lodge. The hymns were accompanied by Fr Thomas and Miss Ogni on guitars.

Fr Benedict continued to employ semi- and full-time volunteers for various outdoor work projects. The swimming pool had last been painted in 1968. Several volunteers were now cementing holes and painting the surface with chlorinated rubber paint. Christmas logs for old folk was another project, as well as leaf-raking.

Abbot Celestine and Fr Maurus were now chaplains at convents at Quidenham, Norfolk and at Talacre, Wales respectively. Fr Edmund was parish priest at Little Malvern, near Worcester. Fr Anselm was assisting at a parish in Coventry and Fr Laurence in Warrington. During the first part of November, Fr Mark preached a retreat to Poor Clare nuns in Edinburgh. He then went to the Passionist community at Coodham, Ayrshire to take part in a Renewal weekend attended by 300 people.

On 4 November came news of the death of Fr Michael Young OSB of Douai Abbey. He was one of a group of young men who made their Novitiate at Fort Augustus in the early 1920s, due to a shortage of space at Douai.

On 6 November Fr Prior officiated at the burial in the monastic cemetery of Andrew MacLaren who had stayed in the Abbey as a boy. At the age of 13 he had wanted to join the Community. From 1922-45 he was MP for Burslem, at first in the Labour Party. He later resigned from it. In London he founded the London School of Economic Science.

On the same day (6 November), Old Boy Fr James Birnie (1924-31) died. Before his retirement he had been parish priest at St Andrew's, Ravelston in Edinburgh. Present at the funeral was Fr Thomas and other Old Boys, Mgr John Barry and Frs Rogerson and Davison.

The following month Fr Francis' amusing production of 'My Three Angels' by Sam and Bella Spewack was given before a large audience made up of the School, parents and friends. Set in a penal colony (the location was authentic enough!) the play featured Raymond Atkinson as Convict 3011, Andrew Mitchelson as 4707 and Malcolm Tenant as 6817. All three did more than justice to their parts. The rest of the cast added to the atmosphere. As usual, the costumes were made by Fr Vincent, while Fr Edward acted as stage manager and lighting director.

The rain and frost almost destroyed the Rugby season. All the later fixtures had to be cancelled. The ground was so unplayable that five-a-side touch Rugby was introduced. The Ness Challenge Cup had to be conceded to Inverness Academy on the basis of their win in September. Bad weather also hindered set games. Play was only possible on the Macdonald pitch. Despite all these handicaps, A. Basigara and J. Dunn were chosen to play Rugby for North of Scotland Schoolboys.

From the beginning of Advent, members of Lovat and Vaughan who attended the Community Mass on weekdays, joined the monks in Choir by sitting in the cross-benches and receiving Communion under both kinds.

On 26 January 1978 Mr Owen showed his film, 'The New Boy', starring David McSherry, made in 1974 by himself and other members of the School. On 8 February Mr Owen presented an audio-visual show which was to be made available to tourists in the Summer.

Following a Forensic Science talk to the Senior School in late January by M. E. Cameron of the Glasgow Police, samples of Fr Benedict's homemade wines were analysed. The chromatograms were interesting: one elderberry wine had a proof reading of 26°. All were comfortingly free of poisons like methanol, or hangover ingredients such as amyl alcohol.

Among the Old Boys it was learnt that Nicholas Coppin (1965-69) was now a member of the Royal Lyceum Theatre Company in Edinburgh and at Christmas played the Lion in 'The Wizard of Oz'. Fiona MacDonald (1971-73) was due to graduate from the Royal Scottish Academy of Music and Drama. Fourteen members of the Edinburgh District had their first meeting at Old Boy Paddy Crossan's hostelry, 'The Tilted Wig'.

On 27 March Calder House presented 'The Sword of General Frapp' by John Harris, produced by Mr Keith. With a cast of around 30, the play told the story of the founder of the Frapp restaurant dynasty whose cooking had cured the Emperor Napoleon.

The Hockey season was interrupted by weather and illness. At no time could the School field a full team. They were beaten by the Old Boys and Robert Gordon's College, but managed to beat Aberdeen Grammar School 6-4.

On 15 May the Community was due to have its Quinquennial Visitation from the Abbot President, Dom Victor Farwell of Worth Abbey. During the previous Summer the General Chapter of the English Benedictine Congregation proposed a reflection by each monastery on its life and work in preparation for the 15th centenary in 1980 of St Benedict's birth. The Council at Fort Augustus decided to set about this with a series of workshops led by invited speakers. One immediate result was the visit of 51 schoolchildren from the diocese in a Catechetical Camp in April.

The 15th centenary in 1980 was also the date chosen for the centenary celebrations of Fort Augustus itself. The Abbot, Council and Community were considering the possibility of launching an appeal for funds to complete the building of the Abbey Church. On 15 March the Community met to hear the architects, Mr Allan and Mr Wells (head of the Wells Organisation), on plans for the Church and a possible appeal.

Mr Bryce, who had been the Maths teacher in the School since 1971, left in March to become a Senior Education Officer in Nigeria.

On the night of 1 April the gnarled old elm tree, which stood so picturesquely opposite the Hospice door, sadly succumbed to age and infirmity. It simply fell over in the course of a nearly windless night. It was said to have been planted in 1746 by the officers of the Fort to commemorate Culloden and to have been the place of execution of a number of Jacobite soldiers.

In April Mr Thomas Flynn, an Edinburgh amateur astronomer, presented his 11½ inch (300 mm) reflecting telescope to the School. It was dismantled and brought up in the Land Rover by Fr Francis and Mr Gavine. With the aid of some stout helpers, it was erected on the roof of the Blessed Sacrament Chapel. This instrument of great optical power would be used for the work of the Duke of Edinburgh awards, 'O' Level, or the British Astronomical Association's lunar programme.

The Camera Club, under the guidance of Mr Gavine and N. O' Flanagan, had been unearthing half-plate glass negatives from the Printing Office for the usual Summer exhibition. Many of them showed the early stages in the building of the Church and the Village as it was towards the end of the nineteenth century.

On 7 May Abbot Nicholas clothed three new Oblates – N. Hurley, A. Hurley and C. Niven. The Confraternity now numbered five. All could be seen on occasions exercising their privilege of taking part in the Community's prayer in Choir.

The West of Scotland Old Boys' group had their last meeting at Eaglesham on 2 May. About 35 attended, including wives. A challenge Hockey match, East versus West, was arranged at the East Kilbride Sports Centre on 30 April.

The School had a visit from J. M. Robinson (1960-66) who came up from London to research old Scottish farm buildings. Since obtaining his DPhil. at Oxford, he had been working for the Historic Buildings Department of the Greater London Council. He had already written a book on the Wyatt family of architects, due to be published by the Clarendon Press.

The standard of Hockey had improved that term. In the Kennedy Cup Six-a-Side tournament in Inverness the 'A' team easily qualified for the semi-finals but were unlucky to lose 2-1 to Highland 'A'. There were three wins, two draws and two defeats over the season. The winner of the new cup donated by Western HC (the Edward Buchanan Memorial Trophy for the outstanding schoolboy player) was V. Gram-Hansen.

In spite of the difficulties of finding time for Athletics practice, eight boys took part in the Northern District AA competition at Inverness. Martin Bell was particularly impressive in his mature approach to competitions. In Golf, four boys played in the Highland Region Golf competition. V. Gram-Hansen had the best round and came fifth equal.

The Junior Proficiency group of the CCF spent a Thursday afternoon in May preparing for a *recce* patrol later the same evening. The area was the Convent woods where three small patrols worked over a triangular course attempting to find the sacred lamps of Conjugation and Declension which marked the groves of Kennedy's 'Primer'.

On 20 May the Senior Cadets took part in an exercise on the Ellice Estate round Leac and the Invervigar burn. Pylons marked the border between Exland, Whyland and Zedland. Patrols from Exland and Whyland were trying to infiltrate Zedland to recover the secret mechanism of a missile which had gone off course and failed to explode.

CHAPTER 18

The Abbey School
1978-81

OVER 60 Old Boys attended the 1978 Reunion, with 48 present at the AGM. Among the guests were Miss Kathleen O'Donnell and Mr Roger Beauchamp, formerly on the Carlekemp staff for many years and now enjoying retirement.

Sporting achievements for the Summer were mediocre. The Cricket XI lost against Gordonstoun (twice) and against the Old Boys, drew against Nairn and Highland CC (Fr Francis, playing for the Abbey, made 58), but beat Inverness Academy. Lovat won the Athletics competition by 218 to 128 points. Vaughan won the Tennis, the Badminton and the Golf.

The 1978 Prize-giving took place on 12 July with Lord Burton of Dochfour presenting the prizes. In his speech the Headmaster, Fr Francis, commented on how successful the amalgamation of Carlekemp with Fort Augustus had been. At the end of the ceremony Abbot Nicholas outlined the proposed Centenary celebrations of the Monastery in 1981 and the plan to raise funds for the completion of the Abbey Church.

The Abbey Printing Press resumed operation after a gap of a few years. For many years under the expert direction of Br Hugh, the Press was a thriving industry, but it finally ceased to function at the death of Br Joseph in 1974. Br Aelred was working it now, but only on a very minor scale. Br Placid continued to be more or less confined to his room, although he was gradually improving.

The Autumn term began on 12 September. There were now 161 pupils in the School, 14 more than in September 1977 and five more than in July the previous term. Mr Andrew Dempster arrived to teach Maths and Miss C. O'Hare came as School Matron.

The CCF returned refreshed from their Summer camp with the Royal Scots in Germany where each Cadet had been able to drive a

Chieftain tank and armoured personnel carriers, as well as enjoy a 'flip' in a Gazelle helicopter.

The Rugby season began well with a 18-14 win over Lochaber High School. Shortly after, the XV lost heavily to Rannoch School 30-6, beat Inverness Academy 18-0, but were overpowered by Keil School 37-3, finally losing to Inverness Academy 10-6.

Other activities flourished: 39 members crowded the Air Rifle Club; 30 joined the Chess Club; the Badminton Club had 40; and the Gun Club acquired a second Spanish AYA 12-bore double-barrelled ejector.

The project for the completion of the Abbey Church to mark the Monastery's Centenary was officially launched by Lord Lovat on 7 October. Following a lunch in the Monastic Refectory for Lord Lovat's guests, the project was discussed in detail by a representative of the fund-raising firm. Groups supporting the project had been set up in the Highlands, Glasgow, Edinburgh, Perth, Dundee, Newcastle, Merseyside and London. Already more than £60,000 (almost a quarter of the £250,000 needed) had been raised, including a generous donation of £10,000 from the Columba Trust at the request of Lord Brand.

News came of monks who were now outwith the Abbey. Fr Thomas McLaughlin had been appointed Cathedral Prior of Rochester. Fr Maurus had completed his second term as Chaplain to the Benedictine Nuns at Talacre. By arrangement with Bishop Conti, he was to be loaned to the Aberdeen diocese for the service of the parish at Cannich (Marydale) where he would replace the recently deceased Fr Bede O'Donnell.

The School play in December was 'You too can have a Body' by Fred Robinson, produced by Fr Francis, with makeup and costumes by Fr Vincent, stage managed by Fr Edward.

The performance of Sasha MacKenzie as the poetic, hypnotic but murderous Maud Tarrant was beautifully done. Her acting gave Raymond Atkinson (the object of her seemingly besotted attentions) a positive character for his portrayal of Chick Wade, TV scriptwriter and buffoon, which really sparkled from the first Act.

The Rugby XV regained the Ness Trophy from Inverness Academy after three years. The final game was won 18-14. The XV followed a disastrous defeat at the hands of Gordonstoun (46-3) with a much more aggressive display against Aberdeen Grammar when they only lost 10-7. Vaughan won the House Match 12-7.

Mr Haines had begun to take members of Calder House under his wing – a gentle stroll up Beinn à Bhacaidh and an equally gentle descent with saucer-like snowflakes, mist and diminishing visibility was one of his outings.

At the National Mod at Oban in October, J. MacKenzie entered the Junior Fiddle competition and his sister Sasha (a future international performer) won two trophies for clarsach – the Elspeth Hyllested trophy for solo playing and the Jean Campbell Memorial Trophy for Clarsach accompaniment to a singer.

The Church Building project had now advanced beyond the initial stages. While Abbot Nicholas had attended meetings in London and Liverpool in the past weeks, Fr Thomas tried to stir up support in the Tayside Region with a meeting in Dundee. The massive foundations of the proposed Church that was never finished had been cleared of the growth of half a century and the sounds of building could be heard mingling with the cheerful whistling of the workmen. To date the walls of the apse had risen to a height of about 15 feet.

The numbers of the resident Community had decreased with Br Placid and Br Wilfrid having gone away for long periods of convalescence.

Then, early on the morning of 29 January 1979, Fr McLaughlin died suddenly. Only the day before he had been up and about as usual, attending Choir and preparing his classes.

Fr Thomas was born in Bombay in 1914. His schooldays were spent at Fort Augustus under Commander Farie, where he excelled in sports. He entered the monastic Novitiate in September 1932. In 1936 he was sent to Rome to study for a doctorate in Theology. The outbreak of the War prevented him finishing the course. He was ordained priest by Bishop Bennett in 1939 and subsequently taught Science and Latin in the School, also training the School Choir. He found time to produce highly successful Gilbert and Sullivan operas. In 1945 Abbot Wulstan made him Prior and Novicemaster. Abbot Oswald appointed him Headmaster of the Abbey School in 1954, a post he held until he was sent as Prior and Headmaster to Carlekemp in 1958. While Headmaster at Fort Augustus, the School roll rose above 100 and the Calder Wing was added. Fr Thomas was also intensely involved in fund-raising for the building of the Abbey Church nave. For those who worked closely with him, he was a tower of strength, a man who understood and forgave.

Outdoor Hockey was impossible because of the weather. However, in the Indoor Six-a-Side Tournament at Kinloss the School team finished third.

With 45 members and a further ten applicants, the Ski Club had grown to embrace a quarter of the senior school. There had been ski outings on all games afternoons to local snow fields, starting with the slope below Culachy House and progressing to the huge drifts at the top of the Suidhe.

From early January the firm of Rushworth and Dreaper from Liverpool had begun to dismantle the Church organ. This was the next step in the process of completing the Church, since the organ had to be resited to release the aisle space and allow the East end to be completed. Recently signs of deterioration had begun to show in the mechanism. Most of the Swell organ had become unusable, woodworm had made inroads into the soundboards, and the old magnetic relays had become noisy in their action. Rushworth and Dreaper's plan for rebuilding involved reducing the organ in size, but also adding other stops to achieve a much better tonal balance and clarity. The whole organ would be accommodated in the organ chamber above the choir, acoustically an ideal place. All the pipework would be revoiced and the action completely renewed and electrified.

Fr Mark Dilworth had been appointed by Cardinal Gray to succeed Mgr David McRoberts as Keeper of the Scottish Catholic Archives and Administrator of Columba House. As this post would involve a considerable amount of work in Edinburgh, Fr Mark would in future be absent from Fort Augustus more frequently, but he would remain as Parish Priest.

Calder House presented 'Hans would not tie his Bootlaces' by Marjorie Randle on 26 March. Mr Keith's production was powerful, so much so that the fuse system, so tenderly nursed by Fr Edward, finally failed in the middle of the show. Kevin Jermy tripped his way to success, while Tony Mather bravely out-croaked the toad in the well. Paul Curran and Dale Thomson vied for the admiring glances of the audience, but Jane Anderson outdid them with no effort at all.

On 22 March Miss Kathleen O'Donnell died. She had held the post of Matron at Carlekemp for nearly 40 years. Not only did she look after the health of the boys, but she also cared for their clothing and general well-being. When she retired from Carlekemp, Cardinal Gray presented her with the Papal award '*Bene merenti*'. She had continued to live at Carlekemp in a cottage in the woods, where the boys delighted to visit her. When the Prep School was brought to Fort Augustus, Abbot Nicholas offered her a home close to the Abbey. There she spent the last year and a half of her life, surrounded by the affection of all who had known her. She was buried in the monastic cemetery among the monks she had served so faithfully all her life.

Mr David Gavine, who had been Geography teacher for nine years, took up the post of Lecturer in Navigation and Astronomy at Leith Nautical College at the beginning of April. In addition to teaching Geography, he also taught Junior Science and successfully presented 'O' Level candidates in Geology and Astronomy. The Astronomy Club was founded and flourished under his knowledgeable guidance.

When the School Matron left at the end of the Summer term, Miss C. O'Hare had taken the post for a term. In January she was succeeded by Miss N. Martelli.

The first Hockey matches only took place in the last week of term. A whole term had passed without any fixtures. It was hardly surprising that against Highland HC the School XI lost 5-0.

In the CCF two Cadets, Kevin Billson and Dana Blanchard, were given a flight with the RAF. Their log recorded:

0700 hrs Friday 16 March. Suitably kitted out we took off from Kinloss in a Nimrod of 206 Squadron on a 7-hour mission to Gibraltar. Nimrods are submarine hunter-killers and our flight out proved most interesting. The mission was to photograph Russian warships leaving the Mediterranean. The relatively new Russian aircraft-carrier 'Kiev' was one of our targets.

The Church Building Fund continued to make satisfactory progress. More than £81,000 was raised by 26 March. Bishop Conti ordained Br Aelred as deacon on 21 March. Two of the young monks from Pluscarden, who had been studying at Fort Augustus, made their solemn profession on 10 March – Brs Hugh Gilbert and Anselm Atkinson.

The CCF was delighted to learn that Lt.-Col. R. D. MacLagan CBE MC (formerly in command of the Cadet branch of the Queen's Own Highlanders) had agreed to become the first honorary Colonel of the Contingent. Colonel 'Chew', as he was affectionately known, had been instrumental in re-establishing the Cadet Force in the School. His dedicated work for Cadets in the Highlands over the previous 20 years was well known.

The improvement in the Hockey XI's skill and fitness was now obvious. They had some excellent games against very stiff opposition. The XI registered four losses and three wins. In the Kennedy Six-a-Side tournament in Inverness at the end of April, the 'A' six were unlucky to be beaten by Highland A on penalty flicks.

Vaughan won the Inter-House Athletics, although Lovat were unlucky to lose two of their leading athletes, Martin Bell and D. Hamilton pulling muscles early on.

After the School's departure for Easter, the Abbey welcomed a group of boys from St David's High School, Dalkeith who were curious enough to give up part of their holiday in order to find out what happens in a monastery. After their departure, 50 youngsters of the Highland Youth Camp came from the small and scattered communities in the diocese to live for a few days in the Abbey. They took part in all the Holy Week services, some acting as servers.

The Abbey Church Centenary Fund passed the first £100,000. The architect of the Church paid a visit to Fort Augustus to discuss the plans. The organ builders were expected back in August to re-erect the refurbished organ.

After an uncertain start, the young Hockey XI again developed well. After two defeats they won the next three matches and drew against Gordonstoun away in the final match. Vaughan won the House Match with a score of 142 for 6. Lovat, however, gained some revenge by winning the Tennis, Badminton and the Golf. The Junior Soccer teams lost 4-3 against the local High School, while the Senior side lost against Invergarry and Glenalban, both experienced men's sides.

The filling of the swimming pool was delayed by the installation of a filter, but it was completed by 8 June. The clean appearance of the water, from which even the suspended peat was now filtered out, was remarkable. The water came from Loch Ness at about 52° F. After a few days of warm sunshine the temperature of the water rose to 68°. But even at the lower temperature some hardy souls swam. A record of seven bathes in a day was achieved by Sally Beaumont.

The girls' Yoga class had taken the place of earlier Music and Movement sessions. Mrs Beaumont had volunteered her services for Yoga and throughout the year the girls had been taught basic movements and postures. Mrs Stone conducted a Sewing class on another day for the girls.

In the Monastery, the recent installation of a wheelchair lift outside the monks' Refectory had proved of great benefit to the older and sicker members of the Community. Fr Cuthbert was now a regular attender at morning coffee in the Calefactory. For many years his only excursion to ground level was to have Christmas dinner with the Community.

Fr Mark, Keeper of the Scottish Catholic Archives, was resident for most of the time at Columba House in Edinburgh, although he came up for two or three weekends every month. He was currently engaged in writing several chapters of a book being prepared in conjunction with an exhibition on St John Ogilvie to be held in the Third Eye Centre, Glasgow. He continued to hold the post of Parish Priest of Fort Augustus. In his absence the responsibilities were shared by Frs Andrew and Benedict.

Fr Andrew was heavily involved in making arrangements for the English Summer School to be held in the Abbey during the holidays. A similar venture the previous year had been a marked success.

Lord Dulverton presented the prizes at Prize-giving, announcing that he would fund a prize for annual award to a pupil presenting a paper on ecology or local natural history. In his speech, Headmaster Fr Francis particularly complimented I.A. Mitchelson who had been offered a place at Pembroke College, Oxford, through the Scottish Special Entrance Scheme. This gave places at English universities to Scottish candidates at the end of their fifth year on the basis of their Highers results.

The first Rugby fixture came only ten days after the School returned. A disorganised and unfit First XV lost heavily to Inverness Academy. Possibly the toughest game of the season followed against a powerful Oban High School side. A strong Jedburgh Grammar School XV on tour was then held to seven points at half time, before the thread of the game was ultimately lost. The most disappointing defeat was by an unusually weak Keil team. In the final match, the Gordonstoun 2nd XV was beaten.

Although the November rain and frost kept fixtures down to a minimum, there were wins against Aberdeen Grammar School for the first time in several years (7-8), and Lochaber High School (18-0). The House Match was tied at 10-10.

Three girls had joined the Gun Club. There were clay shoots on Sunday afternoons and practices on Tuesday evenings. The traps had been relevelled and a new site found for driven birds. This gave good overhead shooting and a wide variety of angles. The Air Rifle Club now had 28 regular attenders, while Archery boasted around 20.

The CCF Summer Camp was at Lochaline in July. Sailing, fishing and hill-walking parties set out each day for different locations, including a two-day outing to Mull. The accommodation, consisting of metal-ridged shelters, was erected in record time. It was a truly adventurous camp which called for initiative and quick thinking, but which provided moments of marvellous relaxation and peace.

The anniversary of the launching of the Abbey Centenary Fund was celebrated by a lunch at the Abbey on 13 October, hosted by Lord Lovat. Over 50 guests were entertained by the Community.

After lunch, Fr Gregory demonstrated the rebuilt and restored organ. The very large pipes and all the workings, formerly located in St Joseph's Aisle, had been removed. The entire organ was now contained in the organ loft above the Choir. The console had been re-sited to provide a larger, more symmetrical space around the altar and to give the organist a better overall view.

The Fund was now approaching three-quarters of the total required. The sum assured was now £170,319. Of this £62,855 had been subscribed by 62 Old Boys. It was the intention of the Community that the Abbey Church should be solemnly consecrated on the Feast of St Benedict, 11 July 1981.

The School play in December 1979 was Knott's 'Wait until Dark', a difficult play to stage. Sasha MacKenzie played the blind Susy Henderson with considerable skill. Kevin Billson, as the easy-going Mike, was always in control. Edward Malloy as Crocker, the 'heavy', conveyed a sense of knuckle-dustered stupidity. Fr Francis and Mr Bill Owen successfully dealt with many of the play's problems, assisted by Fr Vincent (costumes) and Fr Edward (stage-manager).

The first half of the 1980 Spring term saw a concerted effort by builders and craftsmen to complete the first three stages of the Church Building project before 7 June. On the structural work, the apse up to the courses surmounting the encircling lantern windows had been completed. The short addition to the Lady Aisle, and the longer one to St Joseph's Aisle, had also been built and roofed over.

At present, work was afoot in laying the final cladding of conglomerate artificial stone and in roofing the apse. Also in hand was the building out of the sanctuary from the Choir steps.

Because of all this work, the builders had completely taken over the Church. The Community had moved into the Chapter House for Mass and Office. Sunday Mass, meantime, was celebrated in the School Assembly Hall.

Of the overall Building Fund target of £250,000, the generosity of donors and the hard work of the promoters had raised £185,774. The most successful of the area fund-raising groups was the Highlands which had raised £19,779. A further approach to smaller Trusts was about to be made and renewed efforts were planned abroad.

In the School the Ski Club had a record entry: 52 pupils plus the Matron and two Masters. Unfortunately, the snow gods had been slow to respond to such a direct appeal to their favour. Fort Augustus had missed out on most of the low level snow that Winter.

The Gun Club had several shoots, including one over Mr Grant's estate for young shots. It was bright and sunny in the morning and crisp under foot when the guns walked the coverts in line with the keepers and dogs. Few birds were seen before the break for lunch, but the afternoon provided more sport than accuracy. Although the bag totalled only three birds (how some of them escaped the barrages of lead was miraculous), everyone had an enjoyable and instructive time. In the evening the warmth and comfort of Mrs Grant's fireside and lavishly-spread dining table capped the day.

The Hill-Walkers made only one outing – a small party to Glenn Cuaich, finding 800 feet of really hard snow. This provided an opportunity for practising the skills of cutting steps in snow. Indoors, the Chess Club had finished the knock-out tournament and constructed a ladder which would be in operation after Half-Term. The Cubs had been kept indoors by the cold wet weather, but managed to make a start on a mini-assault course in the swamp.

Hockey had been almost unaffected by the bad weather. The First XI had taken some time to settle, because of the large number of young, untried players. Against Gordonstoun at Sweethillocks on a frosty, sporty pitch, they were lucky to escape with a draw. Western won 7-0 in a morning game, but the training session in the afternoon, when the teams were mixed, was useful for all. The A and B sides did reasonably well in the Six-a-Side Tournament at RAF Kinloss.

Old Boy J. M. Robinson (1960-66), formerly architectural editor of the *Survey of London* (1978-79) and now Librarian to the Duke of Norfolk, had his first book published: *The Wyatts. An Architectural Dynasty* (Oxford University Press). N. Blackburn (1961-65) had taken up a lectureship at Manchester University. I. Traquair (1962-67) was director of Logistic Management Services Ltd, Aberdeen. Over the previous four years he had developed a computer-based business mainly directed at North Sea oil companies.

On 21 March the Community celebrated the ordination to the

priesthood of Fr Aelred by Bishop Mario Conti. The whole School and around 50 guests attended. The School sacristan, Chris Stephenson, acted as the principal master of ceremonies, assisted by a full team of altar servers. This was the first ordination at Fort Augustus for several years. Two days later, Bishop Conti confirmed 24 boys during morning Mass.

The Church Building Fund appeal now stood at £194,950. Progress in the construction of the new Church was plain to see. On 19 March the Church was back in use for Mass and Office. The new sanctuary had been built, though not yet tiled in its eventual light green slate. The new altar, on its polished granite columns, had been installed. The walls of the nave and the Lady Aisle and the brickwork above the Choir had all been cemented and covered in a white textured plaster. The workmen were currently putting the roof on the apse.

The First Hockey XI had a hectic series of matches against adult opposition at the beginning of the Spring term. However, the forwards' failure to use their chances was a severe and often fatal handicap. The team finished fifth in the Kennedy Cup Six-a-Side Tournament. They lost 3-1 to Linlathan HC, 5-3 to Ruthrieston HC, and 2-0 to Aberdeen Grammarians. In mid-May the senior Inter-House Athletics Competition resulted in a 47 point win for Lovat

On Saturday 7 June 1980 the three Benedictine monastic communities in Scotland – the Cistercian Abbey of Nunraw in East Lothian, the Benedictine Abbey of Pluscarden in Morayshire, and the English Benedictine Congregation house at Fort Augustus, combined for a joint celebration at Fort Augustus.

Pontifical High Mass was celebrated at noon in the Abbey Church with a congregation of 500. Lunch followed for all in a marquee opposite the School tower. The guests had an opportunity to visit an exhibition of monastic life in Scotland, past and present. The day ended with Pontifical Vespers at 4.00 pm, followed by tea in the marquee.

The guests included Bishop Mario Conti of Aberdeen, Lord and Lady Lovat, Abbot Victor Farwell of Worth (President of the EBC), Abbots John Roberts (Downside), Augustine O'Sullivan (Glenstal), Celsus O'Kelly (Portglenone) and Prior Bede Kilgallon (Prinknash). Abbot Celestine Haworth (former Abbot of Fort Augustus who had now retired there from the Carmelite Convent at Quidenham) was present, along with Abbot Donald McGlynn (Nunraw) and Abbot Alfred Spencer (Pluscarden) with members of their communities.

The School took part in many ways: senior pupils preparing the cloisters, mounting the exhibition, ushering during its display, serving in the church, serving at lunch. Two members of the Camera Club made a photographic record of the occasion. The singing of the whole School and the help in moving furniture contributed to the success of a memorable celebration.

The Appeal for the completion of the Abbey Church continued to receive donations. The £200,000 mark had now been passed.

As the Summer wore on, Badminton had been supplanted by Football – mainly five-a-side. Hill-walking was still popular; there were post-Higher expeditions to Morvich in Kintail, while the Adventure Club set off with Mr MacCallum to walk over the hills to Torgoyle Church in Glen Moriston. There ice formed on the tents during the first night, but on the Saturday the temperature rose to almost 80° F. The group then set off north to Loch na Beinne Bàine high up in the hills of Glen Moriston – a return journey of about 14 miles.

Mr Owen, who had taught Art classes in the Junior forms for several years, resigned. Mrs McCallum took over responsibility for those classes. Following his visit to the United States the previous October, Mr Owen had decided to spend more time in America each year.

Prize Day was held on a fine day, a change from the unpleasant weather that prevailed for most of the term. The prizes were presented by Mr G. S. Gimson, Sheriff-Principal of Grampian, Highland and Islands.

The Headmaster, Fr Francis, celebrated the Mass of Thanksgiving for the School year at 11.00 am. Then sherry was served in the marquee. After lunch, Abbot Nicholas dedicated the renewed organ. An organ recital by Mr David Hardie followed.

In his report, Fr Francis noted that there had been a 100 per cent success rate in English, Latin, French and Biology at 'O' Grade and in French at 'H' grade. He also mentioned the award of a CBE to Old Boy D. A. P. Barry, chairman of the Parole Board, and the selection of R. B. W. Milne for the Great Britain Olympic team at 400 metres.

A variety of reasons reduced the number of Cricket matches that year – poor weather, a union restriction on teachers' extra-curricular activities in Local Authority schools, and the state of the Abbey wicket which would have made real pace bowling very dangerous. The XI beat Gordonstoun and the Old Boys, but lost to Northern Counties. Vaughan won a one-sided House Match, since they had the majority of the XI. Lovat, however, emerged victorious in Tennis, Golf and Badminton.

During the annual Inspection of the CCF rain poured steadily, but the weather failed to detract from a thrilling demonstration exercise in which hostages were snatched from student guards and spirited away amongst the noisiest and most smoke-screened battle fought at Fort Augustus since the '45 Rising!

When the School returned in September, it was to learn that Old Boy Martin Loftus (1931-38) had died. Frank Partridge (1966-71) and Fiona MacDonald (1971-73) had been married in the Abbey Church in late August. They were now living in London where Frank worked at the BBC Sports Desk. Miss Margaret Herraghty had presented a trophy for Music in memory of her brother, Edward. It was a copper bowl, silver gilt, early nineteenth century, inset with coins of George III. The Old Boys had also presented the School with a computer, a 32K PET with a dual-drive floppy disk unit and a cassette deck.

On 1 September Fr Cuthbert Wilson died after a long illness. The School knew him as the blind priest who might be seen sometimes in his wheelchair on the sanctuary, concelebrating Conventual Mass. Fr Cuthbert, however, had had a varied life. He had worked in the London Stock Exchange, studied Canon Law in Rome, been Chaplain to the Highland Light Infantry and Prior of Fort Augustus from 1960-64. He spent two long periods in the USA.

After he lost his sight, his radio and talking books were valued resources. At times he was in much pain, which he endured patiently. The end came quickly. He was 76 years of age, a monk for 53 years and a priest for 42 of them.

The relatively young Rugby XV was the best the School had had for some years. It showed promise, but often played games of two halves and the pack failed to work consistently. There was a defeat and a win against Gordonstoun; a defeat against Keil School and a win against Millburn. In the second half of the term the XV won all of its four games (78 points for, 36 against).

Among the clubs a newcomer was Technical Drawing, taken by Mr Dempster. The Camera Club planned to mount the photographs taken of the 1500th anniversary of the birth of St Benedict in an album as a permanent memorial of the occasion. Music and Movement continued to cater for the girls – L. Olsen, O. Stone, A. Grant, B. Stone, F. MacRae and J. Anderson attended for an hour every week. The emphasis was on posture and graceful movement.

The School play, 'See how they run' by Philip King, an amusing and light-hearted farce, was given at the end of term. It was produced by Fr

Francis. A pet dog added to the fun in its theatrical premiere, managing to impose a refreshing air of sanity until it found it all rather too much and left the stage with its ears laid back along its skull. Then there was an underpainted spectre that ran about brandishing a poke at the most unlikely people. At another juncture, the Abbey's sirens began to wail, forcing several of the part-time voluntary firemen in the audience to leave in great haste.

As for the acting – Amabel Grant and Fiona MacRae were particularly good as the formidable Miss Skillon and the ingenuous agent of order, Ida. Mark Mungavin was a very convincing, but totally confused and outraged Bishop of Lax.

Eight members of the CCF spent a successful weekend on Torr Dhùin (the vitrified fort at Auchterawe). This taste of excitement was more fully realised on the second day with abseiling off the School Tower.

As 1981 dawned there was news of the Assisted Places Scheme. The School administration had agreed to take part in provisions (under the Government's new Education Bill then going through Parliament), to make financial assistance available to parents for tuition costs in independent schools.

The School felt that more and more parents were finding that their work required them to move about the country and even abroad. In such a climate, boarding schools provided a continuity of education for such families. In an increasing number of families both parents had jobs, careers for women being accepted as natural in society. A boarding school could be a blessing in such circumstances. For single parent families the boarding school offered a valuable service. Family business could be time-consuming, and disruptive. The security and routine of boarding school might be essential for the upbringing of the children.

The weather had curtailed Hockey since the beginning of term. In spite of the lack of practice this caused, four matches were won, one drawn and two lost. The Old Boys won 4-2, while Vaughan (with nine of the XI) beat Lovat 3-0. In the Spring term there were three lost matches, one win and two draws.

The hundredth anniversary of the School (and Kilgraston's fiftieth anniversary), was marked by a visit to Kilgraston on Sunday 15 March. A Hockey XI from the Middle School took on the Kilgraston XI after Mass and lunch. The pitch was soft and bumpy. The girls showed more finesse, the boys more strength. In the end the boys won 2-0.

A new set of Stations of the Cross was designed and made by Mr Simon Brown, a relative of Fr John-Baptist. They were etched on polished slate, the material which was used to tile the sanctuary.

At the end of January, Fiona (née MacDonald) and Frank Partridge became parents of twins, Kirsty and Jamie. This was the first time both parents of a new baby had been former pupils.

When the Higher exams finished, two expeditions took place. One of them, led by Mr Court and Mr Haines, went up Creag-nan-Damh, a daunting 3000 feet climb up the old stalkers' path. It revealed beautiful views of Loch Cluanie and some deposits of semi-precious stones, such as amethysts and garnets. The descent followed cairns made by Mr Haines on previous visits.

The Easter holidays saw a Highland Youth Camp of 60 young people from the diocese spend a week in the School. Fr Vincent and Fr Benedict organised and ran it. Fortunately, the weather kept fine.

The Inter-House Athletics competition was held on the last three days in sunshine, heavy rain, thunder and lightning, not to mention interruptions from low-flying Navy helicopters. K. Deady's 25 year old High Jump record of 1.66 metres was finally broken by D. Kiwanuka who cleared 1.67 metres.

The Centenary celebrations of the Abbey centred on the consecration of the Church by Bishop Mario Conti on Saturday 11 July. The previous day the Old Boys had arranged a reception and supper-dance. The Assembly Hall was converted into a dance-floor, with one corner as a bar. The cloisters became a buffet and the quadrangle was laid out in alfresco café style.

The celebrations began with a Pontifical concelebrated Requiem Mass for deceased members of the Community and School. Fr Andrew McKillop, the senior Old Boy in the Community, preached. The reception and buffet supper followed. A planned group photograph and the use of the quadrangle had to be abandoned because of light rain. Over 200 people were present at the supper, while the School had a disco in the School Refectory, to which they had invited girlfriends and sisters.

The morning of Saturday 11 July was given over to last-minute rehearsals and preparations for the afternoon Consecration ceremony. The ceremony began with a procession into the Church, led by Cadets in uniform carrying an embroidered banner of the Abbey's coat of arms. Each Scottish Bishop and Abbot had his own banner and escort, as did also the three British Cardinals (Cardinal Gordon Gray, Cardinal Basil

Hume and Cardinal Tomás Ó'Fiaich) who were present. Cardinal Gray had been appointed special envoy of Pope John Paul II for the occasion, and he was escorted by two Knights Commander of St Gregory and six Knights of Malta, all in full ceremonial dress.

Each of the Scottish Bishops assisted in the consecration of the walls and crosses of the Church. The lay-sponsors of the appeal were present, as was the Lord Lieutenant of Inverness-shire, Sir Donald Cameron of Lochiel and Lady Cameron.

A champagne tea for all the guests was given in a marquee after the ceremony, at which Lord Lovat, Abbot Nicholas and Cardinal Hume proposed the toasts. All the guests received an engraved wine-glass as a memento. The School were given mugs decorated with a picture of the Abbey.

The evening's programme was a Gala which the School had prepared. A pageant of local history, from Celtic to Black monks, written by Fr Vincent and directed by John McGregor, was the highlight.

On Sunday a Mass of Thanksgiving was celebrated by Cardinal Gray, as President, and the Monastic Community. The Cardinal preached in a most inspiring manner. At the Prize-giving in the afternoon he also presented the prizes.

PAX IN VIRTUTE

CHAPTER 19

The Abbey School
1981-85

IT had been a Cricket season of foul weather and cancelled matches. Nevertheless the XI achieved a high batting standard. They beat Inverness Academy (with J. D. Kiwanuka scoring 116 not out) and the Old Boys (with five minutes to spare), but were in turn beaten by Gordonstoun. Lovat won a surprising victory in the House Match.

After the Summer the Rugby XV beat Lochaber High School 20-12 in a scrappy game, but lost heavily to Inverness Academy (20-0). Then followed a 11-10 defeat by Millburn Academy, a 23-0 win against Keil School, a 24-14 defeat by Oban High School, and another by Aberdeen Grammar. Pride was restored with wins over Kelso Academy and Inverness Academy (48-15).

The School play, 'The Happiest Days of Your Life' (produced by Fr Francis), featured Amabel Grant, Fiona MacRae and Miranda Grant as colourful schoolmarms, and David McLaughlin as the laconic and mysterious janitor, Rainbow.

In the Community, Fr John-Baptist was making a good recovery from surgery he had undergone the previous October. Meanwhile, on 14 February 1982, after suffering a stroke, Br Adrian Houghton was transferred to Raigmore Hospital in Inverness. On the day after Ash Wednesday he died, at the age of 72. For generations of schoolboys, he was a cook who provided wholesome and abundant meals. For others, he masterminded the Refectory with Rudolf, Peter and Lily. Latterly, he had been in charge of the Abbey Shop.

In the 1950s Br Adrian ran the poultry farm beside the River Tarff, where Br David could also be spied behind large baskets of eggs or fleeing from the fierce cockerel. The whole Fort Augustus area received a supply of free-range eggs and dressed poultry from the farm.

Br Adrian's day took in other interests, such as rose-beds, pot plants on every window-sill, and cats. For years he trained the altar servers and was in charge of the School cleaning. Four hours' sleep was all he found necessary. He despised siestas.

The Feast of St Joseph (on 19 March) was marked by the Solemn Profession of Br Anthony Hain. This took place during the Conventual Mass at which the entire School was present.

Fr Vincent was honoured by the Northern Fire Brigade with the Good Conduct and Long Service medal, the second member of the Community to receive the medal.

In spite of the poor weather, the Hockey XI remained unbeaten by another school, losing only to Highland HC. Both A. McLaughlin and T. Kelly were chosen to play for the North of Scotland Schoolboys' Rugby XV against a touring Italian Under 19 XV. The visitors won 51-3.

The bowlers in the Cricket XI, meanwhile, lacked spin and outswing and the batsmen had little confidence. Two matches were won and three lost. Vaughan won the house Match.

The Monastic Community learnt with sadness of the death of Fr Aidan Trafford of Downside. He had been Bursar at Fort Augustus during the War. Meanwhile, Fr Denys Rutledge, who had been working in South America for many years, had returned from Chile to Fort Augustus in order to receive medical attention. After spending some time in hospital, he was moved to a convalescent home in Nairn.

In May the Community received the sad news of the death of Lady Abbess Mary Tyler of Holme Eden Abbey, Carlisle. She was the last surviving member of the Community who had been at St Scholastica's, Fort Augustus (the Old Convent) and was in her hundredth year. Her sister was at one time Matron of the Abbey School.

St Scholastica's was shortly to be dispersed. This sad conclusion to the Community's history was the result of a long period without recruits. In February, Fr Edward visited Holme Eden and brought a number of articles back to Fort Augustus. Among these was a fine portrait of Abbot Leo Linse (founder of Holme Eden) which was given a place of honour on the walls of the Monks' Refectory.

Abbot Victor Farwell, Abbot President of the English Benedictine Congregation, conducted a Visitation at Fort Augustus from 7-9 June. As always he was careful, charitable and expeditious.

In June 1982 a party of 50 attended the Murrayfield Youth Rally to welcome Pope John Paul II on his first visit to Scotland. Some of the Community, with local parishioners, also attended the celebrations at Bellahouston Park in Glasgow. Abbot Nicholas was on the dais with the Pope and the Bishops.

At the Annual Old Boys' Reunion on 3 July, a huge crowd squeezed into the Monks' Refectory for supper, followed by a social in the Hospice Gallery. At the meeting it was announced that monies taken at the dance and Gala the previous year amounted to £3000, which was being put into trust for a future School development.

A large number of parents and relatives enjoyed fine weather on Monday 12 July when Bishop Conti presented the prizes. In his speech, Fr Francis said that the Higher results of the second five years were 27 per cent better than those in the first five years. If 1981 were compared to 1970, then the 1981 results were 76 per cent better. He noted that Camping was an increasingly popular activity and added that it was hoped to integrate this more regularly with project work in Biology, Geography and History.

When the School returned in September, Mr Court (who had taught English, coached Rugby, functioned on the CCF, and contributed to School life in many other ways), had moved on to Strathallan. Mr G. McCulloch took his place.

In Rugby the XV beat Millburn Academy 42-6, Inverness Academy 42-0, Keil School 11-4 and Gordonstoun 44-0. Later in the year there were victories over Aberdeen Grammar School (10-3), Oban High School (28-4), and a surprising defeat by Inverness Academy (17-0).

J. D. Kiwanuka, D. G. Nkoma and M. J. Mungavin represented the School in the North of Scotland Schools XV against the South of Scotland Schools at under-18 level. R. L. Giulianotti and A. J. Meldrum were selected for the under-15s team.

In Chess the arrival of R. Sieveking from Hamburg greatly increased the strength of the Club. In theory and practice he was the most exact player the School (staff included) had ever had.

On 21 October 25 boys were guests of the local Hub Youth Club for a Hallowe'en Disco. The girls had prepared an amazing selection of tempting nibbles.

Amabel Grant, meanwhile, and Torquil MacKenzie took part in some successful Eventing. Amabel won the Hayfield Trophy at Royal Deeside Horse Trials, while Torquil won cups and rosettes at the Dunanin House and Dochfour events and, as the only rider to have a clear round and the fastest time, an invitation to a prize dinner party.

'I'll get My Man' was the Christmas play, with two spirited performances from Amabel Grant, David Small, Rory Sullivan and Tony Mather. More of the female parts were taken by boys, which added to the absurdity of the proceedings. As usual the producer was Fr Francis, costumes were by Fr Vincent, and Fr Edward stage-managed.

Many players from the previous year's Hockey team had left the School. This, combined with the wet and windy weather, put great pressure on the team. The Gym was over-used and resounded to the *clack* of hockey sticks. Defeats by Gordonstoun and Highland followed. As the season continued, however, there was a definite improvement in the standard of play. Aberdeen Grammar School, Robert Gordon's College and Gordonstoun were all beaten, although the two former finally managed to take their revenge in the last two games of term.

On 19 January the Vice-President of the Old Boys' Association, Mr Angus J. Macdonald, died at the age of 76. From nearby Whitebridge, he and his brothers were amongst the earliest arrivals at Fort Augustus when the School was re-opened in 1920. His love of Fort Augustus remained with him all his life.

A fine Shinty player as a boy, he passed on his talent for stick and ball to his sons and grandsons, all of whom followed him through the School. It was after the death of his second son, Iain, in 1961 that Angus donated the Macdonald Memorial all-weather Hockey pitch that had done so much to improve the quality of play and players over the previous twenty years.

He was a founding member of the Old Boys' Association and its Glasgow representative on the Committee for many years, during which time the Shrovetide Ball in the Bath Hotel was a highlight of social life in the West.

Latterly, his health broke down and he retired to live with his wife, Grace, and younger son Alasdair in Jersey. To them, to Mhairi and Gay and to Angus junior, who had in so many ways continued the outstanding support of Fort Augustus showed by his father, the sympathy of the School, the Old Boys, and of the Community was extended.

Br Bernard McInulty made his simple profession on 19 March in front of the Community and School. On 20 March, Fr Anthony Hain was ordained to the priesthood by Bishop Conti. His first Mass was celebrated the following day, the Feast of St Benedict.

Once again, Fr Vincent and Fr Benedict organised a Highland Youth Camp in the School. More than 80 youngsters, between 16 and 19, from the dioceses of Aberdeen and Argyll, spent the week 26 March to

2 April at the Abbey. Bishop Conti came for the Sunday and Monday.

The Vaughan Vintners, the exclusive society which had pursued its interest with regularity on Sunday evenings (in the Lodge, courtesy of the Matron), extended associate membership to the Masters' Common Room (full membership was restricted to Vaughan prefects). Two wine tastings were held when Masters and their wives attended.

On Friday 8 April 1983, Fr Vincent Pirie Watson died suddenly but peacefully in his sleep, after an exhausting but exhilarating day in harness. He was born in Edinburgh in 1934. After a brief time at Saint Andrew's Priory in Canaan Lane he came up to Fort Augustus in 1939. He completed his schooling at the Abbey and entered the Monastery, being ordained in 1958. Even before his ordination he was involved in the School, teaching, coaching Rugby and playing vigorously. On the election of Abbot Celestine in 1960, Fr Vincent succeeded him as Housemaster of Vaughan. He remained in that post until his death.

In the following 23 years he undertook an enormous number of tasks. He built up the CCF and established it as second to none in Scotland. He was also in the Fire Brigade and still active as the local Fire Chief. In the 1960s his polyphonic Choir gave pleasure to many. Whenever there was a School play Fr Vincent worked behind the scenes, doing make-up, designing and making costumes. He championed the cultural visits to Fort Augustus arranged by the Scottish Arts Council.

He enjoyed fishing, shooting, stalking. He taught himself to ski. He organised and ran the Gun Club. He loved sailing and gave much time and energy to the Village Youth Club. He was a most dedicated man who did not spare himself; a person of many talents which he used unselfishly in the service of others.

Four hundred people came to Fr Vincent's funeral. A piper, an Old Boy of the School, led the cortège through the monastic garden to the graveside. After Fr Vincent's death, Lt. J. B. MacDonald was appointed the new Commanding Officer of the CCF. Mr Haines took over the duties of Adjutant (Civilian). Fr Benedict took over the Fire Brigade; while Fr Francis and Fr John-Baptist shared the duties of Housemaster of Vaughan.

Early in May, Abbot Nicholas inaugurated an association of Lay-Oblates of the Abbey, based at Pitkerro House near Dundee. A form of lay-community had been established there many years before by Dr A. MacQueen, an Old Boy.

In the 1950s two young men, Peter Hastings and Colin Macdonald, as a contribution to the Lay-apostolate, opened a bookshop/coffeehouse

(The Ogilvie Bookshop), opposite University College, Dundee (now Dundee University), a constituent college of St Andrews University.

A group of young Catholics met in the bookshop and, in the course of regular country walks, found Pitkerro and its chapel. The house was empty, dilapidated and leaking. Colin Macdonald and his assistants lived in poor accommodation in town and the families with children needed more room. This prompted them to look for suitable lodgings within their means.

It was eventually agreed that the group should occupy Pitkerro with the object of setting up a Community. A constitution was thrashed out. The principal aim was to be 'the pursuit of a Christian life of perfection insofar as laypersons with families, and single people too, could do so consistent with their lay state'.

The Office of Compline was said nightly; other prayers were encouraged, particularly attendance at Mass. The most important legal obligation stated that all should agree to be bound by Community decisions.

In 1985 there were 16 resident full members and one non-resident, each in his/her own 'household'. Expenses were shared with respect to common financial obligations such as rates, in accordance with space occupied. In 1974 the house was sold to the Community and its administration placed in the hands of the Pitkerro Trust.

At Fort Augustus the Cricket season was made even shorter than usual by poor weather and Summer camps. The standard of play had little chance to improve and depended more on native talent than practised technique. The Team's apathetic fielding was specially disappointing, as was the lack of practice. There was one victory and three defeats.

In Athletics the old High Jump record of 1.67 metres was equalled by J. D. Kiwanuka and shattered by D. G. Nkoma who cleared 1.77. Hamish MacDonald's Cricket ball record which had stood for 42 years was broken by I. Ifeanyi with a throw of 84.14 metres.

Prize-giving was on 10 July. The principal guest and presenter of prizes was Lord Brand, a Senator of the College of Justice and former Solicitor-General. Fr Francis drew attention to 1982 as having produced the best Higher results ever. He also underlined the significance of Fr Vincent's contribution to the life of the School.

At the Old Boys' Reunion in July (attended by 39 members), it was agreed that in view of the School development Appeal the Committee should be expanded to include invited honorary members from among parents and friends of the School and Community.

In the academic life Old Boys continued to make their mark. J. M. Robinson PhD had been appointed Fitzalan Pursuivant Extraordinary and had also had his third book, *Royal Residences*, published by Macdonald. J. P. R. Moore had obtained his doctorate in Astrophysics at Durham University.

New staff in September included Mr Gordon Wilson (to teach English) and Mr Gary Morris (Geography). During the Summer holidays the project for a Fr Vincent Memorial and the modernisation of the School took a step forward with a preliminary survey by an architectural firm, the Law and Dunbar-Nasmith Partnership of Forres and Edinburgh.

The Rugby XV suffered from inexperience. They lost the first two matches against Inverness Academy and Keil School, but then beat Gordonstoun 6-0. The XV won all their matches in the second half of the term, beating Aberdeen Grammar School, Inverness Academy and Oban High School. The House match was won by Vaughan by a single point. M. Mungavin continued to captain the North of Scotland Schools XV, in which he was joined by P. Mattison, G. Nkhoma and P. Bennett.

News came of Old Boy Andrew Drummond being awarded the first Maurice Ludmer Memorial Prize for a series of anti-Nazi stories published in the *News of the World*. Andrew was now a senior staff reporter in London with a brief on extremist groups and crime. In the course of his research for the anti-Nazi stories, he joined right-wing groups. When posing as a Nazi he was party to meetings of European Fascist groups and ex-SS men on the Continent.

The end of term play was yet another farce, 'Shock Tactics' by John Dole. The story centred round Fred, a home-made computer, and the pandemonium caused in the Shaw household by Fred's permanent and interfering presence. Michael Mungavin was the absent-minded and cranky boffin, George Shaw. Hugh Eaton was the hearty, hard-drinking Uncle Ben with a very convincing limp. Kevin Igoe scuttled through the part of Mrs Trudge, the housekeeper. Miranda Grant played Poppy Blossom, the inquisitive and fascinating reporter. Fr Francis produced the play, Sasha MacKenzie was in charge of the wardrobe, while Hamish MacDonald applied the make-up.

The second term began in normal Winter weather but quickly became snowbound. About 40 families attended the mid-term parent/teacher meeting. Hockey was impossible until 10 February when the first Hockey practice games were played. When the season did get under way, two games were won and four lost.

On the Fort Augustus Locks, unusual work was in progress. M. Lansdowne interviewed the site engineer and reported that the British Waterways Board had engaged Morrison Construction to repair the lock sills on the Fort Augustus section of the Caledonian Canal. The problem in replacing the old wooden sills by concrete ones was the water which seeped up and in from everywhere. This was the first time this work had been done since the construction of the Canal 160 years before. When the Canal was drained some interesting objects were found – pottery bottles, clay pipes, an 1875 shilling and lots of eels.

In January there was a break-in at the Abbey carpenter's shop. All the tools and equipment were stolen. Abbot Holman's car was broken into and maliciously damaged.

Since the School Modernisation Appeal was launched, several consultations had taken place. A survey of the west wing was made by the engineering firm of Dinardo and Partners, draft plans and drawings had been delivered by the architects, and an Appeal brochure produced. The first stage of the general plan, including a Fr Vincent Memorial, had three parts. First, the Lodge would be converted into a guest house of ten rooms and a common room, releasing the Hospice for School development. Second, the Hospice would be converted into a school house for 60 boys in one, two, three and four person studies. Third, a sports hall large enough for indoor Hockey and Tennis, with four Badminton courts, would be built. Later stages included the conversion of the old School to another school house and the renovation of the West Wing.

On 25 March 1984 the School Modernisation Appeal and the Fr Vincent Memorial Fund were inaugurated. Lord Brand, who had agreed to be a principal sponsor, came with Lady Brand to chair the meeting. The 70 guests were welcomed by Abbot Nicholas and Fr Francis on the Hospice gallery. After sherry, a buffet lunch for the Community and guests was served in the Monks' Refectory.

At the meeting, Fr Francis spoke on the educational need for the proposed changes. Mr Capon of Law & Dunbar-Nasmith outlined the structural and building aspects of the plan. He drew attention to the fact that the present buildings were reaching the end of their natural lifespan and that substantial repair work was necessary quite apart from the proposed change of use. The Bursar, Fr Edward, then explained how the work would be done, using the Abbey's labour force as far as possible. Finally, Abbot Holman explained how it was planned that funding for the project would be raised.

Because Easter was so late in 1984, the School came back on Wednesday of Holy Week. The School assisted at the main services after supper on Holy Thursday, Good Friday and Holy Saturday. As usual, a small group of French students had arrived to spend the term in Fort Augustus. They came from Paris, most from St Louis Gonzague, Franklin, which had regularly sent students to the School for the Summer term.

During the period between the end of the bulk of the exams and mid-term, the practice had grown up of organising two or more nights' camp for everyone in the School. The Junior forms had projects or field-work in Geography, History and Science to complete during the camp. The Seniors were more physically taxed as a challenging change from the pressures of the exam period. Mr Haines organised this highly complex fortnight, using CCF resources, while Mr Jones took the important role of chef at the permanent base camp. All members of staff supervised one or more of the ever-changing groups.

The core around which all other activities was constructed was a project in Adventure Training for as many Senior CCF Cadets as possible. Outside Cluanie, Glenuig, Srath Duilleach, virtually every Senior boy enjoyed two or three days rock-climbing and abseiling, two days Hill-walking and two days 'Yomping' (there was a 45 Commando RM Sergeant with them).

Form Three walked to Glenelg from the upper ruined broch on its defensive ridge to the 'redcoat' barracks at Bernera. The second day, spent on the main ridge south of Cluanie Lodge, gave the Geographers an opportunity to sketch glacial landscapes.

Form Two investigated the life of the shore at Loch Hourn – crabs and mussels. Form One, including two girls and four French boys, climbed Creag à Mhaim and revelled in the panorama from the summit.

The Hockey XI did well in the Kennedy Cup Six-a-Side outdoor tournament in April, but succumbed to sustained pressure against an Old Boys XI, losing 6-2. At a second tournament in May, P. Bennett won the Eddie Buchanan Memorial Trophy as the outstanding school-boy player. In June visitors from Augsburg, Inverness's twin town, came with a Hockey team, TSV 1847 Schwaben (whose basic skills were a lesson for any schoolboy). The School lost narrowly, 2-0.

In the Community, meanwhile, all was action and recovery. Abbot Nicholas had just returned from a pilgrimage to Lourdes with the Knights of Malta. Br Stephen had been put in charge of the Monastery and School grounds and staff.

Br Wilfrid returned to the Abbey after a spell in hospital. Br Placid was at Nazareth House, Aberdeen. Br Pascal was receiving special therapy at Strathpeffer for the hip he fractured the previous year.

The Cricket XI suffered badly from lack of practice and coaching for a variety of reasons. None of the bowlers was penetrating; the batting was brittle. Only one match was won. Vaughan won the House Match, while Lovat triumphed narrowly in the Athletics.

Several boys were involved in a Sonar watch from a raft moored off the Horseshoe in Loch Ness. Pairs spent twelve hour shifts, some during the day, some at night, monitoring a Sonar scanner with a visual read-out. The equipment operated from a 42 feet inflated raft moored in 600 feet of water. One group recorded a couple of 'interesting' readings at great depth, well below the thermocline and fish depths.

Prize Day was warm and sunny. Professor Dunbar-Nasmith CBE, Head of the Department of Architecture at Heriot-Watt University, presented the prizes. Fr Francis explained the Project to modernise the School, the architect's drawings for which were on display. Abbot Nicholas, in his concluding speech, gave a progress report on the Appeal since its launch in March. The sum assured in those 15 weeks was £94,000. In an entertaining address, Professor Dunbar-Nasmith offered some thoughts on the formative influence of buildings on life.

On its return in September the School was slightly down in numbers. The roll fell from 108 to 91 according to the Annual Statistical Returns.[1] Mr T. Henry joined the staff as Art Teacher and to take Junior French. Art was now a full time course in the curriculum, offering drawing, painting, graphics, photography, film-making, animation and screen-printing. There was also an Art Club which met on Tuesday evenings.

A. Mitchelson gained a First in Biochemistry at Oxford and had been accepted to study for a PhD in Genetics at Imperial College, London. J. C. Mitchell was studying Drama in Chicago, while D. G. Lyon was at the Royal Military College prior to going to the Staff College. Professor A. Anton, visiting Professor of Law at Aberdeen University, was appointed the UK member of the European Human Rights Commission, the first Scottish lawyer so appointed. W. Shiu, after gaining his medical degree at Manchester and an MRCP of England and of Ireland, was now Lecturer in Medical Oncology in the Chinese University of Hong Kong.

The deaths had occurred of J. A. Kennedy (1923-28) who died in May 1984 at Inverness, and Cedric Greenwood (1942-44) who died in Edinburgh at the end of August after a long illness.

The end of term play was a farce, 'Post Horn Gallop'. This displayed to advantage the manic militarism of Hugh Eaton as Lord Elrood, the skittish boyishness of Ciaran Keaney as George Willis, Scoutmaster (knobbly knees to the fore), and the unquenchable man-hunting femininity of Michael Igoe in the role of Ada the maid. The play was produced by Mr. G. Wilson, with Fr Edward as stage manager and make-up by Hamish MacDonald and Mrs Bryce.

The Rugby XV began with a convincing 24-3 win over Inverness Academy, but then lost to Keil 14-0. Five players went to the North of Scotland trials, of whom R. Giulianotti, P. Bennett, J. J. Knox and E. Grogan were chosen for the squad. Then came a 21-0 win against Aberdeen Grammar School, but the XV succumbed 6-4 to Inverness Academy who reclaimed the Ness Shield in a subsequent game. The School then beat Gordonstoun 9-3. Vaughan won the House match 6-3.

There was Cross-Country success for I. Dunn, who trained conscientiously from the beginning of term. He entered the North of Scotland Schools' Cross Country Championship at Kingussie. Although just over 15, he had to compete in the section including runners up to 18. He did extremely well to come second, beaten by a sixth year pupil from Millburn. Vaughan again won the Inter-House competition.

On 18 November Br Placid Grady died at Nazareth House, Aberdeen. He was born in 1905 at Lemington, Northumberland. After leaving school he worked for a time as a warehouse clerk and acted as organist at St George's, Bells Close, and as secretary to the Society of St Vincent de Paul.

He came to Fort Augustus on 20 April 1937, making his Perpetual Profession in 1941. For a time Br Placid was in charge of both the Monks' and School Refectories, but on 12 October 1944 he had to undergo surgery for the removal of a kidney. On his return he found he was incapable of active work. He took up tailoring and was given charge of the Linen Room in November 1945. At the same time he looked after the Polish men and women who did domestic work in the School. He kept up the tailoring even when his health began to deteriorate. After Dirge and Solemn Requiem Mass, Br Placid was buried in the Abbey Cemetery, his funeral being attended by relatives and by the School, as well as the Community.

A statistical survey of the Old Boys' membership list now revealed that there were 307 senior members, 65 junior members, 21 honorary members and 52 life members. The total of paid-up members was 181.

About 50 parents attended the Annual Parent/Teacher meeting on 14 February, slightly more than the year before. Although the weather was cold, the roads were not affected by ice. Several commented on the beauty of the Highlands as they drove north in the crisp, clear Winter sunshine. The interviews were centralised in the Assembly Hall, a more convenient arrangement than previous occasions.

Five days later tragedy struck the School, with the unexpected death of Biology teacher Mr Donald Angus. He had been suffering from a heavy cold over the Mid-term holiday, but nothing prepared the School when he was found dead on the Tuesday evening.

Mr Angus joined the staff in September 1975. For ten years he had been in charge of all the Biology teaching, presenting candidates at Ordinary and Higher grades with much success. He also took a practical and very useful part in extra-curricular activities – Rugby, Hockey and Cricket sets. He ran the Chess Club, and helped with the Computer Club. More recently he became interested in local history. He was survived by his wife, Anne and daughter, Morven.

On 15 February Rudolf Lipinski died in hospital at Inverness, where he had been taken by ambulance that morning after suffering a heart attack during Mass in the Abbey Church. At the time he was given the sacraments by the celebrant, Fr Andrew.

Rudolf, who described himself as the 'Abbey Pole', was 77 years of age. Before the last War he had been a postman in his native Poland and was very proud of this. Following the Nazi invasion, he was conscripted into the German Army. He was forced to serve until he was able to escape to the British lines during the fighting in Northern France. The story of his escape was exciting and he attributed his survival to the intercession of Our Lady, to whom he had an extraordinary devotion for the remainder of his life. He joined the Free Polish forces and after the War decided to settle in Britain.

Rudolf began his long service to the Fort Augustus Community at Carlekemp, but soon came to the Abbey where he remained for the rest of his life. In due course he became a British citizen, but was able to revisit Poland on holiday and be reunited with the surviving members of his family.

He worked for many years in the Abbey shop and its recent closure had been a heavy blow to him, for there he met many foreign visitors, particularly Germans, with whom he was able to speak in their native language. His interests were wine-making, coins and stamps, gardening

223

and ornithology. He was particularly good at competitions and often won prizes. He was very generous and sent much of his income to his relatives in Poland.

On 31 January, actor and broadcaster John M. MacGregor (1941-46) died in hospital. The School and Community were especially grateful to John for being the director of the Centenary pageant. More recently he had served as a local organiser of the School Development Appeal. John acted with the Royal Shakespeare Company, at one point understudying Sir Laurence Olivier. He also found time to advise on other School theatrical productions.

J. A. Kozlowski was now a priest with the Veritas Foundation in London. Having gained a BSc and MSc in Engineering at London University, he worked as an engineer in Canada, the USA and in Africa. When his wife died, he went to the Beda College, Rome and was ordained in 1981. (Fr Kozlowski subsequently worked in Norway and nowadays is doing parish work in the Ukraine.)

On the first anniversary of the launching of the School Development Appeal, a meeting was held to which benefactors of the Church and School appeals, Old Boys, and past and present parents were invited. Just over 70 guests attended. The main topic of concern was the unexpected decision, recently announced, to close the Abbey School in July 1985 because of the fall in the School roll. This decision had been put to the Community's Council and Chapter by Abbot Nicholas and the Headmaster, Fr Francis, and it was (somewhat reluctantly) endorsed by both bodies.

The parents' meeting was used to explain the reasons for the decision to close the School, to describe how the Community saw its future service to the Catholic Church in Scotland, and to ask that the generous support for the appeal so far given should not be ended in view of the continuing apostolate of the Abbey.

Such was the strong reaction to this by parents, Old Boys and other benefactors (who immediately came forward with extra financial guarantees), that it became clear the policy chosen by the Community was unacceptable and unworkable.

An Action Committee was formed that same afternoon, composed of parents, Old Boys, staff and local councillors. It was agreed that the beginning of Easter week would be the deadline for action. Letters were drawn up, to be circulated to all parents, Old Boys and supporters, explaining precisely what was necessary for the survival of the School.

The response would allow the Committee to report to the School Trustees, so that the decision to close could be re-examined in the light of that response and the outcome reported back to parents in Easter week.

After serving as Headmaster from Easter 1972 to Easter 1985, Fr Francis retired. This was the joint longest anyone had held the post (Fr Ethelbert McCombes had also served 13 years from 1939 to 1952), and it was marked by a steady progress in academic results and good standards on the sports field. He introduced computers into the School which made it possible to analyse examination results more accurately. He also delivered a series of brilliant prize-day speeches that would be long remembered. Fr Francis moved south as parish priest of St Edmund's, Bungay in Suffolk. He was succeeded as Headmaster by Fr Benedict Seed, an Old Boy and Science graduate of St Andrews University. His place as Housemaster of Lovat was taken by Fr Aelred Grugan.

The Action Committee consisted of Mr G. Breatnach (Chairman, a parent), Mr J. Johnstone (District Councillor), Fr Edward (Bursar), Mr J. Dunn (Accountant), Mr S. Dunn (Old Boy), Mr G. Wilson (Master), Mr R. Giulianotti (Old Boy and parent). The Prior (Fr Augustine) and the Headmaster (Fr Benedict) also attended meetings.

By their action and enthusiasm they gathered financial support and an encouraging number of applications for the School. The Committee had the support of Abbot Nicholas and the Community. At a Chapter meeting on 16 April, the Community voted to keep the School open and cancel plans for its closure.

In the Community, Fr Denys Rutledge was appointed Librarian, in succession to Fr Augustine. The latter continued to tend the monastic gardens with their abundance of flowers.

The Hockey XI lost four matches and won the game against Bedstone College on their Scottish tour from Shropshire. They were coached by an Old Boy, Colin Bryce, now on their staff. Lovat won the House Match 2-1. The School finished seventh in the Kennedy Cup Six-a-Side, while the Old Boys were tenth.

The extremely cold and inclement weather, combined with the unhappy state of the teaching profession in county schools, cut the Cricket season to a minimum. The XI beat the Old Boys and Vaughan won the House match in that sport and in Golf and Athletics.

At the Prize-giving, Mrs Winifred Ewing, local Member of the European Parliament, Chair of the Committee on Youth and Education, presented the prizes. She spoke of the importance of fostering harmony among nations. She noted the presence of German, French, Nigerian and Mexican boys in the School and commented that this was a sign of hope. She then presented the School with a copy of the 'Declaration of Arbroath', signed in 1320 by the leaders of Scotland and then sent to the Pope.

Three months after the launch of the Action Committee, a fighting fund of £35,000 had been raised. As a result of an advertising campaign the School received 100 enquiries which eventually led to a dozen completed application forms being submitted. This put the projected roll for the School in September in the low 90s.

When the School year began in October, there were 82 students. Among the staff, Mr A. Dempster left to take up a Maths appointment at Kilgraston. In his place came Mrs M. L. Fletcher whose husband had taken over the Golf View Restaurant (subsequently known as 'The Gallery'). An Old Boy, Mr P. M. Vallot, took over Fr Benedict's Chemistry classes.

By this time the Action Committee had been transformed into an Advisory Board. A number of Inspectors came to advise and to help the School. One outcome was that Ordinary Grade exams would be replaced by Standard Grade.

The Rugby XV were beaten in their opening game by Keil (22-10). Then came a 40-0 victory over Millburn Academy (whom they later beat again 35-8). Against Highland Colts the School lost 9-0. After Mid-term two matches in a row were lost against Wick High School and Aberdeen Grammar School. The final game of the season was an 18-13 win over Highland Colts. Lovat won the House Match.

A number of Old Boys generously gave their time to repair the boathouse roof, the tennis court, the gym floor, the outer wall and the bicycle shelter.

Two prominent Old Boys died: Dr Michael Roden (1937-41) and James Brown (1923-28).

In October and November, Cricketer Ian Botham walked from John o'Groats to Land's End in aid of Leukaemia Research, keeping close links with 'Breakfast Television'. A dozen boys from the School joined the walk in early November between Carrbridge and Pitlochry. The weather was cold, sleety and dreich. The boys raised £1000.

The highlight of the Cross-Country was the breaking of Chris Hall's School record of 23 minutes 13.5 seconds (which had stood since 1946) by I. B. Dunn who finished in 22 minutes 12.33 seconds. His dedication and determination to carry out his training, regardless of weather, was a lesson for all budding athletes in the School.

The Advisory Board had a constructive meeting on 17 November. A constitution was unanimously adopted. Abbot Nicholas thanked the members of the former Action Committee for their hard work and asked the new Board to give every assistance to Br Stephen in his new role as Vocations Director.

CHAPTER 20

The Abbey School
1985-93

THE annual opportunity for parents to meet Staff took place on 14 February. Fifty guests found the face-to-face discussions with teachers a valuable help in assessing the progress of their children.

Meanwhile, the Advisory Board continued to hold regular monthly meetings throughout the term. Much time was devoted to a review of how accounting procedures might be modified to improve the efficiency of the School.

The Board recommended that market research should be applied to improve the effectiveness of the School's advertising. In matters of publicity it was seen as advisable to liaise with Br Stephen in his role as Vocations Director.

Following the meeting on 16 March, the lay-staff joined the Board for a lively and constructive exchange of views. Looking ahead beyond the completion of the Hospice, the Staff were asked for their opinions on the plans for, and function of, the main School Block.

The Army Section of the CCF took part in the Spring Festival at Torgoyle where, over the weekend of 1-2 March, 45 Cadets enjoyed 18° of frost, a brilliant night sky, and some splendid shooting stars. On 12 February both Sections were inspected by the Naval Flag Officer of Scotland and Northern Ireland, Vice Admiral G. M. F. Vallings.

The Rugby First XV enjoyed a very successful end to the season when it went down to spend a weekend at Keil School in Dumbarton. They beat Hillhead School 28-6 and then, in a hard-fought game, also beat Keil 9-7. Except for an injury he sustained in the first match, the School Captain, E. Brogan, would also have been the Captain of the North of Scotland Schools' team. Nevertheless, Fort Augustus was well represented by R. Giulianotti, J. Keaney, J. Mackenzie, C. Wright, M. Masini and M. Giulianotti in the Senior squad.

The Hockey team, without many of the previous year's squad, had a good deal of re-building to do. They lost 2-1 against Highland HC in three half-hour sessions, and lost by the same score to Aberdeen Grammar School. By the second half of the term, the XI had developed into a competent side. They subsequently had two wins, four defeats and one draw.

On Sunday 9 March 22 Kilgraston girls came to visit along with Sister Duffy. Mr I. Keith had also brought along a dozen boys from Strathallan. The latter disappeared into the Monastery to find out about the life of the monks.

The Hockey match was contested in conditions so bad that well-wrapped spectators were driven away. Although they fought hard, the girls were beaten 4-0. After tea there was a Quiz which the girls won 41-40 to the accompaniment of vociferous support.

After delays due to exams and inertia, the Athletics reached full momentum near Mid-term. The House Competition was won comfortably by Vaughan, who nearly broke the record for the 1600 metres. R. Giulianotti was the individual Sports Champion, beating I. Dunn by one point. The latter continued his success by being highly placed in District and National Cross-Country runs. He then won the Scottish Schools 3000 metres and was chosen to represent Scotland in Wales on 19 July.

Cricket activities were cut to a mere three weeks by the over-run of Athletics and Hockey, plus CCF commitments. The School were defeated by the Old Boys (most aged 40 or over). The House Match was won by Lovat.

The Cookery Club, founded in January by Mr Jones the Abbey Chef, met as two groups of Sixth Formers on Tuesday and Sunday evenings. They learnt how to choose, prepare, cook and serve a meal, and capped their efforts by inviting guests to a three-course dinner.

On 25 February Br John Condon died at Nazareth House, Aberdeen. He had come to the Monastery in the late 1920s. Among other things, he was an efficient plumber and won a long-service medal with the Fire Brigade. Latterly he had manned the door and the telephones, as well as being the Monastery's contact with the Village. His kindness to the poor who called at the door, his devout attendance at funerals of numerous local acquaintances, and his care for the troubles of all, deservedly won him high repute. The School swelled the congregation at his funeral on 1 March.

Early in May, one or two warm days prompted thoughts of bathing, so the fire engine was deployed, the swimming pool scrubbed and 60,000 gallons pumped into the pool in four hours. Loch Ness water is brown with peat. After pumping and treating with sodium hypochlorite, the water became crystal clear.

A chance visit by Mr George MacLaren of Dundee, who had masterminded swims of the whole 23 mile length of Loch Ness, inspired a project to swim across the Loch. Abbot Joseph McDonald once completed such a swim, probably over a course from the Abbey boathouse to Glen Doe boathouse.

George advised the boys on training, safety and the application of oil and grease. He then took three boys to his Swimming club in Broughty Ferry and conducted an attempt to swim the Tay estuary. Thus on 8 June, Vincent Igoe, James McLinden and Bobby Brown spent 35, 45 and 85 minutes in the cold, grey, choppy salt water swimming respectively two-thirds of the way across, all the way across, and all the way there and back.

On 28 June Loch Ness fell calm. The two stronger swimmers, James and Bobby, crossed Loch Ness from the Witch's Stone to the Old Railway Pier, each with a boat in attendance. James took 35 minutes and Bobby 28. The crossing was three-quarters of a mile, not so wide as the River Tay. The temperature of the water was 35°F. The boys were only 13 years of age.

Prize Day was on Sunday 6 July. A warm day with long sunny periods welcomed the guests. Sir Robert Cowan, Chairman of the Highlands and Islands Development Board (and a good friend to the Abbey) presented the prizes, while Abbot Nicholas presided. He spoke of the benefits which the School had brought, not only to its members but to the locality, benefits which the HIDB supported with patronage and grants.

Around 35 Old Boys turned up for the Reunion (although only 19 attended the AGM). The Voluntary Week which had been such a success the previous year received little support. Only three Old Boys turned up this time.

As a result of Fr Stephen's vocations work, several young men participated in the life of the Monastery. Five Postulants were expected in the Autumn. The two Summer Schools for foreign students were well supported, with 130 subscribers under the command of Fr Andrew (first) and Fr Francis (second).

When the new School year began, Mr Seamus Coleman was the

new Art Master. He and his wife, Catherine, took over Craig Darroch vacated by Mr Tom Henry. In December Mr Gary Morris, the Geography Master, left for a post in the Army after being at Fort Augustus for more than three years. Mr R. Burnett came to take his place.

At the start of the season the Rugby First XV did not seem to be strong. However, the team developed well in skill and spirit. The first game (against Gordonstoun away) was won 10-0; the return game saw the margin of victory increased to 40-0. In a mini-tour of the North, the XV beat Thurso 44-0 but lost 24-8 to Wick. In the return game the XV beat a combined Wick/Thurso XV 36-0. In a hard game against Millburn, the School won 20-4. This result and a 7-0 win against Aberdeen Grammar School put the Abbey School team into the new Scottish Schools' Cup where the team was defeated 20-11 by Berwickshire High School at Duns. Lovat won the House Match 8-6.

On the last day of the Christmas term the School and Community were entertained by a play and some carol singing, with Fr Gregory on the piano and a cheerful solo on the accordion from John Kendal.

The play chosen was 'Black Comedy' by Peter Shaffer, produced by Mr Wilson, with set and lighting by Fr Edward, costumes and make-up courtesy of Hamish MacDonald, and some furniture loaned by Mr and Mrs Sabin of the Lovat Arms Hotel.

Martin Waugh and Giles Rencontre played Brindsley Miller and Colonel Melket. Vincent Igoe impersonated the beautiful and sophisticated Carol. Garry Buggy's Anglo-Indian accent was hilarious.

For once, Hockey was unaffected by the elements. The opening game of the season against Gordonstoun was a 1-1 draw. Later in the season there were four defeats, two victories and a draw (against the Old Boys). The First XI took sixth place in the Kennedy Cup Six-a-Side. The House Match was a 1-1 draw. The Hockey trip to Strathallan was eventful in that snow fell and blocked the roads home. Far from causing distress, this created another happy evening at the Pine Trees Hotel as guests of Mr and Mrs John MacLellan.

In Cricket the School were defeated by Joe Barry's XI, but they beat the Old Boys. Lovat won the House Match.

After many years of neglect, Football was surprisingly rediscovered. A School team was put together which managed to beat a local outfit 7-1 with a magnificent display of teamwork and individual touches of genius!

Some teachers, responding to insistent advice from the Inspectorate, spent time in other schools to study the content and organisation of their subjects elsewhere. Gordonstoun, Wick, Edinburgh Academy and George Watson's accommodated Fr Benedict, Mr Stone, Mr Vallot and Mr Stephenson.

At Prize Day Mr Charles Kennedy MP took the place of honour and Abbot Nicholas presided. In the presentation of prizes there was a change in the method of making an award. Instead of each subject having a prize each year, the meritorious conduct of a pupil became the criterion and its nature identified. This then became the title under which the prize was awarded (leadership, for example, effort, study and progress, personal commitment, church music).

On 25 August Br David Brooks died. He was nearly 70. He was a person who, once seen, was always remembered. Perhaps his smallness of stature made him approachable, but to a greater extent it was his friendliness, his playful spirit, his sincerity, his loyalty. He liked to meet people. When he raked leaves in the avenue it was more to welcome visitors and passers-by than to tidy the grounds or build a compost heap. When he collected the eggs or fed the chickens for Br Adrian, he feared the cockerels which used to chase him; his rapport was with people.

When he worked as Refectorian it was characteristic that a burden-some bulk milk jug was found to conceal only a cup of tea. It is likely that his guided tours for visitors round the remains of the old Fort, the Catacombs Chapel and the Cloister gave more information about his personality than about history; the tourists learned to love him and consequently to think well of the monks.

Latterly, his health caused him to fall asleep often. When he was once so affected, during a tour, his group wondered with concern whether to wake him, or wait till he awoke, or tiptoe silently away! They did not feel let down or antagonistic. His many correspondents, his friends from school and monasteries and from lengthy travels in Britain and Europe, the bus drivers and couriers, the countless visitors to Fort Augustus, would all miss him.

The Rugby XV beat the Gordonstoun 2nd XV, Aberdeen Grammar School FP Colts, Inverness Technical College, Highland Colts, Oban High School and Millburn, but were defeated by Keil School and the Old Boys. Lovat beat Vaughan 18-3. In the Scottish Schools Cup the Abbey beat the Nicholson Institute in Stornoway 22-0, but lost to Marr in Troon 0-12.

In October the School shared in the Loch Ness Scan which aimed to examine by sonar every part of the Loch. Media representatives surged frenetically around. But Nessie eluded the searchers.

BBC Television filmed twice at Fort Augustus. On 2 November they covered Br Stephen's work for vocations. This appeared at 6.55 pm on 4 November, and again on 'Breakfast TV', and later on Kenya TV and Australian TV. There were also features in the Sunday papers. The filming in April had not yet been broadcast.

These entertaining activities were interspersed with times of sorrow. On 17 October Old Boy Sean Waugh (1984-86) died by accidentally leaving on a chip pan and dozing off in the same room. The fumes overcame him, and some days in hospital on life-support failed to revive him. At School he was notable for his imperturbable good humour and philosophical outlook. He was good at golf. Some boys, Mr Haines, Br Stephen, and many Old Boys attended his funeral which was conducted by Fr Aelred.

Fr Anselm Richardson died on 11 November at Oulton Abbey in Staffordshire and was buried at Fort Augustus eight days later. He was at the School from 1924-29 and then joined the Monastic Community. Most of his work was done elsewhere: as a chaplain in Iceland, or in a parish in England, or as a convent chaplain. He was Abbot Oswald's Prior from 1951-59 and also briefly taught at Carlekemp. His sincere, down-to-earth spirituality, founded on the teaching of the Popes and on devotion to Our Lady, was one chief trait. Another was do-it-yourself practicality symbolised in the home-made unbreakable rosaries he produced. The report that he refused to become Co-adjutor Bishop of Iceland illustrates how hugely he was esteemed. He was a familiar figure striding through the Abbey church, taking snuff and blowing his nose with a large red handkerchief.

Abbot Celestine Haworth died on 7 December 1987. He was at the School from 1927-29 and then in the Monastery from 1929-67. After that he went to parish work and also served as a chaplain to nuns. He succeeded Fr Oswald Eaves as Abbot in 1959 and governed the Abbey for a single eight-year term. He was the first Vaughan Housemaster (1942-59), Mathematics teacher, and a rugged Rugby player up to about 1950.

His very unusual personality ensured that he could not remain unnoticed (although he would have liked to be). In prayer and at Mass he was expressive in gesture and word, trying (as it were) to release the inexpressible. He rather baffled fellow-worshippers who could only partially imitate or follow such devotion. At Mathematics he was similarly intense and inspiring, but he found it a trial to be patient with adolescent understanding. Nevertheless, he made up for his breaks in patience and was counted as perhaps the best Mathematics teacher the School had ever had.

Three new Postulants were welcomed to the Monastery: Br Garry O' Brien, Br Keith Bonnici, and Br Bill Houston. This gave some company to the veteran novice, Fr Ninian (David) Ward.

The 1987 Christmas play was Frederick Knott's 'Dial M for Murder'. Giles Rencontre played the lead Tony Wendice, while Vincent Igoe was his rich wife Sheila. The acting was convincing and carried the audience through the complex fortunes of the characters.

Over Christmas the kindling was chopped in the seclusion and warmth of the boiler room under the Church – an unnerving place if there alone because of the odd noises and automatic control of the boilers. The kindling (about a ton of it) was then distributed to about 70 homes of senior citizens. This was the fifteenth year of this good work. The logs were a gift from the Forestry Commission.

For much of the Easter term the Caledonian Canal was empty from Fort Augustus to Kyltra. At the bottom of the Canal, where the stream still flowed, the boys found boat-hooks, fishing-rods, golf balls and even a driver behind the seventh tee. Black mud covered most of the exposed Canal bottom, and in due course most of the boys too, who had to be hosed down before they could enter the School buildings.

Only for the Seven-a-Side tournament of 23 March was the School able to field a Rugby team. The XV won their match against the only other school team there, but lost to more powerful men's teams.

For the Hockey XI it was a term made frustrating by the weather. It caused the cancellation of all but one fixture. The XI beat Aberdeen Grammar School 5-3 at home. Vaughan won the House Match 4-3 and the Cross-Country.

In April Mr Chris Stephenson (1975-80) married Miss Johanna MacLellan of the Caledonian Hotel. This was a happy occasion joined by past and present pupils and conducted by Fr Andrew.

At the close of the Easter term, the School, staff and friends were entertained by the Junior Forms with a presentation of Richard Tydeman's 'Snow White Special'. Henry Gray was an effective compère, Malcolm Dent a vain, abrasive Queen, and Daniel Gary a Snow White who could easily outdo the Wizard duo of Maghnus Byrne and Andrew Hogg.

The Appeal to set up an Old Boys' Bursary for School pupils, especially sons and daughters of Old Boys, received £3325 in donations, £500 from the Old Boys Association. In addition there was £590 promised in Covenants. This last figure was one-third of the annual fee and would be enough to support one pupil.

The Old Boys' Reunion was held in the last week of June. This was an opportunity to wish Mr Hamish MacDonald and Mr M. Haines well in their retirement after 31 and 22 years of service to the School respectively.

September brought several changes. Fr Edward was appointed Headmaster and Bursar. Mr R. Burnett, Head of Geography, would assist him as Deputy Head. Fr Robert McKenzie left for parochial duties in Canada and was replaced as Housemaster by Mr Julian Shurgold, Head of History. Mr Gordon Wilson left after five years as English master to take up a new appointment in Aberdeen. Mr David Davidson joined the Staff as Head of English.

The new session also saw the Senior boys installed in their new study bedrooms in the recently completed Hospice. The ground floor of the Hospice now housed the reception area, offices for Headmaster and Bursar, and the parlour for guests.

The sudden death of Mike Haines, at his home in Milton on 18 October, cast a deep shadow of gloom and mourning over the Community, his fellow members of Staff, pupils and Old Boys. To those who knew him well, his health had been declining for some time. Nevertheless he continued going quietly about his work, attending at all times to the needs of others, as his labours with The Samaritans showed.

Born in 1925, educated at Weymouth College and Wellingborough School, he graduated from St Andrews University in Modern and Medieval History with English Literature. He served in the Royal Engineers from 1946-48 and was in the Territorial Army until 1953. From 1952 he was House Tutor at Strathallan School, before becoming a Housemaster at Rannoch School in 1959, joining Fort Augustus in 1966.

On Fr Vincent's death he unselfishly took on, with great success, the onerous task of Adjutant in the CCF Contingent, also acting as OC Army Section. There were many pleasant memories among Old Boys and others who remember not only his History classes, but also the hill-walking weekends, post-Higher camps and expeditions. He often said that if he had to die suddenly, he would choose to be on his beloved hills and mountains – possibly his own fireside chair was the next best thing.

During the late Summer, Abbot Nicholas attended a Congress of Abbots in Rome. Brs Bernard and Stephen travelled with him and stayed at the Monastery of St Paul Outside-the-Walls. In recent months several young men had come to see the Monastery. Philip Roche and Robert Baker were two of these Postulants.

On 8 December Bishop Colin McPherson of Argyll and the Isles ordained Brs Bernard and Stephen as priests. The Abbey Church was filled to capacity with people coming from as far as southern England and by the coachload from Glasgow. Many Old Boys were in evidence.

Stephen Dunn, the Old Boy representative on the Advisory Board, was now studying for the priesthood in the Spanish College at Salamanca. The Board conveyed to him thanks for his sterling work and wished him every success in his chosen vocation. Two parents were welcomed to the Board – Mrs McLinden from Motherwell and Mr Maclean from Lochailort.

A video had been produced showing School life and activities. It was primarily intended to help in promoting the School and increasing numbers. The video was made by North Scene Videos, Ardersier, Inverness-shire.

Recently the School had been represented at the ISIS Exhibition in London. The School stand was managed by Br Stephen, Mr Burnett, Mr Giulianotti and Graham Lappin. The photographs and posters attracted much attention, as did the video. The Exhibition resulted in a number of enquiries.

As usual, the Rugby squad turned out to be stronger than antici-pated. Nevertheless, there were gaps in key positions such as stand-off and full-back. The first game was a narrow defeat by Gordonstoun. There followed impressive wins against Oban High School (twice), Millburn and Inverness Academy. The trip north to Wick and Thurso produced a victory against Thurso, but led to a defeat by Wick.

There was very little Football. The Junior boys had played against a team from St Margaret's, Airdrie, drawing 3-3. Normally the Abbey played the local secondary school two or three times a term, and against a Village team once a term. However, due to some ungentlemanly con-duct from both teams, it was necessary to postpone any further Senior Football while the rule book was scrutinised to determine whether or not the Marquis of Queensberry had had anything to do with its writing!

The Photography Club had resurrected itself and was at last up and running. The Club had produced very few finished prints during the previous year. Now they were attempting album covers, landscapes, portraits and experimental photography.

Other popular activities included 'Dungeons and Dragons' (a fantasy role-playing adventure), the Video Club, and the Handiwork Club. The latter was based in an outhouse under the Church and involved the production of go-carts, furniture and tools.

The School Play in December was the exciting murder/thriller, 'The Big Killing' by Philip Mackie. Produced by Mr C. Stephenson, heading a team which included Mr H. MacDonald and Fr Edward, the play, with V. Igoe as the likeable rogue Peter Ashbury, was enjoyed by a large number of parents, pupils and Staff.

On 18 June 1989 a dozen boys rowed down Loch Ness from Fort Augustus to Lochend, a distance of 24 miles. This effort was in aid of the Handicapped Children's Pilgrimage Trust which funded trips to Lourdes for children with special educational needs.

It took the boys ten hours, in temperatures of 80° and more, before they arrived tired but in good spirits, landing at the same spot as St Columba when he sailed out to convert the King of the Picts at Inverness. The row raised the magnificent sum of £1800.

Bishop Colin MacPherson of Argyll and the Isles (the boundary of whose diocese was halfway between Fort Augustus and Invergarry) presented the prizes on 2 July. At the end of the ceremony a cheque for £1800 was presented to the Inverness representative of the HCPT.

Br Wilfrid Atkinson, for many years a regular oblate at Fort Augustus, died in July. He had been resident for a number of years in Nazareth House, Aberdeen. Before joining the Community, Br Wilfrid, who was a native of Preston, had been an Anglican monk and later tried his vocation as a Jesuit laybrother. For many years he coped with the Abbey's plumbing and also manned the door at the Hospice, receiving visitors.

Br Pascal McLaughlin died suddenly in the forenoon of Friday 29 September in his 92nd year. He was born in Clydebank and worked in John Brown's Shipyard before joining the Royal Navy in the First World War. He came to Fort Augustus and made his profession in 1932. He worked at many domestic chores in the Abbey until he fell and broke his thigh in 1985. His last years, when he had to use crutches and also became very deaf, were an inspiration to the Community by his cheerful and steadfast attendance at all monastic duties.

In the first week of October, the Annual Meeting of the Headmasters of the Benedictine Schools of Britain took place in the Abbey. Monk Headmasters from Ampleforth, Belmont, Douai, Worth and Ramsgate took part, together with the Lay Headmasters of Ealing and Ramsgate Senior School. Fr Edward was the host.

On 14 October Br Paul Bonnici, a native of Malta, made his Simple Vows in the presence of Abbot Nicholas. The Mass was attended by the School pupils. Br Paul's parents brought up the Offertory gifts to the celebrant, Fr Augustine.

In October 1989 *The Newsletter* appeared. It was green and A4 in size. It chronicled the arrival of three Apple Macintosh Plus computers fully installed and ready for action in the Computer Room. These were, in fact, the gift of the Old Boys' Association and of Ralph Giulianotti, as decided at the Old Boys' AGM the previous June. So now there were three new computers, plus the two original BBC machines, and one belonging to Mrs Upstone who, with Fr Benedict, took the Computing.

In early October Fr Benedict retired from the Fire Service which he had served on from 1961 – not because he wanted to, but because Fire Service regulations so dictated.

Most in the School would have known the little wooden 'fire station' which in recent years had stood at the top of the roadway leading down to the boathouse. Often its cheerful red doors stood open showing Fr Benedict pottering around the gleaming fire-engine while he carried out the maintenance necessary to make it ready for any emergency.

When the siren echoed round the Abbey precinct, it was followed in a few moments by the *hee-haw* of the engine's klaxon and everyone knew that Fr Benedict and his men were off on another errand of mercy.

The people of the Village showed their appreciation of this long service with a function in the Lovat Arms Hotel. Fr Benedict was given a commemorative Fire Brigade plaque and a cheque to enable him to visit Medjugorje.

In Rugby, M. Lynas was chosen to play for the Glasgow Under-16 team. The XV lost five games but won five, two of them spectacularly – 56-0 (against Fortrose Academy) and 52-0 (against Inverness Academy).

The Senior School play was the exciting Agatha Christie whodunnit, 'The Unexpected Guest'. After an 'unexpected' (but unavoidable delay) at Christmas – and a change of leading actor – the play was performed in front of a large and enthusiastic audience of monks, masters, parents and boys. Paul Douglas was notable as the replacement leading part. R. Pagliari was outstanding as the dead body. The play was produced by

Mr D. Davidson and Mr P-L. Delofeu, with make-up by Hamish MacDonald.

Due to the foul weather in January and February there had only been a few official Hockey practices. Although the very young XI did not win a single game, they competed well. There were six defeats and two draws. Vincent Igoe had an exceptionally good season in goal. Lovat won the House Match.

The Naval Section of the CCF was now the proud owner of a brand new dory powerboat which would be used as the safety boat. The Cadets had been invited to take a launch out on the River Forth for a weekend, giving them the chance to use their navigation skills and practise ship manoeuvres.

At £3 a year for Junior members, the Fort Augustus Golf Club was a tremendous bargain. The greens were good, the situation beautiful, and only the heather rough was displeasing. A new School schedule had come into operation in January whereby all day Saturday was free of Class and Prep periods. This enabled the pupils to golf all morning. About ten boys took advantage of this.

On 18 March the School had its first ever Open Day for prospective parents. A large number of guests were escorted round the School, visiting various teachers in their classrooms. After the success of this day (which resulted in the enrolment of two boys), another Open Day was organised for 27 May.

The warm Summer days of 1990 encouraged some of the School to go diving in the Loch for anything they could find. So far, nothing of value had been found. The swimming pool was filled and frequently used. There were even plans to cover and heat the pool by the beginning of the next School year at a cost of £20,000.

The School term would now end on 10 June, with the School returning in August. This would give a four-term year, as there was now a two-week holiday during October. The Abbey also planned to operate three English Language Summer Schools in 1990.

Since the previous issue of the *Fort Augustus News* Abbot Nicholas had celebrated his eightieth birthday, and a novice, Fr Maxwell, had been clothed as Br Bede. There were now 15 monks in the resident Community and five outside the monastery – Fr Francis and Fr Robert working in North America; Fr Mark in Edinburgh; and Fr Maurus and Br Michael being nursed in Aberdeen and Dundee respectively.

It was Br Michael who had cast the concrete steps in the Monastery garden by which the highest floods were measured – up to the fifth step in 1989 but only up to the second step in 1990. However, the high water lasted several weeks in 1990 and undermined the supports of the main platform in the boathouse. Extensive rebuilding would be needed.

Mr Hamish MacDonald was guest of honour at the 1990 Prize-giving. The Headmaster, Fr Edward, commented:

> *When the boys were asked who they would like as a prize-giver this year, they said they would like a Sports Personality. However, we discovered that all the main sports personalities had gone either to Sardinia for Football or to New Zealand for Rugby. So, when consulting the Advisory Board, they said that if we wanted a Sports Personality, who was more sporting than Hamish MacDonald who looked after our sports for over thirty years.*

There had been only one staff change since the previous year. Mr Cameron Donnelly had come to teach History, and for games and sports, including the (unofficial) Soccer. There would be two internal changes of Staff in the coming term. Mr Burnett was withdrawing from his post of Deputy Head, as he had only intended doing this for two years. Fr Edward had decided that the responsibilities of Deputy Head would be shared. As he himself was no longer Bursar, he planned to take over much of the administrative work himself. Discipline would be in the hands of the Housemasters. The curriculum would be taken over by Mr Coleman, with the title of Prefect of Studies. From August, Mr Stephenson would be over-all Games Master, with Mr Burnett still in charge of Rugby.

The 1990 exam results included 64 Highers sat, with 33 certificates gained at Band 'C' or above. Of the 136 Ordinary Grades sat, there were 110 certificates gained at Grade 4 or above.

About 60 Old Boys attended the Reunion. At the AGM Fr Edward launched an appeal to set up a Bursary Fund. Within a short space of time the Fund got off the ground with contributions amounting to £14,000, mainly from one benefaction of £12,000 from Mr A. McAllister of St Andrews.

At the Requiem Mass the Old Boys remembered Morgan O'Connell (1939), Sandy Young (1938), Bill MacDonald (1939) and James Robertson (1943). There was also tragic news of the accidental death of Alistair J. Sabin (1972-77) in Australia.

Sadly Br Bede Maxwell and Br John Brodie had found they were not suited to the monastic life and had left. The tailoring of the former and the handyman skills of the latter were a great loss.

The English Language Summer Schools (now in their fifteenth year) were held in the unusually long Summer holiday break (ten weeks). The one in June, not coinciding with Continental holidays, attracted only seven students. The July School, with 64 students, was blessed with unusually warm and sunny weather. The third Summer School, with 40 students, was unfortunate to encounter continuously cloudy conditions.

The School year started in August with 20 new boys enrolling. There were 14 resident members of the Monastic Community. Fr Stephen took over the duties of Vaughan Housemaster, while Fr Bernard returned to sacristy work and to the new project of restarting the Monastery shop for tourists. Fr Aelred continued as Lovat Housemaster. The new shop was planned to occupy the same premises that were once used by Fr Aloysius and Br Adrian.

Mr Ronnie Ross, an official of Glenmoriston Gun Club, who had given the School 25 pheasants, invited interested members of the School Gun Club to man the traps at an Open Charity shoot on 15 September. At a practice for this, the automatic remotely-controlled traps with a five-second loading-time rather daunted the five boys who had volunteered their services – they had to load 625 in quick succession.

The day dawned sunny, still and warm. By 11.00 am some 70 guns were in action from four 5-person stances. Encouraged and coached by some local young people, the boys became expert at the traps and performed well all day long.

On the way to the shooting ground, the Sherpa van broke down with petrol-feed problems. In the next eight days Fr Benedict distinguished himself by breaking down again in the red Renault 11 and then in the grey Renault 11.

The Rugby XV started well by winning their first game against Nairn Academy 18-12. The next game, against Oban High School, was lost 26-22. Gordonstoun then beat them 28-10. There followed losses against Millburn Academy (21-12) and Strathallan (16-4). The last game of the season was a 14-4 win against Oban. Lovat won the House Match 32-10. Four of the Under-18s, M. Lynas, H. Gary, D. Gray and S. Rhodes, were selected for the North of Scotland Team, and S. Obern for the Under-15s.

In November 1990 a feathered creature which had not been seen since the 1960s suddenly appeared – albeit in a lesser form. Much thinner, with a different cover (Fr Philip Hynes' mock-Celtic border), and with a less elegant type-face, but nevertheless recognisably *The Corbie* of old, appeared, with a pale blue cover. The new *Corbie* was the joint effort of Fr Aelred and Fr Stephen.

The funeral of Alistair Sabin took place in Fort Augustus on 20 November 1990, his body having been brought from Australia where he had died while on a walking holiday. Among the large crowd of mourners there were teachers past and present, Old Boys and monks. Another Old Boy, Peter Greenfield (1947-52), died on 16 January. The funeral took place in Birtley on 9 February, with Fr Benedict representing the Abbey, but Peter's ashes were to be buried in the Abbey graveyard on 31 March. He and his wife had been regular visitors to the Abbey and he had also tried life as a monk in the 1950s.

Other Old Boys, Gavin Queen (1976-80) and Jason Watt (1987-90) (now in the US Navy), were on service in the Persian Gulf.

In November, Abbot Francis Rossiter (Abbot President and Abbot of Ealing Abbey) conducted the four-yearly Visitation of Fort Augustus. His report on Community life and work was favourable. The only unusual element was that he announced April 1991 as the date for the election of a new Abbot. Abbot Nicholas's third eight-year term had passed quickly, making a total of 24 years in office.

The Senior School play (produced by Mr D. Davidson) was the Derek Benfield farce 'Off the Hook'. After a large number of cast changes, the play was given before an appreciative audience of parents, boys, masters and members of the Community.

Outwith the normal Hockey season, two matches were played. The School was beaten 4-1 by RAF Kinloss, but drew 2-2 with Alness HC. Maghnus Byrne was selected to represent the Midlands Under-18 Hockey team. He played in their crushing defeat of the East (Edinburgh) by 9-0. There followed a 4-0 defeat by Highland HC and a win over Strathallan Second XI (3-1). In the School's first appearance at the Independent Schools' Indoor Hockey (Six-a-Side) Tournament, they were knocked out 5-2 by Stewart-Melville.

An Old Boy get-together organised for Friday 10 May at the Pepperpot Inn, Eaglesham (courtesy of Angus Macdonald) promised the following succulent menu:

Amontillado Sherry with Abbey Soup
Chablis with Loch Ness Salmon

*Fleurie with Carlekemp Beef, Priory Sauce, School Vegetables
    and Potatoes*
Bordeaux Blanc Superieur with Kilgraston Surprise
Brandy, Benedictine and Coffee

★   ★   ★

On 24 April 1991, Fr Mark Dilworth was elected Abbot of Fort Augustus. Born in 1924 and brought up in Musselburgh and Edinburgh,
Gerard Dilworth went to St Andrew's Priory School, Edinburgh. At the
outbreak of war, this school was evacuated to Fort Augustus and the
boys continued their education there. Gerard entered the Novitiate
straight from School and was clothed as Br Mark. On completing his
monastic studies, he was ordained in 1947. After Ordination, he was
sent to Oxford where he took a Master of Arts in Modern Languages.
After a period teaching in the School, he was appointed to his first term
as Headmaster by Abbot Oswald Eaves. A few years later he became
parish priest of Fort Augustus instead. Shortly after Abbot Nicholas'
period as superior started, he was re-appointed Headmaster. But during
all these variations of office, Fr Mark was immersed in historical studies.
Finally, in 1979 he took up the post of Archivist at the Scottish Catholic
Archives in Edinburgh.[1]

In January 1968 Abbot Nicholas Holman had come to Fort Augustus
as its seventh Abbot. As a Chaplain to the Forces, he had served in
Northern Ireland, in France during the disastrous campaign of 1940,
then in Africa, Sicily, Italy and the Balkans. After the War he was Prior-
administrator of Belmont and later worked as Bursar of the Oratory
School. He succeeded Fr Anselm Rutherford as Claustral Prior of Downside under Abbot Christopher Butler, combining that office with responsibility for the parish of Midsomer Norton. In Liverpool he was Rector
of St Mary's, Highfield Street. Scotland, however, was *terra incognita,* and
the Fort Augustus Community was new to him. Respect for the office
he held soon turned to personal regard and affection. In 1975 he was
elected for another eight years, and once again in 1983. Abbot Nicholas
had the courage to propose completing the Abbey Church to mark the
hundred years since the Monastery was solemnly blessed. He had the joy
of seeing it consecrated.

Three days before the Abbatial election, the Chairman of the Advisory Board, Mr Ralph Giulianotti, was presented with the Insignia of a

Knighthood of St Gregory the Great by the Prior, Fr Augustine Grene.

At the prompting of a number of Old Boys, a request that Ralph Giulianotti should be created a Knight of St Gregory the Great was passed on by the Community to the Holy See, through Bishop Mario Conti of Aberdeen. (It should be remembered that in AD 573 St Gregory, the Urban Prefect of Rome, transformed his family home on the Coelian Hill into a monastery dedicated to St Andrew, with a style of living loosely based on the *Rule* of St Benedict.)

The presentation was followed by a meeting of the Advisory Board. In the afternoon the third Open Day took place when some 22 families visited the School.

The Hockey XI began with a 2-1 defeat by Stewart-Melville, followed by others at the hands of Glenalmond (2-1), Grammarians (3-2) and SHC (1-0). In the Five-a-Side SHU Highland District Indoor Hockey Tournament, the School finished in fifth place; in the Kennedy Cup Six-a-Side, the School took third position. Lovat won the House match 5-1.

At mid-day on 10 June 1991, the Abbatial Blessing of Abbot Mark Dilworth took place. Bishop Conti officiated. Attending the Blessing were Archbishop Keith O'Brien of St Andrews and Edinburgh, Archbishop Thomas Winning of Glasgow, Bishop Kevin Rafferty (St Andrews and Edinburgh), Bishop Vincent Logan (Dunkeld), Bishop John Mone (Paisley), Abbot Alfred Spencer (Pluscarden), Abbot Donald McGlynn (Nunraw), Abbess Joanna Jamieson of Stanbrook, and Episcopalian Bishop George Cessford (Moray and Nairn).

The new Abbot presented the prizes at the annual Prize-giving. In his speech, Abbot Mark (as a former Headmaster) underlined his commitment to the School and its prosperity.

After the Summer break, the new School year began on 28 August. Nineteen pupils had left but 21 had arrived in their place. The resident Monastic Community consisted of 13 monks, only four of whom were still below retirement age and fit enough to work full time.

The term started with a solemn votive Mass of the Holy Spirit on the first day back. This was followed by several days of 'Autumn Manoeuvres' during which the new students were settled into their classes and class timetables were adjusted.

New and stricter rules had been introduced covering Prep and study periods generally. Senior boys would now have to earn the privilege of working in a private study.

In Rugby, M. Byrne and D. Gray were selected to represent North of Scotland Schools against South of Scotland Schools at Elgin on 23 September. D. Gray contributed greatly to the North's first win against the South in the 23-year history of the District championships by scoring two tries. The final score was 21-4.

The School XV went on to beat a Gordonstoun Second XV (11-0) but then lost to Elgin Academy and Morrison's Academy Second XV (9-0). Against a combined under-18 team from Eastwood Schools and Clarkston, the School won 19-13.

The final edition of *The* (new) *Corbie* appeared in March 1992. A large advertisement on the final page showed a charging elephant holding a banner which read 'Don't forget the Abbey School Bursary Fund'. Around its middle was strapped a large white cloth which proclaimed 'All contributions large or small to the Bursar please. Raise £50,000 and a Benefactor will double it!! Amount so far £24,000'.

In April Fr Edward relinquished the post of Headmaster, replacing Fr Stephen as Bursar. Fr Aelred became the new Headmaster. In June 40 Old Boys attended the Reunion. On the 11 June the funeral of George Irvine (former police sergeant and long time parishioner) took place in the Abbey Church. The following month was marked by the tragic death of 16 year old schoolboy Louis Innes, killed in a motor accident on the A832 between Poolewe and Aultbea.

The School returned in August with a reduced complement of 52

boys. In September Fr Francis Davidson came back to Fort Augustus after five years at Portsmouth Abbey, Rhode Island, USA. Then Fr Michael Conlin, formerly chaplain to the Old Boys Association, died of cancer on 24 October after a long illness. He was 50.

Michael studied at Ushaw before being ordained by Bishop Wheeler in Leeds Cathedral in 1967. After serving as a curate he became assistant secretary to the Diocesan Schools Commission. In 1972 he was appointed Bishop Wheeler's personal private secretary. In 1982 he became a parish priest in Leeds and then at Yeadon. Despite his many diocesan commitments Fr Michael remained above all a pastoral priest, with an abiding concern for people as individuals and a mischievous sense of humour.

On 17 November 76 year old Fr Augustine Grene passed away. Born in County Tipperary in 1916, James Grene entered the School in 1930 and gained First Class Honours in French and Latin at Edinburgh University. In the Monastery he taught Dogma and served as Prior, Novice Master, Sacristan and was a (prize-winning) gardener. He had two terms as Headmaster of the Abbey School.

On 20 December Willie Doherty (1921-25), Joint Vice-President of the Old Boys' Association, died. Born in 1907, he lived in the west end of Glasgow almost all his life. After a few years early schooling at St Aloysius College with the Jesuits, he was among the first batch of pupils admitted when the Abbey School reopened in 1920.

Willie spent his life in the licensed trade. His father, the late Bailie William Doherty, was one of the first Catholics to enter Glasgow Corporation. On appointment as Chairman of the Scottish Legal Assurance Society, he handed over the management of his licensed premises to Willie and his brother Hugh. In 1938 Willie became the West of Scotland manager for Ushers Beer, an appointment he held until his retirement in 1970.

After a year as a special constable, Willie joined the RAF. He served in India and Burma as a Radar Technician and then in England until 1945. He was an all-round athlete as well; and his services as a member of a jazz band, as a violinist and tenor singer, were also much in demand. His three greatest loves were his family, the Abbey School, and the Catenian Association. One of his closest friends was Bertie McKillop (later Fr Andrew) from Lanarkshire, the oldest remaining priest of the Fort Augustus Community in the year 2000. Fr Andrew celebrated the Requiem Mass for Willie at St Peter's Church in Partick.

On 7 January the funeral took place of John Patrick Brown, also

Joint Vice-President of the Old Boys' Association. He was a Liverpudlian who started at the Abbey School in the early 1920s. In those days the rail journey from Liverpool to Fort Augustus took two full days, with an overnight stop in Glasgow. The boys had to wear either Eton collars and bowler hats, or the kilt. Meeting up with the Glasgow contingent, they would take the train from Queen Street straight to Fort Augustus, alighting at the railway terminal just behind the Lovat Arms Hotel.

During his 70 year association with the School, John Brown was its main ambassador. During the Second World War he was a Captain in the Royal Artillery, serving in Aden and India. He took to life in Asia with gusto, learning to ride a camel and studying Arabic and Urdu. He counted among his friends Sikhs, Jains, Muslims, Hindus and Buddhists.

He had three boys at the School at different times and his brother had two. Fr Laurence Kelly was so confused at the profusion of Browns that he numbered them in Latin *primus, secundus, tertius, quartus, quintus, sextus, septimus* and *octavus*.

After a lapse of a few years, the School received an invitation from the Upper Sixth girls of Kilgraston to go to their Annual Ball, held on 18 January. In order to prepare for the dancing, the School called on Mr C. Stephenson who had long experience of Scottish Country Dancing. After many nights' hard work, the boys felt reasonably prepared.

The Highland Dress arrived on the Friday night. Amidst excitement and laughter, the boys all tried their outfits on. The transformation from Sixth Form students to Highland gentlemen was amazing!

The School party was based at St Mary's Monastery, Kinnoul in Perth where the boys changed for the Ball. At Kilgraston the first part of the evening was given over to Scottish Country Dancing. Then the boys sampled the girls' cooking, prepared earlier in the day. Filled with food, they headed for the dance floor again where a disco had started. Everyone took part with enthusiasm.

The Ball finished just before midnight and the boys returned to Kinnoul. Next morning, after breakfast, the boys headed back to Kilgraston for Mass. Afterwards the Upper Sixth girls took the boys to lunch, followed by a short tour round the school and a game of hockey.

The Senior School play that year was the Tim Kelly farce, 'Soapy Murder Case'. It was enjoyed by an enthusiastic audience. After several deaths – and numerous mix-ups, the play ended with the resolution of all the farcical problems. It was produced and directed by Mr D.

Davidson and featured C. Murray as television soap-opera sponsor, Horatio Tucker.

The Hockey XI was captained by Maghnus Byrne who was selected to play for the Scottish Independent Schools (Scottish Cameleons) against past and current Scottish Under-18s. The School was beaten 2-0 by Stewart-Melville on the Mary Erskine all-weather surface which was incredibly slippery. The School team never settled on a pitch which was so foreign to most of the boys' experience.

On 12 January 1993 Sir Robert Cowan died. He had been a member of the Advisory Board and helped to procure a number of much-needed grants for the School from local funding bodies. By February the Bursary Fund stood at a healthy £67,000.

The sporting highlight of the year was the winning by the School Hockey Six-a-Side team of the Scottish Independent Schools Cup, something which they had never achieved before.

The School play, produced in April by Pierre Delofeu and Mrs Lesley Finlay, was an artistic success.

In May, Fr Richard Rotter (Bursar of the English Benedictine Congregation) and Mr Jonathan Deacon (accountant at Buckfast Abbey), came to advise on the multi-million pound building repair project and on the possibilities of further exploiting the tourism potential of the Monastery and the School. Later in the month alarm was caused by the steady deterioration of Fr Luke Cary-Elwes' wooden Cricket Pavilion, designed many years before by Fr Paulinus Gorwood. Some of the front wall had collapsed and it had sustained other damage to the rear.

Following the Old Boys' Reunion on 5 June (attended by 50 Old Boys), where the School lost the Cricket match, an announcement was unexpectedly made on 8 June that the School was to close forthwith.

Like all the rest of the School, Paul Igoe was deeply affected:

The day began like any other. I'd slept in and was running around my room throwing my uniform on, excuses flying through my head as to what I was going to say to the duty prefect. The term was coming to a close, we had been in Fort Augustus for nine weeks and six days (five to go) and everybody was eager to get home. I had an 'End of Term Exam' that morning – Geography – and it was supposed to be one and a half hours long. However, Dave Smith (a prefect) came in to the study hall in the middle of the exam to explain to us that Fr Aelred (the Headmaster) had called an assembly. In a state of confusion everybody in the exam made their way to the Assembly Hall. I arrived there and took my seat. The Assembly Hall was a large room with red and cream walls. At one end was a stage, at the other two large doors with windows on either side of them stretching out to the sides of the hall. Through these windows you could see a corridor with the Headmaster's room, stairs, the main entrance to the School, the Secretary's office and the Staff common room. I remember those events as if I watched them unfold in slow motion as in a film. An atmosphere of unreality permeated the room. Fr Aelred walked from the Staff common room (he had told the staff first) and into the Assembly Hall. We all rose to his entrance. He raised his hand then dropped it, signalling to us to sit. It seemed as if some ritualistic ceremony was being performed and we were simply spectators. Fr Aelred then told us the bad news. He simply explained that the School hadn't generated enough pupils for the next year and the Abbot had decided that it had to close. We stood, said a prayer – as we did after every assembly – and Fr Aelred left. Usually after assembly everybody would dart off to their class or room or whatever, but this time everyone stood still. For about a minute there was no movement, no sound, nothing, only what seemed like an eternity of shock and dismay. At last people began to move. I turned to my best mate 'Holmsey' who gave a kind of half-hearted smile of disbelief. We walked from the Hall out to the front of the School and sat in front of the Clock Tower. It was a sunny day but the Loch had stirred up a fair breeze to make it just a little 'nippy'. We talked for a while about whether or not to go back into the exam or to attend School for the rest of the week. Then I looked up to the Tower and thought of all the hundreds of pupils who had studied under it and what a dismal shame it was that it had to end. Tears began to run down my face. I realised that I wasn't just losing a school, but I was losing friends and a home, and my plans for the future had been shattered.

With less than 100 boys then in the School, it was projected that numbers would decrease still further when the next term opened in August. Prize-giving was cancelled. Disconsolate, the Staff held a farewell party on 11 June. Sunday 13 June 1993 was Corpus Christi. The boys attended Mass and then it was all over.

Saint Andrew's Priory, Carlekemp Priory and Summer Schools

CHAPTER 21

Saint Andrew's Priory School
1930-45

THE origins of Saint Andrew's Priory lay in Abbot (later Archbishop)
Andrew McDonald's ambitious scheme to construct an educational
and religious complex on the Melville Estate just south of Edinburgh:

> The Abbey School, a boarding-school formerly connected with the abbey, is about
> to be moved (1929) to Edinburgh to the Melville Grange estate on the out-
> skirts of the city. Melville Grange College is to consist of ten boarding-houses,
> each with rooms for 50 boys. A monastery for 100 monks and an equal number
> of lay brothers is planned and a church which can hold 1000 worshippers.[1]

In the event, the Melville Estate was found to be riddled with mine-
workings and unsafe for construction of the kind envisaged; the funds
also proved to be unavailable. After Abbot McDonald became Archbishop of St Andrews and Edinburgh, the new Abbot of Fort Augustus,
Fr Wulstan Knowles, sensibly enough, decided that economy would be
the order of the day.

The site for the new Priory School in Edinburgh's district of Morn-

ingside, had once been known as Streatham House. The buildings were rapidly altered by the architects Reid and Forbes to meet their new function as a school.

On 1 October 1930 the Abbot of Fort Augustus presided over the opening gathering, which included the Archbishop of St Andrews and Edinburgh and Canon John Gray (parish priest of St Peter's, in whose catchment area the new Priory stood).

The School began first, then the Chapel was blessed a few days later; regular Choir Office began on 5 October. Already the new Play Hall and Games room were ready for use, and the playing fields were in the process of being levelled.

The services of Gilbert Harding, an Honours graduate of the University of Cambridge, had been secured. Consequently, when he arrived in January 1931, the School would be able to take in boys up to the age of twelve.

The resident Community consisted of Fr Basil Wedge, Prior and Fr Kentigern Milne, and four junior monks (Brs Denys Rutledge, Edmund Carruth, Ethelbert McCombes and Andrew McKillop) who were to study for their degrees at Edinburgh University. Miss Kathleen O'Donnell SRN, who had been recruited as Matron, Governess, Housekeeper and Caterer, had been introduced to her duties by the Matron of the Abbey School, Miss Tyler. Mr and Mrs MacAllister were the Janitor and Cook, respectively.

Gilbert Harding, after teaching two terms at the School, left to take up a post of lecturer at Antigonish University, Nova Scotia in Canada. He was replaced by Instructor Captain J. G. Green, and then a second master arrived, Mr J. C. Maher MA (Dublin). Later Fr Swithun Bell came to teach French and Religious Knowledge.

In 1933 Fr Basil was replaced as Headmaster by Fr Matthew Stedall. Over the next few years the numbers in the School increased and, as the curriculum was still geared to Higher examinations, more staff had to be engaged. The Priory School was now charging higher fees than the very efficient local non-Catholic schools. As many of the boys were also on reduced fees, this led to the School making a loss of around £2000 a year.

Towards the end of the year Fr Matthew asked the Abbot of Fort Augustus to send him a young monk recently ordained, Fr Oswald Eaves. Commander Farie was also keen to have him on the Abbey School staff. However, he was sent to Edinburgh and was later joined by four other young monks, Frs Gregory, Alban, Aloysius and Joseph.

During the Eucharistic Congress of June 1935, the final open-air Mass was held at Saint Andrew's Priory, Canaan Lane. Outside the walls of the Priory a vocal body of militant Protestant Action members (under the leadership of Town Councillor John Cormack) lined Morningside Road and attempted to disrupt the proceedings, despite the efforts of the police.

Some stones were thrown at departing buses and there were scuffles. Several arrests were made among the activists, but no serious injury resulted, although many of those attending the Congress were put into a state of fear and alarm.

It was by now evident that by taking older boys up to Higher School Leaving examinations, it was financially impossible to compete with the endowed or State-aided schools in Edinburgh who were charging much lower fees.

During the Summer of 1937 the Prep class at Fort Augustus was transferred to Canaan Lane and it opened in its new role of Preparatory School only, with 45 boys. Most of the boys under twelve years of age returned. There were eight new boys. Fr Celestine Haworth and Miss W. Doonan joined the staff. Thirteen boys had gone up to Fort Augustus, one to Ampleforth, and one to Stonyhurst.

The School acquired the mansion and grounds adjacent to the current School property. The boarders took up residence there on 13 November. Four of the rooms had been converted into dormitories and named after English Benedictine Martyrs: Barkworth, Barlow, Gervase and Pickering. The seven junior boarders, along with Fr Oswald, processed to the building in cassocks and surplices and he christened the house. Next morning Mass was celebrated there on a temporary altar. Later there was a permanent altar and Mass was celebrated there every morning.

Among outings were several visits to the Monseigneur Picture House in Princes Street, and a visit to the theatre to see T.S. Eliot's 'Murder in the Cathedral' with Robert Speight as Thomas à Becket.

A Debating Society had been inaugurated that term with Fr Oswald as Chairman. Three meetings had been held to debate travel by road compared to rail travel, the abolition of speed limits, and corporal punishment as an alternative to lines!

One of the activities enjoyed most by the boys was the Horse-riding lessons taken through the Dreghorn Estate, where the young riders managed to get to grips with cantering their mounts. It was hoped that, by the following year, the riders would even be able to jump their horses.

Rugby was the strong point of the School, the boys being taken to watch games at Goldenacre and Myreside. Their opponents were the Royal High School Juniors (whom they beat by 14-3); George Watson's College Juniors (to whom they lost 3-6); Rochester House (another defeat); Loretto (lost by 21-3); and Belhaven Hill (played at Dunbar and lost 23-0).

Events on the Continent, meanwhile, also had their impact on the Priory School. Miss K. O'Donnell, the Matron, recalled:

> In 1938 the persecution of the Jews by the Nazi regime in Germany and Austria was at its height, and refugees were coming to Britain in large numbers. Many of these were children of parents one or both of whom were Jews or of Jewish extraction. Homes were being sought for them, either with families or in schools. Lady Margaret Kerr, always in the forefront where charitable works were concerned, asked Father Matthew [Stedall] to take a small boy aged seven, the son of a University professor who had been sent to a concentration camp. The mother was pure Aryan and was not allowed to keep the child. The arrival of this little boy, Kurt Wallach – scared and tired-looking – is one of the saddest memories I have. I remember so vividly his small canvas trunk packed with such love and care by a mother who had little or no hope of ever seeing him again …. He was a very brave intelligent child, and soon learned English, made friends and settled down. Father Matthew got an older brother of about fourteen years placed in the Abbey School. Towards the end of the War I heard that the father had survived the concentration camp, was released by the Allies, and came to Scotland … he recovered and later got a post in America where he took the boys.

The Easter Term in 1938 saw a new facility made available for the boys. A former laundry had been equipped with carpenters' benches. The room was now littered with newly-assembled toothbrush-racks, pipe-racks and calendars. Much excitement was caused by the School's acquiring a 'real talkie' film projector, a GeBoscope.

The School Gymnasium, meanwhile, was not only put to use for Games but could be turned into a rink for Roller-skating! Weekly Swimming took place at the Drumsheugh Private Baths at the West End. Among the visits made that term were Edinburgh Castle, the Botanic Garden, Edinburgh Zoo and Leith Docks.

The Prep School Boarding House was now known as St Bede's, having been completely re-decorated by the Lay-brother painters.

A House Competition between the four dormitories had begun. Marks were gained or lost for general studies, tidiness, cleanliness, common sense, manners, speech and punctuality.

The annual visit of His Majesty's Inspectors took place in the Summer of 1938. Around the same time Miss M.I. Ellis, who had served the Abbey School for many years, joined the staff.

Corporal T. Sweeney of Redford Barracks trained the boys for the Annual Sports on 4 June. Although it had been raining, the rain lifted for three hours and so allowed the parents to watch the whole event from the terrace as usual. Especially appreciated was the Riding Gymkhana, for which the horses were lent by the Spylaw Riding Academy. Major-General Sir W. Maxwell-Scott travelled from Abbotsford to present the prizes, and the afternoon's activities were privately filmed by Mr D. Grant.

J. S. Lawrie of Trinity Academicals coached the boys in Cricket, the lower sets being assisted by Br Joseph and Miss Ellis. Three of the games were lost, one cancelled and one won by 42 runs (Rochester House).

On the Feast of St Peter and St Paul, 20 boys received the Sacrament of Confirmation at the hands of Archbishop McDonald.

The Annual Speech Day took place on 15 July. The programme consisted of songs, recitations and piano pieces, followed by a sketch in Latin. After the Headmaster's speech, the prizes were distributed by Lady Moncrieff. After the tea interval, the boys presented Euripides' play 'Iphegenia in Tauris', produced by Fr Denis and performed in the Greek Theatre erected on the lawn.

Shortly after the new School year began, the Priory was devastated by an epidemic of chicken-pox which stayed for six weeks and marred studies, games, the mid-term holiday and general activities. Because of the international crisis, the boys were thrilled by being fitted with gas masks and agog at the possibility of having to dig trenches!

The most interesting excursion that year was a visit to the Home Fleet which was stationed in the Firth of Forth. Fr Oswald drove the boys to South Queensferry where they embarked on a small craft which took them all out to HMS 'Royal Oak'. From its deck they were able to get a close-up view of HMS 'Nelson', 'Sheffield', 'Courageous' and the aircraft carriers.

Inside the Priory building, the former woodwork room had been transformed into a bigger Chapel than was possible in the old one in St Bede's House. The boys helped to pull down the walls. Then the sanctuary floor was raised, the arch built and the altar fixed in place. Br Martin took over and completed it in time for the first service of evening Compline on St Benedict's Day, presided over by Archbishop McDonald.

Among the new boys in the Summer of 1939 was Angus Pirie Watson (later to become Fr Vincent[2]). Fr Oswald had bought a 'Home-broadcaster' which he brought into the classrooms for speech-training. The boys were therefore able to give their own concerts 'over the air'.

Speech Day was held on 25 July, Mrs More-Nisbett of Cairnhill distributing the prizes. The Headmaster read a very favourable report from HM Inspectors who had visited the school that term.

On 26 August 1939, 18 Priory boys, evacuated from Edinburgh, boarded the train from Newhaven Station. It took almost ten hours to reach Spean Bridge. It was well after midnight when they finally arrived at Fort Augustus. The rest of the boys followed, one by one.

For their accommodation (as there was none at the Abbey itself), Mr Pimley handed over his home in the Old Convent for classes and dormitories. The 39 boys were transported backwards and forwards first, in the Abbey lorry and then in a luxury coach.

The new boys were captivated by the home farm at the Convent. They roamed the woods or paddled in the trickle of the River Tarff. Some even tried to milk the cows, not always successfully. The Aeronautical Society continued under Fr Oswald, who also took the First Set for Football. In all, Fort Augustus offered activities of many kinds:

The romance of the Fort, the spacious countryside, mountains clamouring to be conquered, ships in the loch and always the possibility of a monster (even though there are no more tourists) – the tale has hardly begun. The days fly past always bringing something new. They are crowded days too, the morning and evening for studies, long afternoons of recreation ringing the changes on rugby, hare and hounds, cubs, model aeroplane competitions, cinema and lectures.

Frs Andrew McKillop and Edmund Carruth joined the staff, while the Matron, Miss Ellis, left the Abbey after 17 years service.

The Aero Society now had 45 flying models. A photograph which appeared in *The Corbie* caused a considerable stir. Captioned 'Our Indoor Squadron', it showed 20 model planes lined up in formation on a billiard table. Evidently, when the film had been sent to be developed in Inverness, someone had suspected it to be the work of a spy, for not long afterwards members of the British security forces visited the School to question Fr Oswald![³]

Every three weeks the Prep School enjoyed a full day holiday. The boys revelled in the many activities open to them – Cricket, Boating, Tennis, Model Aeroplane flying, Mountaineering. There was bathing in the swimming pool, in mountain lochs and streams and picnics in the hills, or at the water's edge.

It was at the Annual Sports Day that the reality of evacuation hit home. Events had to be curtailed. There were no parents and no distribution of prizes.

There were no teams of the same standard to play Cricket against, only the Abbey School Third Set who were beaten by the youngsters 97 runs to 25. Inverness Academy Juniors were older and beat the Saint Andrew's team by 70 runs. Nevertheless, the coaching by Frs Edmund, Gregory and Aloysius led to great improvements.

Winter 1940 marked the second year of Saint Andrew's Priory School at Fort Augustus. Much had been done over the previous twelve months to make the boys' quarters in the Hospice and the Old Convent more comfortable. There was a new classroom and recreation room at the Lodge, new and better changing rooms for Games, and a workshop with many tools and gadgets.

Fr Anselm Richardson left the staff to take up duties as a Chaplain to the Forces. Frs Aloysius, Maurus, Thomas, Jerome and Br John came in his place, accompanied by Mr Wilfred Worden, the well-known pianist.

Sport and recreation continued as before. Although the Priory Rugby teams made great improvements, they were not tested in any fixture with a rival XV. The Hallowe'en party was as great a success as ever. The boys' needs were few: 'A roaring fire in the grate, plenty of toast on the hearth and a big dish of jam on the table.'

On the Feast of the Immaculate Conception the Priory School presented a Nativity Play on the School stage, to the Community, the Abbey School, several parents and friends. 'Come to the Manger' gave great credit to all who took part. Written by Sister M. Milroy SND, with music by Mr Worden, the play was staged by Fr Thomas. Several of the pieces as well as the overture were the work of Mr Worden who also conducted the orchestra composed of Frs Thomas and Gregory (violins), John-Baptist (viola), Aloysius (double bass), Andrew (horn), Cyprian (drum and bells), Br Aidan (clarinet).

Fr Ethelbert McCombes was appointed Headmaster of Saint

Andrew's Priory School. Only one boy left, to attend another Public School – G. Green, who left for Downside College.

Full use was made of the day-holidays with picnics, cycle-runs and a good feed at the end. Each Sunday there was a tea party at the Abbey Lodge, where Mgr Comyn usually brought a few welcome 'extras'.

It was a great joy to the Air Scouts' Group Scoutmaster, Fr Oswald, when the BBC made the official announcement on 31 January that the Aeronautical Society were the first Air Scouts ever. The boys were thrilled when a plane from the HQ of the Observer Corps flew low over the Abbey and dropped a message to the Air Scouts by parachute.

When the Priory boys returned to Fort Augustus for the Summer Term, they found a new Headmaster. Fr Matthew Stedall had been transferred to a new post within the Monastery and it was decided, under wartime conditions, to bring both Schools under one adminis- tration under Fr Ethelbert, with Fr Oswald remaining as Housemaster for the Junior School.

The Air Scouts, who were now joined by Air Cubs, had a packed and varied programme of activity. They made a trip to Evanton where they were shown round by Pilot Officers Brown, Craig and Fryer (father of Kevin Fryer, later a boy at the School).

The new School year 1941-42 began with many new faces among the staff and the pupils. Almost the entire IV Form had been lost the previous term, having joined the Senior School.

Fr Swithun Bell rejoined the staff after many years absence. Mr A. Scott and Mr J. Douglas became resident masters, while Fr Edmund left to become a Chaplain to HM Forces.

Rugby continued to be played every Tuesday and Thursday, but Fr Oswald, who had been Gamesmaster for the previous eight years, resigned and was succeeded by Mr A. Scott.

Although the Spotters' Club was now joined to that of the Abbey School, Saint Andrew's Priory decided to form their own Junior Section, as the Club had grown so rapidly. As so many of the original Air Scouts had passed on to the Abbey School, both troops were joined.

The Cubs were delighted to receive a visit from the Chief Scout Commissioner, Lord Glentaner. The Pack had increased in size and so a new Six was formed.

Old Boys of the Priory were active all over the world. F. Addly was now at the British Embassy, Washington DC, while G. Smith had seen action in Malaya as a 2nd Lieutenant in the Argyle and Sutherland

Highlanders. K. McLennan was a pilot in the RAF, Oswald McDonald was in the USA training to be a pilot, and A. Hodgson was serving as a wireless operator in the Merchant Navy. D. Devlin (Br Kentigern) was a novice at Ampleforth Abbey and A. Fegan a professed Brother of John of God, working in a hospital in Scorton, Yorkshire.

In 1942 an eight year old boy joined the School. Donald Cammell, destined to become one of the finest film directors in the world, came to Fort Augustus where he spent two terms at the Old Convent before leaving.[4] According to his biographer, Sam Umland, 'the time he spent there was very critical for him (he didn't like the experience at all, and in fact ran away once or twice; his maternal grandmother lived in Drumnadrochit)'.[5]

Early in 1943 Saint Andrew's Priory acquired the Abbey Cottage as a boarding house to serve as an overflow to the Old Convent. Miss W. Doonan, who had been First Form Mistress for the previous three years, left for War reasons. Miss D. Stanmore replaced her. Mr J. Douglas, who had been on the staff for a year, departed for further studies at university. Eighteen new boys arrived and eight left to go to the Abbey School.

The boys had been entertained to a large number of 'talkie' films through the generosity of a parent who presented the school with a Rotary Converter.

There was sadness at the news of the death of two Old Boys – Oswald McDonald – killed in the USA while training in night flying; and K. McLennan, also killed in an air accident. There was better news of Gordon Smith – after twelve months suspense it was learnt that he had not been killed in the Malayan Campaign.

On 9 October 1945 Carlekemp Priory School, successor to Saint Andrew's Priory, opened in North Berwick, East Lothian.

CHAPTER 22

Carlekemp Priory School, North Berwick

1945-77

THE reasons that made it necessary to establish a new school were many and varied. For example, it was difficult to restore and re-organise the Abbey School after the hostilities of war ceased. However, it was (as the Editor of *The Corbie* put it) Divine Providence and the leadership of Abbot Wulstan Knowles which overcame all obstacles.

At the end of the War, the buildings and grounds in Edinburgh which had been taken over by the Army (the Royal Corps of Signals) were still not available for the use of the Priory School. In addition too many boys had been accepted for entry in September 1945 to allow the School to go back to the restricted accommodation at Fort Augustus.

Negotiations were actually quite advanced for the purchase of Naemoor, a property at Rumbling Bridge in Kinross. However, this fell through. Then by a stroke of good fortune the Benedictine Abbess of Holme Eden, near Carlisle, formerly the Abbess of the Old Convent at Fort Augustus, and the sister of Old Boy Lord Carmont, told her brother to ask St Benedict to find a buyer for Long Bellenden, a handsome property he owned at North Berwick in East Lothian.

So it was that on 9 October 1945, after a considerable amount of searching for a suitable site, the boys finally came to the mansion house

of Long Bellenden (now reverting to its former name of 'Carlekemp'). Situated on the western edge of the seaside resort of North Berwick, East Lothian, the building had been designed by John Ross in 1898 for the papermaker James Craig.

The walls of Carlekemp were constructed of snecked Rattlebags stone; the interior was an elegant mixture of Gothic, Tudor and Jacobean ornamentation.

Plans were quickly made for the removal of the Junior school from Fort Augustus. On 24 June 1945, Fr Oswald Eaves ALCM was appointed Headmaster. The staff consisted entirely of masters who had worked in the school at Fort Augustus: Fr Maurus Whitehead (Prefect of Discipline), Fr Gregory Brusey (Master of Music), and Fr Edward Delepine (Classics Master). The Matron, Miss K. O'Donnell SRN, Mr A.V. Scott and Miss Stanmore also remained on the staff.

The preparation of the new building, close to the sea and bordered by a golf course, was in the hands of Frs Oswald, Maurus and Gregory and Miss O'Donnell. Br Joseph, Br Pascal, Mrs McCawley, Mrs Tyrell and Miss Moyra McKay, and many others, also assisted. Domestic servants (to clean the building and prepare food) were few at first, but the number gradually increased.

The first bell for classes rang on 10 October, the day Fr Abbot arrived from Fort Augustus. Next day he celebrated a *Missa Cantata* at an altar erected in the Great Hall, boys and monks making up the choir.

Among the new boys were Angus Macdonald, George Davidson (later Fr Francis Davidson OSB, the last Superior of St Benedict's Abbey), Roger Seed, Jamus Smith, John Thorlby (later a member of St Patrick's Missionary Society [Kiltegan Fathers] in Brazil), Owen Halloran, Mike Tyksinsky, Andrew Maczek, John Sclater, the Marquess of Clydesdale (the present Duke of Hamilton), and George Hope of Luffness.

On St Benedict's Day (11 July) the Archbishop of Edinburgh, Andrew Joseph McDonald OSB, attended a celebratory lunch along with the Prior of Nunraw, the Very Rev. M. Sherry OCR, the Rev. Peter Walter OSB, Sir Hew Hamilton-Dalrymple, Col. J. P. N. H. Grant, and Fr Thomas Gallagher, parish priest at North Berwick. In the afternoon, in the presence of many parents, the Archbishop confirmed 22 boys, Sir Hew Hamilton-Dalrymple acting as godparent to all.

During the first Autumn and Winter the School was unable to play Rugby as the ground was still requisitioned by the Air Ministry. To compensate there were regular games of Football on the sands nearby and strenuous games of Rounders.

Cricket was played weekly on the grass in front of the house. In February the Carlekemp Stables were taken over by Mr Guy's Gullane Riding School and soon most of the School were taking riding lessons on the Broad Sands under the expert eye of Mr McRae.

Apart from the Annual Sports, the School enjoyed many other activities – visits to the King's Theatre, Edinburgh to see Gilbert and Sullivan operettas performed by the D'Oyly Carte Company, excursions to Tantallon Castle, Nunraw Monastery and boat trips to the island of Fidra and to the Bass Rock.

Most adventurous of all, however, was the Mid-summer Excursion to France arranged and led by Fr Edward. The visit was made possible through a POW camp in Germany where Fr Gregory's brother had been imprisoned along with a French priest, Fr. Delcourt, a teacher in a French seminary. After the War, Fr Gregory was contacted by Fr Delcourt and the Mayor of Charlieu about bringing over a party of boys.

The boys left with Fr Edward on 26 July, travelling via Newhaven and Dieppe, arriving in Paris next day. After a brief tour they travelled overnight and reached Charlieu on the Sunday morning. Among the highlights of their stay was a pilgrimage to Paray-le-Monial, a 70 kilometre bus tour of the upper Loire Valley, visits to ancient castles and priories, a 40 kilometre cycle run, crowned by a bathe in the Loire. The boys lived with families of the boys they had corresponded with the previous year. They arrived back on 7 September looking tired but healthy!

Throughout the Autumn and Winter terms, between the hours of 4pm and 6pm, the School enjoyed a varied selection of films. Mr Worden came down from Fort Augustus and rigged up a system of loudspeakers in every classroom. He used the amplifier of the film apparatus to relay gramophone, radio or microphone communication.

During the Summer season the boys made good use of North Berwick's open-air swimming pool where Mr McCracken coached the boys individually and in classes.

Every Saturday afternoon the Cub pack met under Cubmaster Fr Gregory, using the woods in the School grounds for happy hunting, sometimes puzzling passing golfers with their enthusiastic howls and other animal noises!

From Autumn 1946 to Summer 1953 no information about Carlekemp was published in *The Corbie*. Hence, none is available (since it does not exist in other sources). Previously known as 'The Preparatory School Notes or Cuttings from the Carlekemp Chronicle', it had by now been changed to the plain 'Carlekemp Notes' and consisted of little more than a page, in contrast to the often very detailed record which appeared up to 1946.

One of the most happy and most memorable events in the history of Carlekemp took place in 1948. The great English golfer, Sir Henry Cotton (1907-87), met Fr Oswald and made several visits to Carlekemp before winning the Open Championship at Muirfield, a few miles west of North Berwick. Matron Miss O'Donnell vividly recalled the event:

The evening before the final round he called as usual and, on leaving, the boys wished him luck and added that they would pray for him. He said (jokingly, we thought), that if he did win, he would come here and show them the cup. Next day, everyone had their ears to a radio set. We were all thrilled to hear he had won. But the excitement was terrific when suddenly a fleet of press, radio and film photographers' cars drove into the drive and it was announced that the great Henry Cotton was on his way. Everyone was outside to greet and congratulate him. The boys danced a Scottish reel round him for joy. Cameras clicked as he held the cup aloft for everyone to see. During the next week the hero, School, Community, Staff and boys were on every film screen in the British Isles. We got messages about it from all over. Later on he gave a Silver Golf Cup to be competed for by the boys. He also very kindly presented a cheque to Fr Oswald, who used it to buy some badly-needed seats for the chapel.

Probably the most unusual game ever played at Carlekemp took place in 1951 when the School took on Angusfield at Soccer. Chris Dunn was in goal and Carlekemp won 4-1. Angusfield was the only school which fielded a *girl* in the Rugby team – the Headmaster's daughter – and she was no pushover, giving as good as she got.

Because of chickenpox and measles Carlekemp's 1953 Hockey season saw only one match played with a full team, against Belhaven Hill at Dunbar. The School performed excellently, winning 2-0, helped by having practised regularly against a boys' team stiffened with masters.

The Summer term began with the prospect of Scholarship and Common Entrance examinations. Already P. J. Smyth had been successful in the Ampleforth Scholarship exam. The Common Entrance was due on the 15 June, but before that there would be a very welcome break for the Coronation holiday. And there was not a little local interest in that event. The sister of one pupil, Lord Binning, was to be one of the Queen's train-bearers at her Coronation in Westminster Abbey. In anticipation, the Saltire was already at the mast-head on the flag-pole high on the School roof.

That term, Golf was especially in favour with the boys. They practised diligently around the School – so much so, that one boy surprised himself and delighted his companions by holing out in one, from the back lawn to the Headmaster's Office via a window pane!

The following year (1954) Prize-giving took place on 17 July. Mgr John Breen gave away the prizes in the Study Hall. After the School song 'For God and St Andrew' had been sung, the Headmaster, Fr Ethelbert, made his annual report. The visitors then heard a number of songs from the School Choir. After tea there was a display of Highland Dancing, presented by Mrs Pearson and her staff. This culminated in a grand massed Highland Fling.

In Rugby the Carlekemp team had little chance against bigger, heavier and older opponents. In Hockey, however, where weight and size did not matter so much, good victories were recorded against Belhaven, Fettes and Loretto. Most of the Cricket matches were also won.

The England Rugby XV and the All Black Touring Team both made use of the School field for practice before their matches against Scotland.

There was a record entry for the Common Entrance examination. Fifteen boys were entered and 15 passed.

Thirteen new boys arrived at North Berwick in the Autumn term of 1954. On the Rugby field, once again, it was clear that the youth of the Priory School team made success unlikely. However, hours of practice and patient instruction on the part of Mr Beauchamp meant that, although all matches saw the School defeated, the boys showed great spirit and went down with honour.

Chess and Monopoly were all the rage. Games that had started but were still unfinished at bedtime were carefully preserved till next day.

On 15 December Frs Gregory and Edward produced the School Nativity Play. One member of the audience wrote:

There was a large cast, and everyone who took part deserves great credit. The speaking and singing were particularly delightful, and no one had any difficulty in hearing every word. Father Edward somehow manages to produce, as if by magic, a most attractive stage complete with an efficient and brilliant lighting system, and wired for sound. The stage springs up like a mushroom growth just before the play, and is dismantled and stowed away just as quickly after-wards.

Fr Edward produced the play and acted as stage manager; Fr Gregory was in charge of the music; Miss Walker costumed the actors.

A recent arrival in the School was a beautiful television set, the gift of Lord Haddington. It was installed on the eve of the Immaculate Conception. The whole School was able to see the Scotland versus Hungary Football Match the following day. The 7.30 pm television News was now a feature of School life, ending with bedtime half an hour later.

On 20 May Archbishop Gordon Gray came to Our Lady, Star of the Sea in North Berwick to confirm 26 candidates from the School. The Priory School Choir, under the direction of Fr Gregory, greeted the Archbishop's entrance with '*Ecce sacerdos magnus*'.

Towards the end of the term came the Annual Sports where the Henry Cotton and McCann Golf Cups were competed for. Local day-boy Garth Morrison excelled himself by winning both Cups, as well as the Parents' Cup for the 440 yards (open). On 16 July the Speech Day ceremony was presided over by the Countess of Haddington.

The 1956 Michaelmas term saw an increase in School numbers to 67, seven of whom were day boys. There were 16 new boys and a quick head count revealed that there were 23 boys in the School who had brothers at Carlekemp or at the Abbey.

Miss M. Walker, First Form mistress, who had been at Carlekemp for four years, left and was replaced by Mrs Gilhooley, a native of North Berwick with many years teaching experience in Linlithgow.

On 8 December the annual Nativity play was performed. That year it was entitled 'Come to the Manger'. Quite a crowd of friends from North Berwick attended. The audience applauded the players, and Fr Edward (who was responsible for the production, training, stage-building and lighting) and Fr Gregory for the fine singing of the Choir.

Recorders were very popular, especially among the lower Forms. Fr Gregory hoped to encourage the formation of a serious recorder group. Five boys were presented for the Royal Academy piano examinations and all passed.

Another innovation was the model electric '00' gauge railway introduced by Mr Beauchamp, and the formation of a Railway Club, limited to 16 senior boys. The whole circuit, together with the carpentry involved, was built up by Mr Beauchamp with the help of Club members. It was a 'Gem' flexible track (double circuit) of 35 feet. There were three engines, a quantity of rolling stock and three controllers.

Of the five Rugby fixtures, one of which (with Belhaven Hill) had to be cancelled because of illness, the School lost 0-9 to St Mary's, Melrose and to Edinburgh Academy 0-20, but beat Loretto 6-0.

Two new boys arrived for the Lent Term 1957. Within a week of the start of term, mumps made its fearsome appearance and stayed until the Easter holidays.

During the term Fr Ethelbert had the ceiling of the chapel distempered and then he himself painted and decorated the rest of the chapel and sanctuary. The walls were painted in *eau-de-nil,* and the sanctuary ceiling and arch with all its carvings were picked out in cadmium red and gold. Red velvet hangings reaching from ceiling to floor around the altar, and new velvet altar hangings and tabernacle veils, completed the renovation.

The highlight of the Term was the visit of the Welsh Rugby team on 1 February, prior to their match against Scotland. The boys enjoyed watching the three-quarters in action on the School ground. This was followed by a stand-up tea in the refectory. The iced cakes were decorated with leeks for the occasion.

Since 1950, Carlekemp had had the privilege of entertaining the English Rugby team four times at Carlekemp before the Calcutta Cup match. The South African Springboks and the New Zealand All Blacks had also visited.

Due to the mumps epidemic all Hockey fixtures were cancelled. The two House runs, however, to Dirleton and Fidra, were held. Both runs were won by R. Morrison, the first in a new record time of 23 minutes 11 seconds. The record for the Fidra run (25 minutes 45 seconds) held by R. N. Godfrey remained unbeaten.

The Welsh Rugby team visited the School on 1 February. Among the celebrities were Ken Jones and Cliff Morgan. The team practised on the Strathearn Road pitch. Afterwards they had tea in the refectory. Cliff Morgan presented the School with his jersey and stockings.

At Half-term (8 and 9 June) Fr Aidan took a party of boys round the Bass Rock. They were fascinated by the many birds nesting on the sanctuary. On the Feast of Corpus Christi the boys sang the Mass. After an early lunch Fifth Form went with Fr Aidan by train to Edinburgh Zoo. Another group was taken on the same day to Dirleton Castle.

Towards the end of May the Archdiocesan Inspectors of Religious Knowledge, Frs McClelland, Glancey and Rhatigan, expressed their satisfaction at the standard reached by the boys. Fr Glancey returned on 21 June for a day's recollection.

At the end of June came the ordeal of the Common Entrance examinations. On 2 July the results were announced. All were successful and D. Davenport was granted a scholarship to Ampleforth College, while J. van Bavel was given one to Fort Augustus.

The Edinburgh branch of the Fort Augustus Old Boys held a Reunion at the School on 23 June. This was followed by a match against the School (lost by the boys by 29 runs).

On the Feast of St Peter and St Paul, after sung Mass, there was an exodus of the Senior Forms for their annual expedition to the Cistercian Abbey at Nunraw near Garvald.

Prize Day was on 20 July. Prizes were presented by Mrs Hope of Luffness. Afterwards the boys, directed by Fr Gregory, gave a concert of choral and instrumental music. This was followed by tea served in the marquee on the lawn. Then, under the direction of Mrs Pearson, the School gave a performance of Highland and Country Dancing.

In Cricket it was an indifferent season: one game won and four lost. In the Sports, V. Di Rollo set a new record of 4 feet 6 inches in the High Jump. The House Shooting Cup was won by Lamb, while the House Games Cup was won on points by Craigleith. The House Golf Competition was won by Fidra. The *Victor Ludorum* was shared between V. Di Rollo and J. van Bavel.

The 1958 year began on 20 September with the arrival of 16 boys making up a School complement of 69. Of the eleven boys who had left the previous term, all but two went to Fort Augustus. This meant that a third of the Abbey School intake came from Carlekemp.

Among the staff Mrs Pearson had retired as dancing teacher. Then Fr Robert McKenzie joined the staff after finishing his studies in Rome.

The first part of the term was marred by a week of Asian flu which affected a large number of boys. Half-way through the term the School was delighted to receive a present of 40 storybooks, annuals, games and jigsaws from Mrs de Winter, mother of an Old Boy.

The lounge at the foot of the great stone stairway had recently been decorated with a number of magnificent old tapestries which also served to keep out the draught. However, they did not prevent the

269

arrival of an unexpected visitor in the early hours of the previous week – a burglar:

He found his way to the Chapel and the collection box there was rifled. The stationery cupboard evidently held promise of great loot for him, for he literally hacked his way through it, only to find a few odd pennies.

For the Rugby season that year the School could only just field a team. Only a few of the previous year's team was left. All games (except for three) were cancelled because of the flu. Outstanding among the forwards was R. Cardosi, while P. Bayliss at centre was a brave and secure tackler in defence.

The Spring Term of 1958 began on 17 January. Soon East Lothian was in the grip of Winter. There were frequent falls of snow which gave the boys great opportunities for snow battles on the New Field. Any of the masters who ventured there took their life in their hands!

At the Mid-term holiday on 22 February Fr Aidan led a small party up the snow-clad North Berwick Law with its whale's jawbone arch. They climbed up the steeper side through a good deal of mist.

The School said goodbye with sorrow to Fr Martin, parish priest of North Berwick, who had been appointed to a new parish at Liberton in Edinburgh. Before his departure he was an honoured guest for lunch at the School.

Garth Morrison, an Old Boy of Carlekemp and a native of North Berwick, was chosen to captain the England under-15 Rugby XV against Wales and scored the winning try. Garth was now at Pangbourne Nautical College, having taken first place in a scholarship exam there.

The three Hockey matches that term (against Belhaven, Loretto and Fettes) were all lost (1-3; 0-3; 3-4). The outstanding player in the team was R. Morrison, ably abetted by H. Shannon, P. Bayliss and C. P. Seed.

There were two visits that year from International Rugby sides. On 12 February the Wallabies, the Australian touring side, came to the School before their games with Scotland. Although conditions were still wintry, the Australians were able to put in a good practice and afterwards exchanged a few friendly snowballs with the boys:

Nobody had quite the effrontery of a certain person, who asked Bob Scott, full back for the All Blacks, to repeat his feat of kicking a goal from the half-way line with his bare feet (which he did, just to oblige him).

The next morning the Wallabies returned for a practice and then met the School over coffee and biscuits in the Fifth Form room. It was interesting to note that six of the team were Catholics.

On 14 March the England XV visited. The first invitation had been made in 1950 by Abbot Oswald and by now the selectors and such veterans as Jeff Butterfield were old friends of the School:

Tea, arranged by the Matron, Miss O'Donnell, followed. In the refectory the England XV noted with interest Mr Beauchamp's framed autographs of past English teams who had visited Carlekemp.

The new term began on 25 April. A month later 25 boys were confirmed in the parish church by Archbishop Gordon Gray. The School choir took over all the singing, which included 'Ecce sacerdos magnus' and 'Veni creator'.

On 24 May the Catalan Hockey team visited the School, accompanied by the Spanish consul and his wife. They were greeted with a rendering of the Spanish National Anthem; there were bright flowers and vivid posters placed everywhere by Fr Aidan. After sherry with the Community and Staff, the visitors went to the Chapel where they sang the famous Montserrat hymn.

Abbot Oswald came down to Carlekemp on 15 June to take part, along with Frs Aidan and Gregory, in the national pilgrimage to Dunfermline.

All three Cricket matches played were won. The rest had to be cancelled. Belhaven (home) were beaten by eight wickets; St Mary's, Melrose by 14 runs; and Belhaven (away) by 12 runs. In the second match H. Shannon took six wickets for 16 runs; in the third, R. Morrison also bowled splendidly, taking 7 wickets for 25.

On Sunday 22 June the Old Boys had their Annual Reunion at Carlekemp. They held the meeting in the refectory, following lunch at the Westerdunes Hotel, before taking part in a light-hearted Cricket match against the School, with the Headmaster fearful for the windows and the juniors' heads!

On St Benedict's Day, Fr Gregory and Fr Robert took a large party for the annual outing to Nunraw. Fr Gabriel at Nunraw welcomed them and the boys spent vast sums in the Monastery shop. At the end of term on 19 July the Abbot of Nunraw, reciprocating the visit, presented the prizes before a concert and a display of Highland dancing.

271

The Autumn term began on Friday 19 September with 16 new boys. Under Headmaster Fr Ethelbert were Fr Gregory, Fr Aidan, Fr Robert and Mr Beauchamp (who not only taught academic subjects but coached all the games with the cunning and quiet determination that only someone who had seen action at sea could muster). Mrs Gilhooley and Mrs J. B. McCulloch (Art) were joined by Mrs Nelson and Miss Cameron (Dancing).

The weather for most of the term was fine and this helped the games programme. The School XV, under its Captain R. C. Morrison at stand-off, won its first match (against Belhaven) by 21–3. There was another win (against Edinburgh Academy) and two defeats (St Mary's Melrose 15–0 and Loretto 35–0). As *The Corbie* commented: 'This game is one that the School will wish to forget.'

The Mid-term holiday was on 1 and 2 November. The Hallowe'en party and games were a great success as usual. In the fancy dress competition Andrew Drummond, in full Cardinal's regalia, caught the eye of the judges.

Miss O'Donnell the Matron had acquired a puppy, a Welsh collie called 'Lassie' who was a great favourite with everyone.

On the last day of term the School gave a concert with carol singing from every Form and recitations from the First Form. There were also piano solos and duets.

East coast *haar* and hard frost set in right from the start of the Spring term on 16 January 1959. Carlekemp was an oasis of health while schools all around were being ravaged by flu. This curtailed the programme of Hockey fixtures. There was one new boy, H. P. Wright.

On 6 February the visit of the Welsh rugby team was a highlight of the term. A substantial tea prepared by Matron awaited the selectors and team after their practice on the School pitch. Mr Beauchamp, of course, was also at hand to gather further international figures for his framed photographs of visiting teams.

On 1 March there was Exposition of the Blessed Sacrament and a day of prayer for the persecuted Church in China. Each Form took their turn in watching and the day ended with Rosary and Benediction.

The Dirleton Run on 10 March was won by C. P. Seed in the very good time of 23 minutes 41 seconds, which was only 30 seconds outside the record. The House placing was: Fidra (first), Lamb (second), Craigleith (third).

The following day a good friend of the School, Sir Hew Hamilton-

Dalrymple of Leuchie, North Berwick, died. Sir Hew had been Confirmation sponsor for generations of Carlekemp boys. Frs Ethelbert and Gregory assisted at the Requiem Mass in North Berwick Parish Church.

Only two Hockey matches were played. The School beat Belhaven 2-1, but lost to Loretto 7-0. Three House matches were played, from which Fidra emerged victorious.

The Spring term began on Friday 17 April, with classes starting the following Monday. As the grounds were not ready for Cricket, Mr Beauchamp organised a 'get-fit' campaign of runs and walks. Others prepared for the annual Sports, marking out the tracks, putting up Hurdles, the High Jump, and cleaning the Long Jump pit. Later in the term a tractor and gangers bought by Mr Beauchamp caused great interest among the boys. Without Mr Beauchamp's constant care and attention the lawns and playing fields would not have been in as excellent condition as they were. Mr Beauchamp, in addition to his teaching and coaching duties, was ever a keen photographer. He had now graduated to colour photography and delighted the boys with slide shows on an automatic projector.

Each Form had its own May Altar in the Form Room where prayers were said every day in honour of Our Lady. Special remembrance was made of the Pope's request to ask a blessing on the forthcoming General Council of the Church.

On Ascension Thursday the Junior Forms went to the beach where the find of a mussel pearl led to keen competition to discover more. It proved a fruitless but exciting search.

On 18 May Mr J. Grant, a former professional at Le Touquet, France gave Golf lessons to the boys. On the first day of the Half-term weekend Abbot Oswald arrived with Mr Henry Cotton. Some of the boys left in the School were fortunate to get Mr Cotton's autograph.

Cricket that year was disappointing. Of six matches played, only one was won. M. R. McLaughlin, the Captain, was the most competent batsman and, as a bowler, kept the best length. The XI only showed their true form towards the end of the season.

Throughout the term there was a plentiful supply of strawberries and tomatoes from the Priory garden, under the care of Mr Haggerty. These were put to good use at the Old Boys' Reunion at Carlekemp on 28 June. The Cricket match ended (catastrophically) with a tie and was the climax of a very enjoyable afternoon.

The term was, however, overshadowed by Fr Ethelbert's illness. Every night the School said the Rosary for his recovery. In his absence, Fr Gregory gave the Headmaster's report and Abbot Oswald presented the prizes at Prize-giving. After tea in the marquee a display of Highland Dancing was given under the direction of Mrs Nelson and Miss Cameron.

The School returned on Friday 18 September. At the beginning of a new term the excitement of the eleven new boys was overshadowed by an awareness that Fr Ethelbert was gravely ill in the Bon Secours Nursing Home, Glasgow. In his place came Fr Thomas McLaughlin who had unselfishly relinquished his post as Headmaster of the Abbey School, Fort Augustus.

A number of improvements had been made around the School and policies. In the changing-rooms, wire lockers now replaced the old wooden ones; a floor-seal had been put down in the Study Hall, Refectory and many of the classrooms. The Cricket square in front of the School had been re-sown.

Mrs T. McCawley had come to replace Mrs Gilhooley (who had taught at Carlekemp for four years) as First Form Mistress. Miss O'Donnell, the Matron, had been to the United States and had a fund of travellers' tales to tell.

At the end of October Abbot Oswald visited the School to accompany Fr Aidan up to Fort Augustus for the solemn profession of Fr Aidan's brother, Dom Fabian Duggan (who would be ordained at the end of term).

The films shown that term were excellent: Laurel and Hardy in 'Bonnie Scotland', Bing Crosby in 'Going My Way', 'The Wizard of Oz' and 'Quo Vadis?'

The Rugby season was a fair one. The XV won two matches, lost two and drew one. The strength of the team was its enthusiasm and energy; its weakness lay in a lack of finishing, particularly in the Backs.

The Nativity Play that year was 'One Night in Bethlehem', given before the School on Sunday 13 December, with a special performance in the parish hall (courtesy of Fr Donoghue) for parents and the parish on Wednesday 16 December.

The beginning of the 1960 Lent term saw one staff change: Fr Aidan (who had been teaching RK, English, Latin and Geography) returned to Fort Augustus. In his place came Fr John-Baptist.

The Hockey fixture list was upset by an outbreak of measles. This was not a good year for the XI, who played three and lost three. On Friday 18 March the England Rugby XV and selectors practised on the School pitch, after which they were photographed with the School. There was great amusement when the English team put on school caps for the photograph.

Abbot Celestine visited Carlekemp shortly after the start of the Summer term. He was warmly welcomed by the boys and celebrated mass in the Chapel.

As the weather was warm and fine, Cricket nets were quickly put up. Until games were properly organised Golf proved very popular. There was a demand for Swimming but the weather was still a little cold. A holiday was given for the wedding of Princess Margaret. Some of the boys stayed to watch the service on television, but most preferred to get outside, down to the town or onto the beach.

The Archdiocesan Religious Inspectors (Frs McClelland, Rhatigan and Lawrence Glancey) came on 18 May and declared themselves satisfied with the standard of Religious Knowledge shown by the boys.

Archbishop Gordon Gray administered the Sacrament of Confirmation to eleven boys in the School Chapel on 26 May, later talking to some of the boys on the lawn. Many photographs were taken. There was a Day of Recollection on Corpus Christi, during which Fr Jock Dalrymple gave a series of talks.

Once again the fine weather enabled Mr Haggerty to produce a plentiful crop of tomatoes and a bumper crop of strawberries. Unfortunately the annual Old Boys' Cricket match could not take place due to the state of the new Cricket square which had been re-sown but had not come on as expected. All home Cricket fixtures had to be cancelled as well. Only two matches were played and both were lost!

Lady Margaret Kerr was to have presented the School Prizes on 23 July. Owing to illness she was unable to come and her place was taken by Abbot Malachy Brasil OCR. He was accompanied by the Abbot of Nunraw. A concert followed the Prize-giving; then tea was served in a marquee on the lawn, accompanied by the customary display of Highland Dancing.

When the School returned on Friday 23 September, it was with eight new boys and two new members of staff. Fr Hubert Varty came after many years' experience teaching in the United States; Miss S. Hyland replaced Mrs T. McCawley as First Form mistress.

From the beginning of term the weather was very wet. Pitches were waterlogged and there was also widespread fog. Nevertheless, this was one of the most successful Rugby seasons for many years. Six matches were played, four of them being won and two lost (one of these was a 62-0 defeat by St Mary's, Melrose!).

The School was proud of the fact that an Old Boy, Garth Morrison of North Berwick, was now Captain of the Rugby XV at Pangbourne Nautical College. Garth was also selected to play for the Scottish School-boys against the English Schoolboys.

On Friday 7 October the boys served Pontifical Benediction when Archbishop Gordon Gray came to perform the official opening ceremony of the La Sagesse nuns' new Convent at Leuchie House, the former home of the Hamilton-Dalrymple family.

The Michaelmas term gave an opportunity for the School to devise its own entertainment. The annual Hallowe'en party was a great success. Most of the boys were in fancy dress, prizes being awarded for the best costumes. A sing-song followed, with party games. With Fr John's encouragement, the Fifth Form put on a sketch, 'Emergency Ward 10' – with a difference. Among the 'props' was a string of sausages! The whole evening was organised by Fr Gregory.

There was no Nativity Play that year, many of the principals having succumbed to coughs and colds. Fr Gregory came to the rescue with an end of term concert, including two French pieces, a carol and a song, both of which had been prepared by the Fifth Form in class.

Although television was not available often, the boys enjoyed 'Wells Fargo', 'The Lone Ranger' and 'Whacko!' Among the popular films were 'Blue Murder at St Trinian's' and 'Scott of the Antarctic'.

Six new boys appeared on 13 January when the School returned after the Christmas holidays. There was no snow until the first days of February, but an outbreak of flu did interfere with the Hockey list.

During the week preceding the match against Scotland, the South African Rugby XV practised on the School ground. Four members of the team were then entertained to tea – Avril Malan (Captain), Michel Antelme, John Gainsford and Keith Oxlee. On 10 February the Welsh Rugby team and selectors visited the School. Several photographs were taken on the pitch with the boys included, as well as a team photograph in front of the School.

It was not an exceptional term for sporting events. The Hockey season produced one victory (Loretto) and two defeats (Fettes and Belhaven). There was a lack of thrust in the forward line and goals were not easy to find. The Dirleton Run was won by N. A. MacLaren (for the second year in succession) in a time of 23 minutes 30 seconds. In the House competition Lamb came first, Craigleith second and Fidra third.

There was considerable excitement when T. G. McErvel received a letter from Norway. It turned out that his correspondent had found a bottle he had put into the sea at North Berwick the previous October. It was picked up off the Norwegian coast in March at a place called Sör Flatanger, after a remarkable journey of about 400 miles.

Mumps were a continuing feature of the 1961 Summer term – not a dramatic epidemic, however, but a prolonged series of minor attacks. This inevitably affected the Cricket and Golf. Both School matches were lost, the first (against St Mary's, Melrose) by 72 runs; the second (against Belhaven) by 120 runs. During the Sports in the middle of May, pulled muscles were a common occurrence.

On 26 May there was great excitement:

Two challenge Cricket matches were played. The first, against the Old Boys, on 18 June, was lost for the first time ever, due mainly to the fine batting of P. C. Barry. On 9 July a Parents' XI was comfortably beaten by the School. F. D. Cummings had the satisfaction of bowling his father out with the first ball of the match!

Prize Day on 22 July was attended by a record number of parents and guests, among whom were Old Boys Abbot Oswald Eaves (on holiday from Sweden) and Fr Alban Boultwood, Prior of St Anselm's, Washington DC. Abbot Wulstan Knowles distributed the prizes.

Fifteen new boys arrived at Carlekemp in late September 1961. There were new faces too, among the staff. After four years in North Berwick, Fr Robert had left to go to Rome to study Sacred Scripture; Fr H. A. Varty had left for Canada where he was to teach at the Cathedral Schola Cantorum in Toronto. In their place, Fr Fabian came from Fort Augustus to take over History and Geography and Mr T. E. Fitzgerald came to teach French, Maths and English.

By September the conversion of the stable block was complete. As well as living quarters there was now a new classroom and a dormitory, known as Fisher and More.

At Hallowe'en the traditional party and fancy dress parade took place, and 'I Appeal to Caesar', a two-act play specially written for the occasion on the life of St Paul was presented. A Nativity Play, 'The

Prince of Peace', was also presented at the end of term, excellently acted and sung. The boys' singing and the musical accompaniment was by Fr Gregory (whose organ piece 'Fantasia on Christmas Carols' was shortly due to be published by Augener).

It was not one of the best Rugby seasons, with four defeats, followed by two victories. Fidra won the House Match competition, while the winner of the Dirleton Run (on 7 December) was N. A. Maclaren in a new record of 23 minutes 11 seconds.

During the Spring term a letter arrived from Henry Cotton. He was returning the autographed photo of the winner of the last Henry Cotton Cup. Writing from the French Riviera, Mr Cotton revealed that he intended to visit the School next time he was in Scotland.

On 16 March the English Rugby team visited Carlekemp. They practised on the field as usual and were then entertained to tea. Photographs were taken of the team with the boys. Unfortunately Colonel Prentice, Secretary of the Rugby Union, was unable to be present for the first time since 1950 as he was seriously ill in hospital. Prior to the English team's visit the lower section of the Strathearn Road field was re-fenced and several trees in the woods felled as they were considered dangerous.

On the last day of term the School enjoyed an hour and a half's entertainment. This consisted of a concert, featuring vocal and instrumental items, a one-act play, 'Storm in an Egg-Cup', and an operetta written by Fr Fabian for the occasion called 'The Magic Wand'.

German measles and flu meant that only two Hockey matches were played. One (against Fettes) was won; the other (against Belhaven) lost.

The School learned, with regret, of the death of Lady Margaret Kerr, a patron of the School since it first opened in Edinburgh who, along with the other patrons, presented the Captain's Shield in 1936.

German measles and streptococcal throats followed by chicken pox bedevilled the Spring term and interfered with Cricket matches. Nevertheless, the School XI won three out of four of their matches. There were some lighter moments – such as the arrival of Mr Beauchamp's new car, a red Messerschmitt in which he made the long journey from Bristol to North Berwick.

Carlekemp had now become a member of the Incorporated Association of Preparatory Schools. Admission to the IAPS had been on the recommendation of the headmasters of Belhaven Hill School and Loretto Prep School.

On Whit Monday Archbishop Gray came to confirm 16 boys, the sponsor being Old Boy solicitor Mr J. P. S. Conacher. On the feast of Corpus Christi, a day of recollection was given by another Old Boy, Fr Norman Baird. The Sisters of Leuchie Convent came down for the Procession of the Blessed Sacrament in the afternoon. On 11 July (the Feast of St Benedict) the boys had their annual outing to Nunraw where they were able to see the progress made on the building of the new monastery.

There were two notable guests that term – Abbot Oswald came for a few days before returning to Sweden, and Commander Farie (on a day of heavy rain, thunder and lightning) came on 21 July to distribute the prizes.

In the annual Sports the *Victor Ludorum* was S. M. J. Janikiewicz, while Fidra won the House Championship. F. D. Cummings not only won the Green Cricket Cup, but also the Henry Cotton Golf Cup.

The new term in September began with a record 19 newcomers. They found a new Prior, Fr Edmund Carruth, who took all Fr Fabian's classes for the whole term during which he was absent.

In October the central heating and domestic water system was changed from coal to oil. This was providential as it coincided with the retirement of gardener and groundsman Jim Haggerty who, for many years, had been in charge of the stoking and care of the boilers.

The Rugby season was a disappointing one. All four matches played were lost. The wing forwards did not cover well and the pack's heeling was not clean enough. In the backs there was little enterprise or efficiency.

Owing to the severe weather at the beginning of January 1963, the Hockey fields could not be used for many weeks. However, a good substitute was found on the sea shore where the hard and level stretches of sand made good pitches.

The young and promising Hockey team won one game and lost two. In goal was Captain O. A. Lane, probably the best goalkeeper the School had ever had.

This term also saw what seemed to be the end of the visits from Welsh or English Rugby teams. Neither came that year, as the larger North Berwick hotels were closed for the Winter.

The end of term concert was composed mainly of three scenes from Shakespeare, two from 'Julius Caesar' and one from 'Macbeth'. This was followed by songs and recorder music.

For days at a time the Firth of Forth coast was shrouded in the notorious East of Scotland *haar* (sea-mist) during the Summer term. This interfered with Cricket and Golf. There were a few hot sunny days, but rain and cold winds were the order of the day.

In Miss S. Hyland's absence, Miss Mullen came to teach the First Form. Among visitors to the School were Abbot Celestine, the Abbot of Roscrae, Dom Eugene Boyland, and the Abbot of Nunraw, Dom Columba Mulcahy. Among the many Old Boys calling in was Dom Gordon Beattie of Ampleforth who was preparing for the priesthood. He was at Carlekemp from 1949-54.

The School watched the funeral of Pope John XXIII on television and later saw the new Pope give his first blessing. The following day was declared a holiday to celebrate Pope Paul VI's election.

After the Common Entrance exams a half-holiday was given in June to mark J. Norman's winning a major scholarship from Ampleforth. Norman also won the Captain's Shield and the Calder Cup.

That term saw the publication of a book of Gaelic prayers on which Fr John-Baptist had been working for some time. This was the second edition of a collection of typical Catholic prayers and devotions, including the text of the Mass [J. Andrew MacBride (editor): *Lùl a' Chriòsd aidh* ('Guidance of the Christian'), Stirling: Learmonth & Sons.]

The School had recently adopted a mission station in Ikot Ene, Nigeria run by the Medical Missionaries of Mary. Raffles and auction sales were used to send a financial contribution to the missionaries.

The 1963 Cricket team was a very young side, as most of the previous year's team had left. This led to nervous and tentative batting and a poor standard of bowling. The one good point of the side was the fielding, which was excellent. All three matches were lost.

In the Annual Sports the House Championship was won by Fidra, who also won the House Relay. *Victor Ludorum* was P. A. Elliot, while G. J. R. Lumsden won both of the Golf trophies.

On 9 July the Third Form's annual outing to Nunraw Abbey took place. The boys rambled over the monastery grounds, playing Football and Cricket, making the long walk to the reservoir and inspecting the progress on the vast new monastery building. Then came an enormous picnic lunch under the trees. After Vespers the party returned to North Berwick.

Prize Day was on 20 July, when the prizes were distributed by Abbot Oswald Eaves, who was on leave from his work in Sweden. A concert followed and, after tea, Mrs Nelson and Mrs Bruce presented an exhibition of Highland and Scottish Country Dancing.

★ ★ ★

Early in September 1963, Fr Thomas McLaughlin was taken ill. He was ordered by his doctors to have complete rest and not return until the New Year.

The School returned on 20 September with eleven new boys. Exceptionally fine weather continued right up to Half-term. A monthly paper, *The Carlekemp Times,* made its first appearance in September, covering all aspects of the life of the School.

Sadly Mr Jim Heggarty, gardener and groundsman at Carlekemp for more than twelve years, died after a long illness. He had retired the year before because of advancing years and ill-health.

Mr Peter Anson, the historian and artist (a number of whose pen drawings of boats hung in the School), came for several days to Carlekemp. Abbot Celestine visited the School at the end of September and said the School Mass. However, he had to cut his visit short when news was received of the death of Fr Basil Wedge, the first Prior of the School when it was founded in Edinburgh in 1930.

Two Old Boys, John Airs and Christopher Rance, who were at Carlekemp together, entered the Dominican Novitiate at Woodchester on St Michael's Day.

The custom for the School to entertain an International Rugby team each year seemed in danger of being broken when the Marine Hotel decided they would close for the Winter and not re-open until the Spring. However, at Mr Beauchamp's instigation the Royal Hotel agreed to open a little earlier than intended in order to accommodate the visitors.

The Rugby season was one of the most successful for some years. Of the six matches played, the School won four and lost two, gaining 86 points, having 40 scored against them. H. E. Murphy (Captain) was the best of the three-quarters, while the strong and lively pack was led by Vice-Captain C. J. Livingstone.

The annual Nativity Play, staged on Sunday 8 December for an hour, was given before around 40 guests, including several of the boys' parents who lived locally. The Headmaster, Fr Thomas, was allowed to attend by his doctors. As usual, the Choir's singing was of a high standard, enriched by recorders and percussion.

Early in January 1965 Abbot Wulstan Knowles came to Carlekemp to recuperate after an illness. Raffles and the sale of *The Carlekemp Times* meant that a substantial sum of money could be forwarded to the Medical Missionaries of Mary at Ikot Ene, Nigeria. Later in the year Fr John McAllister (who was in charge of the Bauchi mission in Nigeria), and Sister Galgani Gunn from Ikot Ene, visited the School. Fr McAllister also gave the conferences on the Corpus Christi day of recollection.

The influence of Fr Gregory was still to be seen in the good music results. All six candidates presented for music theory examinations were successful, B. A. L'Estrange gaining the maximum mark of 99.

On 21 March the England Rugby XV trained on the School field the day before the Calcutta Cup match. This was followed by tea in the refectory.

Seven Rugby matches were played by the School XV, but only two were won. The Hockey season was one of the best in recent years. All three matches played were won. Cricket, by contrast, was a disappointment. Five out of six matches were lost. The main weakness lay in the batting, which was poor all round.

The start of the Summer term saw Fr Anselm Richardson replacing Fr Edmund as Prior. Fr Edmund had been recalled to Fort Augustus to be Prior there. On 3 May Fr Francis Davidson came to Carlekemp to celebrate Mass in the School Chapel. He was the first Old Carlekempian to be ordained a priest.

On 25 May a group of Shakespearean actors from the Osiris Repertory Company visited the School. They performed the murder scene from 'Macbeth' and some of the more comic scenes from 'Twelfth Night'.

Two performances of a Passion Play were given before the Easter holidays. The play (which had been specially adapted and produced by Michael Turnbull, a member of the teaching staff and an Old Boy) lasted for fifty minutes and included the innovative placing of the choir on the study-hall balcony above the stage.

New cricket nets were installed, higher and wider than the old ones, which were in a very poor condition. Archery was introduced, with practices held on the New Field or on the front lawn. Swimming lessons were given again this term in North Berwick pool. About a dozen boys received lessons three times a week from a professional coach.

The 1965 Cricket season was very satisfying. Of the six matches played, four were won and two drawn. Two others were cancelled because of illness. The Old Boys were beaten by one wicket and the Parents' XI by 57 runs.

Three records were broken in the annual Sports. J. A. MacBride set a new record of 12.4 seconds in the 100 yards; L. W. Hogarth broke records in the 220 yards (30 seconds) and 440 yards (71.4 seconds). Hogarth was the *Victor Ludorum*.

On Prize Day, 18 July, the Marquess of Lothian distributed the prizes. Abbot Celestine and Abbot Oswald Eaves were also present.

Fourteen boys left at the end of term, as well as Fr Gregory, Mr Fitzgerald (who had been at Carlekemp for three years), Miss S. Hyland and Mr M. Turnbull.

When the new term began on 24 September 1965, a record 14 new boys appeared, pushing the School roll up to 70. There were also two new members of staff – Miss E. Fagan and Fr Chrysostom – who would teach Geography and Art.

The Rugby season was one of the best. Of the five matches played, four were won and only one defeat was recorded. The team scored 79 points, with 17 against.

During the term Mrs J. McAllister died. She had joined the domestic staff when the School first opened in Edinburgh before the War. During the War, when the School moved to Fort Augustus, Mrs McAllister, with her husband John, stayed on in Edinburgh to look after the build-ings which had been occupied by the Army. When Carlekemp opened, Mr and Mrs McAllister lived in the Lodge.

Two performances of the Nativity Play were staged at the end of term – the first for parents and friends, the second for old folk, some 60 of whom came from homes in the surrounding district.

The Lent term began on Friday 14 January 1966 with a record 77 boys. Two new activities were offered that term: Fr Chrysostom gave lessons to the 14-strong Chanter class and also formed a Stamp Club to help the many collectors in the school. It began with a large membership of 44.

Towards the end of January a great number of trees were felled in accordance with a plan drawn up by the Scottish Woodland Owners' Association, of which Carlekemp was a member. The plan involved the planting of trees over a period of 40 years, by felling in groups and replanting every fifth year. Many of the old trees were either dead or dying. The felling was carried out by Mr Leon from Haddington, one of the foremost experts in the field.

The Hockey season was excellent, every game being won (including one against a girls' team from North Berwick High School). In the last three seasons the School had won every game they had played.

Cricket was equally successful, with five games won and two drawn. One of the victories was against Salford Grammar School, the visitors' first defeat in eleven matches played, six of them against Scottish schools.

Three new records were set during the annual Sports. D. M. Allison broke the records for the First Set 100 yards (11.7 seconds), 220 yards (28.9 seconds) and 440 yards (69 seconds). The House Relay was won by Craigleith, while boys in Lamb House filled the first three places in the Direlton Run.

The School was honoured to receive a plaque from the secretary of the Rugby Football Union, Mr R. E. Prescott, in recognition of Carlekemp's long association with the England XV. Unfortunately, owing to the difficulty of finding accommodation in North Berwick, the team would probably not be returning.

During the Easter holidays Fr Thomas took a group of boys on an educational cruise. Travelling on the *Nevasa*, they called at Madeira, Tangier and Lisbon (including a visit to Fatima).

On 8 July Mr Henry Cotton visited. He was staying at North Berwick during the Open Golf Championship at Muirfield. While at Carlekemp he signed autographs and posed for pictures.

For the fourth year in succession the Henry Cotton Cup for Golf was won by G. J. Lumsden. He knocked 12 off the existing record of 253 set in 1955 by Garth Morrison for the four rounds of 18 holes each.

Prize Day on 23 July began with the singing of the School hymn to Saint Andrew. The prizes were distributed by Lord Wheatley, who also attended the exhibition of Highland Dancing on the front lawn.

Sixteen new boys arrived on 23 September, along with Mr D. McPhail who would teach English, Latin and French. Mr McPhail was formerly on the staff at Fort Augustus. He took the place of Mr Bridge who was going to teach at a Prep School in England.

During the holidays the loft over the garage had been converted into a science laboratory. A staircase had been put in and new glass doors added overlooking the stableyard.

The groundsman, Mr Biskup, had been to visit his native Poland and returned with an icon of Our Lady of Czestochowa which he presented to the School. It was now hanging in the chapel,

There were now 19 in the Chanter group. D. Russell arrived back with his own set of pipes. Later the group learnt their first Strathspey and practised counter-marching in pipe-band style.

A new club was formed to handle the production of plays. It had 23 members and a committee of six. The club prepared a play for Hallowe'en, 'The Red Herring', which told the story of a group of boys on Jersey during the German occupation.

Another new activity was the Discussion Group who met at intervals to discuss world events and current affairs. A daily newspaper was taken in the Reading Room so that senior boys could keep up to date with the main news items.

Early in October six boys took part in the trials for the Scottish Schools National Swimming championship. P. J. Dalton and L. J. Duthie qualified and competed at Warrender swimming baths in Edinburgh.

On 18 October Colonel E. E. Toms and Major J. Gray of the Gordon Highlanders gave a two-hour talk on the sinking of the 'Scharnhorst', with the aid of wall charts and other illustrations. Each spoke from the opposing point of view, German and British.

The School bought a large quantity of hockey, rugby and cricket equipment at a sale in Thornton's Sport Shop, Edinburgh.

The Nativity Play chosen was 'Thou Bethlehem'. It lasted just over an hour and had a large cast of 29. There were two public performances, one for parents, the other for old people from homes in the district.

The School learnt with sadness of the death of Miss D. Stanmore. During the War years, Miss Stanmore was on the staff when the Prep School was at Fort Augustus. When Carlekemp opened, she joined the staff there.

A gale in the middle of January brought down 16 trees, a roof from one of the sheds in the old piggeries was torn off and several slates dislodged from the main building.

Six boys sat the Townsend-Warner history exam in February. Five of them were mentioned in the results. The Historical Society's magazine, *Carlekemp Historian*, was published during the term.

The 1967 Rugby season was a good one, with five out of six matches won. Eleven members of the XV were awarded colours. Hockey was a similar story. Because of cancellations, only four games were played. The XI won all of these, scoring 26 goals with only one scored against.

The boys' Day of Recollection in Holy Week was given by Fr F. D. Crowley, an Old Boy and at the time a teacher at St Vincent's Junior Seminary, Langbank. For the first time all the Holy Week services were held at Carlekemp. The Choir sang in both Latin and English.

Two new boys arrived at the start of the Summer term.

The vegetable garden was once again under cultivation, after lying idle for a couple of years. The gardens and paths were cleared of weeds and the greenhouse tidied up. Potatoes had been planted, as well as rows of other vegetables.

Towards the end of April a freak tide at North Berwick took the sea nearly a mile out from the shore. One man walked within 70 yards of the island of Lamb, usually a mile out to sea.

The School acquired several pieces of furniture from the Helpers of the Holy Souls who had moved to new premises from their Convent in Drummond Place, Edinburgh. Among these were two refectory tables, a large vestment cupboard, chairs and a trunkful of stage costumes. Mrs McEvoy of Stanbrook Abbey also obtained a very large assortment of first class costumes, the gift of the Women's Institute, Callow End, Worcester.

The Corpus Christi procession took place in fine weather with the nuns from Leuchie Convent. Fr Anselm carried the Blessed Sacrament in the Procession through the woods, which had been cleared of nettles and undergrowth by the boys.

A cheque for £100 was sent to the School's adopted mission at Ikot Ene, Nigeria. The sum was raised from the sale of *The Carlekemp Times* and other activities. In July *The Carlekemp Historian,* no. 8, was published.

The Cricket season was one of the poorest, with two thorough defeats, two wins and one match drawn.

In the Sports competition, E. Scott cleared 14 feet 8 inches in the Long Jump, beating the previous record by 7 inches. By coincidence, M. T. Turnbull, who had held the record since setting it in 1954, called in on a visit just in time to see Scott make his winning jump.

Mr McPhail ended his temporary teaching engagement on 23 June and Mr J. McGroarty arrived to take Art and general subjects. An Old Boy, John Macqueen, came to take the Senior boys for a concentrated Science course.

On Midsummer's night, the boys of the Third Form performed part of Shakespeare's 'A Midsummer Night's Dream'. It was staged in the open, on a grassy square on the fringe of the woods.

On 16 July the School Mass was offered for Old Carlekempian John Gordon Beattie who was ordained the same day, in the presence of Abbot Oswald. Fifteen of the leavers had been accepted by Fort Augustus, two by Ampleforth.

The annual Prize-giving was held on 22 July. Abbot Oswald, on holiday from Sweden, presented the prizes. Also present were the Abbot of Nunraw and Fr W. D. Hamilton (formerly on the teaching staff at Fort Augustus).

Eighteen new boys started on 22 September 1968. There were changes in the Community: Fr Anselm, Prior for the previous two years, had returned to parochial work in England. Fr Thomas was now Prior as well as Headmaster. Fr Mark had also left to take up the Headship at Fort Augustus. Miss Moira Grego joined the staff to take Latin and English.

At the end of November the Abbot President of the English Benedictine Congregation, Dom Victor Farwell, accompanied by his secretary, Fr Benedict Sankey of Worth Abbey and Abbot Celestine, came to visit the Community. The Abbot President 'observed that Carlekemp could be developed, as it was in an admirable position geographically for development, and he foresaw a very bright future for the School'.

The 1968 Rugby season was very successful, with five wins and only two losses out of seven games played. Hockey saw mixed fortunes with two draws, one win and one defeat. The Cricket XI had four victories and two defeats. Fidra won the House competition.

There were 15 new boys in all during the 1968-69 year, bringing the School roll to 70. Fourteen boys left in July 1969.

The Nativity Play was given twice (once to 130 guests) and was reckoned to be the best ever given at the School. The Choir was trained by Mr Cosgrove, while Miss Fagan accompanied the carols at the piano. A Passion Play was also staged in March, written, produced and directed by Fr Fabian.

The new Science Laboratory was opened in the loft above the garage, so launching a Science course for the Fourth and Fifth Forms.

The Rugby season was a very good one. Six out of eight matches were won. Both Hockey matches were also won. Cricket, however, was less successful with only three victories and four defeats.

At the annual Prize-giving, Bishop Hart of Dunkeld distributed the prizes. Fr Mark, Headmaster of Fort Augustus, was also present. An exhibition of Scottish Country Dancing on the front lawn, including a massed Highland Fling, the 'Dashing White Sergeant' and a Sword Dance, followed a concert of songs and instrumental music in the Study Hall.

New members of staff in the Michaelmas term included Mr W. F. Flynn, who took Mr Bennet's place, and Mr P. Simpson who took over piano and singing from Mr Cosgrove. There were 13 new boys.

A new feature in the *The Carlekemp Times* was the appearance of the 'Fort Augustus News', a regular monthly feature produced by Fr Vincent, which was added to the back of *The Times*. One of the facts the news sheet highlighted was that there were now 34 boys from Carlekemp in the senior houses at Fort Augustus.

The first fixture of the season was a 17-13 defeat by St Mary's, Melrose. There then followed a 18-6 defeat by Edinburgh Academy and a 15-8 one by Loretto. Things improved marginally later. The School drew with Edinburgh Academy and then beat Belhaven 12-6.

Two Old Carlekempians were in the news. Lord James Douglas Hamilton had been admitted a member of the Faculty of Advocates; Cedric Shackleton had received his PhD in the Faculty of Science at Edinburgh University and was now at the Karolinska Medico Institutet in Stockholm.

The Christmas play was 'The Bells of Bethlehem', with 41 boys on stage (two-thirds of the School) at the one time. More than 50 old folk attended the first performance.

On 21 February 1970 a new priest, Fr Hugh Shannon, was raised to the priesthood at St Mary's Cathedral by Cardinal Gray. He became the second Old Carlekempian to be ordained, the first being Fr Francis Davidson. Four days later Fr Hugh returned to Carlekemp to say one of his first Masses in the Chapel. He spoke to the boys afterwards and gave each one of them his blessing.

In the first Hockey match of the season the School were beaten 4-0 by Belhaven and 6-0 in a second game. However, the School went on to beat Fettes 4-0 and Loretto 2-1.

On 20 March the England Rugby XV arrived. Strathearn Road was lined with cars when the players began their serious training session, watched by a good crowd. Among them was Bill McLaren, the well-known rugby commentator.

At the end of Lent, the Passion Play, 'The Cross and the Empty Tomb', was given three performances. Written by Fr Fabian Duggan, it also featured Choirs trained by Fr Thomas.

The first Cricket match, against Belhaven, was won by five wickets. But the season went on to become one of the most disappointing on record – five out of six fixtures were cancelled through illnesses at other schools. In the Sports, however, a new High Jump record of 4 feet 8 inches was set by James Toms.

After the Summer, there was a record enrolment in what was the School's jubilee year. There were now 72 boys in the School – the highest ever – and there had been a record intake of 16. Among those who sent a special message of congratulations was Her Majesty the Queen.

Among new members of staff were Mr A. Twist who replaced Mr Flynn, Mrs W. Turner (piano) and Mr G. Roberston who taught singing.

In the first Rugby matches there were wins against St Mary's (16-9) and Elingham (14-9). Edinburgh Academy beat the School 13-0, but Loretto were beaten 17-13 and Belhaven 26-3.

In November 1970 Mr Roger Beauchamp celebrated 21 years at Carlekemp. Educated at Clifton College, Bristol and at Cambridge (where he took a degree in Modern Languages, History and International Law), he joined the Royal Naval Voluntary Reserve at the beginning of the War. After serving in the Mediterranean (where he was awarded the Distinguished Service Cross), he taught at Mill Mead School, Shrewsbury and came to Carlekemp on 13 November 1949.

Commented Fr Thomas:

It would be difficult to find a better example of Christian living than he has shown to all .... Words are inadequate to express our debt of gratitude for all that Mr Beauchamp has contributed to the School.

After an absence of ten years, Fr Robert McKenzie returned to Carlekemp to allow Fr Fabian to go to Australia as a Chaplain to visit his mother there. Fr Robert was until recently in charge of Junior House at Fort Augustus. Fr Fabian was to be one of four Chaplains on RHMS 'Ellinis' Chandris Lines. He wrote from Las Palmas on 19 May that, with 180 Catholic families on board, he was busy but enjoying a smooth voyage.

Mr Beauchamp represented Carlekemp at the Centenary Dinner of the Rugby Football Union, held in London at the Hilton on 17 April. About 1000 guests were present, with HRH Prince Philip, Duke of Edinburgh, proposing the toast.

In the first Cricket fixture Carlekemp suffered a four wicket defeat by the Fettes Junior Colts team. Then the dreaded *Mumps* struck. No matches against other schools could be undertaken. In Athletics, Golf and Shooting, Lamb was the victor. B. Dick won the Henry Cotton and also the McCann Cup. The former was presented by Henry Cotton in person, as he was commentating on The Open at Muirfield.

During the Summer holidays, Mr Beauchamp and his sister spent some time at Fort Augustus in their caravan. Miss O'Donnell also stayed there for a while before visiting her home in Ireland. Fr John was in hospital before going to recuperate at the Abbey where he was joined by Fr W. D. Hamilton of Drygrange, attended by one of the students.

By October, 13 leavers had transferred to Fort Augustus (only two going to other schools). There were 14 new boys. New members of staff were Miss J. Ward (who replaced Miss E. Fagan who had now retired) and Dr C. O'Riordan who came to teach the violin.

The Rugby season opened with a 42-10 defeat by St Mary's, Melrose. After several team changes, this was followed by a 28-4 victory over Edinburgh Academy.

On 30 March 1993 Douglas, 14th Duke of Hamilton, died. Fr John represented the School at the Service of Celebration and Thanksgiving held at St Giles High Kirk, Edinburgh. The lesson was read by the actor Tom Fleming; the Gospel was proclaimed by Fr Jock Dalrymple.

The links between the late Duke and Carlekemp went back to the days when the Prep School was evacuated to Fort Augustus under the headmastership of Fr Oswald Eaves. Fr Oswald had been anxious to begin Air Scouts and the ATC. This work was begun in 1940-41 and it was the Duke of Hamilton who put the units on their feet. The friendship between the Duke and Fr Oswald was maintained throughout the War. It gave the Duke great pleasure to know Fr Oswald had acquired Carlekemp, so close to his own home at Lennoxlove, near Haddington. He sent three of his sons to school there. Indeed, in the Carlekemp Visitors' Book were the signatures of the Duke and the Duchess on 12 February 1946, when they were staying at Holyrood Palace on one of the several occasions when the Duke was Lord High Commissioner at the General Assembly of the Church of Scotland. On 20 May 1946 the name of 'Angus Clydesdale' appears, their eldest son, signed before he came to school. In June 1949 Lord James Douglas-Hamilton wrote his name when he came with his parents.

The friendship between the Duke and the Headmaster was maintained after Fr Oswald was elected Abbot of Fort Augustus. As Abbot, he later visited Lennoxlove.

During the Easter holidays the Community were in Fort Augustus and all the staff on holiday. They returned on Easter Monday to find that Matron's cottage had been broken into. Matron, who had spent the holiday in North Wales, took it very well, even saying that in clearing up the mess she had been able to dispose of a great deal of unwanted things she had forgotten she had.

When the boys came back they found that the old vegetable garden had been ploughed up, levelled and sown with grass. More wildlife than usual had taken over the woodland. As well as the familiar Mallard Ducks, there were partridges, pheasants and hares. The latter had been stripping the bark from young trees. The rabbits had multiplied. They no longer burrowed but lived under the ivy in the Woods. A gorgeous cock pheasant, resplendent in gold, green and blue took a stroll every morning outside the School Office window, apparently admiring the view over the Firth of Forth.

When the General Assembly of the Church of Scotland ended in Edinburgh on 30 May, Abbot Nicholas, who had represented the Bishops of Scotland at the Assembly, came to stay for a couple of days and gave an interesting description of the proceedings.

On 11 June 15 boys sat the Common Entrance exam, supervised by Sr Hyacintha from Leuchie. The following day the official School photograph was taken.

For the second year, the School Cricket team was unable to play any inter-school games because of illness. The only competitive games were the House Matches. In the Sports, C. Grainger won the Senior Hurdles, the 400 metres, the Senior Long Jump, the 100 and 200 metres. Lamb won with 38 points, and also won the Golf Competition.

On the Feast of St Benedict, Cardinal Gordon Gray came for his first Confirmation ceremony as Cardinal. He celebrated Mass in the Study Hall with the Choir at the chapel door so they could lead the singing, accompanied by Mr Robertson on the organ. Afterwards he presented the Papal Award, *Bene merenti,* to the Matron, Miss K. O' Donnell for her long years of service to the Priory School since its opening in Canaan Lane, Edinburgh.

In his homily, Cardinal Gray spoke of North Berwick as he knew it as a boy. He described how he used to watch the fishermen preparing their long lines at the harbour. Our Lord, the Cardinal reminded those present, had spent many days by the sea in the company of fishermen.

News of the death of the Hon. Mrs Stirling of Keir was received with regret. Mrs Stirling was one of the original patrons of the School, along with Lord Moncrieff, the Lady Cecil Kerr and the Lady Margaret Kerr. Mrs Stirling was the daughter of Simon, Lord Lovat, who gave Fort Augustus to the Community.

During the Summer holidays Fr Thomas and Fr John went to Switzerland to stay with the monks in the Abbey of Engelberg. They made a pilgrimage to the Shrine of Our Lady at Einsiedln and another to the tomb of St Nicholas.

After the retiral of Miss O'Donnell as Matron, Miss J. Turner was appointed in her place. Mr M. Ferguson replaced Mr Twist and Mrs J. Gunn came as secretary in place of Mrs C. Mills. Fr Mark Dilworth had also come to join the Community at Carlekemp.

On 27 October 1973 over 100 guests from many parts of Britain converged on Carlekemp to honour Miss O'Donnell by their presence at a sherry party, during which tributes were paid to her and a presentation made.

Among the guests was Abbot Nicholas, Fr Francis Davidson, Fr Dominic Milroy and Fr Gordon Beattie, both from Ampleforth.

In a message sent from Karlstad, Sweden, Abbot Oswald wrote:

> *I think of her as Teacher, Housemother, Catering expert and 'Mistress of the Wardrobe', but pre-eminently Nurse, not only to generations of schoolboys but even to members of the Community. How many owe her a debt of gratitude.*

After the presentation of a cheque and an illuminated address, Dr D. Shannon spoke about Miss O'Donnell:

> *I first saw Matron standing in Powell Dormitory surrounded by the usual beginning of term chaos – one child silently weeping, two locked 'in mortal combat' and others jumping on beds or unpacking cases. Over the years since then I have sat in her room and listened to her reading a bedtime story to the first year pupils. I have watched her supervise evening ablutions. I have listened to her yelling from the Headmaster's study at boys on the front lawn, telling them to come in immediately and change their wet stockings. Throughout her professional life, Matron has given unstintingly of her time, her experience and her love in fulfilling the most demanding of Christian vocations.*

On Friday 1 February a large bus drove up to the front door of the School. From it came a party of individuals, many of whom were recognisable as they had been on television playing Rugby for England. When they had changed, they were given a short talk by D. L. Sanders and then took their places in a group to be photographed with their coach in front of the School.

It was 24 years since the England players and reserves were first at Carlekemp the day before the Calcutta Cup game at Murrayfield. In the

Refectory were the framed photographs of visiting International XVs. The autographed souvenirs were displayed in the Refectory. Players signed their names on a drawing of a rugby field in the position in which they played. The officials accompanying the team also added their names – off the 'field'. All the Selectors but one had once been at Carlekemp as players.

On the Friday, from his classroom window, one of the First Formers saw members of the England squad going out of the changing-room towards the field. He declared that it was 'quite unfair that Carlekemp should have to play against such giants'!

Seeing D. L. Sanders, the Chairman of the Selectors, give a stray rugby ball a mighty punt from the tarmac in front of the School far across the lawn, it was hard to realise that he had an artificial leg. Two of the players were brought back from the Strathearn Road field to the Marine Hotel by the doctor accompanying the group. Unfortunately, one of them, Roger Uttley, was not able to play against Scotland. Mr Beauchamp, using a ticket which he had been kindly given, found himself sitting in the Murrayfield stand near Uttley who recognised him.

On the evening of 11 January the School telephones went out of order – a Scots pine had blown down on top of the wires in the Woods. In all, seven Scots pines were felled or severely damaged. New trees (spruce, fir, larch, beech and sycamore) were planted in their place.

On the 21 March, Miss K. O'Donnell returned to her quiet little cottage in the Woods at Carlekemp from her home town, Omagh in County Tyrone.

During the term the actor Peter Finch came with his wife to see Fr Thomas, with a view to getting his son into the School. Mr Finch had been very friendly with an Old Boy, Alex Macdonald, who was at Fort Augustus in Fr Thomas' day.

It was a disappointing Hockey season as two games with Loretto, one with St Ninian's, and one with Cargilfield, had to be cancelled either because of illness (not at Carlekemp) or weather. Of the five matches played, two were won and three lost.

As a result of a Fire Inspection the previous term, the Senior dormitories were moved from the first floor to the ground floor and the classrooms then moved upstairs. The new classrooms were brighter and provided a magnificent view of the sea and islands in the Firth of Forth.

Visitors in May were Lt.-Col. and Mrs D. E. C. Russell. Mrs Russell was a great-niece of Mrs Kennedy, from whom Lord Carmont purchased Carlekemp. As a small girl in the 1920s Mrs Russell spent several holidays at Carlekemp.

The Cricket season was a disappointing one. All the fixtures had to be abandoned because of illness or transport difficulties during the fuel crisis. The only match played was against Belhaven. The School lost 51–101.

Mr Michael Ancram (the Earl of Ancram), Member of Parliament for East Lothian, accepted the Headmaster's invitation to give out the prizes.

After 14 years of work in Sweden, news came that Abbot Oswald Eaves was to return to Britain and live in Carlekemp. He had been working in the province of Värmland when Bishop Ansgar Nelson suffered a heart attack. Abbot Oswald was called to be Vicar General in Stockholm, to carry out the Bishop's episcopal functions. Shortly afterwards he was made Administrator of the Cathedral in Stockholm. When a new bishop was appointed, Abbot Oswald returned to Värmland, where he was assisted in his work by eight Dominican Sisters. His parish was the size of Belgium!

Eighteen boys had left in the Summer and 14 new boys came in their place. Mrs Reynolds had joined the staff, along with Mr Samuels.

The Rugby XV had a mixed season. They beat Loretto (14-8) and Belhaven (12-4), but were beaten by Edinburgh Academy, Cargilfield and Craigflower (53-0).

Two Christmases had passed without the traditional Nativity Play. That year, to save the immense amount of organisation required, there were only six boys in the cast. The Choir sang from the gallery and Miss Ward accompanied the boys on stage with her guitar.

Two new members of staff joined in January 1975. Mr D. C. Collins came to teach Science, English and take games; Miss Law came in daily to take the Second Form for English. Miss Grego (whose book *Italian for You* had sold 9000 copies) continued her good work.

Abbot Oswald Eaves came back from Sweden to Carlekemp. It did not take long for him to settle down in the School. In August 1973 he had a slight stroke (the reason he left Sweden). This left him slightly weakened and without his old vigour and drive. He took two Forms for Religious Knowledge, celebrated Mass at Leuchie Convent daily, and also went to offer Mass in the parish church at North Berwick or at Luffness on Sundays.

He was not really fit. He suffered from arthritis in the hips and also sinus trouble. Though invited to get up later, he was always at Morning Office in Choir. He was not accustomed to giving in to physical discomfort and had been very strong and healthy until the previous year.

When the Winter term ended, he went south to visit his niece and other friends. Miss O'Donnell had a letter from him on 7 January in which he said he had had a very happy Christmas, had met lots of friends, and was looking forward to returning and taking a more active part in life at Carlekemp.

Sadly, he died shortly after. Many friends of Abbot Oswald wrote to ask that a memorial to him be established at Carlekemp. After discussion and consultation it was decided that what he would have liked best would be a Bursary in his name, the income from which would help in the education of a boy.

In the School, meanwhile, outdoor activities continued. The Hockey season included a memorable 8-0 win over Belhaven. Golf took up a good deal of free time and the Sports were held during the Games periods.

On 17 May Fr Francis Davidson, Headmaster of Fort Augustus, came down to interview boys who were going there in September. The first Scholarship for Fort Augustus through the Common Entrance Exam in June 1975 was gained by I. A. Mitchelson.

The artist and writer Peter F. Anson died and was buried at Nunraw Abbey on 14 July. Mr Anson had been a member of the Anglican Benedictine Community on Caldey Island, almost all of whom came into the Catholic Church in 1913. They transferred from Caldey to Prinknash, Gloucestershire, from which Abbey Pluscarden Priory (now an Abbey) was founded. Mr Anson entered Fort Augustus as a novice, but did not remain there. He presented Carlekemp with some of his water-colours of Scottish fishing boats while the School was in Edinburgh.

During the Summer holidays some 40 girls from a school in Liverpool spent eight days at Carlekemp. In September six new boys arrived. For the first time, sons of Old Boys of Carlekemp were entering the School – Richard Sidgwick, for example, was the son of Iain (1955-54) who was tragically killed in a car accident; Iain Macdonald was the eldest son of Angus (1954-50) whose father, Angus, was an Old Boy of Fort Augustus.

Another arrival was Fr Andrew McKillop, who had once lived at Saint Andrew's Priory while taking his degree at Edinburgh University. In the Summer holidays, in order to make ends meet and use Carlekemp's facilities to the full, it was proposed to run a course in English for foreign students. Fr Andrew was to be in charge of the organisation.

Now that the new central heating boiler had been installed, it had become possible to use the basement again. One of the table-tennis tables had been put up there for use in the dark evenings.

On the morning of 7 October, Mr John P. Mackintosh, the MP in whose constituency Carlekemp was located, paid a visit to the School. Abbot Nicholas, who happened to be there, met him, as did boys of the Fourth and Fifth Forms. Professor Mackintosh answered the boys' questions on a wide range of political, economic and moral issues.

The Rugby season was particularly unsuccessful. The School XV lost all their major fixtures, beaten by large scores (Belhaven 46; Loretto 39; Edinburgh Academy 52), although they beat King's Meadow Primary School 38-4. The School pack was a very light one, tackling was poor, and half the team were inexperienced.

The Christmas play, 'Baby born in the Barn', was performed on two afternoons in December. Most of the action took place in a disused barn somewhere in Germany just before the Second World War. Among the audience were infirm patients brought by ambulance and car. On the Saturday, girls from Kilgraston helped serve the tea.

On the evening of 16 December the School had the traditional Christmas Dinner by candlelight. The Refectory had been decorated by the Fifth Form. Afterwards all gathered around the Christmas tree in the Hall and up the Grand Staircase and sang carols, accompanied by Mr Robertson. When these were over, the Headmaster gave out the presents from the tree. Later there was Christmas cake and fruit.

It was disappointing that, in the 1975-76 Rugby season, the England XV did not visit Carlekemp. Since the hotels in North Berwick closed for the Winter and could not therefore accommodate them, they went elsewhere.

During the 1976 Lent Term, Mr J. Hamilton Dalrymple (later Fr Jock Dalrymple jr) came to the School to give tuition in Maths and English to small groups and individuals who had made good progress. He was also most enthusiastic about Rugby, having been coached at Ampleforth by J. G. Willcox, England's former full-back. He introduced the boys to caring for the sick at his former family home, Leuchie (now Leuchie Convent), where they helped the Servite nuns by entertaining the residents (sufferers from Multiple Sclerosis and other diseases) three times a week. Mr Dalrymple also acted as one of three judges in the

Mid-term Debate on the aeronautical merits of Concorde, chaired by Miss Grego.

There were heavy gales in January. Some of the trees lost branches; others were totally destroyed. One of the rugby posts on the Strathearn pitch was blown down. But there was no snow and little fog or frost. However, on the evening of 17 February North Berwick was shaken by a series of loud bangs. The cause was unknown. At first it was thought to be an earth tremor, but this was ruled out. By coincidence the Monks and some of the boys were at that time singing Compline, praying to be delivered from 'the plague that prowls in the darkness'.

The Hockey team had a moderately good season. They played one, won one, lost one and drew four games. In preparation for the next season several Rugby afternoons were held each week. Their improvement was due mainly to Old Boy Mr T. Kelly who came down every Sunday. A new activity, Orienteering, was developed by Fr Andrew.

Courtesy of Mrs Hope of Luffness, Aberlady, some 50 new rose bushes were planted. All the garden beds by the East Lodge had been cleaned out and dug over. A new grass verge was made in front of the School. Large stones were put there to prevent cars parking on the grass.

On 23 May the Eastern Area of the Fort Augustus Association met at Carlekemp. A large gathering attended. After the Cricket match against the School the Old Boys went to Benediction, where they were led by Abbot Nicholas.

The Summer of 1976 was full of memories. The weather was beautiful, allowing the boys to swim as often as they wanted. Most evenings the Seniors went down onto the beach. Sometimes, after a very hot day, the sea was silky and cool.

The tradition of having a Corpus Christi Procession was revived. Lanterns and canopy were lent by Canon Ward. Fr Andrew carried the Blessed Sacrament as the Procession went around the lawn, the trees in the Woods still dripping with moisture from a sudden shower. Benediction was given at an altar erected in the porch.

On the Feast of St Peter and St Paul, the School went by bus to Luffness, near Aberlady, where Mrs Hope made all welcome. Skittles, croquet and clock golf were played on the lawn. The ruined Priory with its Crusader's tomb was visited. Mass was celebrated in the Chapel in the evening.

Fr Gregory visited for one night. He featured on the television programme broadcast on 8 June about the Loch Ness Monster. Fr Gregory was now one of the key witnesses to the existence of Nessie. In the *New York Times* of 12 June he was quoted as saying: 'We ought to leave the Monster alone. In this technological age, we've placed a label on everything. I am a champion of the unknown. Mystery intrigues people, and so it should remain.'

On 29 May Mr Beauchamp, Miss O'Donnell and Fr John were invited to Haddington for a preview of an exhibition of paintings by Arthur Forrest of North Berwick, who was at Carlekemp when Abbot Oswald was Headmaster. There was news, too, of John Smyth (1962-68) who gained a First at Cambridge. While he was at Carlekemp he won the top scholarship to Ampleforth.

The 1976 Cricket XI was unbeaten. Of the six matches played, four were won and two drawn. Craigleith beat Lamb in the House Match. A parent had kindly donated a petrol-driven 12-inch lawn mower which was ideal for putting finishing touches to the Cricket pitch before a match. In the Sports, Craigleith won.

Since she had come back from training teachers in Nigeria, Carlekemp had been fortunate to secure the services of Miss Moira Grego. She took classes each morning. Miss Grego was determined to educate the boys, not just to 'teach' them. Now she had retired and her place was taken by Mr I. J. Keith. Mr D. C. Collins was replaced by Mr B. S. Dick.

Between 7 and 20 November 1976 there came a procession of worries. First, Fr Thomas was told by the Doctor to rest. Then the deep freezer broke down, followed by the domestic hot water boiler. The fire alarm refused to function, the central heating packed up, the gauge on the fuel tank for the main central heating jammed, so that there was no heating for two days. Feverish colds laid boys low.

On 21 November, the Feast of Christ the King, at about 4.00 pm, the sky in the east turned a beautiful orange, slowly changing to yellow farther north, then fading into a light blue. In the west it was dark blood-orange red, gradually turning a deep purple. Rapidly this turned into grey. Many thought there was going to be a huge thunder storm, but nothing materialised. These colours cast a strange light on the earth. The grass seemed to jump out; it was darker than usual and seemed to glow. In the east there was an incredible rainbow, standing out from the yellow sky. At around 4.30 pm this wonderful sky left. It grew dark, but the experience was not forgotten.

The day after the Feast of St Andrew, Winter arrived during the night. The world fell still and frost crept in, reaching minus 10°. North

Berwick Law, and even the Bass Rock, were covered in hoar frost that glittered dazzlingly in the brilliant sunshine.

On the same day, 1 December, Duncan Hay made Rugby history for Carlekemp. He was chosen to play hooker for the Dandylions, the Preparatory Schools of East Scotland, against the Preparatory Schools of West Scotland. The Dandylions won 18-7. Not so fortunate was the School Rugby XV, which managed to lose all five of its games.

On 8 December the School held its Christmas celebrations. The Fifth Form decorated the Refectory and Christmas Tree. At 4.30 pm everyone sat down to roast turkey, stuffing, brussel sprouts, potatoes and Christmas pudding. Mrs Gibson had baked three magnificent cakes, but it was decided to leave them until the following day. Abbot Nicholas arrived by rail in time for the Christmas Tree. After carols had been sung, he distributed the presents.

'We could go in' was the title of Dr John Morrison's Christmas Play which was performed on the 10, 11, and 12 December, produced by Mr I. Keith, with piano accompaniment by Mr G. Robertson. The second performance was for the old people from various Homes in North Berwick. Dr Morrison came with Parents and friends for the last performance.

When the 1977 Lent term opened there were two changes of part-time teaching staff. David Scott replaced Stewart Wilson as piano-accordion teacher and Mr G. Robertson replaced Mrs Walker as piano instructor, while still continuing to give singing lessons twice a week.

Part of the traditions of Carlekemp was the legend of the 'White Lady' which often caused new boys to shudder when in bed at night. The legend claimed that a man and his wife were said to have arrived at the house one stormy night. They were given what became Powell dormitory to sleep in. While thunder crashed and lightning flashed, the two had a heated argument, during which the man murdered his wife. He hunted frantically for a place to hide his wife's body until he saw the fireplace which was not in use. He stuffed the body up the chimney. However, the corpse was discovered and he confessed his crime. In later years it was said that the White Lady could be heard walking around the School.

Of the five Hockey matches played in the Lent term, one was won, one drawn and three lost. The father of a potential pupil visited the School on 13 March. He did not call in or speak to anyone, but just looked round the grounds and watched the boys playing six-a-side

Hockey. Father and son were so impressed that both decided to put the boy's name down for the School.

Then – a bombshell. Parents were informed by letter that Carlekemp was to be closed in July and the School amalgamated with Fort Augustus. The Headmaster, Fr Thomas, wrote:

> *I think I know how parents of present boys feel …. In fact, less are leaving than I expected and the vast majority are coming north …. Only those who know the whole story can understand the reasons for our leaving Carlekemp. The parents have been told that 'overheads' will be reduced by being taken down from two to one – catering, heating etc and fees should not have to go soaring …. We are sorry that all the staff cannot come with us and we offer them our very sincere sympathy …. I hope and pray that all those who find the closing – or moving upwards – of Carlekemp a trying crisis may be consoled and strengthened now and, in time, recognise it as a blessing in disguise.*

One of the staff for whom the closure of Carlekemp meant instant retiral, was long-time teacher and Games master, Roger Beauchamp DSC. An inspired coach in Rugby, Hockey and Cricket, 'Beachy' (as he was affectionately known) trained generations of boys in the highest standards of sportsmanship.

Meanwhile, boys at the School were invited to visit Fort Augustus by the Headmaster, Fr Francis (himself a former pupil and head boy at Carlekemp), who had come down to North Berwick on 14 May to see the parents.

The Fort Augustus Council unanimously decided Carlekemp had to be closed as it was not paying its way. This was confirmed at a Chapter meeting, where the proposal received a large vote in favour of closure.

On 22 May a record number of Old Boys gathered together for the last time at Carlekemp. In his address, Fr Thomas reminded the Old Boys that they had put before them principles and standards and they should be different – and recognised as different. They, as Old Boys, owed this to the Abbey and should acknowledge it. They were also indebted to the Monks in another way. When he himself went to the Abbey School in 1926 the fees had been only £33 a term. It was the Monks who had subsidised the boys' education.

Prize Day was cancelled. Fr Francis interviewed the seven Common Entrance candidates. Fr Edward, Bursar at the Fort, came down at Mid-term to look over the property.

K. G. Clarke (1961-66) read of the impending closure of Carlekemp, jumped into his car and drove from Lancashire to North Berwick, arriving in time for supper.

On 11 July, St Benedict's Feast Day, a farewell dinner was held for the staff and friends of Carlekemp. After the meal, local GP Dr J. Walinck thanked the Community. Then Fr Matthew Donoghue, parish priest of North Berwick, added that he knew how much the Benedictines would be missed in the area.

CHAPTER 23

Summer
Schools

IT was on 6 October 1975 at Carlekemp that the idea of an English Language Summer School was first mooted. Abbot Nicholas, in a conversation with Fr Andrew McKillop, suggested this in order to widen the role of the School, and to utilise the School buildings, Staff and some of the Monks during the long Summer vacation and even during the other two vacations.

The reason for this initiative was the need for the School to generate more income in order to keep up with inflation. It had to be an operation exclusively in the hands of the School.

The first step was to determine what kind of programme a Summer School could offer. Then a list of the best foreign newspapers and mag-

Source: Ordnance Survey Map 1900

azines in North West Europe could be drawn up where advertisements could be placed – principally in Belgium, Holland, France and Germany.

On 1 August 1976 eight students arrived for the first three-week Summer School. Fr Andrew was in charge; Miss Ward and Fr John-Baptist helped with the teaching. Three Fort Augustus boys came as companions to the students and helped in many ways. They were David Blair, Lawrence Vallot and Colin Coupar.

The students came from France, Germany and Switzerland. Classes were given in the mornings, and the afternoons were devoted to sightseeing. The venture was a great success. The following year, twelve Spanish students came – six boys and six girls.

In 1978 the Summer School was held at Fort Augustus. This was preceded by an intensive series of recruiting letters sent to a great variety of European contacts. The School opened in the middle of July with 33 students.

The 1979 Summer School had 19 students – six Belgians, five French, four German, three Swiss and one Spanish. Their average age was 17 1/2.

Hannes Thurm-Meyer, now a dental practitioner in Bremen, Germany, still remembers the effect the Summer Schools had on him:

> I was booked in for the 1980 Summer School. I arrived in Inverness by train. There I met Hamish MacDonald. In the course of conversation I discovered he had just come back from playing hockey in my hometown of Bremen. We drove along the shore of Loch Ness. The beauty of the countryside was overwhelming.
>
> This was to be a Summer that I would not forget for the rest of my life. Father Andrew and Father John were in charge and Chris Stephenson and Derek Cardiff were the helpers.
>
> The next year two of us got the chance to come back as helpers – Eva Buch Andersen from Denmark and myself. Five more Scottish Summers in Fort Augustus followed for me until 1987 – Summers full of valuable experience, fun, interesting people and good spirit.

By 1980 there were again 33 students, 45 came the next year and 57 in 1982. Thirty German students, ten Danish, eleven Italian, nine French, 13 Dutch, three Austrians and two Swiss turned up in 1983, paying £360 for the three-week course. Eighty-three students arrived at Fort Augustus in 1984 and, when a second Summer School was added in the Easter of 1985, there were an additional 33 students, a figure which had jumped to 75 by 1989.

As well as being the prime mover of the Fort Augustus Summer Schools, Fr Andrew McKillop was awarded the MBE in 1995 to honour him and his predecessors' climate observations. These were undertaken at the Abbey since 1884, Fr Andrew's observations dating from 1929. From time to time he was assisted by others, including Fr Benedict Seed.

Old Boy Chris Stephenson, by this time a teacher at the Abbey School, recalled the many happy hours spent as a member of the Summer School staff, along with other Old Boy instructors (such as Photographer Mike Drummond and Sailing supervisor Vincent Igoe):

We worked and we played hard. Fr Andrew was behind it all. The locals called him Father Flat Out *because they constantly saw his car whizzing around the Village or setting off for Inverness. The students called him* The Flying Scotsman. *I know we made £30,000 profit on our last Summer School (that is, £10,000 a week profit).*

Sports Colours

1925   T. McArdle (c), H. Doherty, R. McKillop, T. White, W. McLean, J. Eaves,
        M. Carty, D. Duffy, J. McCombes
1926   J. Eaves (c), R. O'Connor, W. McLean, G. Carruth, J. McCombes
1927   R. O'Connor (c), J. Carruth, H. Boultwood, W. Young, J. Dunn
1928   J. Dunn (c), H. Boultwood, J. Carruth, W. Young, D. Matheson, F. Froes,
        I. Kennedy, G. Whitehead, D. Carruth
1929   D. Matheson (c), D. Carruth, G. Whitehead, J. Birnie
1930   G. Whitehead (c), J. Brusey, J. Birnie, J. Harrower, P. Shiel, E. Herraghty,
        J. McLaughlin, J. O'Hara, P. Byrne
1931   J. McLaughlin (c), P. Byrne, J. O'Hara, P. Shiel, J. McFall, P. Reilly, J. Foy,
        J. Stephen, P. Murphy, B. Beers, D. Kelly
1932   P. Byrne (c), J. Stephen, J. Foy, P. Reilly, B. Beers, D. Kelly, M. Walsh
1933   P. Byrne (c), J. Rogers, J. Lewis, R. Phoenix, J. Jennings, A. Macdonald
1934   R. Phoenix (c), J. Barry, J. Rogers, M. Reilly, J. MacLennan, W. Mackay,
        G. Bartlett
1935   W. Mackay (c), P. Mohan
1936   P. Mohan (c), M. Loftus, W. Christopher, F. Taylor, A. MacQueen
1937   M. Loftus (c), W. Christopher, A. MacQueen, D. Barry, R. Levack, H. Curran,
        F. MacQueen, W. Kelly, W. MacDonald
1938   R. Levack (c), W. MacDonald, F. MacQueen, H. Curran, O. Walsh, J. Laverty,
        A. Watson, F. Sutherland
1939   F. Sutherland (c), T. Crawford, P. Barry, O. Flynn, V. Birch, J. Dalgleish
1940   R. McLernan (c), R. Anderson, J. Dalgleish, R. Di Rollo, N. McGregor
1941   R. Di Rollo (c), N. McGregor, J. Dalgleish, N. Baird
1942   N. Baird (c), M. Keegan, M. Couttie, J. Harris, I. Di Rollo
1943   I. Di Rollo (c), D. Atkinson, K. Murray, T. Herd, D. Korczynski
1944   D. Atkinson (c), K. Murray, D. Korczynski, J. Locke. P. Crossan, J. Marin, C. Hall
1945   C. Hall (c), C. Di Giacomo, A. Greco

1946	D. McKay (c), A. Greco, H. Cardosi, M. Crawford, J. Korczynski
1947	M. Crawford (c), J. Caruana, D. Dando, J. McEachin
1948	J. Caruana (c), L. Murray, R. Baird, J. Malone, C. Barrett
1949	J. Malone (c), L. Caruana
1950	J. Malone (c), L. Caruana, F. Whitehurst, R. Seed, F. Chapelle, R. Duncan, T. McLaughlin
1951	F. Whitehurst (c), T. McLaughlin, R. Duncan, B. Paton, V. Macari, A. Haworth
1952	F. Whitehurst (c), R. Duncan, B. Paton, V. Macari, P. Mooney, A. Haworth
1953	P. Mooney (c), W. Mackenzie
1954	G. Martin (c), R. Swift
1955	R. Swift (c), K. Deady, J. Kelman, R. Beith
1956	J. Kelman (c), A. Duncan, M. Cipolato, E. Di Rollo, B. Spary, G. Dupuis
1957	A. Duncan (c), C. Dunn, M. Cipolato, E. Di Rollo, B. Spary, G. Dupuis
1958	M. Cipolato (c), I. Daly
1959	R. Sinclair (c), I. Macdonald, J. van Bavel
1960	J. van Bavel (c), I. Atkinson, R. Godfrey, G. McGlynn
1961	G. McGlynn (c), A. Young
1962	H. Shannon (c), J. Marshall, A. Burns
1963	R. Drummond (c), P. Perrin, I. Campbell, W. Chisholm, R. Cardosi
1964	J. Slight (c), H. Walker
1965	J. Edgar (c), D. Shannon, C. Campbell
1966	D. Haworth (c), P. Diviani
1967	A. Cousland (c), P. Doyle, K. Janik
1968	P. Doyle (c), C. Donne, C. Grieve
1969	P. Doyle (c), P. Greco, J. Doyle, V. Chlebowski
1970	J. Doyle (c), V. Chelbowski, J. Edgar, B. Lanni, P. Dalton
1971	J. Edgar (c), P. Dalton, B. Lanni
1972	M. Doyle (c), R. Grant, M. Copolla, G. Squires, M. Mortali
1973	J. Collins-Taylor (c), S. McRory, C. Wilson
1974	C. Wilson (c), I. Sunderland, C. Grant, M. Dalton, P. Squarey
1975	P. Murray (c), L. Vallot, S. Ross
1976	L. Vallot (c), A. Sabin
1977	C. G. Bryce (c), A. L. Basigara
1978	B. P. Robinson (c), J. P. Stephenson, D. P. Cardiff
1979	P. Vallot (c), J. T. Welsh, D. J. Blanchard, P. O'Shea, G. A. J. Semple, D. A. Ogilvie, N. R. Robertson
1980	D. A. Ogilvie (c), I. S. Phillips, A. W. McLaughlin, J. D. Kiwanuka, A. M. Mungavin, A. N. Blanchard
1981	A. W. McLaughlin (c), T. L. Kelly, T. R. Welsh, P. R. Westcott, D. G. S. Nkhoma, J. D. Kiwanuka, D. Boyle
1982	J. D. Kiwanuka (c), D. Boyle, D. G. S. Nkhoma, A. J. O'Sullivan, S. P. Kiwanuka, M. J. Mungavin, P. R. Protte
1983	M. J. Mungavin (c), D. G. S. Nkhoma, C. MacLellan, A. J. Meldrum
1984	P. F. Bennett (c), S. D. Murphy, J. K. Knox, R. L. Giulianotti
1985	E. Brogan (c), R. L. Giulianotti, C. Keaney
1986	M. A. Giulianotti (c), C. Smith, M. Waugh, S. Risi, J. B. Dunn
1987	A. MacMaster (c), M. S. Masini, M. J. Hughes
1988	M. J. Hughes (c), R. Brown, G. M. P. Lappin
1989	M. A. J. Robson (c), V. F. Igoe
1990	M. J. Lynas (c), J. H. M. Gray
1991	S. Rhodes (c), D. F. M. Gray, M. P. Byrne, C. Murray

HOCKEY

1930	G. Whitehead (c), J. Brusey
1931	P. Murray (c), P. Reilly, P. Byrne, J. Stephen, B. Beers, J. O'Hara, J. McLaughlin
1932	J. Stephen (c), B. Beers, P. Reilly, P. Byrne, J. Paterson, J. Lewis, H. Lyall
1933	H. Lyall (c), J. Lewis, P. Byrne, S. Bartlett, J. Barry
1934	S. Bartlett (c), J. Barry, H. Lyall, J. Rogers, R. Phoenix, W. Mackay, T. Barry
1935	T. Barry (c), W. Mackay, W. Young, A. MacQueen, L. Lyall, F. Taylor, P. Mohan
1936	T. Barry (c), F. Taylor, A. MacQueen, W. Young, P. Mohan, M. Loftus, R. Levack
1937	A. MacQueen (c), R. Levack, M. Loftus, G. Davidson, F. MacQueen, O. Walsh, W. MacDonald, W. Christopher, W. Kelly
1938	O. Walsh (c), F. MacQueen, W. MacDonald, V. Birch, R. Anderson
1939	V. Birch (c), R. Anderson, F. Sutherland, R. McLernan, P. Barry, C. van Zeller, R. Smith
1940	R. Anderson (c), R. McLernan, H. MacDonald, T. Sutherland, R. Di Rollo
1941	H. MacDonald (c), R. Di Rollo
1942	R. Baird (c), J. Harris
1943	R. MacGrath (c) I. Di Rollo, K. Murray, D. MacFarlane, P. McGregor
1944*	
1945	C. Hall (c), C. Di Giacomo
1946*	
1947	M. Crawford (c), T. McGregor, J. McClusky, D. Dando
1948	J. Caruana (c), R. Baird, S. Tyskinski, M. Kerrigan
1949*	
1950	K. Smith (c), L. Caruana, T. Eastham
1951	F. Whitehouse (c), J. Malone, R. Seed, P. Laing
1952	F. Whitehouse (c), B. Paton, R. Duncan
1953	F. Whitehouse (c), R. Duncan, B. Paton, R. Chisholm
1954	G. Martin (c), P. Smith, M. McCabe
1955	G. Martin (c), K. Deady, A. Fava
1956	K. Deady (c), G. Davidson, R. Beith, P. Gordon Smith, A. Duncan
1957	P. Gordon Smith (c), A. Duncan
1958	A. Duncan (c), E. Di Rollo, I. F. Macdonald, I. Daly
1959	I. Daly (c), M. Cipolato, I. F. Macdonald
1960	I. F. Macdonald (c), N. C. Taylor, M. Turnbull
1961	R. N. Godfrey (c), J. G. van Bavel, B. J. Mathieson
1962	H. G. Young (c), P. C. Bayliss, A. J. Burns
1963	J. P. Marshall (c), R. C. Drummond, A. J. Burns, H. D. Shannon, P. R. Perrin

1964   R. C. Drummond (c), P. R. Perrin, E. F. Foley, D. I. Colquhoun
1965   J. H. T. Slight (c), I. S. Brown, P. J. Diviani, D. M. Waters
1966   T. J. Murphy (c), D. Shannon, C. T. Campbell
1967   D. L. Haworth (c), P. A. Diviani, H. E. Murphy, J. A. MacBride
1968   P. Doyle (c), H. E. Murphy, J. A. MacBride
1969   P. Doyle (c), P. Greco, A. Cunningham, W. Chapman
1970   P. Grego (c), G. T. Lumsden, W. M. Chapman, J. Doyle, D. M. Allison, R. Mazzoni
1971   J. Doyle (c), G. T. Lumsden, W. M. Chapman, F. A. Partridge, H. P. MacDonald,
       J. J. Murphy
1972   D. W. Butchart (c), K. Slowey, M. M. McLoughlin
1973   G. S. Squires (c), A. J. Whitehead
1974   D. I. Campbell (c), M. G. Chapman, P. M. Couttie
1975   P. M. Couttie (c), C. V. Grant
1976   L. Vallot (c), S. L. Ross, A. J. Sabin, D. R. Milne, C. A. Job
1977   L. Vallot (c), A. J. Sabin, G. A. Hay
1978   C. G. Bryce (c), A. L. Basigara, V. J. Gram-Hansen
1979   V. J. Gram-Hansen (c), B. P. Robinson, A. V. Campopiano, D. A. Seed,
       A. H. Nicol
1980   J. T. Welsh (c), A. V. Campopiano, I. S. Phillips
1981   A. V. Campopiano (c), T. L. Kelly, I. S. Phillips, D. A. Ogilvie, A. M. Mungavin,
       T. R. Welsh, P. N. Bettosi
1982   T. L. Kelly (c), T. R. Welsh, P. R. Westcott, F. E. Ogilvie
1983   D. K. Kiwanuka (c), D. G. Nkhoma, P. F. Bennett
1984   D. G. Nkhoma (c), P. F. Bennett, J. K. Knox, P. T. Mattison
1985   P. F. Bennett (c), R. L. Giulianotti
1986   R. L. Giulianotti (c), M. A. Giulianotti, S. Phillips
1987   M. A. Giulianotti (c), A. O. Knox
1988   M. J. Hughes (c), M. S. Masini
1989   M. J. Hughes (c), G. M. Lappin
1990   M. A. Robson (c), V. F. Igoe, M. P. Byrne
1991   M. P. Byrne (c), J. H. Gray, M. J. Lynas, D. F. Gray, C. Murray

[*NB: Colours were not awarded in 1944, 1946 or 1949.]

CRICKET

1923   R. McKillop (c), B. O'Callaghan, T. McArdle, A. Macdonald
1924   T. McArdle (c), R. McKillop, B. O'Callaghan, A. Macdonald, T. White,
       D. Gargan

1925	T. McArdle (c), R. McKillop, B. O'Callaghan, T. White, D. Gargan, J. McLean
1925	T. McArdle (c), R. McKillop, B. O'Callaghan, T. White, D. Gargan, J. McLean
1926	T. McArdle (c), R. McKillop, W. McLean, G. Carruth, H. McDonnell
1927	J. McCombes (c), G. Carruth, J. King, H. Boultwood
1928	H. Boultwood (c) J. Carruth, J. Dunn, J. Birnie
1929	H. Boultwood (c), J. Dunn, J. Carruth, J. Birnie, J. Richardson
1930	J. Birnie (c), J. Brusey, D. Carruth, J. Harrower, J. O'Hara
1931	J. Birnie (c), J. Brusey, J. Harrower, J. O'Hara, J. McLaughlin, P. Murphy
1932	P. Murphy (c), J. O'Hara, J. McLaughlin, M. Walsh, H. Lyall
1933	M. Walsh (c), H. Lyall, J. Rogers, J. Lewis.
1934	H. Lyall (c), J. Rogers, J. Lewis, W. MacKay, J. Barry
1935	J. Rogers (c), W. MacKay, J. Barry, T. Fletcher
1936	T. Fletcher (c), W. MacKay, W. Young
1937	T. Barry (c), W. Young, G. Davison
1938	M. Loftus (c), G. Davison, A. Maqueen, O. Walsh
1939	O. Flynn (c), W. MacDonald, V. Birch, R. Anderson
1940	V. Birch (c), O. Flynn, R. Anderson, H. MacDonald, P. Barry
1941	R. Anderson (c), H. MacDonald, J. Dalgleish
1942	R. Baird (c), H. MacDonald, J. Dalgleish, L. Baxter
1943	R. Baird (c), G. Harris,
1944	R. Magrath (c), I. Di Rollo, K. Murray, P. McGregor
1945	D. Atkinson (c), K. Murray, J. McCormick, A. Korczynski, C. Hall
1946	C. Hall (c), D. Makay, M. McCormack, J. McCluskey
1947	M. Crawford (c), J. Korczynski, D. Gordon-Dando, J. McCluskey, T. McGregor
1948	M. Crawford (c), J. McCluskey, T. McGregor, M. Kerrigan, R. Baird
1949	L. Murray (c), M. Kerrigan, R. Baird
1950	K. Smith (c), Rankin, D. Grant
1951	A. Moore (c), F. Whitehurst, F. Chapelle
1952	A. Moore (c), F. Whitehurst
1953	F. Whitehurst (c), Paton, V. Macari
1954	G. Martin (c), G. Davidson
1955	G. Martin (c), G. Davidson, K. Deady, A. Duncan
1956	G. Davidson (c), K. Deady, P. Kelly, A. Duncan
1957	A. Duncan (c), B. Spary
1958	A. Duncan (c), B. Spary, I. Daly, L. Paterson
1959	I. Daly (c), L. Paterson, I. Macdonald
1960	I. Macdonald (c), M. Turnbull, M. Coppin
1961	J. van Bavel (c), R. Godfrey, M. Coppin, H. Young
1962	H. Young (c), M. Coppin, R. Drummond, H. Shannon, V. Di Rollo
1963	R.C. Drummond (c), H.D. Shannon
1964	R.C. Drummond (c), J.H.T. Sleight
1965	J. H. T. Slight (c), N. Johnston Stewart, H. Anderson

APPENDIX II

Notes to Chapters

NOTES TO CHAPTER 1

[NB: Unless otherwise specified all from 'Jottings from the School Chronicle' in *The Corbie, Fort Augustus News* or *The Carlekemp Times*. SCA = Scottish Catholic Archive; SRO = Scottish Record Office.]

1 John Gifford: *Architecture: The buildings of Scotland: Highlands and Islands*, pp 168–173.
2 Gordon Donaldson and Robert S Morpeth (eds): *A Dictionary of Scottish History*.
3 John Prebble: *John Prebble's Scotland*, p 90.
4 Joseph Mitchell: *Reminiscences of my life in the Highlands* (London: Unwin Brothers, 1883).
5 Aelred Grugan: *Red Coats and Black Habits: The Early History of Fort Augustus* (n.d.).
6 Alban Boultwood: St Anselm's Abbey Newsletter (Summer 1980).
7 David McRoberts: 'A Coat of Arms for Fort Augustus' in *Scottish Catholic Herald* (29 May 1959).
8 Cyprian Gibson: 'Fort Augustus Abbey. Benedictine Almanac and Guide', 194-3.
9 Psalm 131:14 (which occurs every Tuesday at Vespers); Psalm 131 in the Vulgate, 132:14 in the Revised Standard Version (Greek/Septuagint numbering versus Hebrew numbering): 'For Yahweh has chosen Zion, desiring this to be his home, "Here will I say for ever, this is the home I have chosen".'
10 Cyprian Gibson: op. cit., pp 194-5.
11 *The Tablet* (15 September 1876).
12 *Catholic Directory* (1879).
13 *The Dublin Review* (October 1879).
14 Ibid.

NOTES TO CHAPTER 2

1 Scottish Catholic Archives (SCA) ED 3/127/14
2 Basil Whelan: *The Annals of the English congregation of the Black Monks of St Benedict (1850-1900)* (1st edition 1932; 2nd edition 1942; reissued 1971), pp 228-29.
3 Ibid: p 229.
4 SCA ED 3/91/3: James Campbell, Rome to Archbishop Strain (12 December 1882).
5 See G Reid Anderson: *Abbeys of Scotland* (London: James Clarke & Co, 1939), pp 8-9 (the first electricity supply installed in the Highlands was built by the monks

themselves by the damming of the river and the building of a lade); and David Oswald Hunter Blair: *In Victorian Days* (London: Longmans, 1939), p 226 ('the motive power was steam at first, though we later obtained power from one of our mountain streams').

6   Fr Ambrose Geoghegan was wounded on 17 August 1918. See Tom Johnstone and Tom Hagerty: *The Cross on the Sword; Catholic Chaplains in the Forces* (London: Geoffrey Chapman 1996), p 171.

7   War Journal of Lionel G. Smith, France and Belgium 1915-17, AWA in the Archives of St Edmund's College (series 12, 167A, 291-92) quoted in Johnstone and Hagerty: *The Cross on the Sword*, p 129.

8   Michael MacDonagh: *The Irish at the Front* (London: Hodder & Stoughton 1916), p 120 (quoting *The Spectator*).

9   SCA: Odo Blundell: 'Crannogs', unpublished typescript, pp 2-3 (see also PSAS vol. XLIII 1908-9, pp 159-164).

10 Hugh A Fraser: 'Investigation of the artificial island in Loch Kinellan, Strathpeffer', PSAS (1916-17), pp 48-99 and PSAS XLIII (1908-9), pp 159-164.

Note to Chapter 3

1   SCA: Abbey School, *Fort Augustus Chronicle* (1920-23).

Note to Chapter 4

1   *A Pronouncing Dictionary of Scottish Gaelic* (Edinburgh: W & A. K. Johnston Ltd, 1932). *Shinty: a short history of the ancient Highland game* (Inverness 1932).

Notes to Chapter 5

1   Edward Delepine: *Outline History of Fort Augustus Abbey* (unpublished MS, 1999).

2   Francis Lindley: *Lord Lovat* (London: Hutchison 1935).

3   Bulloch: *The Sunday Times*.

4   David Oswald Hunter Blair: *A Last Medley of Memories* (London: Edward Arnold, 1936).

5   SRO ED32/283: Report on Fort Augustus, the Abbey School, 22 June 1938.

Notes to Chapter 6

1   SRO ED32/283: Report on Fort Augustus, the Abbey School, no.V, 1938.

2   Sir David Oswald Hunter Blair (born Dunskey, Ayrshire on 30 September 1853), son of Sir Edward Hunter Blair, Bart and Elizabeth Wauchope. He succeeded to the estates of Dunskey and Brownhill, Ayrshire on 12 December 1857. From 1899-1909 he served as Master of Hunter Blair's Hall, Oxford where he guided the academic and spiritual development of Benedictine novices. He also made several journeys

to Brazil (1896 and 1909) to help the fledgling Benedictine house near São Paulo. He was elected Abbot of Fort Augustus in 1913 until his resignation from ill-health in 1917. It was largely to his generosity that the Abbey possessed so fine a library. His literary output was prolific, ranging from a critical edition of the *Rule of St Benedict* to a translation of Bellesheim's *History of the Catholic Church in Scotland from earliest times.*

3   Denys Rutledge (born 7 January 1906; died 7 November 1997), buried in the Abbey Cemetery.

4   Cyprian Gibson (born 10 June 1893; died 28 January 1960). Thomas McLaughlin (born 23 October 1914; died 29 January 1979). Laurence Kelly (born 16 January 1915; died 8 February 1987). John-Baptist McBride (born 8 May 1914; died 24 April 1998).

5   Fr Anselm was the first Prior of Worth and later was Headmaster of Downside. Subsequently he was Sub-prior and Master of Theological Studies.

6   Abbot Wulstan Knowles (born 28 March 1881; died 13 April 1965) is buried in the monastic cemetery at Fort Augustus.

NOTES TO CHAPTER 7

1   John McFall's grave is at the graveyard at Sidi Barrani.

2   Fr Kentigern Milne (born 8 October 1856; died 7 March 1942), buried in the Abbey cemetery.

NOTES TO CHAPTER 8

1   Fr Luke Cary-Elwes (born 9 January 1866; died 16 July 1946).

2   Fr Julian Stead: Letter to Author (29 July 1999).

NOTE TO CHAPTER 9

1   John Cornwell: *Hitler's Pope – The Secret History of Pius XII* (London: Viking 1999), p 410.

NOTE TO CHAPTER 12

1   At New Year 1953 a BBC TV film was shown (produced by Stanley L Russell of the Thames and Clyde Film Co, Glasgow for BBC). Then on 16 June, at 3.00 pm, there was a broadcast of Vespers of the Feast of the Sacred Heart, featuring the monks, boys and Fr Gregory, with commentary by Abbot Oswald Eaves. This was the first full-length service broadcast from the Abbey. In 1954 (broadcast October 5, at 8.05pm) there was a BBC TV programme of ten minutes duration. In 1955 (broadcast in June, Scottish Regional Service), there was a Religious Service that featured a short talk by the Abbot, with the school choir singing hymns and monks

singing plainchant.The BBC produced a short film on Fort Augustus Abbey in 1957 featuring Polly Elwes' interviews with the Abbot and Br James. On 20 February 1957, the BBC broadcast Votive Vespers of St Andrew, prefaced by a short talk by Abbot Oswald on Fort Augustus and monastic life. On 15 November 1959 there was a BBC Scottish Programme, 'Morning Service', with the School contributing congregational singing and the polyphonic choir singing Palestrina's '*O sacrum convivium*' under the direction of Mr Calvert.

NOTE TO CHAPTER 13

1 Fr Denys' Publications include: *Catechism through the Liturgy,* London: Douglas Organ, 1949; *In Search of a Yogi: Himalayan Pilgrimage,* London: Routledge and Kegan Paul, 1962; *Cosmic Theology: The Ecclesiastical Hierarchy of Pseudo-Denys,* Staten Island, NY: Alba House, 1964; *The Complete Monk. Vocation of the Monastic Order,* London: Routledge and Kegan Paul, 1966; *Basic Christian Communities* London: CTS, 1993.
2 *The Glasgow Herald* (8 March 1961).

NOTE TO CHAPTER 16

1 'Everything till now' (edited by A. J. Sabin, M. E. Ward and S. C. Ross) was followed in 1974 by 'Fug 320' (edited by Michael F. Lombardi and Hubert C. L. S. Lorin). In 1975 'The Clarts Plodger's Yearbook' appeared (edited by Mux W. McCullough, Peter J. Murray, Sjoerd Vogt, Colin V. Grant and Mark A. Rankin).

NOTES TO CHAPTER 17

1 Letter from Thomas McLaughlin (8 February 1975).
2 Frytol was the trade name for a cooking oil. The company's oil drums made useful waste-paper baskets, but with towels stretched over them they could also serve as musical instruments.
3 Abbot Nicholas Holman writes that 'a sufficient proportion of leavers [from Carlekemp] were not reaching Fort Augustus, and it did not really pay its way', Chapter 37, unpublished Autobiography, 1999.

NOTE TO CHAPTER 19

1 SRO ED32/414.

Note to Chapter 20

1   Abbot Mark Dilworth's publications include *Scottish Monasteries in the Late Middle Ages* (Edinburgh University Press 1955), *The Scots in Franconia: a century of monastic life* (Scottish Academic Press 1974), *In the heart of his house* (Kevin Mayhew 1979), and 'Scottish Catholic Archives: summary handlist of holdings up to 1878' (Columba House 1986).

Notes to Chapter 22

1   *The New Catholic Dictionary,* London: The Universal Knowledge Foundation, 1929, p 810.
2   Fr Vincent Pirie Watson (born 12 January 1934; died 8 April 1983).
3   Told to the Author by Abbot Oswald Eaves.
4   Edinburgh-born film director Donald Seton Cammell (1934-96). His films include: 'La Collectionneuse' (1966); 'Demon Seed' (1977); 'Duffy' (1968); 'Lucifer Rising' (1981); 'Performance' (1970); 'Tilt' (1978); 'The Touchables' (1968); 'White of the Eye' (1986); 'Wildside' (1999). 'Performance', made with Nicholas Roeg, was named as 48th in the British Film Institute's best British films of the twentieth century (1999).
5   E-mail to the Author (30 July 1999).

Note to Chapter 23

1   Christopher Stephenson: E-mail to Author (19 January 2000)